Making a Scene

Making a Scene

The Contemporary Drama
of Jewish-American Women

Edited and with an Introduction by

Sarah Blacher Cohen

Syracuse University Press

Copyright © 1997 by Syracuse University Press
Syracuse, New York 13244

All Rights Reserved

First Edition 1997
97 98 99 00 01   6 5 4 3 2 1

The paper used in this publication meets the minimum requirements of American National Standard for Information Sciences—Permanence of Paper for Printed Library Materials, ANSI Z39.48-1984. ⊗™

Library of Congress Cataloging-in-Publication Data
Making a scene : the contemporary drama of Jewish-American women /
    edited and with an introduction by Sarah Blacher Cohen. — 1st ed.
        p.   cm.
    Includes bibliographical references.
    Contents: Isn't it romantic / Wendy Wasserstein — A shayna maidel
/ Barbara Lebow — The ladies locker room / Sarah Blacher Cohen —
Nobody's gilgul / Lois Roisman — Whither thou goest / Barbara Kahn
— The night the war came home / Hindi Brooks — Across the Jordan /
Merle Feld.
    ISBN 0-8156-2713-0 (alk. paper). — ISBN 0-8156-0404-1 (pbk. :
alk. paper)
    1. American drama—Jewish authors. 2. Jewish women—United
States—Drama. 3. Jews—United States—Drama. 4. American drama—
Women authors. 5. American drama—20th century. I. Cohen, Sarah
Blacher.
PS628.J47M35   1996
812'.540809287'089924—dc20   96-21140

Manufactured in the United States of America

To the indispensable women in my life:
my loving mother, Mary Blacher;
my devoted sisters, Bess Rosen Lichterman
and Dorothy Seidelman;
and my nieces and grandnieces,
who will someday write their own plays

Sarah Blacher Cohen is professor of English at the University at Albany, SUNY, and is a leading scholar of Jewish-American literature and an accomplished playwright. She is the author of *Saul Bellow's Enigmatic Laughter* and *Cynthia Ozick's Comic Art: From Levity to Liturgy.* Her plays include the musical *Molly Picon's Return Engagement* and *The Old System.* Professor Cohen collaborated with Isaac Bashevis Singer on *Schlemiel the First* and coauthored, with Joanne Koch, the musicals *Sophie, Totie & Belle; Sophie Tucker: Red Hot Yiddishe Mama; Soul Sisters;* and the screenplay *Belle.*

Contents

Illustrations

Acknowledgments

WERE I TO CITE all the memorable women in my life, their winning traits and special contributions would fill another volume. Rather, let me pay tribute to the most unforgettable characters in my personal drama: my loving mother, Mary Kaminsky Blacher, who gave me life and a Jewish sense of purpose in that life; my devoted sisters, Bess Rosen Lichterman and Dorothy Seidelman, who often delayed fulfilling their own desires to pamper and praise their baby sister; my nieces, Sheryl Pelc, Lynn Hurwitz, Nancy Shimon, Sandy Bernstein, Liza Blacher, Monique Pommier Blacher, Roberta Rosen, Barbara Blacher, and Dianne Blacher, who were models of maturity, amazingly sensible and sensitive for their years, and my grandnieces, Julie Pelc, Sari Pelc, Ellie Pelc, Mara Hurwitz, Adina Hurwitz, Rachel Shimon, Lauren Rosen, and Lisa Rosen, who dazzled me with their agility of body and imagination.

I wish also to thank the women at the Albany Jewish Community Center Locker Room who inspired me to create the principal characters of *The Ladies Locker Room:* Sophie Geller, my ninety-years-plus friend, who became Sophie, the cheerleader and midwife from Bialystok; Bess Becker, the stylishly attired octogenarian, who became Emily, the elegantly outfitted cantor's daughter; and Edith Kolmin, the energetic Viennese realtor, who became Greta, the resilient survivor of the Holocaust and breast cancer.

To the women who helped me transform *The Ladies Locker Room* into a "theatrical bath-house," I owe yet another debt. My gratitude to President Karen Hitchcock of the University of Albany, for approving my innovative sabbatical usage to hasten the completion of my anthology. Especially grateful am I to my *dramaturges:* Cynthia Ozick, omniscient *rebbe* and mentor supreme, and Joanne Koch, my gifted collaborator on other plays. Of invaluable assistance were my *critics and kibitzers:* Helen Moshak, Nancy Schiff, Elaine Safer, Joyce Ladenson, Myra Sklarew, Judith Baskin, Elizabeth Ruthman, Lillian Lux, Zelda Batt, Roz Alexander, Renee Matthews, Helen Elam, Judith Fetterley, Judy Johnson, Joan Schulz, Sara Freifeld, Tanya Clyman, Rhoda Feldman, Evelyn Aronson, Carol King, Francine Frank, Gloria DeSole, Barbara Lebow, Eleanor Koblenz, Charlotte Abrams, Leslie Diamond, and Sara Harris; *sponsors:* Joyce Pogoda, Adult Program director of the Albany Jewish Community Center and Nancy Bellowich Negron, director of the University at Albany's Disabled Student Services; *directors:* Kit Goldman, San Diego's Gaslamp Theatre, Sally Chasnoff Kahan, Northwestern University, and Frieda Scott, University of Georgia.

To help me create a home for *The Ladies Locker Room* in my anthology, *Making a Scene: The Contemporary Drama of Jewish-American Women,* I am indebted to the following women: Ellen Schiff and Judy Barlow, editors of their own excellent drama anthologies; Mimi Brodsky, typist; Cheryl Schoonmaker, graduate research assistant; and Cheryl Reeves, copy editor and proofreader.

In conclusion, I cannot fail to mention two male laborers working selflessly behind the scenes to lend support and substance to my dramatic endeavors: the accomplished and trustworthy director of Syracuse University Press, Robert Mandel, and my dependable and loving husband, Gary Cohen.

Sarah Blacher Cohen

Albany, New York
August 1996

Making a Scene

Introduction

Characters

PROFESSOR SARAH, a somewhat pedantic English professor whose conversations inevitably sound like lectures.

BUBBE SORELE, her Yiddish Eastern European alter ego whose earthy humor and common sense candor puncture Professor Sarah's inflated intellectuality. Speaks in a Yiddish accent.

Setting

The study of Professor Sarah, which is strewn with books, plays and newspapers—a mess.

PROFESSOR SARAH. *(Wringing her hands and pulling out her hair.)* Why did I edit this anthology: *Making a Scene: The Contemporary Drama of Jewish-American Women?*

BUBBE SORELE. Yes, why? What kind of foolishness is this anthology? You could have made some gefilte fish and done something important.

PROFESSOR SARAH. What I've done *is* important. I've gathered together very talented women playwrights who face a difficult challenge. They must rely on often flawed interpreters—actors, directors, set designers—to convey their meaning. They are not afraid to expose their vulnerabilities in the most public of art forms.

BUBBE SORELE. Expose their vulnerabilities—it doesn't sound kosher to me. But don't men playwrights do that, too?

PROFESSOR SARAH. Yes, but the words they speak are valued by society. They are praised for creating universal art, genuine art which is not limited by gender. But women playwrights are denounced for producing narrow, domestic art. They are chastened for speaking up in a male-controlled theater world that attempts to silence them.

BUBBE SORELE. You mean, they're trying to be big-mouths like me.

PROFESSOR SARAH. No, they want to draw upon their unique sensibility to communicate their vision of reality. They do not want to be dismissed as intellectual lightweights who merely capture "the fleeting words of everyday life" but "rarely hit the high note of great drama" (Mersand 1937, qtd. in Barlow, viii). They resent being called "playwrights in petticoats" (Nathan 1941, qtd. in Barlow, viii) who could not equal or excel the best of our male dramatists.

BUBBE SORELE. Who says such nonsense about "playwrights in petticoats?" What about "men playwrights in pajamas?" They don't know nothing. Some of them can't even tell a bagel from a bialy. Without the women, something is missing.

PROFESSOR SARAH. You're right. Women make up half the human race, yet women's words do not exist in equal numbers, nor are they transmitted from century to century. If women's words had been appreciated, we would not have lost them and would have a richer civilization because of them.

BUBBE SORELE. Didn't your writer friend, Cynthia Ozick, say something like that?

PROFESSOR SARAH. In a way, but she was referring to the tremendous loss of Jewish women's contributions to the intellectual life of the community: "If Jewish law aids in suppressing women scholars who can grow to create it . . . that is akin to cultural self-destruction." What we have then is a "Jewish half-genius," which causes us to listen with "only half an ear" and speak with "only half a tongue" (Ozick 1988c, 140).

BUBBE SORELE. With "half an ear" and "half a tongue"—they should see a doctor quick!

PROFESSOR SARAH. Maybe that's one of the reasons I edited this anthology, to restore the "Jewish half-genius" in women's drama concealed behind the *mehitzah,* the ritual partition separating men from women.

BUBBE SORELE. Now you're getting to something I can understand: *mehitzah*s. That's where we women tried to pray, "shushed" the children, and envied the men who read from the Torah.

PROFESSOR SARAH. Come to think of it, those ritually privileged men resemble those Jewish-American male playwrights whose works receive preferential treatment. Investors take the financial risk to produce them, theatergoers attend their performances, presses publish them, and educators teach them.

BUBBE SORELE. Now, professorke, you gotta admit. These men playwrights must have some talent. They didn't get ahead just cause they were Jewish men whose mothers loved them too much.

PROFESSOR SARAH. True. Theater critic Ellen Schiff does remind us that "since the establishment of the Tony awards in 1947, plays and books for musicals written by Jews have been nominated virtually every year; by 1990 some thirty had won. Elmer Rice, the first Jew awarded the Pulitzer Prize for drama . . . in 1929, heads a roster that currently includes seventeen Jewish laureates" (1995, xviii).

BUBBE SORELE. Not bad. Some of them know how to write about women, besides. Could it be that a few of their lady characters become more alive in their dramas than in the dramas by the women playwrights?

PROFESSOR SARAH. Whose side are you on?

BUBBE SORELE. What's true is true. What about that Bessie Berger? Doesn't that *boychik* who created her—a Clifford something—

PROFESSOR SARAH. Odets, Clifford Odets.

BUBBE SORELE. Yes him. Doesn't he have her say that she's "not only the mother" in the house, "but also the father." That's a pretty big job. You need a special lady to do that.

PROFESSOR SARAH. You're right. Bessie Berger is a special lady with admirable strengths. She has great resourcefulness, great energy, great shrewdness, great emotional depths. But she also has her weaknesses. She's stingy, opportunistic, vindictive. She is desperately afraid of poverty and prevents her son from marrying a poor orphan. She's overly concerned with middle-class propriety and forces her daughter to marry a man who is not the father of her baby. She smashes her father's recordings, his dreams of utopia, because she projects onto him her son's contempt for her unethical behavior.

BUBBE SORELE. It seems like this lady is a *mishmash* of good and bad.

PROFESSOR SARAH. Exactly. That's what makes her a fully rounded character. That's not the case with Sylvia Regan's female protagonist, Becky Felderman, in *Morning Star,* written in 1940, just five years after *Awake and Sing* (1935). She is more saintly than human in her magnanimous acceptance of so many personal tragedies: the death of her daughter in the Triangle Shirtwaist Factory fire and the loss of her son in World War I. She is so thoroughly virtuous in keeping her remaining family together that she resembles the unsullied heroine of melodrama.

BUBBE SORELE. You mean she is too good for her own good?

PROFESSOR SARAH. No, I mean she's too good to be believable as a character. Not so with Bessie Berger. Odets permits her to be the embodiment of a life-denying capitalism, along with being the maternal villain of the play. At least that's what the Marxist and misogynistic critics claim she is.

BUBBE SORELE. What means misogynistic?

PROFESSOR SARAH. Woman-hating. But Odets makes us feel compassionate for Bessie as well. He makes us see her as a victim of the Depression. He shows us what a great personal sacrifice she makes to enable her family to survive economically. In one of her final speeches, she exclaims: "My whole life I wanted to go away too, but with children a woman stays home. A fire burned in *my* heart too, but now it's too late. I'm no spring chicken. The clock goes and Bessie goes. Only my machinery can't be fixed" (Odets 1995, 279).

BUBBE SORELE. I know what Bessie is talking about. My machinery can't be fixed neither.

PROFESSOR SARAH. The fact that you can identify with her means that she is a fully realized character.

BUBBE SORELE. If she lived in my shtetl, I'd be a friend of hers. Too bad she wasn't created by a Sadie Odets. Then you could have included her in your women's anthology. What about that girl Yentl created by my Yiddish writer friend, Singer, Isaac. She's not fat, but she, too, is what you call a fully rounded character. How about having her in the anthology?

PROFESSOR SARAH. In many ways she is an ideal candidate. She is grappling with problems of identity confronting Jewish women in late-nineteenth-century Poland, problems that have not been resolved in our own century. Her love for studying Torah vies forcefully with her love for a man. Her yearning for mental and spiritual liberation is strongly at odds with her need for physical and emotional union. She suffers the painful consequences of the need to choose one alternative.

BUBBE SORELE. I, too, had difficult decisions. Should I make a beet borscht for the family or study the Torah?

PROFESSOR SARAH. The feminist treatment of Yentl's conflict between love and learning can be attributed primarily to Singer's female collaborator, Leah Napolin. Singer's attitude toward Yentl was a traditionally religious and masculine one: Yentl errs by trespassing in the male's learned domain. By dressing in men's clothes to do so, she also damages her own God-given femininity. She must be routed from the community because she is not dependent on a man to define her identity and, therefore, does not provide a model for man's dependence on God. Considering herself the accomplished rival of any man, she encourages man to view himself as the accomplished rival of God.

BUBBE SORELE. Poor Yentl! She was not treated very well by Mr. Singer. He'd not only have to change his sex, but change the way he looks at things before I would let him into our anthology. Maybe Barbra Streisand with her screenplay of *Yentl* you should ask to join us.

PROFESSOR SARAH. I don't think so. Her version of *Yentl* is too simplistic. At the end Yentl goes to America and effortlessly has it all: an independent fate as a scholar and love, too, in the promised land.

BUBBE SORELE. And she's singing while she's doing both. I guess we don't need singers of Singer who do a poor imitation of him. (*Sighs*) There must be some well-known Jewish women playwrights. What about that Stein lady who said "a nose is a nose is a nose."

PROFESSOR SARAH. You mean Gertrude Stein, who said "a rose is a rose is a rose." Of German-Jewish extraction, she did write a few memorable plays, such as *Four Saints in Three Acts* (1934), *Dr. Faustus Lights the Lights* (1922), and *The Mother of Us All* (about Susan B. Anthony) (1932), but they were more concerned with her identity as an American lesbian or a member of the literary avant-garde than as a Jew. Her plays encouraged women to defy social codes to achieve personal fulfillment, to employ idiosyncratic language to convey their idiosyncratic views of authority figures. Stein was committed to making sense out of nonsense, and was known for her comedy of language, her puns, her elaborate wordplay, and her ingenious nonsequitors, which wittily served to mask an underlying moral seriousness.

BUBBE SORELE. Doesn't sound too Jewish to me. What about Hellman, Lillian? Isn't she supposed to be America's most famous Jewish woman playwright?

PROFESSOR SARAH. Like Gertrude Stein, Hellman has Jewish-German origins, but Jews are conspicuously absent in her plays, though the Hubbard family in *The Little Foxes* (1939) and *Another Part of the Forest* (1946) are based in part on her mother's Jewish relatives. They are portrayed as rapacious Southerners, however, not as Jews. Even in Hellman's World War II plays, *Watch on the Rhine* (1941) and *The Searching Wind* (1944), there were no Jewish characters nor any direct reference to the persecution of the Jews. Undoubtedly Lillian Hellman's a-Semitic dramas were a response to the period's unwritten censorship of things Jewish in the arts. But they also reflect her own anti-Jewish feelings. Her memoirs reveal that she wanted to banish objectionable Jews and Jewish traits from her life, and she apparently wanted to banish them from her plays as well. The notable exception is her adaptation, *My Mother, My Father and Me* (1963), of Burt Blechman's novel, *How Much?*, where she focuses on the Jewish middle class but then indicts them for their hypocrisy and philistinism. In her original dramas what she values most is the physical and emotional bravery of Gentiles, a kind of Hemingwayesque "grace under pressure" in contrast to the Jews in her life, whom she sees as unduly fearful and self-seeking. Thus Hellman's "negative image of the Jew, coupled with her Hemingwayesque world view, suggests a flight from her own Jewishness" (Lyons 1986, 109).

BUBBE SORELE. That was a lecture, not an answer. I still don't understand what makes a Jewish-American lady's play? Hellman is Jewish but she doesn't write about Jews in her plays.

PROFESSOR SARAH. For that reason, she doesn't belong in my anthology.

BUBBE SORELE. What if a lady is not Jewish but writes about Jews?

PROFESSOR SARAH. You mean someone like Ann Nichols, the Protestant playwright who wrote about Jews and Gentiles. Her 1922 *Abie's Irish Rose,* the most popular play of the times, was an amiable comedy of Jewish and Irish-Catholic star-crossed lovers and their feuding fathers.

BUBBE SORELE. Sounds like a good play. Was it good for the Jews?

PROFESSOR SARAH. You tell me. The Old World prejudices and exaggerated dialects of the stereotypical immigrant parents, Solomon Levy and Patrick Murphy, provide the engaging humor of the piece. The New World triumph of romantic love and brotherhood over religious clannishness contributes an even more winning sentimentality. To make intermarriage acceptable, Ann Nichols has two ultraliberal clergymen, Father Whalen and Rabbi Samuels, give their respective blessing to the happy couple and try to gain the parents' approval. Assuming that all faiths are the same, both clergymen express pleasure at the merging of customs and ceremonies in the young couple's home. Ann Nichols succeeds in abolishing the distinctive aspects of

Jewish tradition and Irish Catholicism. So the play ends with "a Christmas tree in the parlor, kosher food in the cabinets, and a ham in the oven."

BUBBE SORELE. Doesn't sound so good for the Jews . . . or the Irish Catholics. I guess you won't have her in your anthology.

PROFESSOR SARAH. You're right. And I won't include Jewish women playwrights whose subjects or characters are not explicitly Jewish, even though their themes and values have a Jewish flavor to them.

BUBBE SORELE. You mean they got to be kosher, not kosher style.

PROFESSOR SARAH. Not exactly. Those dramatists whose works are not explicitly Jewish are kosher in their own right. Playwrights like Karen Malpede, Emily Mann, and Susan Yankowitz are, in a way, secular prophets deeply committed to exploring ethical issues of their time. Their drama rails against the perversion of justice, the brutality of war, the abuses of patriarchy. Their drama is, however, an impassioned expression of their political-poetic activism, not their Jewishness.

BUBBE SORELE. Who, then, are you going to put in your anthology? So far it's a pretty empty book.

PROFESSOR SARAH. There's no doubt about one person whose play I'm going to include: Wendy Wasserstein, winner of both the Pulitzer Prize and the Tony Award.

BUBBE SORELE. Oh, she's one of those ladies what knows everything.

PROFESSOR SARAH. Yes. She has created what one critic calls "comedies of feminine survival that explore the ambiguous effectiveness of the woman's movement during the past quarter of a century. Using the pattern of her own life . . . she has dramatized with a sharply satiric wit the problematic intersection of the individual experience and the collective feminist ideology that would explain and transform it" (Alter 1994, 449).

BUBBE SORELE. That critic uses a lot of fancy words but they don't help me understand this Wendy's plays. What's Jewish about them or does she only write about roses, like that Stein lady?

PROFESSOR SARAH. The Jewishness Wasserstein represents is "ethical and secular: a fact of character, a linguistic marker, the condition of family, community, and culture rather than the theological discipline of a practiced faith" (Alter 1994, 450).

BUBBE SORELE. Again with the fancy words. How can I find this Jewishness in Wendele's plays?

PROFESSOR SARAH. In *Isn't It Romantic* (1983), my choice for the anthology, she dramatizes her protagonist Janie Blumberg's declaration of independence. She has her recognize the infantilizing effects of her ubiquitous Jewish parents, the smothering attentions of a demanding Jewish doctor boyfriend, and the self-centeredness of her Gentile best friend. She has Janie realize that no one else can make her life meaningful, that she alone can become the grown-up Jewish woman who can fend for herself and enjoy her own company.

BUBBE SORELE. Sounds like a pretty serious play.

PROFESSOR SARAH. Yes, it's serious. Still it's a wonderful comedy, one filled with the wry self-deprecation of Jewish humor, which is the principal reason I selected this play for the anthology.

BUBBE SORELE. Is she the funniest Jewish lady writing plays today?

PROFESSOR SARAH. Without a doubt.

BUBBE SORELE. Then why is she funny?

PROFESSOR SARAH. I'll let Wendy Wasserstein answer that question. She best defined the nature of the humor in *Isn't It Romantic* in one of her interviews:

> WENDY: Janie Blumberg is totally trapped by her own sense of humor . . . composed of very witty one-liners. . . . Janie is a character who has a problem expressing her feelings and she desperately wants to be liked.
>
> INTERVIEWER: Is Janie's humor a way of protecting herself?
>
> WASSERSTEIN: It's a protection, but it's a vulnerability as well. . . . Janie . . . tells joke, joke, joke and then finally explodes. Finally she discovers her own strength. And furthermore, there is a strength in being comedic. It's a way of getting on in the world, of taking the heat out of things. Humor is a life force. (Betsko and Koenig 1987, 419)

BUBBE SORELE. That Wendele knows what she's talking about.

PROFESSOR SARAH. She surely does. She understands the dynamics of humor and the psychological benefits her characters derive from it. "Janie Blumberg's humor," she claims, "gives her the ability to distance herself from situations. But she simultaneously endears herself to people by being amusing" (Betsko and Koenig 1987, 420). However, Wendy Wasserstein also relies on her comedic sense to retaliate against victimization.

BUBBE SORELE. What means victimization?

PROFESSOR SARAH. It means troubles.

BUBBE SORELE. Troubles. Do I have troubles! Let me tell you about my troubles.

PROFESSOR SARAH. Later. Now we're discussing *Janie's* troubles, her victimization by patriarchal society in her post-college "bachelor girl" world. But her world is largely devoid of painful historical events.

BUBBE SORELE. You should have another play about that. I don't mean to nudge you, but that's too important to forget about.

PROFESSOR SARAH. Don't worry. I haven't forgotten about it. I'm including the poignant Holocaust-survivor play, *A Shayna Maidel* (1987) by Barbara Lebow.

BUBBE SORELE. *Shayna maidel,* that's what my mother called me.

PROFESSOR SARAH. The play is about such a mother who was killed in the Holocaust because she stayed behind to care for her sick young daughter. Her husband took their other child, a baby girl, with him to America and promised to send for them when he got established.

BUBBE SORELE. It's not so easy for a refugee to get what you call "established."

PROFESSOR SARAH. Because he couldn't earn a living and was too ashamed to borrow money, time ran out for him to save his wife. But the daughter, Lusia, now grown up, was liberated from a Polish concentration camp and came totally unexpected to the United States to live with her father and her American sister, Rose Weiss.

BUBBE SORELE. How does this Barbara Lebow know from this? Was she a Holocaust survivor, too?

PROFESSOR SARAH. No, she was a "witness-through-the-imagination" (Rosen 1974, 58). Born and raised in Brooklyn, she was singed by the flames from afar. She interviewed many survivors of the Holocaust but focused not on their horrific experience in the camps but on their trying periods of adjustment after their liberation. Because she herself was not an actual victim, she became one of those American writers about the Holocaust "that bears the scar without the wound, sustaining memory without direct experience" (Cohen 1981, 2).

BUBBE SORELE. That's good. As long as she doesn't write about what she doesn't know about, like so many of those *Shoah*-business people.

PROFESSOR SARAH. She would never do that. Her focus in the play is on the psychological accommodations the American sister must make to find room in her sheltered life for her Holocaust-ravaged sister. She vicariously experiences Lusia's grim past—the murder of her child and the death of her best friend. Through overhearing Lusia's agonizing nightmares, Rose becomes reacquainted with her dead mother and the decimated shtetl she lived in. Rose is able to mourn the incalculable losses she never knew she had. Etching the concentration camp numbers in her own skin, she becomes the sentient Holocaust victim herself.

BUBBE SORELE. Oy that poor girl.

PROFESSOR SARAH. Not necessarily. In sharing her sister's sorrow, she is able to fulfill the obligation of confronting the most heinous event of this century and, in so doing, gain some understanding of it. This knowledge enables her to give birth to a new, more profound self.

BUBBE SORELE. Isn't that what happens in your own play, *The Ladies Locker Room?* A Gentile girl with a good body gives birth to a baby with the help of a Jewish girl whose body is not so good.

PROFESSOR SARAH. Not quite as simple as that. In my play about disability and the Jewish woman, the midwifery of the disabled Dr. Susan enables her to give birth to herself, but she doesn't do it alone. She gains an appreciation of herself as a capable though physically challenged person through the collective wisdom of her older locker room companions, especially the eighty-some-year-old Sophie Gold from Bialystok.

BUBBE SORELE. Sophie Gold from Bialystok. Maybe she's a relative of mine. You know I come from Bialystok.

PROFESSOR SARAH. Yes I know. You're a lot like her. You're both Yiddish humorists. You each have the capacity to laugh off the cruel ironies of your own lives. You both can wittily undercut the foolish pretensions of academics.

BUBBE SORELE. Oh, that's what I'm supposed to be doing here?

PROFESSOR SARAH. Maybe. But Sophie Gold does more than that. Dr. Susan, who "walks funny," finds kinship with Sophie, who "talks funny," but who "didn't have no accent until she moved to America." In the ladies locker room, this place of enforced intimacy, Sophie acts as Dr. Susan's cheerleader, spurring her on to triumph over adversity and self-pity. She shows Dr. Susan how to exercise the whole body, how to make challahs, and how to deliver babies. She is optimistic about Dr. Susan's future. She encourages her to "enjoy the sunshine" and let the "budding relationship with the botanist" boyfriend grow into something.

BUBBE SORELE. What a miracle worker that Sophie is.

PROFESSOR SARAH. Yes, for Sophie, existence is a miracle. "Life," she says, "is the biggest bargain. We get it from God for nothing."

BUBBE SORELE. Oh how the audiences will love that happy ending. I'm sure you're going to put this locker room play into your anthology.

PROFESSOR SARAH. (*Grinning*) I guess I will.

BUBBE SORELE. Pardon me if I sound like what you call "the under-cutter." But I was wondering. Are you doing this whole anthology just so you can publish your own play in it?

PROFESSOR SARAH. Perish the thought! A thousand times, no! How can you think such a thing?

BUBBE SORELE. I know you. That's why.

PROFESSOR SARAH. I assure you. There are a number of other worth-while plays by contemporary Jewish-American women dramatists that deserve to find a home in this anthology. You know it's the only one on this subject. So I was able to choose from the very best of emerging new voices that reflect the multifaceted realities of Jewish women's lives.

BUBBE SORELE. All right. I believe you. I believe you. Now tell me about some of these plays.

PROFESSOR SARAH. One of them, *Nobody's Gilgul* (1994), by a New Hampshire playwright, Lois Roisman, contains some of your shtetl wit and wisdom.

BUBBE SORELE. What means *gilgul?* I forgot already. I remember my mother telling me to be a good *gilgul* or did she say be a good girl.

PROFESSOR SARAH. A *gilgul* is the bodily home for a wandering soul.

BUBBE SORELE. You mean like a *dybbuk?*

PROFESSOR SARAH. No. In Jewish folklore a *dybbuk* is the spirit of a dead person that possesses the body of a living person. The *gilgul* is the body which houses that spirit. In Lois Roisman's play, Lily, the descendant of biblical Lilith, the disobedient wife of Adam, is the contemporary feminist woman. She is devoid of a soul and, without knowing it, searches for one to make her a complete human being. Eva, the descendant of the biblical Eve, the compliant wife of Adam, is the soul of an orthodox shtetl creature from the distant past. She is searching to inhabit the body of a contemporary woman.

BUBBE SORELE. Lily and Eva sound so different. How could they ever get together?

PROFESSOR SARAH. That's the source of the play's comedy and the-matic content. Especially when they each have such different reality instructors telling them what to do—the ancient rabbis insisting that Eva be subservient to men and Lily's psychiatrist urging her to be self-reliant.

BUBBE SORELE. I think she should listen to the rabbis.

PROFESSOR SARAH. I think she should listen to the psychiatrist. You see, the play captures the dilemma of today's Jewish woman who gains pleasure from performing the rituals of orthodox Judaism, yet she feels restricted by them. She strikes out on her own and is exhilarated by her innovative departures from tradition, yet she misses the sense of Jewish continuity.

BUBBE SORELE. I did not have what you call those "dilemmas." I knew who I was and what I had to do. And people respected me for that.

PROFESSOR SARAH. That's not a luxury all Jewish women have, especially Jewish lesbian women.

BUBBE SORELE. Who are they? I never heard of them.

PROFESSOR SARAH. You never heard of them because Jewish law does not acknowledge the existence of Jewish women whose sexual preference is other women. They're there, but nobody wants to admit they're there.

BUBBE SORELE. You mean they're invisible? What about Jewish men who like too much other men? In the Torah they spoke up against that.

PROFESSOR SARAH. You're right. "The Old Testament (and current Israeli law) prohibits male homosexuality, calls it an abomination, an unnatural act. But neither Jewish law nor sacred literature ever mentions love between women" (Freedman 1982, 211).

BUBBE SORELE. If they don't mention it, it can't be forbidden. Being invisible is not bad, then.

PROFESSOR SARAH. It's bad. "Having to hide is a sure sign of danger" (Beck 1982, xv).

BUBBE SORELE. Very dangerous?

PROFESSOR SARAH. "Jewish invisibility is a symptom of anti-Semitism as surely as lesbian invisibility is a symptom of homophobia." Evelyn Beck, the author of *Nice Jewish Girls*, reminds us "that invisibility has a trivializing, disempowering and ultimately debilitating effect on its members" (1982, xv).

BUBBE SORELE. You're a smart professorke, what can we do about this invisibility?

PROFESSOR SARAH. We can make the lives of Jewish lesbians more visible by getting to know them and by appreciating their unique contributions. I'm going to include a new play about them by a

Jewish lesbian playwright, Barbara Kahn. Her drama, *Whither Thou Goest* (1995), sequel to *Unorthodox Behavior* (1992), which is about a Jewish young woman's rebellion against the shtetl's patriarchy, is about this same woman's immigrant experience in America.

BUBBE SORELE. Sounds a little like me. What kind of work did she do?

PROFESSOR SARAH. Simi Lasser, born Cyma Lozawick, is a staff member at the Hanna Lavanburg Home for Immigrant Girls. Her job is to help Rachel, one of her charges, make her way in the world. She cautions her not to fall prey to vanity, not to give her name away like it was "a piece of candy," not to act backward and speak only in Yiddish. Rachel, in turn, is hopelessly smitten with Simi, who is totally unaware of the teenager's lesbian affection for her. Simi has also unwittingly evoked a similar response from a woman her own age, Charlotte Lobell, the spoiled daughter of a controlling German-Jewish philanthropist.

BUBBE SORELE. Only in America can this happen.

PROFESSOR SARAH. The play depicts the conflicts within and among these three women. It traces the intricate development of their complex Jewish and lesbian identities. Its title, *Whither Thou Goest,* echoing the Book of Ruth, hints at the play's ending: one woman accompanies another woman on a journey to a new locale where they find fulfillment. There they no longer need to hide. Knowing who they are, they feel safe.

BUBBE SORELE. I like plays with happy endings. Have some more of them in your anthology.

PROFESSOR SARAH. I'm afraid that's not always possible in a play about Blacks and Jews, especially in the one I'm anthologizing: *The Night the War Came Home* (1993), by Hindi Brooks. The 1992 Watts Riots of Los Angeles, Brooks's current home town, prompted her to remember the painful 1943 race riots of her native Detroit. This time the riots were ignited by the volatile tensions between the Whites and Blacks who came from the South to work in the Detroit defense plants. When they experienced austerity, rather than prosperity, their fury erupted against the Jewish slum landlords and shopkeepers.

BUBBE SORELE. Sounds like pogroms to me.

PROFESSOR SARAH. Not exactly. The principal black characters are the friends, not the enemies, of the play's central Jewish family. In fact, the daughter is secretly married to a black soldier, who was her former classmate at Wayne State. He returns from the army to protect her family from the rioters and looters.

BUBBE SORELE. You're right. A cossack would never do that.

PROFESSOR SARAH. Also, the family's frightened son, a deserter from the army, accidently kills a black friend. Not the other way around. Much of the play deals with the Jews coping with their fears of black villains and pleading with innocent Blacks to forgive them.

BUBBE SORELE. You would expect a Black to write such a play, not a Jew. And for sure, not a Jewish woman.

PROFESSOR SARAH. Hindi Brooks grew up with Blacks, had strong black friendships and persuaded her parents to reverse their negative opinions of Blacks. Her play, written at a time when a "color-blind" America was still a possibility, holds out the hope for a cessation of hostilities and the restoration of trust and respect between Blacks and Jews. In this drama by a Jewish woman playwright, the Jewish daughter and Jewish mother are the most forceful in combating the internal and external war threatening to undermine the viability of the Jewish family. But more important, they insist we "enlarge our vision beyond our particular pains" (Lester 1994, 177).

BUBBE SORELE. Sounds like a happy ending to me. Better than all that fighting between Blacks and Hasidim in Crown Heights.

PROFESSOR SARAH. Let's say the play reflected "a better age when the common histories of oppression and degradation served as a springboard for genuine empathy and principled alliances" (West 1994, 145). But everything was not neatly resolved. There were still problems.

BUBBE SORELE. Problems, do I have problems.

PROFESSOR SARAH. But not like the problems still erupting between Blacks and Jews or hostilities escalating in Israel between Arabs and Jews.

BUBBE SORELE. You got a play about that, too? I thought American Jews only gave money to Israel. They didn't make up dramas about it.

PROFESSOR SARAH. True. Since its founding as a nation in 1948, the economic "survival of Israel has been the paramount concern of organized Jewish life and probably the paramount source of Jewish identity" in America (Solotaroff 1988, 33). But Israel as subject matter has not seized the imagination of very many Jewish-American creative writers.

BUBBE SORELE. Why is that?

PROFESSOR SARAH. They find its biblical antiquity remote, its Semitic nature strange. Critic Leslie Fiedler tells us: "I feel myself . . . a foreigner in Jerusalem and Tel Aviv and the Holy City of Safed. . . .

Israel remains for me . . . an abstraction, a metaphor from a dull, half-forgotten sermon" (Fiedler 1991, 8).

BUBBE SORELE. So how come this American Jewish lady does not feel like a stranger in Israel and can write a play about it?

PROFESSOR SARAH. This lady, Merle Feld, is a prize-winning playwright and poet who spent a sabbatical year (1989–90) in Israel, where she organized dialogue groups for Israeli and Palestinian women from the West Bank to discuss how to obtain lasting peace and sisterhood. Her play, *Crossing the Jordan* (1994), is an outgrowth of that experience.

BUBBE SORELE. So how can you have a play about ladies sitting together and saying "let's be friends."

PROFESSOR SARAH. It may end that way, but it doesn't begin that way. *Crossing the Jordan* is a play about enemies. It dramatizes the story of two women from opposite sides: Daphne, a liberal young Israeli lawyer assigned to defend Najah, a militant twenty-year-old Palestinian college student accused by the Israeli military establishment of terrorism and murder.

BUBBE SORELE. A Jewish woman lawyer, I like that.

PROFESSOR SARAH. The play also has a parallel plot based on the lives and destiny of two biblical adversaries: Sarah, the legitimate though barren wife of Abraham, who gives her handmaiden to her husband to provide him with an heir, and Hagar, the dark Egyptian beauty who bears him a son, Ishmael. But when Sarah has her own son, Isaac, Hagar suffers the rage of her jealous, unforgiving mistress, who cruelly banishes her and her son.

BUBBE SORELE. The Hebrew Sarah is not very nice to the Egyptian Hagar.

PROFESSOR SARAH. But as historian Judith Baskin says, in many "biblical narratives reprehensible human actions, driven by the most elemental emotions, are seen to fulfill a larger predetermined plan" (Baskin 1994, 216).

BUBBE SORELE. What kind of plan is that? All I know is stalling plans where you pay little by little.

PROFESSOR SARAH. "The divine plan that Isaac, not Ishmael, will carry on the everlasting covenant that God has established with Abraham" (Baskin 1994, 219). Sarah is making sure that will happen.

BUBBE SORELE. I understand. But still the Hebrew Sarah could have been a little kinder to the Egyptian Hagar.

PROFESSOR SARAH. Maybe that's one of the main points of the play.

BUBBE SORELE. Supporters of Israel will not like that point. They're going to be mad on Merle.

PROFESSOR SARAH. Too bad. Merle Feld, like the other dramatists in this anthology, is a playwright of integrity who refuses to be a public relations agent, to tell the public only the good things about Jews. Like the prophets, she's committed to telling the truth as she sees it. She refuses to be censored or silenced.

BUBBE SORELE. You mean like all those lady playwrights you mentioned before, the ones who wouldn't be "shushed?"

PROFESSOR SARAH. Yes, like those who refused to tone down their loud voices, who insisted on singing the songs they wanted to sing, who kept their humanity intact and their talent flourishing, and who fought against being Jewish half-geniuses.

BUBBE SORELE. Enough with the talking about these geniuses. Let them make a scene already and speak for themselves.

PROFESSOR SARAH. Any other orders, Director Sorele?

BUBBE SORELE. Yes. Enjoy! Enjoy!

Photograph by James Hamilton

Wendy Wasserstein

I DON'T SPEND MUCH TIME thinking about being funny. For me it's always been just a way to get by, a way to be likeable yet to remain removed. When I speak up, it's not because I have any particular answers; rather, I have a desire to puncture the pretentiousness of those who seem so certain they do" (Wasserstein 1991, 184). The youngest of four children, Wendy Wasserstein initially functioned as the funny girl who punctured the pretentions of her upwardly mobile Jewish family—her textile manufacturer father, Morris, and her dance enthusiast mother, Lola, who moved from Brooklyn to Manhattan in 1962, when she was twelve years old.

Wendy, named after the heroine in James M. Barrie's *Peter Pan,* left the yeshiva at Flatbush to attend Calhoun School, Manhattan's exclusive prep academy, and to study with the June Taylor School of Dance on the weekends. In 1971 she graduated with a degree in history from Mount Holyoke College, an elite Ivy League women's school, which had very few Jewish students. She did not go on to become a lawyer, as her parents wished, but returned to New York to earn a master's degree in creative writing at City College in 1973. Instead of attending Columbia University's Graduate School of Business to train to take over the family business, she pursued an MFA in play writing at Yale University. While there, she felt like she was "trying to catch the train to Moscow," but kept missing it (Betsko and Koenig 1987, 427). Nonetheless, among the group of predominately male aspiring playwrights, she flourished. Taking issue with the "Yale point of view" that "the pain in the world is a man's pain" (Betsko and Koenig 1987, 426), she wrote as her master's thesis a one-act play about a woman's pain and a woman's humor, which turned out to be the kernel for her first major full-length play, *Uncommon Women and Others.* "I made the decision to write a play with all women after seeing all that Jacobean drama, where a man kisses the lips of a woman's skull and drops dead. . . . I wanted to write a play where all the women were alive at the curtain call" (Betsko and Koenig 425–26).

Beginning with *Uncommon Women and Others* (1977) based on her Mount Holyoke experiences, Wendy Wasserstein has emerged as "the preeminent chronicler of the momentous changes in the lives of women over the last generation" (*Current Biography Yearbook* 1989, 610). Her evergrowing and highly acclaimed plays include: *Isn't It Romantic* (1981/1983), whose protagonist's parents are modeled after Wendy's parents; *The Heidi Chronicles* (1989), which won all the major drama awards: the Pulitzer Prize, the Tony, the New York Drama Critics Circle, Outer Critics Circle, and the Drama Desk "Best New Play" honors; and *The Sisters Rosensweig* (1992), an in-depth Chekovian portrayal of middle-aged women patterned after her own sisters, a play that reflects the maturation of Wasserstein's prodigious talents. Seattle Repertory presented a workshop production of her new play, *An American Daughter,* in spring 1996 in preparation for a Broadway production.

Isn't It Romantic opened at the Phoenix Theatre in 1981 and received mixed reviews, but Wasserstein's revised version, which was produced by the Playwrights Horizon in 1983, was unanimously praised and enjoyed a run off-Broadway just short of two years. Of the new, improved version, Mel Gussow writes, "Wendy Wasserstein has added a sweet humanity to her comic cautionary tale about a young woman's ascent to adulthood. . . . With careful rewriting, the playwright has turned the tables on her own play. . . . It is now a nouvelle cuisine comedy." Janie Blumburg, fashioned after Wendy herself, is a female *schlemiel* figure, mocking herself for the habitual mistakes she makes. Although she often behaves as a dependent ingenue, she matures in the course of the play. She chooses meaningful work over marriage to a Jewish doctor who infantilizes her. She can also separate herself from her Jewish mother and concludes "it's just too painful not to grow up." To cope with the pain, Wendy still believes "in comedy, in its spirit, and its ability to lift people off the ground" (Betsko and Koenig 1987, 431).

In *Isn't It Romantic,* the lyrics from "Isn't It Romantic" by Lorenz Hart and Richard Rodgers, copyright 1932 by Famous Music Corporation, copyright renewed 1959 by Famous Music Corporation, are reprinted by permission. The lyrics from "Sunrise, Sunset" (Jerry

Bock, Sheldon Harnick), copyright 1964 by Alley Music Corp. and Trio Music Co., Inc., are used by permission, all rights reserved. The lyrics from "I Will Follow Him," English lyrics by Norman Gimbel and Arthur Altman, original lyrics by Jacques Plante, music by J. W. Stole and Del Roma, copyright 1962, 1963 by Les Editions Jacques Plante, Paris, France, rights administered by MCA Music Publishing, a division of MCA Inc., New York, N.Y. 10019 for the U.S.A. and Canada, are used by permission, all rights reserved.

Isn't It Romantic was commissioned in 1979 by the Phoenix Theatre in New York. It was originally presented by the Phoenix Theater on May 28, 1981. The cast was as follows:

Alma Cuervo	Bernie Passeltiner
Laurie Kennedy	Barbara Baxley
Fritz Kupfer	Peter Riegert
Jane Hoffman	Bob Gunton

Director: Steve Robman
Scenery: Marjorie Bradley Kellogg
Costumes: Jennifer von Mayrhauser and Denise Romano
Lighting: Spencer Mosse

Isn't It Romantic was presented by Playwrights Horizons in New York on December 15, 1983. The cast was as follows:

Cristine Rose	Timmy Geissler
Lisa Banes	Kevin Kline
Chip Zien	Swoosie Kurtz
Betty Comden	Patti Lupone
Stephen Pearlman	Ellis Rabb
Jo Henderson	Meryl Streep
Jerry Lanning	Jerry Zaks
Tom Robbins	

Director: Gerald Gutierrez
Scenery: Andrew Jackness
Costumes: Ann Emonts
Lighting: James F. Ingalls
Sound: Scott Lehrer
Music Coordinator: Jack Feldman
Choreography: Susan Rosenstock
Production Stage Manager: J. Thomas Vivian

Isn't It Romantic
1981/1983

André and Gerry made it possible for me
to dedicate this play to my parents.

Characters
In order of appearance:

JANIE BLUMBERG
HARRIET CORNWALL
MARTY STERLING
TASHA BLUMBERG
SIMON BLUMBERG
LILLIAN CORNWALL
PAUL STUART
VLADIMIR
Voices:
CYNTHIA PETERSON
OPERATOR
JULIE STERN
HART FARRELL
CAPTAIN MILTY STERLING
SCHLOMO STERLING
TAJLEI KAPLAN SINGLEBERRY

Scene

The play takes place in 1983 in New York City. The action is set in
various locations in Manhattan, and the set should reflect the variety
of locales. In the Playwrights Horizons production, four men dressed
as moving men, then waiters, joggers, and so on, shifted the sets for
each scene. Thus the scene changes were incorporated into the production and often concluded during the phone-message segments.

Prologue

*Against the New York skyline, music and sounds of Manhattan fade into a
voice on a phone machine. Phone-machine segments occur between scenes. There
is no action during the prologue messages.*

Telephone Machine 1

JANIE. Hi, this is Janie Blumberg. I'm not in right now, but if you leave your name and number, I should be able to get back to you sometime today or tomorrow. (*Sings.*) "Isn't it romantic, merely to be young on such a night as this? Isn't it romantic every something something is like a . . ." (*The machine cuts off. Ring. Beep.*)

TASHA AND SIMON. (*Sing.*) "Is this the little girl I carried? Is this the little boy at play? I don't remember growing older, when did they?"

TASHA. This is your darling mother. I wanted to welcome you to your new apartment. Call me, sweetheart. Your father wants to talk to you. (*Ring. Beep.*)

HARRIET. Hi, Janie, it's Harriet. I can't help you unpack tonight. I have a job interview early tomorrow morning. Can you have breakfast with me afterward? I'll meet you across the street from Rumpelmayer's at ten. Oh, I ran into Cynthia Peterson on the street; I gave her your number. Please don't hate me. Bye. (*Ring. Beep.*)

SIMON. Uh, Janie, it's your father. Uh, er, uh, call your mother. (*Ring. Beep.*)

CYNTHIA PETERSON. Janie, it's Cynthia Peterson. Harriet told me you moved to New York. Why haven't you called me? Everything is awful. I'm getting divorced. I'm looking for a job. There are no men. Call me. Let's have lunch. (*Ring. Beep.*)

TASHA AND SIMON. (*Sing.*) "Sunrise, sunset. Sunrise, sunset. Quickly flow the day . . ." (*Dial tone.*)

OPERATOR. Please hang up. There seems to be a receiver off the hook.

ACT I

Scene 1

Central Park South. Janie Blumberg, twenty-eight, is sitting on a park bench. Her appearance is a little kooky, a little sweet, a little unconfident—all of which some might call creative, or even witty. There is a trash can down right. Harriet Cornwall enters from left, singing the "Charlie Girl" commercial. She could be the cover girl on the best working women's magazine. She is attractive, very bright, charming, and easily put together. She spots Janie.

HARRIET. I think I got the job. Hi, Janie. (*Hugs her.*)

JANIE. Hi, Harriet.

HARRIET. Thank God you're here.

JANIE. Of course I'm here. I got your message last night.

HARRIET. The man I interviewed with was very impressed I took a year off to look at pictures in Italy. I liked him. He was cold, aloof, distant. Very sexy. Can I have a hit of your Tab?

JANIE. Sure.

HARRIET. I can't stay for breakfast. I told him I could come right back to Colgate for a second interview. Janie, I think our move back home to New York is going to be very successful.

JANIE. It is?

HARRIET. Of course there's absolutely no reason why you should believe me.

JANIE. You have an MBA from Harvard. Of course I believe you.

HARRIET. You sound like your mother.

JANIE. No. Tasha would believe you 'cause you're thin. Look at us. You look like a Vermeer and I look like a extra in *Potemkin.*

HARRIET. Janie, I think someone's watching us.

JANIE. (*Fluffs her hair.*) Do I look all right? You know what I resent?

HARRIET. What?

JANIE. Just about everything except you. I resent having to pay the phone bill, be nice to the super, find meaningful work, fall in love, get hurt. All of it I resent deeply.

HARRIET. What's the alternative?

JANIE. Dependency. I could marry the pervert who's staring at us. No. That's not a solution. I could always move back to Brookline. Get another master's in something useful like Women's Pottery. Do a little free-lance writing. Oh, God, it's exhausting.

HARRIET. He's coming. (*Marty Sterling enters down left. He is Janie's mother's dream come true: a prince and a bit of a card.*)

MARTY. Hi.

HARRIET. Hello.

MARTY. You're Harriet Cornwall. I sat behind you during Twentieth-Century Problems. I always thought you were a beautiful girl. (*Extends his hand.*) Marty Sterling.

HARRIET. (*Shakes it.*) Hi. And this is Jane Blumberg.

MARTY. Sure, I remember you. I saw you and Harriet together in Cambridge all the time. You always looked more attainable. Frightened to death, but attainable. I'm not attracted to cold people anymore. Who needs that kind of trouble?

HARRIET. I don't know.

MARTY. So what do you do?

JANIE. Oh, I scream here on Central Park South. I'm taking a break now.

HARRIET. Janie and I just moved back to New York together. Well, at the same time. I lived in Italy for a year, and Janie was lingering in Brookline, Mass.

MARTY. Good old Brookline. Ever go to Jack and Marian's restaurant? Unbelievable kasha varnishka.

HARRIET. Excuse me?

MARTY. Kasha. Little noodle bow ties with barley. Uh, my father's in the restaurant business. Are you familiar with Ye Olde Sterling Tavernes?

HARRIET. Sure. That's a national chain.

MARTY. My father's chain.

HARRIET. (*Impressed.*) Well!

JANIE. Well.

MARTY. Well.

HARRIET. Well.

MARTY. Well. I'm on call. I'm a doctor. Kidneys.

HARRIET AND JANIE. (*Very impressed.*) Well!

JANIE. Look, maybe you two should sit for a minute and reminisce about Twentieth-Century Problems.

MARTY. I wish I could. Good-bye.

HARRIET. Good-bye. (*Marty starts to exit, stops, turns.*)

MARTY. Janie Blumberg. Is your brother Ben Blumberg?

HARRIET. Yup. That's her brother, Ben.

MARTY. I went to Camp Kibbutz with Ben Blumberg when I was nine.

JANIE. Yup, that's my brother, Ben.

MARTY. Would you tell your brother Murray Schlimovitz says hello.

JANIE. Who's Murray Schlimovitz?

MARTY. Me. Before my father owned the Sterling Tavernes, he owned the Schlimovitz Kosher Dairy restaurants in Brooklyn. But around fifteen years ago all the Schlimovitz restaurants burned down. So, for the sake of the family and the business, we changed our names, before I entered uh . . . Harvard. Nice to see you. Bye. (*Exits.*)

HARRIET. What were you doing? "Maybe you two should sit and reminisce about Twentieth-Century Problems!"

JANIE. Marty Sterling could make a girl a nice husband.

HARRIET. Now you really sound like your mother.

JANIE. Hattie, do you know who that man's father is?

HARRIET. Uh-huh. He's an arsonist.

JANIE. No. He's a genius. Mr. Sterling, the little man who comes on television in a colonial suit and a Pilgrim hat to let you know he's giving away free popovers and all the shrimp you can eat at ye Olde Salade and Relish Bar—that guy is Milty Schlimovitz, Marty Sterling's father.

HARRIET. It's all right. I can make do without Dr. Murray Marty and his father's popovers. I have to get to that interview. My friend Joe Stine, the headhunter, says they only have you back if they're going to hire you.

JANIE. Well, if you don't marry Marty Sterling, I'll marry him. Wait till I tell my parents I ran into him. Tasha Blumberg will have the caterers on the other extension.

HARRIET. I'm afraid marrying him isn't a solution. Will you walk me back to Colgate?

JANIE. Sure. If I can get myself up.

HARRIET. Do I look like a successful single woman?

JANIE. (Sizing her up.) Well.

HARRIET. What, well?

JANIE. Hattie, you know the wisdom of Tasha Blumberg?

HARRIET. Which one?

JANIE. Always look nice when you throw out the garbage; you never know who you might meet. Put on your jacket, sweetheart. Always walk with your head up and chest out. Think, "I am."

HARRIET. I am. (Puts on her jacket, lifts her head and chest.)

JANIE. Now I can be seen with you. (Slumps. They exit arm in arm.)

Telephone Machine 2

Ring. Beep.

HARRIET. Janie, I got the job. Sorry I got you up so early. I love you. Bye. (Sings.) "School bells ring and children sing; it's back to Robert Hall again." Bye. (Ring. Beep.)

JULIE STERN. Miss Bloomberg. This is Julie Stern at *Woman's Work* magazine. We read your portfolio. Our readers feel you haven't experienced enough women's pain to stimulate our market. Thank you. (Ring. Beep.)

CYNTHIA PETERSON. Janie, it's Cynthia. There's a Lib/Men, Lib/Women mixer at the Unitarian church on Friday. It got a four-star rating in *Wisdom's Child.* My cousin Felice met an anthropologist there and she's in much worse shape than either of us. Wanna go?

Scene 2

Janie's apartment. She is asleep on the sofa. Tasha Blumberg enters in a cape with an attaché case. She looks over the apartment with disdain, sets the case down on some crates, and sits next to Janie. Tasha sings and strokes Janie's hair.

TASHA. "Is this the little girl I carried? Is this the little boy at play?" (*Louder.*) "I don't remember growing older, when did they? . . ." (*Janie, waking up, turns and screams.*)

TASHA. Good morning, sweetheart. (*Kisses Janie.*) Congratulations on your new apartment.

JANIE. What?

TASHA. Your father and I came over to celebrate your new apartment. What kind of place is this? There isn't a doorman. Is this place safe for you?

JANIE. Oh, Jesus, what are you doing here?

TASHA. I came to celebrate. You know your mother. I like life, life, life. I came over yesterday and you weren't home, so I got worried. I had the super give me the key. I thought maybe something happened with the movers.

JANIE. Nothing happened with the movers. Mother, it's seven o'clock in the morning.

TASHA. Isn't that nice? You can have breakfast with me and your father. (*Opens the attaché case, turns on a Jazzercise tape, takes off her cape to reveal her tie-dyed exercise leotards, and starts to warm up.*)

JANIE. What are you doing?

TASHA. I'm warming up for my morning dance class. Why don't you get up and do it with me? If you exercised, you'd have the energy to unpack your crates. (*Continues to exercise.*)

JANIE. Mother, I've only been here two nights. I'll unpack them later.

TASHA. Janie, people who wait, wait. I like go-go. Watch, I'll show you how to do it. (*Demonstrates.*) The girls at dancing school admire me so much. They tell me they wish their mothers had so much energy.

JANIE. Their mothers probably wear clothes.

TASHA. Why are you so modest?

JANIE. I'm your daughter. I shouldn't be seeing you in tie-dyed underwear.

TASHA. You're making fun of me.

JANIE. I'm not making fun of you.

TASHA. (*Still dancing.*) One, two, three, hip. One, two, three, hip.

JANIE. Where's Daddy?

TASHA. I sent him to pick up some coffee.

JANIE. Do the girls at dancing think it's strange you order breakfast from a coffee shop every morning?

TASHA. (*Turns off tape.*) Sweetheart, when you get married, you make breakfast at your house and invite me. Anything you make will be fine. You want to make sausages, I'll eat sausages. Do you know what sausages are made of? (*Janie lies back on sofa.*)

TASHA. Janie, please don't lie there like a body. You have everything to look forward to. When you were in high school, the other mothers would stop me on the street and say, "You must be so proud of Janie. She's such a brilliant child. If only my daughters were like Janie."

JANIE. What are the names of these mothers? I want names. (*Doorbell rings.*)

TASHA. There's your father with the coffee. (*Opens door. Simon Blumberg, Tasha's partner, a very sweet father, though not chatty, enters with a bag containing coffee and a sandwich.*)

SIMON. Janie, is this place safe for you? There isn't a doorman. Why don't you put in the lock I bought you in Brookline?

JANIE. I left it there.

SIMON. You left it in Brookline? That lock cost fifty dollars.

JANIE. I have it, Dad. I have it.

SIMON. You want to split this egg sandwich with me?

TASHA. Simon, please, there's a proper way to do this. First we have to toast Janie's new apartment. (*Hands out the coffees.*) I remember my first apartment in New York. Of course, I was much younger than you and I was already married to your father. (*Toasts.*) To Janie. Congratulations, welcome home, and I hope next year you live in another apartment and your father and I have to bring up four coffees.

JANIE. You want me to have a roommate?

TASHA. I want you to be happy. Talk to her, Simon, like a father with a daughter. Maybe she wants to tell you her problems.

JANIE. I don't have any problems. How's the business, Dad?

SIMON. Your father always with the business, right? You want to see something, Janie? (*Pulls out an envelope.*) Smell this.

JANIE. (*Smells the envelope.*) It's nice.

SIMON. I can't make them fast enough. And then those jerks ship me a million envelopes without any perfume. You know what that's going to do to the Valentine season? Your father always with the headaches.

JANIE. It's all right, Dad. I like the envelope. Smells like the state of Maine.

SIMON. You want to come down to the business today and see whether it interests you? Then I'll take you skating after work.

JANIE. I can't, Dad. I have to follow up some leads for clients here. Some other time I'd like to. (*Puts on a sweatshirt over her flannel nightgown.*)

TASHA. Is that an outfit? Simon, from a man's point of view, is that what you'd call an appetizing outfit?

SIMON. If you were a lawyer, like your brother, Ben, then it makes sense to go out on your own. But I don't understand why a girl with your intelligence should be free-lance writing when you could take over a business.

TASHA. Christ is thinking of going to law school when the children get a little older.

JANIE. Who?

TASHA. Your sister-in-law, Christ.

JANIE. Chris, Mother? It's Chris. I'll come down and see your place next week, Dad. I promise.

SIMON. Take your time, honey. Whenever you're ready.

TASHA. My two big doers. If not today, tomorrow. I can't sit like you two. (*Dances.*) One, two, three, hip. One, two, three, hip. (*Goes over to Janie.*)

JANIE. (*Turns away.*) I won't dance. Don't ask me.

TASHA. Look at those thighs. I'm dying.

SIMON. What's-his-name called our house last night looking for you.

TASHA. (*Stops dancing.*) Who? Who?

SIMON. The popover boy. He called Ben, because they went to summer camp together. And Ben didn't have your new number, so he told him to call us.

JANIE. Ben told Marty Sterling to call you?

TASHA. Please, sweetheart, look nice. It's important. Even when you throw out the garbage. I like this Marty Sterling.

JANIE. You don't even know him.

TASHA. He comes from nice people.

JANIE. His father is an arsonist.

SIMON. Believe me, you can have a nice life with him. Sounds like a very nice boy. He said to give you a message to call him at the hospital. He was in the Emergency Room at Mount Sinai.

TASHA. I told you he was a nice boy.

JANIE. Don't get too excited. He probably wants Harriet's number.

TASHA. What does Harriet have to do with the popover boy?

JANIE. He's *her* friend.

TASHA. Why do you belittle yourself all the time? What kind of attitude is that? Why don't you walk into a room with your head up and your chest out and think, "I am." (*Demonstrates.*) Am I right, Simon?

SIMON. What is it?

TASHA. Sweetheart, stop thinking about those envelopes and look at your daughter. From a man's point of view, isn't that some beautiful face?

JANIE. I am beautiful. People stop each other on the street to say how beautiful I look when I throw out the garbage. And when Marty Sterling proposes, he'll say, "Janie Jill Blumberg, I want to spend the rest of my life with you because every member of your family calls me the popover boy and I want to be near your mother in her tie-dyed underwear."

TASHA. She's making fun of me again.

JANIE. I'm not making fun of you. It's good to be home. (*Kisses them.*) If I was still in Brookline—what time is it? Seven-fifteen—if I was still in Brookline, I'd be sleeping. Here, by seven-fifteen, there's a catered meal and a floor show.

TASHA. The girls at dancing say you can always have a good time with Tasha. Honey, it was wonderful to see you. Thank you for having us, I loved your cooking, and I'm sure you'd like me to stay and chat all day, but your father isn't the only one who has to get to work. I'm demonstrating in class today.

SIMON. Have a nice day, Janie. (*Kisses Janie and starts to exit.*)

TASHA. Where are you going? Give her some money so she'll buy a lock.

SIMON. (*Gives Janie some bills.*) Honey, I'm sorry if I seem preoccupied. Mother walks me to work every morning now. Once I walk a few blocks, my mind gets stimulated. You know, Janie, I used to have the same trouble with my legs as you do. I would have to sit in bed and rest all the time. But you know what makes the difference? Ripple soles. You get a pair of shoes like these and then you're in business. (*Gives Janie more bills.*)

JANIE. Thanks, Daddy.

TASHA. So you'll call this Marty Sterling?

JANIE. (*Pats Tasha's head.*) I will call him. I will call him.

TASHA. Am I getting shorter? I'm getting shorter.

JANIE. You're fine, Mother. (*Flops back on sofa.*)

TASHA. Body, please, don't get back into bed. You have everything ahead of you. You can have a family, you can have a career, you can learn to tap-dance!

JANIE. Are you taking tap dancing?

TASHA. It's part of life. I'll teach you. (*Taps quite smoothly calling out the steps.*) "Flap, heel, flap, touch."

SIMON. (*While Tasha dances.*) I told your mother she could run her own dancing school.

TASHA. (*Ending dance.*) Two lessons. (*Puts on her cape and takes her attaché case.*)

SIMON. Don't you think your mother looks nice? That's a new attaché.

TASHA. I'm an executive mother.

JANIE. It looks very nice.

TASHA. You want it?

JANIE. You keep it, Mother.

SIMON. Let's go, dear. Remember, Janie, ripple soles. (*Exits. Janie flops back on sofa again and sighs.*)

TASHA. Janie, please! Only old ladies sigh. (*She sighs and exits.*)

Scene 3

Lillian Cornwall's office. Lillian Cornwall, an impressive, handsome woman, whose demeanor commands respect, is seated behind her desk. She is speaking on the phone.

LILLIAN. Obviously, Dick, our only choice is to go national with this. I don't care what some kid in your department says about numbers. Hold on a minute, will you? (*Pushes a button on the phone.*) Lillian Cornwall. (*Yells offstage.*) Pauline, no one's picking up the phone here. (*Hits another button.*) Dick, trust me on this one. I'm not being too harsh. No, I didn't think so. Thank you. (*Hits another button.*) Lillian Cornwall's office. (*Yells offstage.*) Pauline! (*Back on the phone.*) I'm sorry, Mrs. Cornwall isn't in. Can I take a message? Oh, Dick, it's you. Well, tell the kid in your department I appreciate his confidence. What can I say? I'm a beautiful, successful, brilliant woman. Dick,

I'm simply not a kid. (*Phone buzzes.*) Hold a sec, will you? (*Pushes another button.*) Yes, Pauline. (*Pushes another button.*) Dick, my lovely daughter is here. Gotta go. (*Hangs up. Harriet enters in a stylish business suit. She is carrying a gift box.*)

HARRIET. Hello, Mother.

LILLIAN. Hello, baby. It's nice to see you. (*They kiss.*)

HARRIET. You're looking well.

LILLIAN. What brings you here? Would you like me to order you a salad or some lunch? I'd call Tom and get us into Four Seasons, but I have a meeting in a few minutes.

HARRIET. That's all right. I have to get back to the office. Um-mmm. (*Takes out three noisemakers and blows them as she hands Lillian the present.*) Happy birthday, Mother!

LILLIAN. Hmmmm?

HARRIET. Happy birthday. I bought this for you in Italy before I ran out of money.

LILLIAN. O, God, I bet that meeting is a birthday thing. Thank you, Harriet. It's very handsome. (*Puts the gift back in the box.*) How are things at Colgate?

HARRIET. Fine.

LILLIAN. Don't say fine, Harriet. You're a Harvard MBA. I expect an analysis.

HARRIET. We're changing the test market from Sacramento to Syracuse.

LILLIAN. Makes sense. And your personal life?

HARRIET. Mother!

LILLIAN. I don't have much time to catch up. I have a meeting.

HARRIET. My personal life is okay.

LILLIAN. Is that better or worse than fine?

HARRIET. It's okay. Janie's back in New York, and that's nice. I see my friend from Harvard, Joe Stine, the headhunter.

LILLIAN. Nice boy.

HARRIET. Nice. A little dull.

LILLIAN. Sweet though. No, you're right. A little dull.

HARRIET. And I'm sort of interested in some guy in my office.

LILLIAN. Is that a good idea?

HARRIET. I'm not seeing him. I'm just attracted to him.

LILLIAN. Sounds like a pleasant arrangement. What does he do?

HARRIET. Mother!

LILLIAN. His job, baby! What does he do?

HARRIET. He does all right. He's my boss's boss.

LILLIAN. How old is he?

HARRIET. Around forty.

LILLIAN. Around forty? He should be further along than your boss's boss.

HARRIET. Happy birthday, Mother.

LILLIAN. Harriet, you can ask me questions about my life right after I'm finished with yours. You're not making this easy, baby.

HARRIET. Sometimes you're hard to take, Mother.

LILLIAN. So they say. (*Answers intercom.*) Bill, I'll be there in a minute. My daughter is with me. Can she be present at this meeting? I thought so. Thanks, Bill. (*Hangs up.*) It *is* a birthday thing. Harriet, why don't you come with me? You can be my date.

HARRIET. Mother, do you remember when you took me to group sales meetings in Barbados? And I appeared in Mary Janes as your date at candlelit dinners by the ocean.

LILLIAN. You were a wonderful date. Interesting, attractive, bright. Certainly more suitable than what was available.

HARRIET. Mother, you're so crazy. I hope I'm going to be all right.

LILLIAN. You'll be fine. Don't dwell on it. Your generation is absolutely fascinated with itself. Think about science. Technology is going to change our world significantly. So, do you want to come?

HARRIET. Sure.

LILLIAN. God, I dread going to this kind of thing.

HARRIET. Me too.

LILLIAN. I'm not being too harsh?

HARRIET. No, you're not being too harsh.

LILLIAN. Comb your hair, baby. I like it better off your face. (*Pushes Harriet's hair off her face.*)

Scene 4

Italian restaurant. Marty and Janie are seated. "Volare" is playing in the background.

MARTY. Do you want dessert? Because if you don't like the dessert here, my father is giving away free popovers in the Paramus Mall. So what do you think you're going to do now?

JANIE. With my life? At this restaurant? Tonight?

MARTY. Now that you've come home.

JANIE. I don't know. Retire. I sent away for some brochures from Heritage Village.

MARTY. I think about retirement. Not that I don't like being a doctor, but I don't want to get trapped. You know what I mean? First, you get the Cuisinart, then the bigger apartment, and then the Mercedes, and the next thing you know, you're charging $250 to Mrs. Feldman, with the rash, to tell her, "Mrs. Feldman, you have a rash."

JANIE. Whenever I get most depressed, I think I should take charge of my life and apply to medical school. Then I remember that I once identified a liver as a heart. Really. I demonstrated the right auricle and the left ventricle on this liver.

MARTY. I left medical school after my first year to do carpentry for a year.

JANIE. Your father must have liked that.

MARTY. He wants me to be happy. I'm very close to my parents.

JANIE. That's nice. (*Pauses.*) I'm sorry. I was thinking about my parents.

MARTY. Are you close to them?

JANIE. In a way. She's a dancer and he's very sweet. It's complicated.

MARTY. My father started out in show business. He used to tell jokes at Grossinger's. That's why he does the popover commercials himself. Now he's the toastmaster general for the United Jewish Appeal.

JANIE. Have you every been to Israel?

MARTY. I worked on a kibbutz the second time I dropped out of medical school. Israel's very important to me. In fact, I have to decide next month if I want to open my practice here in New York or in Tel Aviv.

JANIE. Oh.

MARTY. Why, are you anti-Israel?

JANIE. No. Of course not. I just preferred the people my parents' age there to the younger ones. The people my age intimidated me. I'd be sleeping and they'd go off to turn deserts into forests. The older ones had more humanity. They rested sometimes.

MARTY. I think Jewish families should have at least three children.

JANIE. Excuse me?

MARTY. It's a dying religion. Intermarriage, Ivy League colleges, the *New York Review of Books.* (*Pauses.*) So, how's Harriet?

JANIE. She's fine.

MARTY. She's not sweet, like you.

JANIE. Harriet is wonderful.

MARTY. She's like those medical-school girls. They're nice but they'd bite your balls off. You think Israelis have no sense of humor? Believe me, women medical students are worse. (*Takes Janie's hand.*) Janie, you're one of the few real people I've ever met in a long time. Most of the women I meet aren't funny.

JANIE. (*Quickly.*) Marty, I think I should tell you I find the fact that you don't like women doctors extremely disturbing and discriminatory. I support the concept of Israel and would probably be a much happier, healthier person if I could go out into the desert and build a forest, but I am far too lazy and self-involved. I have very fat thighs, and I want very badly to be someone else without going through the effort of actually changing myself into someone else. I have very little courage, but I'm highly critical of others who don't.

MARTY. (*Sweetly.*) Is that it?

JANIE. And I want you to like me very much.

MARTY. Do you like me?

JANIE. Yes.

MARTY. Sounds tentative. Most women fall in love the minute they hear "Volare." Maybe this will help. I bought it for you when I was in Rome. (*Hands Janie a swizzle stick.*)

JANIE. I was wondering why they have swizzle sticks in the wine.

MARTY. (*A la the Godfather.*) I got connections in the restaurant business. (*Takes Janie's hand.*) Should I take you home, Monkey?

JANIE. What?

MARTY. Want to go home?

JANIE. No. My interior decorator is there.

MARTY. Want to come to my parents' house? They should be out late tonight. After Paramus, there's a UJA testimonial dinner for my father. It means a lot to him, because he's been giving away so much shrimp at the salad bar they almost revoked his job as toastmaster.

JANIE. It's weird going to someone's parents' house. Shouldn't we have mortgages and children?

MARTY. Let's go, Monkey. You'll be all right. I'll help you. (*Takes Janie's hand.*)

JANIE. (*Rises.*) And what'll I do for you?

MARTY. (*Rises.*) Be sweet. I need attention. A great deal of attention. (*Lights fade as Marty embraces Janie.*)

Scene 5

Harriet's apartment. Harriet and Paul Stuart enter. Paul is about forty. He looks very corporate and appealing. Harriet takes their coats and tosses them on a chair. She exits into the kitchen. Paul moves to the sofa, takes out Binaca, gives himself a hit, and sits. Harriet enters, pushing a rolling bar.

PAUL. You remind me a lot of my first wife.

HARRIET. Mr. Stuart, would you like something to drink? I don't have much. I just moved here.

PAUL. Scotch on the rocks. My first wife hated office Christmas parties.

HARRIET. I'm sorry. Did I make you leave?

PAUL. Definitely not. You're one of the most amusing people I've met at Colgate in a long time. Can I tell you something as a friend? You don't have to call me Mr. Stuart.

HARRIET. I think it's funny your name is Paul Stuart. If your name was Brooks Brothers, I'd call you Mr. Brothers. (*Hands him a napkin, with a cracker and a plate.*) Pâté?

PAUL. (*Takes it.*) Where are you from originally? (*Cracks up.*) Have you ever noticed when you try a conversation opener like "Where are you from originally?" you always sound like a jerk?

HARRIET. I grew up in New York. My mother still lives on East 69th Street.

PAUL. East 69th Street. You were a rich kid.

HARRIET. No. Upper middle class.

PAUL. Only rich kids know what upper middle class is.

HARRIET. Well, I wasn't spoiled. Definitely not spoiled.

PAUL. Your father was a lawyer?

HARRIET. No. My mother's an executive.

PAUL. Is your mother Lillian Cornwall?

HARRIET. Yup.

PAUL. Jesus. I interviewed with your mother once. That woman has balls. Do you know what it took for a woman in her time to get as far as she did?

HARRIET. Yup.

PAUL. Poor baby, I bet you do. (*Lights her cigarette.*) Would you like me to spoil you a bit? Relax. For a girl with such a good mind, you get tense too easily. (*They both start laughing.*)

PAUL. Why are you laughing?

HARRIET. You're amazing. First you tell me how amusing I am, then you want to spoil me, and now you tell me what a good mind I have. What are you going to do next? Ask me to come up and see your etchings? (*Paul moves away to his drink.*)

HARRIET. I'm sorry. This is making me a little uncomfortable. Office romance and all that. You're my boss's boss.

PAUL. Harriet, do you know that forty percent of the people at McKinsey are having interoffice affairs?

HARRIET. How do you know that?

PAUL. Friend of mine did the study. Look, I live with a woman, so no one will know. Is that an incentive?

HARRIET. Cathy? Do you live with Cathy?

PAUL. How do you know Cathy?

HARRIET. She calls the office three times a day.

PAUL. You've been paying attention.

HARRIET. I'm a smart kid.

PAUL. (*Pinches Harriet.*) Smart woman.

HARRIET. (*Pulls away.*) Paul, I generally try not to get involved with unavailable men.

PAUL. You've never been with a married man? How old are you? (*Chokes and coughs.*)

HARRIET. Are you all right?

PAUL. Jesus, were there any nuts in that pâté? My doctor told me not to eat nuts. I've got this stomach thing. I tell you, Harriet, when you get older you really gotta watch it. But you'll take good care of me, right, Beauty? (*Pauses.*) Are you excited?

HARRIET. Where are you from originally?

PAUL. You're excited. Don't be embarrassed, Beauty. I'll be wonderful for you, Harriet. You'll try to change me, you'll realize you can't and, furthermore, I'm not worth it, so you'll marry some nice investment banker and make your mother happy.

HARRIET. I don't think my mother particularly wants me to get married. I don't particularly want me to get married.

PAUL. You'll change your mind. Career girls, when they hit thirty, all change their minds. Look, whatever is happening here, we better do it quickly, because Cathy is expecting me home with the laundry at eleven. I'm very attracted to you, Harriet.

HARRIET. Forty percent of the people at McKinsey, huh?

PAUL. And those are just the ones crazy enough to fill out the questionnaire.

HARRIET. Get out of here.

PAUL. C'mere. Deal from strength, Harriet. Men really like strong women. (*Pulls Harriet toward him. There is no struggle.*)

Scene 6

Janie is in her apartment, typing. The doorbell rings. She opens the door. Harriet enters with a package.

HARRIET. Congratulations on your new apartment!

JANIE. Harriet, I've been living here three months.

HARRIET. That's why I came to celebrate. I decided this morning it was time for you to unpack. Did I walk in with my right foot first?

JANIE. I don't know.

HARRIET. Then I have to do it again. (*Exits, rings doorbell, and reenters when Janie opens the door.*) Congratulations on your new apartment!

JANIE. What are you doing?

HARRIET. I looked all this up very carefully in the *Oxford Companion to Jewish Life.*

JANIE. I'm not familiar with this companion.

HARRIET. You have to walk into a new apartment with your right foot, to set you off on the right foot. I also brought you a house-warming gift. But you cannot open it till we get you settled in.

JANIE. Harriet, you know I can't postpone gratification.

HARRIET. Janie, you have to make a home for yourself. Now, what are we going to do with these crates? (*Picks up two crates.*)

JANIE. Harriet, what are you doing? You're flying around the room.

HARRIET. (*Exits with the crates.*) It's Saturday.

JANIE. The day of rest. Didn't they tell you that in the *Oxford Companion?*

HARRIET. It's Paul Stuart's day at home with Cathy. You want me to put the typewriter in the bedroom? (*Picks up the typewriter.*)

JANIE. (*Stops her.*) No. I'm working. Marty's father hired an actor to play a popover at the opening of the new Sterling Taverne, in the Green Acres Mall, and Marty got me a job writing the popover's opening remarks. Hattie, don't you mind not seeing Paul on the weekend?

HARRIET. No, it's okay. As I see it, Paul Stuart is fine until I find the right relationship. It's similar to the case method. And he's great in bed.

JANIE. Marty claims he slept with more than a hundred visiting nurses when he was at Harvard.

HARRIET. (*Sits.*) Really!

JANIE. I just told you that so you'd sit down. (*Sits too.*)

HARRIET. So, is it something with Marty?

JANIE. He decided to open his practice here next month and he's invited me to his parents' house for Chanukah. Some days I walk down the street and think if I don't step on any cracks, I'll marry Marty. What ever happened to Janie Blumberg? She did so well; she married Marty the doctor. They're giving away popovers in Paramus. (*Pauses.*) Hattie, do you think I should marry Marty?

HARRIET. I've always hated women who sit around talking about how there are no men in New York. Or everyone is gay or married.

JANIE. What does this have to do with my marrying Marty?

HARRIET. These women would tell you, "Marry him. He's straight, he'll make a nice living, he'll be a good father." Janie, what women like Cynthia Peterson don't understand is, no matter how lonely you get or how many birth announcements you receive, the trick is not to get frightened. There's nothing wrong with being alone.

JANIE. Harriet, do you remember when we used to listen to "My Guy" and iron our hair before going to a high school dance?

HARRIET. Oh, God, I've blocked all of that.

JANIE. I remember arriving at the dance, looking over the prospects, and thinking: When I'm twenty-eight, I'm going to get married and be very much in love with someone who is poor and fascinating until he's thirty and then fabulously wealthy and very secure after that. And we're going to have children who wear overalls and flannel shirts and are kind and independent, with curly blond hair. And we'll have great sex and still hold hands when we travel to China when we're sixty.

HARRIET. I never thought about any of that. Maybe it's because I'm Lillian's daughter, but I never respected women who didn't learn to live alone and pay their own rent. Imagine spending your life pretending you aren't a person. To compromise at this point would be antifeminist—well, antihumanist—well, just not impressive. I'm not being too harsh?

JANIE. No. Just rhetorical. (*Doorbell rings.*)

HARRIET. Who's that?

JANIE. I don't know. (*Answers door.*)

VLADIMIR. (*About thirty, a Russian taxicab driver enters, holding a bar with a safari motif.*) Hello, hi.

JANIE. Do you have the right apartment?

VLADIMIR. You are Miss Bloomberg?

JANIE. Yes.

VLADIMIR. For you. I am Vladimir. I am filmmaker from Moscow. I drive taxi now. (*Enters with bar, sees Harriet.*) Hello, hi.

SIMON. (*Enters with bar stool.*) Janie, do you like this bar? Hello, Harriet. We thought you might need something to entertain with at home.

TASHA. (*Enters with another stool.*) Don't force her, Simon. Hello, darling. (*Notices Harriet.*) Harriet, you look terrific. Are you seeing anyone?

HARRIET. Sort of.

SIMON. We met Vladimir on the cab ride down here. He came from Moscow six weeks ago.

JANIE. That's nice. Do you like it here?

VLADIMIR. Hello, hi.

SIMON. He doesn't speak very much English.

TASHA. That doesn't matter. If you like people, you speak every language. I can get along in any country. If you smile, you dance, anyone will understand.

JANIE. My mother identifies with Zorba the Greek.

VLADIMIR. Zorba. Yes. Thank you.

TASHA. Harriet, do you like the bar? I saw another one, but I was afraid Janie would say it's too old, it's too new, it's gold.

HARRIET. I like it very much. It's primitive.

SIMON. Vladimir, maybe you want to stay and put the bar together, and Mrs. Blumberg and Harriet and I can bring you up some coffee.

VLADIMIR. Coffee. Regular.

TASHA. Sit. Harriet, join us. Harriet's with Colgate-Palmolive.

SIMON. (*Takes Janie aside.*) He's a nice boy. Don't you think he's a nice boy, Janie? Seems intelligent too. I thought maybe if things didn't work out with you and Marty, I'd take him into the business.

JANIE. You're kidding. This man is here six weeks and he gets a wife, a business, and a dancing mother-in-law?

SIMON. What's wrong with giving a guy a break?

JANIE. (*Makes a sign to get Vladimir out.*) Dad . . .

SIMON. Vladimir, thank you. We'll take the taxi uptown to Rockefeller Center.

TASHA. Every Saturday I take Mr. Blumberg skating.

SIMON. My partner keeps me in shape.

TASHA. Harriet, you look terrific. Who is it you're seeing?

JANIE. She's seeing someone who's married.

TASHA. Let's go, dear. (*Tasha and Simon exit.*)

HARRIET AND JANIE. Good-bye. Good-bye. Nice to see you.

VLADIMIR. (*To Harriet.*) Good-bye. (*To Janie.*) Good-bye. (*Exits.*)

JANIE. One of these days, I'm going to write a book: *My Mother*

Herself. I'm sorry, Hattie. That was the only way I could get them out of here.

HARRIET. (*Looks at the bar.*) Did Tasha go on safari?

JANIE. No. She went hunting at KMart. Harriet, they brought over a Russian taxicab driver for me to marry! Maybe I should move back to Brookline tomorrow.

HARRIET. You can't leave me here with Lillian and Paul Stuart. I gave Lillian a birthday present that I bought with my last lire in Italy. She hardly opened it. She couldn't wait to get back to the intercom to harass Pauline. Janie, sit; it's the day of rest. It's time for you to open your present. (*Harriet gives her the bag, and they sit on the sofa. Janie puts the bow on her head and from the package takes out a loaf of challah bread, a box of kosher salt, sugar, matches, and a candle.*)

JANIE. What kind of diet are you on?

HARRIET. According to the *Oxford Companion,* this is what your family brings when you move into a new home. Bread—the staple of life. Sugar—something sweet in your life. Salt—a little spice in your life.

JANIE. (*Looking at the bar.*) I have that.

HARRIET. And a candle to light the way. (*Lights the candle.*) Janie, you know what I remember more than those mixers?

JANIE. What? (*Puts her arm on Harriet's shoulder.*)

HARRIET. Remember when you and I would meet for dinner because Lil was at a meeting and Tasha only had brewer's yeast in the refrigerator. I always thought, Well, I do have a family. Janie's my family. In fact, that still helps a lot. I always assumed it was some sort of pact.

JANIE. It is a pact. (*Both break a piece of bread from the loaf.*)

JANIE. Hattie, thank you for my gift from my family. (*Picks up the salt as if toasting.*) Cheers.

HARRIET. (*Picks up the sugar.*) Lechayim. (*They clink the boxes together.*)

Telephone Machine 3

Ring. Beep.

HART FARRELL. Janie Blumberg, this is Hart Farrell, in the personnel department at *Sesame Street.* A temp in our office recognized your name from a part he played at Green Acres Mall. I read your pieces. I'm going to pass them on to Tajlei Kaplan Singleberry. Nice song, luv. (*Ring. Beep.*)

CYNTHIA PETERSON. (*Crying.*) Janie, it's Cynthia. Thank God you have your machine on. I'm home, I'm broke, my trainer is on retreat, I've been rejected by every man on the Upper West Side, and I'm about to get drunk. Janie, do you know a good dry cleaner?

Scene 7

Janie's apartment, left: sofa and TV on a crate. Harriet's living room/bedroom, right: foldout bed, ottoman, TV. Paul and Harriet are in bed. Light goes up on Janie's apartment.

JANIE. (*Enters.*) I fucked up Chanukah.

MARTY. (*Enters.*) You were sweet.

JANIE. I'm sorry I spilled horseradish on your sister-in-law. They have a nice baby. Really, Schlomo is very sweet. I'm sorry I spilled horseradish on Schlomo.

MARTY. You worry too much. You're just like my mother. My mother says you're shy and a little clumsy because you're very angry with your family. But she says don't worry, you'll grow out of it. I told her your mother was a bit cuckoo.

JANIE. Martin, I'm reflective and eager to please, and my mother is a pioneer in interpretive dance. (*Exits into bedroom.*)

MARTY. Don't be so defensive, sweetheart.

JANIE. (*Offstage.*) Everything by you is so simple.

MARTY. Everything by you is harder than it has to be. You think my sister-in-law knew what she was doing when she married my brother? (*Janie enters. She has changed from her dress into sweatshirt and overalls.*)

MARTY. That didn't come out right, did it?

JANIE. That's okay.

MARTY. You know what I mean. My sister-in-law had even less direction than you do, and she's a bright girl too. But she met my brother and now she's a wonderful mother, and, believe me, when Schlomo is a little older, she'll go back to work in something nice. She'll teach or she'll work with the elderly—and she won't conquer the world, but she'll have a nice life. Monkey, I don't want to be alone. But I think it's going to be all right with us. I love you. (*Pauses.*) I put a deposit down on an apartment for us in Brooklyn today.

JANIE. What?

MARTY. I figured if I waited for you to make up your mind to move, we'd never take anything, and I need a place to live before I open my practice. You don't have to pay your half of the deposit now. I can wait a month. Is that okay?

JANIE. Sure.

MARTY. I decided we should live in Flatbush or Brighton Beach, where people have real values. My father never sees those people anymore, the *alta kakas* in Brooklyn, the old men with the accents who sit in front of Hymie's Highway Delicatessen. I miss them. My father and mother never go to Miami anymore. They go to Palm Springs or Martinique with their friends from the Westchester Country Club. My father thought my brother was crazy when he named his son Schlomo. He kept asking my brother, "So what's his real name?" And my father will think I'm crazy when we move to Brooklyn.

JANIE. Marty?

MARTY. What is it, Monkey? Are you angry?

JANIE. No. I like the *alta kakas* in Brooklyn too. I always thought Herman Wouk should write a novel, *Young Kaka*. I don't know.

MARTY. What don't you know? Janie, you're twenty-eight years old. What I'm saying is, either you want to be with me—you don't have to; you should just want to—or, if you don't want to, then we should just forget it.

JANIE. I want to.

MARTY. So, what's the problem?

JANIE. No problem.

MARTY. Uh-oh. What time is it? I promised my father we'd watch his new commercial. (*Turns on the TV. Paul turns on the TV at the same time.*)

HARRIET. I know that man.

MILTY VOICE-OVER. This is your Captain Milty Sterling. I'm here at beautiful Green Acres Mall with the popover boy and my grandson, Schlomo. What are we giving away today, Schlomo?

CHILD'S VOICE-OVER. We're giving away shrimp. We're giving away lobster tails. We're giving away coleslaw.

MILTY VOICE-OVER. How do you like that shrimp, Schlomo?

CHILD'S VOICE-OVER. It's good, Grandpa.

ANNOUNCER. Sterling Tavernes are now located in Green Acres, Syosset, Paramus, Albany, Plattsburgh, Marine Park, Midwood, Madison, Bethesda, and the Bergen Mall. (*Lights fade on Marty and Janie and come up on Paul and Harriet.*)

HARRIET. (*Laughing hysterically.*) I can't believe I know him!

PAUL. Why are you laughing? The man's a marketing genius. He's giving away shrimp. He's giving away coleslaw. I never heard of such an incentive program. How much do you think he can give away and still make a profit? (*Kisses Harriet.*) It's good, Grandpa. (*Gets up.*)

HARRIET. Where are you going?

PAUL. It's late.

HARRIET. You could spend the night.

PAUL. Cathy.

HARRIET. Do you love Cathy?

PAUL. She's devoted to me.

HARRIET. Does Cathy exist?

PAUL. Of course Cathy exists.

HARRIET. I thought maybe Cathy was an answering service you hired to call you three times a day.

PAUL. (*Sits back on the bed.*) Did I tell you to deal from strength?

HARRIET. Yes.

PAUL. Sometimes I'm a jackass. You're sweet, Harriet. You know that? You're a sweet woman. A lot of people never get off in their entire life. Do you think your mother's had good sex?

HARRIET. My mother likes to watch *The Rockford Files* reruns at eleven. (*Gets out of bed.*) Paul, I don't think people spend as much time thinking about sex as you do.

PAUL. (*Follows her.*) Tell me what you like, Beauty.

HARRIET. The other day I was standing in front of your office with my PERT charts, and you called your secretary "Beauty," you called whoever called you on the phone "Beauty," and I think you called the ninety-year-old messenger boy from Ogilvy and Mather "Beauty."

PAUL. I see what's going on here. It's the old "I'm afraid of turning thirty alone and I'm beginning to think about having a family."

HARRIET. Wanting two nights a week or a sleepover date isn't quite a family.

PAUL. Baby, I'm older than you. I've been through this with a lot of women. You want a man who sees you as a potential mother, but also is someone who isn't threatened by your success and is deeply interested in it. And this man should be thought of as "intelligent" by your friends. But when you need him, he should drop whatever it is he's doing and be supportive.

HARRIET. I'm not asking for that. Why are you so bitter?

PAUL. Don't be naïve. Everything is a negotiation, Harriet. Everything. When I graduated from Yale, I thought I'd find a nice wife who would cook me dinner, we'd have a few kids, and I'd support the family; and a few years up we'd get a house in Madison, Connecticut, for weekends. The girl I married never cooked, and she wasn't lucky, like you. Girls didn't assume they'd have careers then. My wife was just very bright and very unhappy. And the girls I date now—the ones like you, the MBAs from Harvard—they want me to be the wife. They want me to be the support system. Well, I can't do that. Harriet, I just wasn't told that's the way it was supposed to be.

HARRIET. Paul, I never knew which way it was supposed to be.

PAUL. What do you mean?

HARRIET. I don't really expect anything from you.

PAUL. You and I are a lot alike, Harriet. We don't want to be alone and we don't want to move forward. So we serve a perfect function blocking each other's lives.

HARRIET. I like you, Paul.

PAUL. My poor baby. (*They kiss and get back in bed as the lights fade down on them and up on Janie and Marty.*)

MARTY. I'm hungry. What do you have to eat, Monkey?

JANIE. We could order up a sandwich. I have the phone number of every coffee shop on the Upper East and West Sides—Four Brothers, the Four Brothers on the Acropolis, the Four Brothers on the Parthenon, the Four Brothers . . .

MARTY. (*Cuts her off.*) That's all right, I'll go to the supermarket, get some chicken and some lettuce and stuff.

JANIE. No, no, no. We can order up a salad.

MARTY. Monkey, you don't know how to cook a chicken?

JANIE. I do. I do. I do. I can make Teflon chicken.

MARTY. You shouldn't put yourself down like that. (*Gets up to go.*)

JANIE. Marty, I love you. We can take the place in Brooklyn. I just want to be with you. (*Marty kisses Janie, crosses to the front door, and exits triumphantly. Janie goes to the phone and dials. The phone rings in Harriet's apartment. Harriet picks it up.*)

HARRIET. Hello.

JANIE. Hattie, how do you cook a chicken? Marty's coming back here in five minutes with a chicken.

HARRIET. Do you want Florentine or something nice?

JANIE. Hattie, hurry. I can't tell him I don't know how. Marty took an apartment for us in Brooklyn, and I can't tell him we have to order up chicken.

HARRIET. Why Brooklyn?

JANIE. He likes Hymie of Hymie's Highway Delicatessen.

HARRIET. Excuse me?

JANIE. He likes the *alta kakas*. (*Janie's doorbell rings.*)

JANIE. Marty, just a sec. Hattie, how do you cook a chicken?

PAUL. (*Gets up.*) Beauty, do you have any Di-gel?

HARRIET. In the cabinet. (*Janie crosses to the door.*) Janie, what are altered kakas? (*Janie opens the door. Vladimir is there.*)

VLADIMIR. Hello, hi. I am in neighborhood. So I drop in. Want to see *The Sorrow and the Pity?*

JANIE. (*Into phone.*) Hattie, I have to go. Vladimir is here. He wants to see *The Sorrow and the Pity.* When can I see you?

HARRIET. I don't know. I don't have my book here. (*Janie's doorbell rings.*)

PAUL. What's wrong with this mouthwash?

HARRIET. It's a Colgate product. (*Vladimir answers the door. Simon enters with a coffee table.*)

SIMON. Oh, hello, Vladimir. How are you?

VLADIMIR. Fine. Thank you. How's it going?

SIMON. Janie, I brought over a coffee table.

PAUL. I better go, Beauty. Cathy.

HARRIET. Me too. *The Rockford Files.* (*Marty enters with a bag of groceries. Paul and Harriet engage in a long kiss.*)

MARTY. Monkey, I got the chicken.

JANIE. Marty, this is my father, Simon Blumberg, and Vladimir.

SIMON. Very nice to meet you. Mrs. Blumberg will be so sorry she missed you.

JANIE. (*Desperately, into phone.*) Harriet!

VLADIMIR. Hello, hi.

SIMON. (*To Marty.*) Vladimir is *my* friend. Janie doesn't even *know* him. He's a filmmaker from Moscow. Let's go, Vladimir. (*Starts pulling Vladimir out the door.*) Nice to meet you. My best to your family.

PAUL. (*At Harriet's door.*) I think we have a pretty good thing going. Think about it. (*Paul, Simon, and Vladimir exit simultaneously.*)

HARRIET. Janie!

MARTY. Who's the filmmaker?

JANIE. Friend of my father's.

MARTY. I'm hungry. Are you sure you can cook a chicken? (*Hands Janie a chicken wrapped in butcher paper.*) I'll go warm up the oven.

JANIE. I'll get the stapler. (*Back on the phone, as Marty exits into the kitchen.*) Hattie!!

HARRIET. Janie, you never mentioned an apartment. When did you see it?

JANIE. I haven't seen it. Marty told me about it tonight after I spilled horseradish on baby Schlomo.

HARRIET. Janie, people named Homo and Schlymie! I feel our move back to New York has been very successful. I've met a sadist vice president and you've become involved in a shtetl.

MARTY. (*Offstage.*) Monkey!

JANIE. Be right there, Marty. (*With desperation.*) Hattie, *how do you* cook a chicken?

HARRIET. You just put it in the broiler.

JANIE. Who told you this? Thank you, Harriet. Bye. (*Hangs up.*)

HARRIET. Bye, Janie. (*Janie unwraps the chicken on the coffee table. She lifts it up by the two wings, over her head, and stares at it.*)

PAUL. (*Enters.*) Beauty, Thursday the laundry's open till midnight.

MARTY. (*Enters.*) Janie, the oven's ready. (*Janie and Harriet cross to Marty and Paul respectively as the lights fade. Janie cradles the chicken like a baby; Harriet is carried off by Paul. Both couples kiss as they exit. A string version of "Isn't It Romantic" is heard.*)

ACT II

Scene 1

Central Park South. Tasha enters wearing earphones connected to a Walkman tape player. She is listening to music that makes her dance as she walks. She sits on a bench, opens her attaché case, and wipes her face with a towel. Lillian enters, eating a hot dog, and sees Tasha.

LILLIAN. Mrs. Blumberg? (*Tasha doesn't hear her.*)

LILLIAN. Mrs. Blumberg!

TASHA. (*Loudly.*) Yes.

LILLIAN. Lillian Cornwall.

TASHA. (*Removes her earphones.*) How are you? Please excuse my appearance. I just got out of class. A real workout I had today.

LILLIAN. You look marvelous. How's Ben?

TASHA. Ben is doing very well. He's a lawyer with Korvette's. I mean Cravath.

LILLIAN. And Simon?

TASHA. Simon is with his business. He would love for Janie to take over, but Janie says she's happy free-lance writing.

LILLIAN. I always liked Janie. She's such a bright girl.

TASHA. I tell her people stop me on the street to tell me how bright she is, but she doesn't believe me. Janie tells me Harriet has a nice job.

LILLIAN. Yes. She's at Colgate-Palmolive.

TASHA. She going to be an executive mother, like you. Very nice. Do you see the girls much? My daughter, whenever I call her, I get the machine.

LILLIAN. I reach Harriet's secretary, or, rather, my secretary reaches Harriet's secretary.

TASHA. She's always been a hard worker, your Harriet.

LILLIAN. Harriet tells me Janie's been seeing a nice boy.

TASHA. He's a very nice boy. But so what? Harriet and Janie are very nice girls. They deserve a little *naches*. You know what I mean by *naches?* A little happiness. Well, I don't want to keep you. I know you're a busy woman. You probably have appointments.

LILLIAN. Actually, I thought I'd surprise Harriet and take her to a nice lunch, but her secretary told me she was in a meeting. So I thought I'd treat myself to a frankfurter in the park. I haven't had a frankfurter in the park since I lived in England, thirty years ago.

TASHA. Can I tell you something? I'm sorry, I forgot your first name.

LILLIAN. Lillian.

TASHA. Lillian, maybe it's none of my business, but you shouldn't eat frankfurters. You know what frankfurters are made of? Have some string beans. (*Takes a bag of string beans from her attaché case.*) All the young girls at dancing school carry plastic bags with string beans.

LILLIAN. (*Takes a bean.*) Thank you.

TASHA. (*Sits and sighs.*) Excuse me. I always tell my daughter only old ladies sigh. My husband has an expression, "Everything presses itself out." Believe me, Harriet will find a nice boy, she'll get married, she'll work, she'll have a nice life. I don't understand why they're fighting it so hard.

LILLIAN. I don't think Harriet thinks about marriage very much.

TASHA. These days they "live together." That's the latest. Believe me, it's the same thing as being married.

LILLIAN. Harriet told me she doesn't particularly want to live with anyone. I don't live with anyone.

TASHA. You can't listen to your children all the time. My daughter tells me I don't wear clothing. I'm wearing clothing. My daughter, Janie, thinks I call her in the morning to check up on her. Yesterday she answered the phone and said, "Hello, Mother. This morning I got married, lost twenty pounds, and became a lawyer."

LILLIAN. That's funny.

TASHA. Oh, you can always have a good time with Janie. But you know what's sad? Not sad like a child is ill or something. But a little sad to me. My daughter never thinks I call because I miss her. The girls at dancing school tell me their problems: they tell me about their parents, their boyfriends, what they ate yesterday, what they're going to eat tomorrow. But they're not my children. Sure, I'd like Janie to be married, and if she were a lawyer that'd be nice too, and, believe me, if I could take her by the hand and do it for her I would. I'm that sort of mother. I remember when Janie was in high school and she'd slam the door to her room and say, "Mother, what do you want from me?" Lillian, what do I want from her? I just want to know that she's well. And to give her a little push too. But just a little one.

LILLIAN. (*Reassuringly.*) Sooner or later you can have everything pressed.

TASHA. It's "everything presses itself out." I tell you, life isn't like those Ivory Snow commercials with the mother and daughter comparing hands. Maybe your life is like that, but at seven-fifteen in the morning, my Janie and I don't get up to play golf together.

LILLIAN. Harriet and I don't get up to play golf either. (*Pauses.*) Do those string beans really fill you up?

TASHA. You're an intelligent woman, Lillian; how could a bag of string beans really fill you up?

LILLIAN. Do you ever go to Rumpelmayer's, across the street?

TASHA. I take my granddaughter when she's in the city.

LILLIAN. Rumpelmayer's always sold the nicest stuffed animals. I never liked those Steiff toys at F. A. O. Schwarz.

TASHA. They're made in Germany.

LILLIAN. How many grandchildren do you have?

TASHA. Just one. But I'm looking forward. I'll tell you what's nice about grandchildren. You don't have to worry about them every day, and they don't *hoc* you a *chinic*. That means they don't bang on your teakettle.

LILLIAN. Would you join me at Rumpelmayer's for a sundae? I have twenty minutes before I have to go to a meeting. I'm sure you can get an iced coffee and some fruit.

TASHA. Why should I have fruit when they have such nice ice cream? I don't care what restaurant you go to, the fresh fruit cup is never fresh.

LILLIAN. I haven't gone for a sundae in the afternoon since I was at Vassar. This is a big day for me. A frankfurter in the park, a sundae at Rumpelmayer's. I'm having a wonderful time.

TASHA. The girls at dancing school always say you can have a good time with Tasha.

LILLIAN. Do you like James Garner?

TASHA. Who?

LILLIAN. Do you ever watch *The Rockford Files?*

TASHA. I put the television on sometimes when I'm waiting for Simon to come home after my classes, but I don't really watch it. Just educational broadcasting and the Barbara Walters' specials. Did you see her with Richard Nixon the other week? That man did all right for himself.

LILLIAN. I beg your pardon?

TASHA. Both his daughters married well, he has a nice house, he travels. And what was he before? A Quaker.

LILLIAN. Excuse me?

TASHA. A Quaker. Listen, I know you people don't like to get very intimate, but since our daughters are such good friends, I want to tell you I always admired you. You were always on time to all the parent-teacher meetings. Not that you and I both aren't smarter than all those teachers combined. But the other mothers would always come in late with the Louis Vuitton bags, and the manicures, but you, the only one who had something else important to do, you were always on time.

LILLIAN. Thank you.

TASHA. What are you thanking me for? You worked very hard. We both worked very hard. That's why we put out such nice products. (*They walk off arm-in-arm, chatting.*)

TASHA. (*As she exits.*) Do you remember that girl Cynthia Peterson?

Telephone Machine 4

Ring. Beep.

TAJLEI KAPLAN SINGLEBERRY. Miss Bloomberg, this is Tajlei Kaplan Singleberry, at *Sesame Street.* Could you come in and see us next week? 288-7808, extension 22. Thank you. (*Ring. Beep.*)

HARRIET. Janie, it's Harriet. Would you do me an enormous favor? Would you and Marty come to dinner tomorrow night? Paul Stuart will be there. Don't ask. (*Sings.*) "I love him. I love him. I love him. And where he goes I'll follow, I'll follow, I'll follow . . .

Scene 2

Harriet's apartment. Janie, Marty, and Harriet are having drinks.

HARRIET. My mother identifies with Jean Harris.

JANIE. I think Jean's mistake was stopping with Dr. Tarnower. On her way to Scarsdale she should have taken care of all of them: Dr.

Atkins, Dr. Pritikin, the nut in Beverly Hills who says it's good to live on papaya.

MARTY. Monkey, Jean Harris should stay in jail for life. (*His beeper goes off.*) I hear you, Mrs. Rosen. I hear you. (*To Harriet.*) I was up all night with her. She thinks the dialysis machine is connected to my telephone. Do you have a private one I could use?

HARRIET. In the kitchen. (*As Marty exits, he looks back at Janie.*)

HARRIET. He's sweet.

JANIE. He's very sweet. Sometimes I look at Marty and think he's such a nice young man, I must be a nice young girl.

HARRIET. You are.

JANIE. I never meant to become one. Last week, when we were driving up from yet another Sterling Taverne opening on the Island, I had my head in his lap, and he stroked my hair and called me Monkey. And at first I thought, Janie Jill Blumberg, you've been accepted; not even on the waiting list. So he calls you Monkey. You'd prefer what? Angel? Sweetheart?

HARRIET. Beauty?

JANIE. And I thought, It's settled, fine, thank God. And I bet I can convince him that Schlomo is not a name for an American child. We were driving along the L.I.E. I was fantasizing if we'd make the Sunday *Times* wedding announcements: "Daughter of Pioneer in Interpretive Dance Marries Popover Boy." And it was just as we were approaching Syosset that I thought, I can't breathe in this car, and I promised myself that in a month from now I would not be traveling home from the Island in this car with Marty. And as soon as I thought this, and honestly almost pushed open the car door, I found myself kissing his hand and saying, "Marty, I love you." I don't know.

HARRIET. I don't know either. Maybe Lillian is right. Maybe life is easier without relationships.

JANIE. Hattie, do you think I should live with Marty?

HARRIET. Well, if you live with him, you won't have to wonder who'll hold you at night, what will happen if you don't pay your taxes, or even, if you want children, who you could possibly get to be the father. You won't read articles in magazines about single women and have to think of the fifty different reasons why you're different from that. You won't begin to notice younger men on the street, or think I'm not really hurting a married man's wife if I have an affair with him, because if it's not me, it'll be somebody else. But Janie, how could you sleep next to a man as nice as Marty and lie to him and say I love you?

JANIE. I do love him. Maybe I'm just frightened.

HARRIET. I thought we had a pact. There's nothing wrong with being alone. We can wait till it's right. (*Marty enters.*)

HARRIET. How's Mrs. Rosen?

MARTY. She died. . . . Just kidneying. Actually, she's not happy with her donor, so I'm driving her home to Rye.

HARRIET. Oh, I'm going up to Rye next week for a planning conference. My friend Joe Stine is driving me up there. (*Doorbell rings.*)

HARRIET. Maybe we can take Mrs. Rosen with us. (*Goes to the door.*)

MARTY. Actually, I can't stay for dinner. The hospital wants me back in a half hour. (*To Janie.*) Who's Joe Stine?

JANIE. Some friend of Harriet's. I've never met him.

PAUL. (*Enters. His shoulder is held stiff against his ear.*) I think I got whiplash on the cab ride down here.

HARRIET. I'm sorry. Are you all right?

PAUL. There's no way to get around safely in this city. Goddamn taxi driver went over a pothole.

JANIE. Do you want Marty to have a look at your neck?

PAUL. It's not my neck. It's my left arm. Oh, my God. Maybe I'm having a heart attack.

MARTY. Really, I don't mind having a look at it.

JANIE. Marty's a resident at Mount Sinai.

PAUL. Nice to meet you. (*Shakes his hand.*)

MARTY. And this is Janie Blumberg.

PAUL. The only other possibility is, my doctor says I've been taking too many amateur massages.

HARRIET. Paul, how about a drink?

PAUL. I better not, with this neck thing.

MARTY. I can recommend a chiropractor.

JANIE. I thought chiropractors were quacks. My mother says chiropractors are quacks. She's a dancer.

PAUL. Your mother's a dancer? What company is she with?

JANIE. She's an independent.

HARRIET. Sweet gherkins? Paul, remember the TV commercial we saw? Well, Marty's father's the one who was giving away the shrimp.

PAUL. Oh, I loved it. I loved it. Is that kid's name really Schlomo?

MARTY. Yes. The UJA is really pissed at my father for making Schlomo eat shrimp on television.

PAUL. (*Cracks up.*) I love it. I love it.

HARRIET. More Brie, Marty? (*To Paul.*) How are you feeling?

PAUL. I don't know, honey. I have this sensation in my foot. Maybe this is a neurological thing.

JANIE. Well, maybe.

MARTY. Doesn't seem to be.

PAUL. What's your specialty?

MARTY. Kidneys.

PAUL. The kid's name is really Schlomo? (*He cracks up again.*) I love it.

JANIE. You're in marketing, aren't you?

PAUL. Yes. But it's too boring to talk about.

HARRIET. I don't think it's boring. (*To Marty.*) Have some gherkins? (*Pause.*)

PAUL. Anyone seen anything good recently?

MARTY. God, I haven't been to a film in ages. If I get any time, I try to read.

JANIE. Did you read the article in the *Times* about artificial insemination? I can imagine myself at thirty-six, driving cross-country to inseminate myself with a turkey baster.

PAUL. Turkey baster?

JANIE. Uh-huh. I'm going to give birth to a little oven-stuffer roaster. (*Janie, Marty, and Harriet laugh.*)

PAUL. (*Gets up.*) Well, I have to be going.

JANIE. Aren't you going to stay for dinner? There's Chicken Marengo.

MARTY. Really, I wouldn't rush off because of the whiplash.

PAUL. Nice meeting both of you. Cathy, er, Beauty, I'm just a little tired. (*Kisses Harriet on the cheek, picks up his coat, and starts to leave.*)

HARRIET. Paul, I don't think we should see each other anymore.

PAUL. (*Stops.*) Excuse me?

HARRIET. I want to stop.

PAUL. (*Moves down to Harriet and whispers.*) We've been through this before.

MARTY. Harriet, do you want Janie and me to get dessert?

HARRIET. No.

PAUL. C'mon, Harriet. I've got this neck thing. Your friends are here. We'll talk about it tomorrow. We'll have breakfast. What's the matter, Beauty, do you have your period?

MARTY. (*Stands, with Janie.*) See you later.

HARRIET. Don't go. (*They sit.*)

HARRIET. Paul's leaving to catch up on his laundry.

PAUL. You knew what the parameters were here. You're a very appealing woman, Harriet. It's nice meeting both of you. Thanks for helping me with this neck thing. Beauty, calm down. You're a good kid. (*Snaps his fingers as if to say "see you later" and exits.*)

MARTY. He's crazy. He didn't have whiplash. Harriet, he's the least gracious man I ever met. In fact, he's a real douche.

JANIE. Hattie, I'm sorry.

HARRIET. What are you sorry for?

JANIE. I shouldn't have told him about artificial insemination.

HARRIET. I'm going for a walk.

JANIE. When are you coming back?

HARRIET. Janie, you sound like Tasha. I don't know when I'm coming back. (*Exits through the front door.*)

JANIE. Well, this was a real nice clambake. I'm mighty glad *I* came.

MARTY. Why is she seeing that guy?

JANIE. The sadist vice president of Colgate-Palmolive? I don't know.

MARTY. Monkey.

JANIE. What?

MARTY. My father wants to know if we're coming to dinner tomorrow. It's my brother's anniversary. The whole family will be there.

JANIE. I can't. I got a call from *Sesame Street.* They want to interview me. I have to stay home and put together some sketches for the giant bird.

MARTY. So you'll do it next week. What?

JANIE. Nothing.

MARTY. What nothing, Monkey?

JANIE. Nothing. Nothing.

MARTY. You want to interview at *Sesame Street,* fine. They do nice work. But don't let it take over your life. And don't let it take over our life. That's a real trap.

JANIE. Marty, I haven't even interviewed there yet. (*He rubs her back intermittently, tapping as if he's checking her heart.*)

MARTY. You're a sweet woman. You don't want a life like that.

JANIE. Like what?

MARTY. Look, I have plenty of friends who marry women doctors because they think they'll have something in common. Monkey, they never see each other. Their children are brought up by strangers from the Caribbean.

JANIE. That's a nice way of putting it.

MARTY. I have nothing against your working. I just want to make sure we have a life.

JANIE. Marty, I like my work. I may have stumbled into something I actually care about. And right now I don't want to do it part-time and pretend that it's real when it would actually be a hobby. But I want a life too. Honey, my mother takes my father skating every Saturday. Simon and that dancer have struck up a partnership. I'm their daughter. I want that too.

MARTY. Janie, I made arrangements with the Sterling truck to move us to Brooklyn next Saturday.

JANIE. We're gonna move with a lot of shrimp and lobster tails?

MARTY. What are you trying to do, entertain me like you tried to entertain Paul Stuart?

JANIE. I was just trying to . . .

MARTY. You know what, Monkey? You're a little disorganized; I'm a little bit of a nudge. So if I don't make the arrangements, what's going to happen? You'll live alone or maybe you'll meet someone who's even more of a nudge.

JANIE. Marty, if I'm one of the few real people you've ever met, why do you call me "Monkey"?

MARTY. Jesus, Janie, I'm just trying to move forward. I gotta go. I'm on call this week. I'll see you on Saturday. (*Snaps his fingers as if he's imitating Paul and exits. Janie walks around the sofa, slowly turns, and gasps.*)

Telephone Machine 5

Ring. Beep.

VLADIMIR. Hello, hi. This is Vladimir. Hello, hi. Uh, I have tickets for Bruce Springsteen. I will return call. (*Ring. Beep.*)

CYNTHIA PETERSON. Janie, it's Cynthia Peterson. I met a man on a plane to Houston. Keep your fingers crossed.

Scene 3

Four Seasons restaurant. Harriet and Lillian are seated at a table. They have finished their entrées. Harriet is distracted.

LILLIAN. Everything all right with you?

HARRIET. Fine. I guess. I made a presentation to my boss a week ago. He told me my ideas were too theoretical. Then the next day, at a meeting, my friend Joe Stine said, my boss presented my ideas as his own and got them through.

LILLIAN. Good for you.

HARRIET. Mother, I work very hard. I don't want that man stealing my ideas.

LILLIAN. You think it would be better to be married and have your husband steal your ideas?

HARRIET. What?

LILLIAN. I was just cheering you up with a depressing alternative. Look at Jean Harris. That guy would have manipulated her for the rest of her life. Do me a favor, baby. Go in tomorrow and tell your boss, whoever he is—Ron, Rick, Dick—I am sorry but you stole my ideas, and I hold you accountable. Do you want dessert? Have some chocolate velvet cake, and I'll take a taste.

HARRIET. Mother, you haven't finished not eating your lunch. You haven't picked all the salad dressing off your salad or removed all the potatoes from your plate.

LILLIAN. Tom, we'll have the chocolate velvet cake.

HARRIET. I remember when you brought me here as a little girl. I told everyone in my class we were going to the Four Seasons for lunch, because you told me it was very special. I always loved coming here, and I thought you were very beautiful in your subtle blue suits, calling all those grown men Tom, Dave. I mean, they never really knew the other women in the room, but they knew my mommy. My mommy was important.

LILLIAN. She is. Harriet, you can't blame everything on me. I wasn't home enough for you to blame everything on me.

HARRIET. Clever.

LILLIAN. I thought so. (*Waves to someone.*) Hi, Bill.

HARRIET. Are you proud of me?

LILLIAN. Of course I'm proud of you. Are you proud of me?

HARRIET. Yes. Very.

LILLIAN. I didn't cheat you too much.

HARRIET. No.

LILLIAN. Have children, Harriet. It's one of the few things in life that's worthwhile. (*Waves at another man.*) Hi, Kip.

HARRIET. Mother, when do you stop hoping that there will be some enormous change, some dam breaking, and then you'll start living your life? You know what I'm tired of? I'm tired of the whole idea that everything takes work. Relationships take work, personal growth takes work, spiritual development, child rearing, creativity. Well, I would like to do something simply splendidly that took absolutely no real effort at all.

LILLIAN. Harriet, your thinking is all over the place today. What is it? Are you having an affair or something?

HARRIET. My boss's boss. The one you said should be further along. But it's nothing.

LILLIAN. Forty percent of the people at McKinsey are having affairs.

HARRIET. I know that.

LILLIAN. See how nice it is to have a daughter in your own field? If you want me to, I'd like to meet this guy.

HARRIET. It's over. He once had an interview with you. He said you have balls.

LILLIAN. Don't be offended, baby. Your father said the same thing. (*Waves again.*) Hi, Ken. Where's our cake? I have a meeting at two-thirty.

HARRIET. Mother . . . ?

LILLIAN. What is this, "Youth Wants to Know"? Honey, I'm an old lady. I don't know all the answers to these things.

HARRIET. I have just one more question. Just one.

LILLIAN. To get to the other side.

HARRIET. What?

LILLIAN. I was giving you the answer.

HARRIET. That's not funny.

LILLIAN. I'm not a funny woman. Ask me, baby. I've got to go. Where is that man? I can't sit around here like this.

HARRIET. Calm down.

LILLIAN. What's your question? Harriet, I'm in a hurry.

HARRIET. Mother, do you think it's possible to be married or live with a man, have a good relationship and children that you share equal responsibility for, build a career, and still read novels, play the piano, have women friends, and swim twice a week?

LILLIAN. You mean what the women's magazines call "having it all"? Harriet, that's just your generation's fantasy.

HARRIET. Mother, you're being too harsh. Listen to me. What I want to know is if you do have all those things—my generation's fantasy—then what do you want?

LILLIAN. Needlepoint. You desperately want to needlepoint. (*Pauses.*) Life is a negotiation, Harriet. You think the women who go back to work at thirty-six are going to have the same career as a woman who has been there since her twenties? You think someone who has a baby and leaves it after two weeks to go back to work is going to have the same relationship with that child as someone who has been there all along? It's impossible. And you show me the wonderful man with whom you're going to have it all. You tell me how he feels when you take as many business trips as he does. You tell me who has to leave the office when the kid bumps his head on a radiator or slips on a milk carton. No, I don't think what you're talking about is possible.

HARRIET. All right. When you were twenty-nine, what was possible for you?

LILLIAN. When I was your age, I realized I had to make some choices. I had a promising career, a child, and a husband; and, believe me, if you have all three, and you're very conscientious, you still have to choose your priorities. So I gave some serious thought to what was important to me. And what was important to me was a career I could be proud of and successfully bringing up a child. So the first thing that had to go was pleasing my husband, because he was a grown-up and could take care of himself. Yes, baby, everything did take work; but it was worthwhile. I never dreamed I'd be this successful. And I have a perfectly lovely daughter. Baby, I have a full, rich life.

HARRIET. Mommy, what full, rich life? You watch *Rockford Files* reruns every night.

LILLIAN. If a man more appealing than James Garner comes into my life, I'll make room for him too. Okay, baby?

HARRIET. Well, I've made up my mind. I'm going to try to do it: have it all.

LILLIAN. Good for you. For your sake, I hope you can. (*Pauses.*) What's the matter, Harriet? Did I disillusion you?

HARRIET. No. I'm afraid I'm just like you.

LILLIAN. Don't be afraid. You're younger.

HARRIET. Mother, you're trying my patience.

LILLIAN. You sound just like me, dear.

HARRIET. If you were younger, I'd say something nasty.

LILLIAN. Whisper it late at night. It will give you guilt and anxiety. Your sweet old mom who worked for years to support you.

HARRIET. Fuck off, Mother.

LILLIAN. Don't tell that to your boss. Pay the bill, will you? Comb your hair, baby. I like it better off your face. Call me Sunday. Pretend it's Mother's Day. (*To waiter.*) This young lady will take the check, please. I love you, Harriet. (*Kisses her on the cheek.*)

HARRIET. I love you too.

LILLIAN. Sometimes.

HARRIET. Sometimes.

LILLIAN. (*As she exits.*) Lovely lunch, Tom. Thank you. (*Harriet sits alone at the table and takes out her American Express Gold Card. She lays it on the table.)*

Telephone Machine 6

Ring. Beep.

SIMON. Janie, it's Dad. Do you want to meet us at Oscar's for brunch? (*Ring. Beep.*)
MARTY. Monkey, sweetheart, are you there? Pick it up. Pick it up. I have to do my father a big favor tomorrow in Central Park. You and I will have dinner in Brooklyn.

Scene 4

Central Park. Sousa's "Washington Post" is heard. Marty enters, to cheers. He picks up a mike. Camera flashes go off.

MARTY. (*Into microphone.*) This is Dr. Murray Schlimovitz, standing in for my father, Captain Milty. I'm here at beautiful Central Park to inaugurate the first annual Sterling Marathon. That's right. He's giving away spring water, he's giving away seltzer, he's giving away carob bars. (*Janie enters left.*)
MARTY. And you know what my father always says: "You should only live and be well." (*Waves, as the crowd cheers, puts down the mike, and moves to Janie.*) Janie?
JANIE. Hi, Dr. Murray Schlimovitz.
MARTY. I decided to open my practice in Brooklyn under my real name. What are you doing here?
JANIE. I was in the neighborhood. They accepted my sketches for the giant bird. Does Mount Sinai know you're here?
MARTY. I'm here because it's my responsibility to my family. (*Pauses.*) Oy, I'm such a schmucky nice doctor.
JANIE. You're not such a schmucky nice doctor. What's the matter?
MARTY. I don't understand you. I call you all last night to coordinate the time for the moving truck to arrive at your house today. You don't return my calls, and then you arrive here today ready to crack jokes. Janie, what are you, a home-entertainment unit? Honey, go home. The moving truck will be at your house in an hour.
JANIE. Marty, do you ever get the feeling that everything is changing and you don't know when you decided to make the change?
MARTY. Nothing's changing. I'm offering you love, I'm offering

you affection, I'm offering you attention. All you have to do is put your crates that you never unpacked on that truck and get on the Belt Parkway. You just move forward.

JANIE. I can't just move forward.

MARTY. You know what I think? I think you're frightened to try. You think it's a compromise. You think you're not grown-up yet. That's bullshit. Maybe you think I'm not special enough.

JANIE. I think you're very special. But I want us to decide to move when we decide together. Marty, you took an apartment and you didn't even tell me about it first. None of it had anything to do with me. I don't want to sneak around you and pretend that I'm never angry. I don't want to be afraid of you. I guess to a man I love I want to feel not just that I can talk, but that you'll listen.

MARTY. Do you think I don't listen to you?

JANIE. You have all the answers before I ask the questions.

MARTY. You picked a hell of a time to bring this up. You want to give the answers, fine. You make the decision right now. Either you move in with me tonight or we stop and I'll make alternate arrangements.

JANIE. Marty, by you everything is much more simple than it has to be. You want a wife; you get a wife. You drop out of Harvard twice; they always take you back. You're just like me. We're too fucking sweet. I'm so sweet I never say what I want, and you're so sweet you always get what you want.

MARTY. Not necessarily. Why do you think I'm thirty-two and not married? All I want is a home, a family, something my father had so easily and I can't seem to get started on. Why? I'm a nice Jewish doctor. Women want to marry their daughters off to me all the time. Sure, I want to know where I'll live, who'll take the children to the nursery, but I wanted something special too. Just a little. Maybe not as special as you turned out to be, but just a little. Janie, I don't want to marry anyone like my sister-in-law.

JANIE. I never liked her. Honey, I wish we could throw a wedding at the Plaza. And your father could be toastmaster general, and Harriet would select my pattern, and my mother would dance, and baby Schlomo could carry the ring in one of my father's gold-seal envelopes.

MARTY. (*Cuts her off suddenly, quite angry.*) Goddammit, Janie, make a decision! You want to have children with a turkey baster, that's fine. You want to write sketches for a giant bird at two o'clock in the morning, that's fine too. You want to come home to Cynthia Peterson's phone calls, great. You want to find out what it's like to take care of yourself, good luck to you. But it isn't right for me. And I'll tell you something, Janie: it isn't right for you either.

JANIE. (*Softly.*) Marty, you're not right for me. I can't move in with you now. If I did that, I'd always be a monkey, a sweet little girl.

MARTY. (*After a pause.*) I have to get back with the starting pistol.

JANIE. (*Stops him.*) Honey, it's complicated.

MARTY. No. It's simple. You don't love me enough. (*Exits.*)

JANIE. Marty . . . (*Janie is left alone as Marty, speaking through a microphone, is heard offstage.*)

MARTY. This is Dr. Murray Schlimovitz, at the first annual Sterling Marathon. Runners ready. On your mark. Get set. Go. (*Janie is left alone on the stage as lights fade.*)

Telephone Machine 7

Ring. Beep.

HARRIET. Janie, I have good news. No; great news. Can you and Marty come over to dinner Sunday at six? There'll be Chicken Marengo. Bye. (*Ring. Beep.*)

HARRIET. Harriet again. Where are you? If you guys don't show up tomorrow, I'll "hock your china." I miss you. (*Dial tone.*) \

OPERATOR. Please hang up. There seems to be a receiver off the hook.

Scene 5

Harriet's apartment. Lillian and Harriet sit with drinks.

HARRIET. I thought you'd tell me I was insane.

LILLIAN. You're not insane. Impetuous, but not insane. Does Janie like Joe?

HARRIET. Janie's never even met Joe.

LILLIAN. You should talk to her about him. It's important to discuss your life choices with your friends.

HARRIET. Mother, you're so full of homespun advice today.

LILLIAN. I got my hair done yesterday. I read a lot of those women's magazines. You and Joe will have to come over next week for some Jell-O. (*Doorbell rings.*)

JANIE. (*Offstage.*) Harriet, it's me, Janie.

HARRIET. (*Opens the door.*) Hi.

JANIE. (*With a bouquet of flowers.*) These are for you. I was afraid you'd say they're too old. They're too new; they're gold.

HARRIET. No, they're perfect.

JANIE. How are you, Mrs. Cornwall?

LILLIAN. Janie, I'll know you the rest of my life and you'll still call me Mrs. Cornwall. Makes me feel good, baby. The kids in my office call me Lillian and pretend we're colleagues. We're not colleagues. I'm a person of moral and intellectual superiority.

HARRIET. My mother deals from strength.

JANIE. Speaking of strength, guess who called me? Paul Stuart. He said to tell you he really likes you very much and he doesn't understand why you won't return his calls. I'm *awfully* glad he has my number.

LILLIAN. Is this your boss's boss? The one who was so impressed with my potency.

HARRIET. Well, he's my boss now. I was promoted.

HARRIET AND JANIE. Yeah!!!! (*They hug.*)

JANIE. I knew there was good news here. I got the Chicken Marengo message and I said something good was happening. I've been trying to call you, but you weren't home, and then I was busy sending the letter *B* to the Bahamas. *Sesame Street* hired me part-time!

HARRIET AND JANIE. Yeah!!!! (*They hug again.*)

LILLIAN. Perhaps I should feel threatened. I'm surrounded by a generation of achieving younger women.

HARRIET. I don't think Janie's threatening to anyone. That's her gift.

LILLIAN. Well, she's impressive. Where's your nice young man? Harriet said she invited him to dinner tonight. I was looking forward to meeting him.

JANIE. Uh, Marty's busy tonight. There's a testimonial dinner for his father at Szechuan Taste. One day they'll find out which rabbi he's paying off and close down those places.

LILLIAN. Harriet, maybe Marty's father should cater your wedding? It'll be a first for the Carlyle. And we could keep it in the family.

JANIE. (*Looking from Lillian to Harriet.*) Excuse me?

HARRIET. Janie, do you remember, at my whiplash party two weeks ago, I told you I was driving up to a planning conference with Joe? He's the headhunter who got me my job at Colgate. He was a year ahead of me at Harvard. Well, I've been spending a lot of time with him recently. And yesterday he asked me to marry him.

JANIE. What?

HARRIET. (*Stands up and announces with pride.*) I'm going to marry Joe Stine. (*Pause.*)

LILLIAN. He'll be all right for a first husband. I'm just kidding. You know I'm thrilled, baby.

JANIE. Congratulations!

HARRIET. I would have told you earlier, but I didn't even know it was happening. And my time with Joe has been so intense, I wasn't able to call you.

JANIE. That's wonderful!

LILLIAN. Janie, you and I will have to plan the shower together. Well, I'm off to the Ming Dynasty.

HARRIET. What?

LILLIAN. I'm taking an Oriental Studies class. Not for credit. Your mother is broadening herself. I'll leave you girls to your dinner. Harriet, for the sake of your marriage, move beyond chicken marengo. Bye-bye, girls. (*Exits.*)

JANIE. She's in a good mood.

HARRIET. She's been reading *Redbook.* So, what do you think?

JANIE. It's wonderful. *Mazel tov.*

HARRIET. (*Going to the kitchen.*) I didn't mean to surprise you like this. I wanted to have you and Marty to dinner. Are things okay with Marty?

JANIE. Yeah. Fine.

HARRIET. You okay?

JANIE. Harriet, have you thought about living with Joe first? Better yet, maybe you should have dinner with Joe first.

HARRIET. (*Exuberant.*) I want to marry him! Janie, he's the only person who's even cared about me in a long time. He listens to me. Tasha's right. You and I deserve a little nachos.

JANIE. *Naches.*

HARRIET. Joe makes me feel like I have a family. I never had a family. I had you and Lillian, but I never felt I could have what other women just assumed they would get.

JANIE. I want to know one thing. I want to know why when I asked you about my living with Marty, you told me you didn't respect women who didn't learn to live alone and pay their own rent? And then, the first chance you have to change your life, you grasp it.

HARRIET. What? Marrying Joe is just a chance that came along.

JANIE. I see. You've been waiting for some man to come along and change your life. And all the things you told me about learning to live alone, and women and friendship, that was so much social nonsense. I feel like an idiot! I made choices based on an idea that doesn't exist anymore.

HARRIET. What choices?

JANIE. Never mind.

HARRIET. Janie, when I told you that, I didn't know what it would be like when Paul Stuart would leave at ten and go home to Cathy and I would have to pretend I wasn't hurt. I didn't know what it would be like to have lunch with Lillian and think I'm on my way to watching *Rockford Files* reruns. Of course you should learn to live alone and pay your own rent, but I didn't realize what it would feel like for me when I became too good at it. Janie, I know how to come home, put on the news, have a glass of wine, read a book, call you. What I don't know is what to do when there's someone who loves me in the house.

JANIE. I could throw this table at you.

HARRIET. Why? Janie, we're too good friends for you to be jealous.

JANIE. I'm not jealous.

HARRIET. Don't blame me for your doubts about Marty.

JANIE. Harriet, I don't blame you for anything. I'm sorry. Right now I just don't like you very much.

HARRIET. Why? Because I'm leaving you? Because I'm getting married?

JANIE. Because our friendship didn't mean very much to you. You bring me the sugar, the bread, and the salt, and you stand there and tell me you never had a family. Harriet, you never really listened to me and you never really told me about yourself. And that's sad.

HARRIET. Janie, I love you. But you want us to stay girls together. I'm not a girl anymore. I'm almost thirty and I'm alone.

JANIE. You lied to me.

HARRIET. I never lied to you. I lied to myself. It doesn't take any strength to be alone, Janie. It's much harder to be with someone else. I want to have children and get on with my life.

JANIE. What do you do? Fall in with every current the tide pulls in? Women should live alone and find out what they can do, put off marriage, establish a vertical career track; so you do that for a while. Then you almost turn thirty and *Time Magazine* announces, "Guess what, girls? It's time to have it all." Jaclyn Smith is married and pregnant and playing Jacqueline Kennedy. Every other person who was analyzing stocks last year is analyzing layettes this year; so you do that. What *are* you doing, Harriet? Who the hell are you? Can't you conceive of some plan, some time-management scheme that you made up for yourself? Can't you take a chance?

HARRIET. I *am* taking a chance. I hardly know this man.

JANIE. You don't have to force yourself into a situation—a marriage—because it's time.

HARRIET. You're just frightened of being with someone, Janie. You're just frightened of making a choice and taking responsibility for it.

JANIE. That sounds romantic.

HARRIET. That's life.

JANIE. Harriet, you're getting married to someone you've been dating for two weeks. I am much more scared of being alone than you are. But I'm not going to turn someone into the answer for me.

HARRIET. Then you'll be alone.

JANIE. Then I'll be alone. (*Pauses.*) I better go. I have to get up early with the letter *B*. If they like this, they'll hire me full-time. In charge of consonants.

HARRIET. Give my love to Marty.

JANIE. I can't. I told him I won't move with him to Brooklyn.

HARRIET. So you'll get an apartment in Manhattan.

JANIE. (*Starts crying.*) We broke up. I decided not to see him anymore.

HARRIET. Won't you miss him?

JANIE. I missed him today when I saw someone who looks sweet like him walking down the street, and I'll miss him late tonight.

HARRIET. Maybe you should call him.

JANIE. No.

HARRIET. Life is a negotiation.

JANIE. I don't believe I have to believe that.

HARRIET. Janie, it's too painful not to grow up.

JANIE. That's not the way I want to grow up. (*Kisses Harriet and starts to go.*)

HARRIET. You don't have to separate from me. I'm not leaving you.

JANIE. (*Picks up the trash.*) Want me to throw this out for you?

HARRIET. Sure.

JANIE. Do you really think anyone ever met someone throwing out the garbage? (*They both shake their heads no. Janie exits.*)

Scene 6

Janie's apartment. Janie is alone, sitting in front of her crates, wrapped in her blanket, holding the swizzle stick that Marty gave her. A romantic version of "Isn't It Romantic" is heard. Janie suddenly begins to cry. The doorbell rings. Janie doesn't answer it.

SIMON. (*Offstage.*) Janie, Janie.

JANIE. (*Softly.*) What? (*Doorbell rings once more.*)

SIMON. Janie. Janie. It's Dad. Can we come in?

JANIE. Just a second.

TASHA. (*Offstage.*) Janie, the super said he doesn't have the key.

JANIE. I changed the lock.

TASHA. What?

JANIE. Mother, you can't come in until you repeat after me: My daughter is a grown woman.

TASHA. Simon, she's crazy.

JANIE. My daughter is a grown woman.

TASHA. My daughter is a grown woman.

JANIE. This is her apartment.

TASHA. Of course, it's your apartment.

SIMON. For Christ's sake, just tell her . . .

TASHA. This is her apartment.

JANIE. I am to call before I arrive here.

TASHA. I always call. I get the machine.

SIMON. Janie, we can leave this with the doorman.

JANIE. There isn't any doorman here.

TASHA. Simon, maybe she wants to be alone.

JANIE. (*Opens the door.*) It's all right, Mother. The six truck drivers just left out the back window. (*Tasha and Simon enter. He carries a box.*)

SIMON. Sorry to bother you. We tried calling, but you don't return our calls.

JANIE. I've been busy, Daddy. I'm going on location with the letter *C* to Canada. They seem to like me.

TASHA. Of course they like you. You're my daughter.

JANIE. I don't think they know *you*, Mother.

TASHA. Simon, give her the package and let's go. (*Simon puts down the box.*)

TASHA. Your father said, "Janie will look like a model in this."

SIMON. You don't have to keep it unless you like it. (*Janie opens the box. It contains a mink coat.*)

SIMON. Do you like it?

TASHA. Give your father a little pleasure. Try it on. (*Helps Janie put it on. It is very small, a size four. Janie hunches to pull it around herself.*)

SIMON. I think it's very nice to your face. The girls are wearing the sleeves short now.

TASHA. I see girls your age wearing theirs to walk the baby carriage.

SIMON. Don't say you like it if you don't like it.

JANIE. I like it. I like it. If I was thirty-six and married to a doctor and a size three, this would be perfect for me.

TASHA. So why aren't you?

JANIE. Do you really want to know why I don't call you? You expect me to dial the phone and say, "Hello, Mother. Hello, Father. Here I am in my mink coat. I just came home from wearing it to walk the carriage. Everything is settled. Everything has worked out wonderfully. Here are your *naches*. Congratulations. I appreciate you."

TASHA. Why do you speak so much Yiddish? We never spoke so much Yiddish around the house.

JANIE. Look, I'm sorry. Things didn't work out as you planned. There's nothing wrong with that life, but it just isn't mine right now.

SIMON. What are you getting so emotional about? Sit. Relax. Look at me. I never get so emotional. Janie, all we did was give you a coat. You'll wear it when it's cold. And if you like, you'll wear it when it's hot, like the old ladies in Miami. That's all. No big deal. Are you taking drugs? Your eyes are glassy. Dear, look at her eyes.

TASHA. I don't want to look at her eyes. You know, Janie, I'll never forget when I sent you, as a child, to Helena Rubenstein Charm School. And you were always late, with your hair in your eyes and your hem hanging down. And Mrs. Rubenstein told me you were an ungrateful child.

JANIE. Mrs. Rubenstein never told you I was an ungrateful child.

TASHA. Simon, what did she tell us?

JANIE. The receptionist at Helena Rubenstein told you I was an ungrateful child. Mother, what do you want from me? You give me a mink coat, and I know you think any other daughter would appreciate this. Helena Rubenstein knows any other daughter would appreciate this. Georgette Klinger's daughter would appreciate this. I am a selfish, spoiled person. Something is the matter with me.

TASHA. (*Gets up.*) Something *is* the matter with you. Simon, I have to go dance. I have to work her out of my system.

SIMON. Dear, relax.

JANIE. I don't see how I can help you understand what I'm doing. Neither of you ever lived alone; you never thought maybe I won't have children and what will I do with my life if I don't.

TASHA. All right. You're the smart one. I'm the stupid one. I haven't taught you anything.

JANIE. (*Furious.*) Mother, think about it. Did you teach me to marry a nice Jewish doctor and make chicken for him? You order up breakfast from a Greek coffee shop every morning. Did you teach me to go to law school and wear gray suits at a job that I sort of like every day from nine to eight? You run out of here in leg warmers and tank tops to dancing school. Did you teach me to compromise and lie to the man I live with and say I love you when I wasn't sure? You live with your partner; you walk Dad to work every morning.

TASHA. Now I understand. Everything is my fault. I should have been like other mothers: forty chickens in the freezer and mah-jongg all afternoon. Janie, I couldn't live like that. God forbid. You think your father would have been happy with one of those women with the blond hair and the diamonds? And I'll tell you something else: you and Ben wouldn't have come out as well as you did. I believe a person should have a little originality—a little "you know." Otherwise you just grow old like everybody else. Let's go, Simon. Honey, you don't have to call us. You don't even have to let us know how you are. You do what you want. (*Starts to go.*)

JANIE. Wait a minute.

TASHA. I'm a modern woman too, you know. I have my dancing, I have your father, and I have my beautiful grandchild and Ben. I don't need you to fill up my life. I'm an independent woman—a person in my own right. Am I right, Simon?

SIMON. Janie, as for me, what I want is some Sunday before I come over here with a coffee table or a mink coat, you'd call me and say, "Dad, let's get together, I'd like to see you."

TASHA. She doesn't want to see us. (*Pause.*)

JANIE. (*Looks at her parents.*) I do want to see you. But you don't have to call every morning to sing "Sunrise—Sunset," and you don't have to bring a mink coat or a coffee table, or even a Russian taxicab driver for me to marry.

SIMON. Whatever happened to him? He was a nice boy.

JANIE. All you have to do is trust me a little bit. I believe a person should have a little originality, a little "you know"; otherwise you just grow old like everybody else. "And you know, Janie, I like life, life, life." Mother, sit, relax, let me figure it out.

TASHA. But, honey, if I sit, who's going to dance?

JANIE. Everything presses itself out.

TASHA. Unfortunately, Janie, the clock has a funny habit of keeping on ticking. I want to know who's going to take care of you when we're not around anymore.

JANIE. I guess *I* will. (*Takes her mother's hand.*) Mother, don't worry. I'm Tasha's daughter. I know; "I am."

TASHA. That's right. "I am." (*Janie touches Tasha's cheek. They embrace.*)

SIMON. And, Janie, from a man's point of view, the next time someone wants you to make him chicken, you tell him I was at your sister-in-law Christ's house the other day and she ordered up lamb chops from the Madison Delicatessen. How hard is it to cook lamb chops? You just stick them in the broiler. If Christ can order up lamb chops—and she's a girl from Nebraska—you don't have to make anybody chicken. Believe me, you were born to order up.

JANIE. Sounds like manifest destiny.

SIMON. In fact, I have the number. We could have a family dinner right now.

TASHA. No, Simon. Let's go home.

SIMON. (*Kisses Janie.*) Good-bye, Janie.

JANIE. Good-bye, Daddy.

TASHA. Good-bye, honey.

JANIE. Mother, one more thing. Take back your mink. (*Takes it off and puts it over Tasha's shoulders.*)

TASHA. Fits me perfectly.

JANIE. Fits you perfectly.

TASHA. Where's my partner? (*Sweeps up to Simon, and, arm in arm, they exit. Janie takes a deep breath in the silence. She picks up her blanket and folds it neatly, picks up the mink box and sets it on a crate. It's time, finally, to unpack. She lifts blanket, box, and crate and starts to exit into the bedroom. The telephone rings.*)

CYNTHIA PETERSON. (*On phone machine.*) Janie, it's Cynthia Peterson. It's my thirty-fourth birthday. I'm alone. Nothing happened with Mr. Houston. I should have married Mark Silverstein in college. Janie, by the time I'm thirty-five, this is what I want.

JANIE. (*Flaps her foot.*) Flap.

CYNTHIA PETERSON. I want a hundred thousand dollars a year, a husband, a baby. Janie, are you there? I hear breathing.

JANIE. (*Takes another step.*) Flap heel.

CYNTHIA PETERSON. I think someone's there. Whoever you are, there's nothing there worth taking.

JANIE. (*Moves and taps.*) Flap, flap, flap, touch. Flap, flap, flap, touch.

CYNTHIA PETERSON. Janie, I met a man at the deli last night. He asked me if I wanted to have a beer in his apartment at one o'clock in the morning. Do you think I should have gone? (*Janie starts to tap with some assurance as the tape continues.*)

CYNTHIA PETERSON. There was an article in the *New York Post* that there are 1,000 men for every 1,123 New York hubby hunters. (*Music comes in, "Isn't It Romantic," as Janie crosses and picks up a hat and umbrella.*)

CYNTHIA PETERSON. And there was this picture of an eligible man. He's an actor and he likes painting. I like painting. Should I call him? (*Music gets louder. Janie dances as Cynthia fades. A spot picks up Janie dancing beautifully, alone.*)

CYNTHIA PETERSON. I could take him to the Guggenheim on my membership. How many of these 1,123 women are going to call him? How many are members of the Guggenheim? I don't know if I want to marry an actor. Maybe I should wait for tomorrow's eligible bachelor. (*Spot fades on Janie twirling with the hat and umbrella.*)

END

Photograph by Bernard Cohen

Barbara Lebow

BARBARA LEBOW WAS BORN in Brooklyn in 1936, attended ethical culture schools in Manhattan, and graduated from Vassar College. In the early sixties she moved to Atlanta, Georgia, where she became affiliated with the Academy Theatre Developmental Workshop, teaching playwriting and directing other people's new dramas. She also headed the Academy's human service program and directed group-development plays with the homeless, the addicted, the disabled, and the imprisoned.

She has written well over twenty plays of her own, many of which were premiered at Atlanta's Academy Theatre. The most successful of them include: *Little Joe Monaghan, The Adventures of Homer McGundy, A Shayna Maidel,* * *Trains,* and *Tiny Tim is Dead. A Shayna Maidel,* however, is her only play to be successfully performed in New York. It received wide acclaim for its 1984–85 fifteen-month run off-Broadway and was cited in the *1984–1985 Best Plays* yearbook.

"I was originally from Brooklyn," Barbara says, "but by 1946 we were living in Manhattan. I'm Jewish and some of my relatives were in concentration camps. When I was ten at the end of the war, we were visited by third cousins who stayed with us for a few months. I know that my reactions to them found themselves into the character of Rose in *A Shayna Maidel*" (Botto 1984, 48).

"The idea for my play germinated for about three years," she recalls. "I did a lot of research—not in libraries—but by interviewing survivors of the Holocaust. I did not focus on their experiences in the camps. There is no mention of atrocities in my play. I was more interested in what happened to these people after they were liberated

*Translates literally as "a pretty girl." It describes inner beauty and is an expression of love and of yearning hope.

from the camps" (Botto 1984, 48). "A woman told me she gorged on food and took a doll from a captured Polish home, recently abandoned by the Germans. Lusia is patterned on this woman who also told me that for years she felt guilt for surviving. . . . There was nothing heroic in this woman's eyes about her experience," Lebow says. "'All I did was live,' she told me" (Koblenz 1992, 2).

"I often wonder, could we have stood it? What if it had been us? We really know so little of what was going on. Just as most of us in this country know so little of persecution. What would be our reaction if it should ever happen to us?" Lebow asks (Koblenz 1992, 2).

The play does not didactically answer this question. By interspersing dramatized scenes from the present with memory scenes and fantasy scenes, *A Shayna Maidel* artfully forges a connection between the living and the Holocaust dead. Opposed to the use of flashbacks, Lebow explains,

> I have memory scenes in my plays—not flashbacks. There's a big difference. A flashback is objective. A memory scene has some reality, but the facts are somewhat distorted or colored by the person's mind who is remembering. Fantasy scenes, which I also use, are events that never happen at all, but which the thinker wishes could have happened. Sometimes the memory of a true event can trigger a fantasy. The mind just jumps around that way, and I try to capture that thought process in my plays. (Botto 1984, 51)

In addition to the play's complex thought process, the kind of language Lusia uses may be equally confusing. Lebow clarifies this confusion. "Whenever Lusia is speaking Yiddish, I start her off with a Yiddish sentence, then have her speak the rest in flawless English to indicate that she's speaking in her own tongue" (Botto 1984, 51).

What is compellingly apparent is the play's emotional impact. According to Mel Gussow of the *New York Times*, "*A Shayna Maidel* acts, finally, as a cathartic release for the audience. A feeling of quietude, not to be mistaken for placidity, suffuses the evening. Neither the author or the cast oversteps into sentimentality. . . . Even as the family is brought together in a tearful homecoming, one cannot forget the missing."

A Shayna Maidel was first produced at the Academy Theatre's First Stage New Play Series, April 18, 1985, with the playwright as director. The script was completed during the Academic Theatre's Mainstage production, April 9, 1986. The play was supported in part by grants from the Georgia Council for the Arts and the City of Atlanta, Bureau of Cultural Affairs, and was selected by Theatre Communications Group for Play in Progress 1984–85.

The Equity premiere was produced at Hartford Stage Company November 15, 1985, with the following cast:

Lindsey Margo Smith	Ray Dooley
Mary Margolis	Kate Fuglei
Gordana Rashovich	Maggie Burke

Director: Robert Kalfin
Costumes: Eduardo Sicango
Lighting: Curt Osterman
Sound: David Budries

The New York premiere was produced at Westside Arts Theatre, opening October 29, 1987, with the following cast:

Melissa Gilbert	Jon Tenney
Paul Sparer	Cordelia Richards
Gordana Rashovich	Joan MacIntosh

Director: Mary B. Robinson
Set Director: William Barclay
Costumes: Mimi Maxmen
Lighting: Dennis Parichy
Sound: Aural Fixation

Playwright's Notes

When memory or fantasy creates a time or place other than Rose Weiss's apartment, this is indicated by changes in the lighting. Music may also be used to parenthesize fantasies. Imagined characters should appear realistically within scenes, not be removed by scrims or other illusions. However, they may enter from places outside the realistic entrances on the set.

At times throughout the play, there can be an interweaving of one or more disembodied *Voice/s* with the action of the play. Usually there is only a suggestion of acknowledgment, a look, a slight hesitation, by the actors since the sounds are internal rather than external, reflections of feelings and memory. Whatever sounds, human or other, are used for these voices are recognizably related: growing from the same line, Mama's lullaby, since they form a continuum of awareness.

The action of the play occurs *before* and *after* time lived in the camps. It is important that any references to life and death in the camps be filled in by the audience. There should be no visual or auditory images suggesting a concentration camp. Any temptation to play tragedy, sentiment, or melodrama must be avoided at all costs. The characters should be perceived by actors and director simply as members of a family who cannot communicate. They do not know the Holocaust is behind them.

Except for Rose, all the characters have a Yiddish accent when they are speaking in English. However, in the memory or fantasy scenes where these characters are assumed to be speaking in Yiddish, the actors should shift into unaccented English. Some Yiddish is used in the play, and translations are provided in footnotes for words and phrases not otherwise translated in the text, to assist those working on, or reading, the play. In performance, most of the Yiddish dialogue will be understood by a non-Yiddish speaking audience as long as the actors know what they are saying. Spoken, many of the Yiddish words resemble their English translations. Gesture and intonation will help clarify meaning and the words give no important new information. The Yiddish flavor is what matters.

Music

The text of the song, "O, di velt verren shayna" by Morris Winchevsky is included by courtesy of The Workmen's Circle Education Department from the record *Songs of Freedom and Resistance* by the W. C. Chorus, directed by Zalmen Mlotek. For permission to perform the song, and to obtain a copy of the record, write Joseph Mlotek, Education Department, The Workmen's Circle, 45 East 33rd St., New York, NY 10016; (212) 889-6800.

Suggested for Mama's lullaby: *Rozhinkes Mit Mandlen* (traditional).

A Shayna Maidel
1988

Characters

ROSE WEISS, early twenties
MORDECHAI WEISS, her father, almost seventy
LUSIA WEISS PECHENIK, her older sister, late twenties (younger in memory scenes)

DUVID PECHENIK, Lusia's husband, thirty (younger in memory scenes)
HANNA, a childhood friend of Lusia, age ranges from fourteen to late
  twenties
MAMA, mother of Rose and Lusia, various ages
MIDWIFE
MOTHER
DAUGHTER
MAN, daughter's husband
*The last four characters appear only in Act I, Scene 1 and are doubled with
  other roles.*

Time

Prologue: 1876; Acts I and II: March 1946

Place

Prologue: A small Polish village.
Acts I and II: Rose Weiss's apartment, New York City, West Side

ACT I

Scene 1

*The main action of the play takes place in Rose Weiss's apartment in New
York City in 1946. The living room of the apartment is center stage with
raised platforms stage left and stage right to serve as bedroom and dinette.
There are doorways which lead from the dinette to the offstage kitchen and
from the bedroom to the offstage bathroom and closet. Upstage center an entranceway from the living room leads off on one side to the bathroom and
closet and off on the other side to the front door. There are no working doors
onstage.*

*As the play begins, the stage is in darkness. It is 1876 in a Polish
shtetl.* The scene has a dreamlike surrealistic quality. Illumination of the
characters is no more than that from a single candle. The daughter, whom we
do not see, but whose voice is heard clearly in labor, is attended by her mother
and a midwife, dressed in long skirts, with their heads covered. Her husband
wears a prayer shawl. In addition to the urgency of the imminent birth, all
are frightened of something outside. There are moments when they freeze, like
the moment of suspension when an animal senses danger. At times these mo-*

---

*Village.

ments are precipitated by something of which only the characters are aware; sometimes a distant shout or noise is audible to the audience. Growing out of the darkness, the first sounds in the scene are the words of a quietly intoned Hebrew prayer.

HUSBAND. *Hashem yish-mereynu mikhol ro veyishmor ses nafsheynu.* *
(*This is repeated throughout the scene at a small distance away from the other activities. When the prayer has been established, it is joined by the heavy breathing and muffled cries of the Daughter.*)

MIDWIFE. *Licht. Mir muzn hobn licht!*† (*The single candle is lit. The following lines and actions are spaced and played under the conditions described above.*)

DAUGHTER. Mama! Mama! (*Mother hushes and comforts the Daughter.*)

MOTHER. (*In response to an outside noise.*) Cossacks! (*Out of one of the silent freezes, a baby begins to cry, creaking like an old door.*)

MIDWIFE. A boy! A blessing on him. (*The baby is wrapped and held.*)

MOTHER. (*Quieting the infant.*) Sha, my child. Sha, sha. (*The baby is quiet.*)

DAUGHTER. You must tell my husband.

MIDWIFE. Reb Weiss . . . (*The praying stops for the first time.*) Reb Weiss, you have a son.

HUSBAND. (*Holding the baby stiffly.*) We shall call him Mordechai.‡

DAUGHTER. Itzik, look! He already knows not to cry. (*A sound in the distance. Another frozen moment.*)

MIDWIFE. *Di licht!* (*She blows out the candle. In the darkness, galloping horses come closer and ride by. Growing out of this sound, and taking over for it as it fades, is a knocking on the door and the loud and insistent ringing of a doorbell.*)

Scene 2

The apartment. Near midnight. The first doorbell ring is followed by intermittent knocking and ringing. Light in the bedroom. Rose, awakened, is startled.

MORDECHAI. (*Offstage.*) Rayzel! Open up the door!

ROSE. Papa? (*She grabs a robe.*)

*May God protect us from all evil and May He protect our souls.
†Light. We must have light!
‡Pronounced with guttural "ch" when in Yiddish mode, or by Lusia. In American mode, as if Mordekai.

MORDECHAI. Who else? Hurry up, Rayzel! What's taking so long? (*Rose goes to open the front door and returns to the living room, followed by Mordechai Weiss. Though he has been a hard worker all his life, Mordechai is a dignified and elegant man with an aristocratic look. He carries a cane, used for style and emphasis rather than for aid in walking, since he moves easily. He wears a coat over a well-pressed dark suit. He removes his hat and scarf, automatically gives them to Rose, who puts them down as they begin speaking.*)

ROSE. I was asleep, Papa. What's the matter? It's the middle of the night.

MORDECHAI. (*He has an old-country Yiddish accent, incongruous to his appearance.*) I got big news. Important news. Sit.

ROSE. (*She sits as ordered; speaks to him as she always does, unconsciously picking up some of his inflection.*) Well, what is it, Papa? Tell me. You're scaring me to death.

MORDECHAI. Glass water first, please. (*Mordechai sits down, pulling papers from an inside pocket, opening, reading and arranging them as Rose goes for water and returns. He sips a little, places the glass down carefully, motions for her to sit again, clears his throat.*) Thanks to God, I found your sister.

ROSE. (*Stunned, speaks softly after a moment.*) My sister! When, Papa? Where? How? How is she?

MORDECHAI. Came these letters from Red Cross and from Hebrew Immigrant Aid Society both together today. To Mr. Mordechai Weiss in Brooklyn. (*Carefully hands papers to Rose.*) She went from concentration camp Poland to hospital Sweden. I make lots phone calls from Greenspan's to be sure and I'm down to immigrant office waiting with more people on same kind business. She comes here by boat in three more weeks. Thanks to God they left one from the family alive.

ROSE. I can't believe it.

MORDECHAI. Is truth. From centuries, from Cossacks to Hitler— *Ich hob im in drerd!**—they tried to wipe out everybody! But you I got away in time and now your sister . . .

ROSE. (*Reading.*) Lusia Weiss Pechenik?† She must be married.

MORDECHAI. A married woman. . . . Last we seen her she was this big.

ROSE. I don't remember her. Or my mother.

---

*He should rot in Hell! (Literally, "I have him in dirt!")

†Lusia—pronounced as if *Lewsha;* Pechenik—as if Peh-*cheh*-nik (ch as in "chew").

MORDECHAI. Soon you'll remember. When she comes, she'll stay here with you.

ROSE. But Papa, wouldn't it be better if she stayed with you at Greenspans'?

MORDECHAI. If it came out different, maybe. If someone else was saved. If we was going to be a family again, we should all be under one roof. Even you. But it didn't come out different. So, in three weeks from now, you'll take a vacation from work.

ROSE. I just got the position, Papa.

MORDECHAI. The boss, he'll understand. Your sister is more important. They give you any trouble over this big, New York po-si-tion, I'll go myself and talk to them or you'll quit because if they don't see the point, they're no good anyway!

ROSE. I'll work it out, Papa.

MORDECHAI. You got to be with her every minute. Take care like a nurse her health, her sleep, her food, everything.

ROSE. But I don't even know her.

MORDECHAI. Is your flesh and blood.

ROSE. Why can't *Tanta** Perla—

MORDECHAI. Your *Tanta* Perla has a bad foot. She sits all day in a chair on the front porch. Anyway, she done her work with you. Now you take care your sister. (He *stands, putting on hat and scarf.*) Every day I'll come visit.

ROSE. But Papa, the place is so small! There's no room for anyone else.

MORDECHAI. Don't let me hear such a thing! (He *walks around, pointing with his cane as Rose tries to get a word in, but can't.*) Lusia sleeps in there. You here on sofa. Is your flesh and blood. A blessing from God on this family saved her life so no more words from you. Brooklyn's not good enough for you anymore so maybe Brooklyn's not good enough for your sister, too. (*Indicating kitchen with cane.*) And from now on you'll keep kosher like you're supposed to, like you was taught.

ROSE. I told you I—

MORDECHAI. Don't tell me nothing. I know what goes on. A hundred percent kosher from this minute. Perfect. Everything like she's used to. I want she should feel at home.

ROSE. But, Papa—

MORDECHAI. (*Overlapping.*) When such a miracle happens and you got now a sister, you don't say the word "but."

*Aunt.

ROSE. I know, Papa. I'm really very happy, but we don't know each other. We're strangers.

MORDECHAI. (*Pounding floor with cane.*) Shvesters! Ain flaish!* (*Mordechai moves toward the front door.*) I come to the boat with you, three weeks Tuesday. You find out what time, the details. Greenspan can live without me a half day. . . . Gai schlofen,† Rayzel. It's late. (*Mordechai exits. Rose grabs the water glass from where he left it and walks quickly toward the kitchen. In the dinette, she stops suddenly. She stands, unmoving. As the light fades to black, the voice of a woman (Mama) is heard singing sweetly in Yiddish: a lullaby.*)

Scene 3

Two-and-a-half weeks later. A Friday near midnight. A phone rings loudly. It rings again. Rose is awakened suddenly. Bedroom light rises.

ROSE. (*Answering phone sleepily.*) Hello. (*In another area of the stage Lusia appears, tightly lit. She speaks uncertainly with a very thick Yiddish-Polish accent. Her voice is gentle.*)

LUSIA. Rayzel Weiss.

ROSE. Hello?

LUSIA. Rayzel Weiss.

ROSE. What did you say? Who is this?

LUSIA. I want speak Rayzel Weiss, please you.

ROSE. I think you have the wrong number. (*Rose is about to hang up, unsure. Lusia looks helpless and confused.*)

LUSIA. Wait, please.

ROSE. Yes?

LUSIA. (*She speaks very slowly.*) I want to speak *mit* mine *shvester*, Rayzel Weiss. Mine *shvester*—sis-ter—Rayzel Weiss.

ROSE. (*Sits up fast. Waits. She speaks tentatively, amazed and frightened.*) Lusia? Is this Lusia?

LUSIA. Lusia Pechenik. Is Lusia Weiss Pechenik.

ROSE. Lusia! This is me. It's Rose. Rayzel. Your sister. Where are you? I didn't expect to hear from you till Tuesday. Where are you calling from?

LUSIA. In New York City. (*Reads from a card.*) Hebrew Immigrant Aid Society. I was on airplane instead of boat.

ROSE. You're four days early. I can't believe it!

*Sisters! One flesh!
†Go to sleep.

LUSIA. Is truth. Believe, please.

ROSE. (*Laughing.*) Oh, I didn't really mean . . . It's just an expression. Forget it. (*Beginning to speak more rapidly.*) Now, I don't know exactly what to do. I didn't expect to see you for a few more days yet. I'm not ready. Papa's not here since we thought you were coming later. But you've got to come right away, no matter what.

LUSIA. I got no place else.

ROSE. Of course you don't. Can you tell me the address? The street. The number where you are. (*She finds a pen and paper in the night table.*)

LUSIA. Four-two-five La-Fay-ette Street.

ROSE. Now, it'll be a few minutes. It's late and getting a taxi may take a while, but I'll be there. (*Holding phone with her chin she tidies the bed.*) Papa won't, you understand. I can't call him. He won't answer the phone on Sabbath, *Shabbes,* you know. What a funny time for you to come. Of course, it doesn't make any difference to me. . . . Oh, wait a minute! This is silly. I'll see you soon and we can talk then. A lot. Anyway, I don't know how *you* feel about it . . . about anything, except you were traveling on Friday night, but it was an emergency . . .

LUSIA. Friday same like Monday, like Thursday.

ROSE. Lusia. Lushke, right?

LUSIA. Mama used to call me.

ROSE. (*Obviously uncomfortable, she pauses.*) Listen, Lusia, I'll be right there. Goodbye now.

LUSIA. Goodbye now. (*Lusia vanishes as Rose hangs up.*)

ROSE. What am I supposed to do? (*She takes an extra blanket and throws it on the living room couch.*) Thanks, Papa! (*Rose turns on the radio, which takes a while to warm up and start playing. She is both tearful and angry, talking intermittently. She comes and goes, dressing herself, bit by bit, in quite stylish clothes, paying nervous attention to her appearance.*) Thanks a lot, Papa . . . Anything for you, Papa . . . What am I gonna do with her? . . . It's not fair! (*Almost ready to leave, Rose faces the audience, brushing her hair in an unseen downstage mirror in the bedroom. Suddenly she stops, looks at her "reflection" for several seconds, then speaks to herself very softly.*) It could've been you, Rose. (*She stares at herself for another moment, then slams down the brush.*) It's all your fault, Papa! (*Picking up her coat and purse.*) Why can't you leave me alone! (*She takes a deep breath, rehearses a smile in the mirror, takes the H.I.A.S. address and goes into the living room. She makes the sofa look as if she had been sleeping there. The radio is still playing when she leaves. The lights dim. The sound of the radio continues for a while, then fades out.*)

Scene 4

Less than an hour later. The radio fades in again with a different tune. The lights brighten as Rose enters, followed by Lusia, who is pale and thin, wearing out-of-date, hand-me-down clothing: a blouse, skirt, and shapeless cardigan sweater. Rose holds Lusia's worn suitcase. Lusia carries an old black handbag and a child's stuffed clown doll. Rose's discomfort and self-consciousness are well-covered by her all-American prettiness and cheeriness. Lusia is cautious and reserved, aloof, at times confused. She speaks softly and with little expression, a sharp contrast to Rose's effusiveness.

ROSE. (*Beginning offstage; rapidly, running on, as she turns off the radio and shows Lusia around.*) It's not very big, but it's mine, at least, and I can do with it what I want, you see, and it's so much better than when I was living with Papa at the Greenspans' in Brooklyn. I'm sure you've heard of them. It was only supposed to be temporary, but that turned out to be sixteen years and the minute I hit twenty-one I moved out. This is the dinette and the kitchen's in there. (*Lusia follows and stands at the doorway, looking into the kitchen. Rose goes off into kitchen. Offstage.*) All the appliances came with the apartment. The newest kind of everything. There's nothing to it anymore—cooking and cleaning and keeping it all nice. You'll get used to it. You know, everything you see here, anything you want, just take it. It's all yours, too. Are you hungry? I mean do you want a sandwich . . . (*voice, only a wisp*) . . . or an apple, maybe? Or something to drink? (*Lusia turns, looks away from doorway as Rose enters.*) A glass of milk or some juice or tea? I'll bet you drink tea, don't you, in a glass, like Papa? (*Lusia nods. Rose offers fruit from the table, Lusia shakes her head.*) But if you're not hungry, let me show you the rest. Now, I was saying about the Greenspans, they're really very nice people, very old-fashioned, like Papa, but different. I know they're cousins or something, but I never could get the story straight. (*Proudly.*) That's called a Picture Window Convector in that window . . . you know, a heater. It keeps it warm in the winter. I think they're third or fourth cousins, whatever that means, or she is, anyway, and I'm sure they'll want to meet you, but we can worry about that later. (*Rose and Lusia are in the bedroom.*) This is your room. (*She finally puts down the suitcase for the last time, and waits for a reaction.*)

LUSIA. Is nice.

ROSE. In here's the closet. And the bathroom. It goes right through to the front hall. (*She goes off. Lusia catches a glimpse of herself in the mirror, is surprised by her appearance, turns away from it quickly. Rose returns with a stack of towels.*) Here's some clean towels. This is the big one for a bath or shower and this one's a face towel and here's the washcloth. See, I got them monogrammed . . . Oh, I'm sorry, Lusia. I'm just so excited. I'll slow down, I promise. (*She does, for a while, trying to be aware of Lusia's possible difficulty in understanding, but gradually she will start rushing nervously again.*) What I mean to say is I had my initials put on them, all matching. And I just had "R. W." put on so when I get married, all I have to do is add another initial.

LUSIA. *Mazel tov.**

ROSE. What?

LUSIA. For your *t'noyim.*†

ROSE. (*Puzzled, repeats the word unsurely.*) T'noyim?

LUSIA. Your marriage coming.

ROSE. (*Laughs, too much.*) Oh, not now, Lusia. I just meant *whenever.*

LUSIA. You don't have *hartseniu?*

ROSE. *Hartseniu?* Oh, you mean sweetheart. Well, no. Not really. There are several people I'm seeing, I mean going out with, spending time with . . . on dates . . . but nobody special. Do you want me to help you unpack? (*Indicates doll as she opens the suitcase. At first taken aback by what she sees, she awkwardly removes a plain, worn robe and pajamas, laying them out on the bed.*) You can put that on the bed or on the chair over there. I used to have doll I slept with for years, a kind of rabbit or something. Mrs. Greenspan got it for me. Papa never would. She was very sweet sometimes. I always call her *Tanta* Perla. Even now when I visit. (*Lusia puts the doll on a chair or dresser.*)

LUSIA. I save it over here. (*Rose brings a wrapped package from the closet.*)

ROSE. Here. This is for you.

LUSIA. (*Holding the present as if it might explode, staring at it.*) Thank you.

ROSE. Well, open it up. (*Rose starts to help Lusia undo the wrappings. Lusia, still staring at the gift, brushes Rose's hands away and continues opening it on her own. She takes out a beautiful and elegant nightgown.*) I didn't know what you had. (*She is suddenly somber, embarrassed.*) What they gave you. I thought you might like it.

LUSIA. *Shayn.* Pretty. Too pretty.

ROSE. Oh, nothing can be too pretty!

---

*Good luck.

†Engagement.

LUSIA. I mean to say, how much pretty.

ROSE. *So* pretty, then. "So," not "too."

LUSIA. So pretty. To sleep with. I cannot believe. So pretty.

ROSE. I'm glad you like it. Now, why don't you go wash up, I mean bathe, and I'll fix something to eat. I'll bet you're hungry, really. And you wear the nightgown. There's a real nice robe in the closet you can use to go with it. I have extras, honestly. And while I'm making lunch—I know it's the middle of the night, but it feels like lunch to me—you can freshen up and wash away all your traveling. You've come so far, in such a short time. I know you're tired, but we need to fatten you up a bit and get the roses back in your cheeks.

LUSIA. *(Refolding the nightgown.)* Di roizn oif di bekelech* . . .

ROSE. I guess it's something like that. What are you doing? *(Lusia has put the nightgown back in its box and is rewrapping it.)* Don't you like it?

LUSIA. Thank you. *(She takes the box and puts it next to the doll.)* I save it here.

ROSE. *(Urgently.)* Oh, Lusia, wear it! Wear something pretty. You deserve something pretty *(picks up pajamas)*, not these awful things. *(Her voice is breaking.)* It's all so terrible! . . . You don't have . . . *(Lusia looks away from Rose, pretending interest in something else.)* There's nothing! . . . I don't know what . . . *(All at once, she stops, then continues speaking smoothly, in control.)* What I mean is you deserve something pretty. Like you. You could be so pretty.

LUSIA. *(An attempt at lightness.)* A shayna maidel? No.

ROSE. A pretty girl. That's right. That's who you are.

LUSIA. Mama used to say about you. "Ah, Rayzel . . ." *(She sighs, imitating Mama. Voice.)* "a shayna maideleh." *(Rose turns away rapidly. Lusia watches her for a moment, then pats the box.)* I save it here. *(Lusia picks up the stack of towels, fingering the monogram first, then the robe and pajamas, and goes into the living room. She turns back to Rose, who is following her.)* Where you sleep?

ROSE. *(A forced cheerfulness, as before.)* Me? Oh, I sleep over here, on the sofa. So I can keep that as a guest room. You know, in case someone comes for a visit or wants to stay over. Sometimes I think Papa might not want to take the subway all the way back to Brooklyn at night. Or *Tanta* Perla, when she visits. Really, I like to curl up out here. It means less to clean up and you know with me working

---

*The roses in the cheeks.

there's hardly time to take care of things right. That's your room. Really it is and I sleep here all the time. Now, wait just one minute more. (*Rose disappears into the bathroom. Lusia looks around slowly, as if catching her breath. She reaches out and almost touches the furniture. Rose returns in a flurry.*) I started the bath for you, so no more dillydallying. It smells wonderful. I put some bubble bath in it . . . "Night of Surrender" . . . can you imagine? (*Rose is pushing Lusia towards the bathroom. Lusia understands little of what's being said, but acquiesces, puzzled and a bit amazed.*) It makes a whole lot of bubbles. It's absolutely sinful, really, it's so good! (*Lusia is now offstage. Shouting after Lusia.*) Stay in there a long time. As long as you like. We can sleep late tomorrow. There's nothing to do all day! (*Rose quickly starts setting the dinette table. Then she goes to the sofa, tidies the blanket. She suddenly stops, sits, grabs a sofa pillow and hugs it tightly, rocking slowly back and forth. Lights fade.*)

Scene 5

An hour or so later. As lights rise in the bedroom, wearing her faded robe, Lusia is fantasizing she is with her husband, Duvid.* She calls him softly. Duvid appears, lights change to a fantasy glow.

LUSIA. Duvid. Duvid . . . *Ich hob a sorpriz far dir.*† (*Not looking at Duvid. He remains behind her. She sees him only in her mind.*)

DUVID. (*Looking at Lusia.*) *Vel ich es lib hobn?*‡

LUSIA. *Yo.*§ (*Lusia and Duvid now start speaking in unaccented English, setting the pattern for all the following scenes where characters are assumed to be speaking Yiddish.*) I *know* you'll like it.

DUVID. Let me see it. (*They are close together but not facing one another. Duvid appears younger than Lusia, filled with humor and energy, in his early twenties, as Lusia remembers him. She is wearing the gift nightgown hidden under her robe, although the package remains undisturbed.*)

LUSIA. First I want to tell you about my sister Rayzel. She doesn't feel like my sister. She's nervous with me. A stranger.

---

*Pronounced as if *Doo*vid (as in "good").
†I have a surprise for you.
‡Will I like it?
§Yes.

DUVID. Tell me why, Lushke.

LUSIA. It's because . . . *I'm* the stranger. I've invaded her house, but what can I do?

DUVID. Be yourself.

LUSIA. But Rayzel is afraid of me. She tries to hide it, avoids looking at me as one avoids a cripple. Or she does the opposite, stares at me and forgets to speak, like she's looking into a deep mirror. Then I'm scared.

DUVID. You're safe now.

LUSIA. (*Turning to look at him.*) Not until I find you.

DUVID. Can I see the surprise already?

LUSIA. All right, Duvidl. Turn around. (*He turns away. She takes off her robe.*) Now look.

DUVID. (*Turning to her, smiling.*) It's beautiful. You're beautiful. But so expensive! Can we afford it?

LUSIA. Rayzel gave it to me. A present. She gave it to me with innocence. With a longing, it seemed to me. But I didn't know how to thank her. I thought, "It's really a present for Duvid." It makes me feel closer to finding you . . . having something waiting for you. To give you. Like the clown for our baby. That was from Hanna. I told you already.

DUVID. (*Quietly.*) It's a handsome clown.

LUSIA. For a handsome child.

DUVID. A beautiful child.

LUSIA. Yours and mine.

DUVID. From you and me and your parents and mine and theirs, all the way back to Adam and Eve. A very important baby.

LUSIA. One of the most. (*Pause.*) Duvidl, lie down here, beside me. (*Lusia reclines, Duvid follows.*) I want to tell you what I miss, here in my sister's bed in New York City. I miss it more than all the love and happiness between us.

DUVID. All right, Lushke. Tell me.

LUSIA. When we're asleep, with you all around me, like a warm shell, and I'm the egg safe inside, then I feel your dreams. Sometimes your foot twitches, sometimes a small sigh touches the back of my neck and I know you're running away or calling in your dream place. It's the most private place there is, the most secret, and you let me be there with you. This is what I miss most, Duvid . . . feeling your dreams. Even in a bed we've never shared, I miss going with you to your dreams.

DUVID. Man and wife are one life.

LUSIA. (*Sleepy.*) So many beds. And no beds. (*Duvid gets up, lowering Lusia's head to the pillow.*)

DUVID. *Gai schlofn, aiele.* * (*Light begins to fade slowly.*)

LUSIA. (*Giggling.*) *Mir kenen machn a kugel.* †

DUVID. (*Tucking her in.*) *Gai schlofn, maideleh.* (*Duvid disappears in the fading light.*)

LUSIA. (*Her voice fading, too.*) *Ich schlof . . . ich schlof . . .* (*Silence in the darkness. Both sisters are asleep. Slight movements come from Lusia's bed. Gradually, her activity increases. She breaks the silence intermittently, whispering at first, then crying out.*) No. No! Mama. Mama? *Sprinze! Sprinzele!* (*Lusia's voice grows louder and she is more active in her sleep. A dim light on Rose in the living room. She sits up on the sofa and listens, not sure what awakened her.*) *Loz mir oich gain! Ich vil oich gain! Nein! Siz avek! Nein!*‡ (*Rose gets up, moves towards the bedroom, uncertain whether or not to wake Lusia. There are stronger sounds, moans, deep anguished cries from Lusia.*) *Vu . . .? Ich ken zai mer nit zen!*§ *Ma—maaaa!* (*Rose turns on the radio and tries to listen to the music so as not to hear Lusia. As Lusia's nightmare continues, Rose twice turns up the radio in order to drown it out.*) *Avek! Aibik un aibik! Got!*‖ *Mama! Mayn maideleh! Sprinze!* (*Lusia's words are almost impossible to distinguish, more of a continuous wail. With the radio at full volume Rose sits with her hands over her ears, trying to hide from Lusia's nightmare. Light fades to black. The radio continues to blare briefly, through the climax of the music.*)

Scene 6

The following day. Saturday, midmorning. Rose is heard softly humming a popular song. The morning light slowly comes up on her. She is wearing a robe and slippers, but looks dressed up. She is setting the table, trying to be quiet so as not to wake Lusia, although Lusia is not in sight and her bed is made. Rose enjoys arranging the small feast. The doorbell rings, startling her. She goes to the front door.

ROSE. Lusia! (*Rose follows Lusia as she puts down her handbag. Lusia is wearing the same clothes as when she arrived.*) I thought you were still

*Egg.
†We could make a pudding.
‡Let me go, too! I want to go, too! No! She's gone!
§Where? I can't see them anymore!
‖Forever and ever! God!

sleeping. I've been tiptoeing around. What were you doing? Where could you go?

LUSIA. To place I come to first. Where you come to get me.

ROSE. Whatever for? Did you forget something? I'm surprised they're even open today. You went all by yourself?

LUSIA. (*Struggling with language.*) I go read list. In books they got. And new names every day. People they find yet from the camps. Some coming yet from out woods where they been hiding.

ROSE. I know. I know, Lusia. But surely by now—

LUSIA. New names every day. And so I make *mine* list. You see? And sometimes maybe I find a person some place alive, some family, some friend. And this how I find Duvid, or he finding me, too.

ROSE. But that would take a miracle.

LUSIA. Is no miracle. Duvid is a . . . a *mensch.** Is only knowing Duvid is alive.

ROSE. (*Covering her discomfort.*) I see. Come, you'll tell me more. We'll eat. (*Rose proudly leads Lusia to the laden dinette table. Lusia shrinks back, overwhelmed.*)

LUSIA. Too much food! *So* much. No, *too* much, I think.

ROSE. You must eat, Lusia. You've got to eat enough. And there's plenty, really. (*Piling food on Lusia's plate.*) I know you're the big sister, but you've got to let me take care of you, for now. Then, when everything's normal again, you'll be the big sister. (*Rose pours a glass of milk. Lusia sips at it, picks at the food. As they continue talking, they remain contrasted in manner. Lusia is still, Rose animated, using her hands a lot.*)

LUSIA. Funny, big sister, baby sister. I have baby sister one time, long time . . .

ROSE. Ago.

LUSIA. Long time ago. So beautiful I think, and I take for walk in . . .

ROSE. Carriage?

LUSIA. Carriage, yes. I take for walk and show to friends mine baby *shvester.* Make me feel good. Happy. Then gone. And many years no sister but picture from America and letter from Papa and lady who takes care of.

ROSE. Mrs. Greenspan. *Tanta* Perla.

LUSIA. Yes. And then no more letter. No more sister. (*Voice.*) And

---

*A real man.

carriage stays empty for too much years. . . . And baby *shvester* woman now who want take care *me*.

ROSE. I don't remember at all. I wish I did.

LUSIA. You don't remember even Mama? (*Rose shakes her head.*) Nothing?

ROSE. I was only four when we left. It's so strange that you have memories of me, that I was part of your life. That I was born in another world. I don't remember any of it. Just a feeling, maybe. Sometimes there's a particular smell when something's cooking or a song comes on the radio and all of a sudden I feel different, like I'm in another place.

LUSIA. How you feel then?

ROSE. Warm. Safe. Sad.

LUSIA. Mama, that is. The feeling from Mama. (*Rose and Lusia look at one another silently across the table, each mirror to the other for a moment.*)

ROSE. Eat some more, Lusia. You're not eating enough. (*Pause while Lusia picks at food.*) Lusia, have you wondered about it, thought why you got sick and not me?

LUSIA. Mama says was plan from God. But she keeps hold our passage, our tickets, till could not read no more. Till thin like old leaf. Till long time after no good, no one . . . they no loz no one . . . no one . . . (*She is frustrated, trying to find the English word.*)

ROSE. Allowed.

LUSIA. Allowed leave Poland no more.

ROSE. And I was playing stickball and going to the movies and eating Mello-Rolls!

LUSIA. What means this?

ROSE. Oh, it doesn't matter. (*She pushes away from the table, gets up.*) He should have gotten you out!

LUSIA. Mama told how whole America changes mind, wants no new Jewish, no new people no more. All fast like this (*snaps her fingers*) something happens no one got money. From streets with gold to nothing. And everyone, not just mine father.

ROSE. That was the Depression. It kept you away, but it didn't make any difference in my life. I remember having bad dreams when I was little, but I don't know what about. Everything else stayed the same; the food, the stories on the radio and Tanta Perla, like a bird chirping around me trying to give comfort after the bad dreams. But she never could.

LUSIA. *De varemsteh bet iz de mamas. Farshtaist?**

ROSE. Yeah, but how could I tell? Mama wasn't real to me. They'd never say her name, or yours. They called you "Them," talking in whispers or in certain looks so I could just pick up little bits of what was going on. And when I was older and could have understood, I knew it was forbidden. Papa wouldn't talk. Not about you, not about Mama. He would just say he was working it out or, later, that Roosevelt would take care of everyone over there. I tried to make myself a family out of the photographs and letters, but they were in Yiddish and I only learned to read English. Tanta Perla used to read them to me and translate. Papa never would. Then, when there were no more letters, I began to forget completely. By the time the war came, it was as if there had been no one there at all . . . until Papa found you. I still don't know exactly how to feel. I mean, I've had it pretty easy and you—

LUSIA. Mine father don't know I'm here yet?

ROSE. He'll be in *shul*† all day. We can call him tonight or even go out there.

LUSIA. No. Tues-day I suppose to come on boat.

ROSE. Papa was going to come with me to meet you. He'll be mad if we don't let him know you're here.

LUSIA. This I remember good about Papa. He gets so mad. He makes a big voice, everybody is . . . (*She shakes.*)

ROSE. Nervous.

LUSIA. Nervous.

ROSE. In that way, he hasn't changed.

LUSIA. I remember him. Papa was a man very . . . pretty?

ROSE. Handsome? Papa?

LUSIA. Handsome. And I know from pictures, too. But everything must be certain way or he is so mad. And very . . . (*She gestures.*)

ROSE. Strict.

LUSIA. Strict. But very proud when we all dress up. You, too. And Mama. Family all go out together. I see his face and I'm thinking how happy he is, how proud. He don't say nothing, but I can see. You know this face?

ROSE. I've never seen that look. (*Pause.*) We'll have to call him tomorrow.

---

*The warmest bed is the mama's. Understand?

†Synagogue.

LUSIA. We wait for Tuesday. Same as plan. Mine father is mine . . . (*She holds out her arm.*) Like you and me?

ROSE. Flesh and blood.

LUSIA. Mine father is mine flesh and blood. On Tuesday, even, he will be mine flesh and blood. Now I got time to look some more for Duvid.

ROSE. But Lusia—

LUSIA. I look for Duvid so mine father could meet mine husband.

ROSE. (*Beginning to clear some of the food onto a tray.*) Can't you rest a little while? Let me take you around. You might get lost. It's such a big city. (*She picks up Lusia's milk.*) Here. I'm going to fix this so you'll drink it. With chocolate.

LUSIA. (*Rising to stop Rose.*) Big world, we find us each other, no? Here yet better. Listen. (*Rose sits.*) I think big world hates Jewish. Today I go to office. I want to go, but don't know go this way or this.

ROSE. Left or right.

LUSIA. Don't know left or right. Everyone says in America police is good, will tell how to go. Safe. So, there's a police with a . . . suit like army . . .

ROSE. A uniform.

LUSIA. The police with uniform sits high up on horse on street talking to children. I think must be safe. I try talking, to make the words right, but was too feared . . .

ROSE. Frightened.

LUSIA. I want to say, "How you get to this place," but instead it comes out Yiddish, "*Vu iz di gaz?*" and I show card with office on. He looks at card and looks at me and goes over, like this, so he touches mine arm here. I think it's better I run away. Then he says something. You know what he says? (*Clears her throat, imitates policeman.*) *Me nemt dem bos oif di gaz, un aroisgayn oif—**

ROSE. (*Amazed.*) In Yiddish? He gave you directions in Yiddish! I'll bet you almost fainted! *Me . . . nemt . . . dem . . . bos . . .* (*Lusia joins in with Rose, starting over.*)

LUSIA AND ROSE. *Me nemt dem bos oif di gaz . . .* (*Rose starts laughing. She exits to the kitchen with the milk and tray.*)

LUSIA. (*Sitting down, amazed.*) America! (*The laughter continues.*)

*You take the bus here, and get off at—

Scene 7

The action continues from the previous scene but now, in Lusia's memory, it is Chernov,* Poland, 1932. The lighting gradually begins to change to a soft glow as Rose's laughter is picked up offstage by Lusia's childhood friend Hanna. Hanna enters conspiratorially from the kitchen, bringing a piece of honey cake for herself and for Lusia. Mama, Lusia's mother, enters behind her. Hanna is about fourteen years old in this scene, pretty, blonde, and lively. Mama is in her mid-thirties. They are dressed as they would be in a small town in Poland in 1932. Lusia and Hanna are the same age, but Lusia, as always in her memory scenes, appears as she is in the present. As Mama enters, the girls are laughing and hiding their stolen cake. There is an easy physical affection between them.

MAMA. *Fun tsu fil essen vert men crank*† than from *under*eating. (*Lusia and Hanna giggle some more.*)

LUSIA. *Ober,*‡ Mama, s'iz not a famine.

MAMA. *Gai farshtai a maidel!*§ Crying all night because some boy calls her a dumpling and now she can't stop eating! (*She shows she is aware of the stolen cake.*) Far be it from me to starve my own flesh and blood.

HANNA. Or me.

MAMA. What's the difference. You might as well be sisters. (*She suddenly stiffens, listens.*) Oy! The soup is boiling over! (*She runs into the kitchen. From time to time we hear her singing offstage.*)

HANNA. I love your mother. (*Lusia nods.*) Only I wish she wasn't so sad. Even when she's joking, like now, I can see she's sad underneath.

LUSIA. (*Shrugging.*) She misses my sister. And Papa, I think. But mostly my sister.

HANNA. It seems like such a long time to be missing anyone.

LUSIA. Four years is nothing, Mama says. A child is part of your body you never stop missing. Sometimes she goes like this . . . (*quick intake of breath, hand to solar plexus*) and she says, "Rayzel is sick, I can feel it," or "Rayzel is frightened. She's crying for her mama." It's the same as when someone's foot gets cut off and it still itches.

HANNA. What about you? Do you still miss them?

LUSIA. Rayzel, maybe. A little bit. I used to very much. I missed

---

*Pronounced as if *Chair*noff (ch as in "chew").

†From overeating one gets sicker.

‡But.

§Go understand a girl!

her and I was even jealous. Rayzel and Papa going to America and I was sick with scarlet fever. My hair all fell out. I looked terrible. I always thought we'd be going soon, too, and we still might, any day now, but then I'd miss you and I know you better than my sister. (*They lean across table, close together, holding hands.*) She's just a baby, anyway. Eight years old. So everything is good the way it is.

HANNA. (*An admission.*) I'm glad you got scarlet fever.

LUSIA. I'll tell you a secret, Hanna. . . . Me, too. (*Looks toward kitchen before she goes on.*) You must swear never to tell this to anyone, ever . . . (*Hanna nods. They take an apparently oft-used swearing position.*) I'm glad I have Mama all to myself! When I was little and scared in the night she wouldn't let me in, with Papa there and the baby crying. But then, when they left, she would open the covers like a great wing and pull me close to her. She's different without Papa here. She sings. And she never made jokes when he was around. I don't remember her laughing out loud. Papa used to make us be quiet. He would get angry all of a sudden and you never knew when. (*Hanna and Lusia continue glancing toward the kitchen through the following dialogue.*)

HANNA. Do you suppose she loves him?

LUSIA. I don't know. It's hard to think of your mother that way. I think she does, from far away. Maybe more, from far away. You know, my father's a whole lot older than she is.

HANNA. He is?

LUSIA. Around fifty-something.

HANNA. I think that's very romantic.

LUSIA. I don't.

HANNA. To have someone like that to take care of you, who knows more than you do. With silver-gray in his hair. My parents aren't romantic at all.

LUSIA. Your parents are just short. They don't look romantic, that's all. It's not their fault.

HANNA. But they never talk, except about business, and they sleep in two different beds.

LUSIA. They do? (*Hanna nods.*) Mine used to have one. I thought everyone's parents did.

HANNA. I will.

LUSIA. Me, too.

HANNA. With Duvid Pechenik?

LUSIA. Shhh!

HANNA. He called you "dumpling."

LUSIA. That means he likes me.

HANNA. But he's just your age.

LUSIA. A year older!

HANNA. He has pimples.

LUSIA. So do you.

HANNA. Stop it! (*The girls' voices are getting louder. They stand up.*)

LUSIA. You stop it!

HANNA. Dumpling!

LUSIA. Midget parents!

MAMA. (*Calling from offstage.*) What's going on in there?

LUSIA AND HANNA. Nothing.

MAMA. (*Enters from kitchen.*) You know, one old friend is worth ten new ones.

LUSIA. I know, Mama, but if she just wasn't so picky.

MAMA. If your grandma had a beard, she'd be your grandpa.

HANNA. We understand. (*Lusia and Hanna smile, giggle, and shake their heads.*)

MAMA. *Kum mit mir,* * Hannele. This time I'll *give* you *dem kuchen!*† (*Lusia and Hanna look at each other, laughing, holding hands, as Mama exits. Hanna kisses Lusia on the cheek and runs after Mama, giggling. Rose, continuing her laughter at the policeman story, comes from the kitchen with the chocolate milk she promised Lusia at the end of the previous scene. The lighting returns to normal as she speaks.*)

ROSE. (*Smiling.*) Here. See how you like it this way. (*Lusia looks at Rose, surprised, as the lights fade to black.*)

Scene 8

Tuesday afternoon. A forties song is heard on the radio in the blackout. The lights come up in the bedroom and in the living room, where Rose is pacing and calling to Lusia, who is in the bedroom.

ROSE. Hurry up and let me see!

LUSIA. (*Offstage.*) Not right. Is mistake!

ROSE. Well at least let me see! (*Rose sits on the sofa. As she waits impatiently, Lusia is coming into the bedroom very slowly, facing directly toward the audience and looking at herself in the unseen mirror. She is uncomfortable, wearing a modish dress and shoes, which fit well but look out of place on her. She wobbles on the shoes.*)

*Come with me.
†The cake.

LUSIA. You stay in living room. I come in there. Don't laugh. Is big mistake. Should be wearing this, Ginger Rogers. (*Lusia comes unsteadily into the living room. Rose jumps up, pleased.*)

ROSE. Well, call up Fred Astaire! You look great! Turn around. It's perfect. Very American. All we need to do is fix your hair and you'll look like you were born here.

LUSIA. Was born in Poland, like you.

ROSE. (*Turning off radio.*) But, don't you want to look like you belong, Lusia?

LUSIA. (*Her hand on her chest.*) When feeling here I am home, then I look like belonging more. Before war I have pretty dresses Mama made. I get some again when I can buy myself. No more from you. Everything you want to give me. Already such a present and your bed, even, I sleep in. Yesterday before . . .

ROSE. The day before yesterday.

LUSIA. Yes. You bring me with to movie all day. Ginger Rogers. Cost a lot money. And food, food, food. All the time giving me to eat. And now clothes. No. Is too much. I get it myself.

ROSE. But you have nothing. Everything was taken.

LUSIA. You don't took it! I have suitcase, clothes from Red Cross. Same what everyone get. Soon one day, I go pick out new something. In store. And it has on it . . . what tell how much . . .

ROSE. A price tag.

LUSIA. A price tag on. No one wore it yet. (*Rose looks at Lusia quietly for awhile.*)

ROSE. At least let me fix your hair, OK? Won't cost a penny. You won't know yourself. (*She sits Lusia on a chair, begins fussing over her hair.*) I'm real good at this, I promise. Everyone at work thinks I get it done, but I always do mine myself. And I know you want to look your best for Papa. Now, don't worry, there's plenty of time. After he finishes at the store, he'll have a shave and maybe get his suit pressed, even though it doesn't need it, and get a shoeshine, too. Papa's always turned out like a gentleman. He's getting off early today to come and pick me up so we can meet you at the boat—but not yet. Sit still.

LUSIA. (*After a while.*) Rayzel, letters coming through front door say for Miss Rose White.

ROSE. I changed it, but not really. It's an exact translation.

LUSIA. Why?

ROSE. Just to sound like everyone else. For instance, you could change your name to Lucy.

LUSIA. What your father thinks to change his name, Weiss to White?

ROSE. His isn't changed. I've never told him I use the other. He probably wouldn't like it.

LUSIA. To change the name don't make you safe, anyway.

ROSE. (*Cheerfully brittle.*) What do you mean?

LUSIA. Someone knows Rose White is Rayzel Weiss, no matter. A new name don't make no difference.

ROSE. But that's not why—

LUSIA. They come take you when they want.

ROSE. It's just easier this way. I don't have to spell it for people.

LUSIA. Even you should wear a cross around neck, they know who you are. Always with Jewish, they find out the truth.

ROSE. (*Shaky, making an effort at being light.*) The truth is . . . your hair is all finished. Come and see. (*Rose and Lusia go to the bedroom "mirror." Rose stands back as Lusia looks at herself with an expression of surprise, pleasure, and bewilderment.*)

LUSIA. If I go in street like this—

ROSE. A very attractive young woman.

LUSIA. If Duvid walk near to me, he wouldn't know who I am!

ROSE. But you would know him.

LUSIA. Maybe he different, too. Thin or hair falls out maybe. Or hurt and walks different.

ROSE. But certainly before the war—

LUSIA. Before they take Duvid, already things was bad. Hungry all the time, sickness, everyone frightened. And this was six years ago. I am still a girl your age in little place, not big city. No Ginger Rogers yet. Already I look too much different only from time. I want Duvid should know me, or a friend of him he shows a picture, maybe.

ROSE. I see.

LUSIA. Thank you for pretty dress and shoes and for try to make me look pretty, too. After I find— (*Doorbell, followed by an impatient knock on the door.*)

ROSE. Papa! (*Lusia looks about, panicked, runs off into bathroom. Rose stares after her. The bell and knocking continue.*) Just a minute, Papa. I'm coming! (*She goes to front door.*) Hello, Papa. (*Mordechai follows Rose into the living room, gives her his hat and scarf. She puts them down while they speak. She is trying to be natural, but is wary and nervous.*) You came early.

MORDECHAI. Greenspan closed up early.

ROSE. Was it crowded? The subway, I mean.

MORDECHAI. What do you think? Like always.

ROSE. It's getting warmer outside?

MORDECHAI. Warmer, colder. With spring in New York, who can tell? When does she get in?

ROSE. Sit, Papa. (*Mordechai sits on the sofa, formally.*) You want some schnapps? (*She moves toward the kitchen.*)

MORDECHAI. A half only. With a piece rye bread if you got it.

ROSE. (*Calling from offstage.*) Coming right up!

MORDECHAI. So, when does she get in? (*Rose returns from kitchen with a shot glass half filled, a plate with two pieces of bread on it, and a napkin. She puts it on the table in front of Mordechai.*)

ROSE. Here you are, Papa. You want something else? (*Mordechai picks up one of the pieces of bread, puts it on the napkin and gives it to Rose.*)

MORDECHAI. You don't understand English? One piece only, I said. (*Calls after her as she takes bread to kitchen.*) Is a sin to waste even one piece bread and give me extra when in Europe they don't got nothing! (*Mordechai murmurs a brief prayer over the food, dips a corner of the piece of bread into the schnapps, then alternately sips and eats in a deliberate manner. Rose returns with the napkin. She smiles, prepares.*)

ROSE. Papa, try not to be upset by this—

MORDECHAI. (*Interrupts his sipping/eating pattern.*) Something's the matter?

ROSE. No. Everything's fine. Really good. It's good news about Lusia. (*Mordechai looks at Rose, waits. Trying to be cheerful.*) Papa . . . She's here already.

MORDECHAI. (*Looking around him.*) Here? In this house?

ROSE. Yes. She came already.

MORDECHAI. When? Today earlier?

ROSE. (*Uncomfortable.*) Before.

MORDECHAI. (*Demanding.*) So where is she?

ROSE. She's getting dressed. She's a little nervous about seeing you.

MORDECHAI. Nervous from her father?

ROSE. She's been through a lot, Papa. All alone. And she's been waiting for such a long time—

MORDECHAI. What? I didn't try with everything what's in my power to get them out?

ROSE. That's not what I—

MORDECHAI. From a father she shouldn't be nervous. (*He rises.*) How long she's been in New York? Why you didn't tell me?

ROSE. I'll go and get her. Maybe she doesn't know you're here.

(*Rose hurries into the bedroom. Mordechai checks his appearance, sits, finishes the schnapps and wipes his mouth delicately. He assumes a distinguished waiting pose. Calling softly.*) Lusia . . . It's Papa. He's waiting. Lusia! (*Lusia, dressed in her own clothes again, comes into the bedroom, walks as if pre-set toward the living room, stops.*)

LUSIA. Please, Rayzel, you come with me.

ROSE. I think it's better if you go alone. (*Lusia sits on the foot of the bed, looking straight ahead, unmoving. Rose, standing between the two rooms, looks from Lusia to Mordechai and back again. The two of them are waiting stubbornly, in the same position. Rose is trapped.*) Oh, all right. I'll come with you. (*Lusia stands, walks ahead of Rose, who follows at a distance, waits behind her. Lusia enters the living room where Mordechai sits motionless, looking straight ahead, waiting.*)

LUSIA. *Tateh?*

MORDECHAI. (*Looks at Lusia, rises. He does not know her.*) Mine *tuchter,** Lusia Weiss?

LUSIA. (*Nods.*) Pechenik.

MORDECHAI. (*Moving towards Lusia a little, still unsure of her identity.*) Lusia Weiss Pechenik *fun Chernov, Poyln?* (*Lusia nods. They are at arm's length now. Rose is watching unobtrusively. Mordechai takes Lusia by the shoulders as if to embrace her. She is passive, unsure of her response. He keeps her at arm's length, then turns her around studying her.*) You look different. You was only so . . . up to here, when I seen you the last time.

LUSIA. *Du oich zaist ois andersh.†*

MORDECHAI. *Red nisht kein Yiddish.‡* Here we should speak American always. You, like your sister Rayzel. You become real American. Your *taten,§* he does pretty good, but not so much as children. It took too long to get you over here, but you still can learn. You're young yet. (*Pause.*) You look a lot like my sister, Berta.

LUSIA. Everyone says this.

MORDECHAI. You know your aunt Berta?

LUSIA. I . . . knew . . . her.

MORDECHAI. Sit. (*Lusia sits carefully, apart from Mordechai, who joins her on the sofa. As if reproaching Rose.*) Maybe you should come with me

---

*Daughter.
†You look different, too.
‡Don't speak Yiddish.
§Father.

to live at Greenspans'. You wouldn't get the right food here. *Tanta Perla* will fatten you up, even with her bad foot.

LUSIA. I stay with Rayzel. Until soon when I'll have mine own home. With Duvid.

MORDECHAI. And where is this Duvid?

LUSIA. Looking for me.

MORDECHAI. He knows your family is here?

LUSIA. He knows Weiss, Mordechai and Rayzel. Maybe he knows Greenspan in Brooklyn, too. I tell him such long time ago. But Duvid is so smart, we find each other. Until then, I stay with Rayzel.

MORDECHAI. And your sister . . . what does she think of the arrangement?

ROSE. (*Joining Mordechai and Lusia.*) It's good like this, Papa. And I've got two weeks with no work . . .

MORDECHAI. You are not *shvesters.* (*Silent, shocked reaction.*) I mean to say, you ain't nothing alike. (*To Rose.*) You take after . . . *fun* different sides the family.

LUSIA. Rayzel is like Mama. (*Pause.*)

MORDECHAI. (*Abruptly, to Lusia.*) Does she give you enough to eat? (*To Rose.*) Make sure it's the best. Kosher. (*Takes some bills out of his pocket and gives them to Rose. To Lusia.*) Or does she make you sick with too much? From overeating you suffer more than from undereating. (*After another pause, suddenly.*) Go get your coats. We're going.

ROSE AND LUSIA. Where?

MORDECHAI. To eat in a restaurant. A big celebration.

ROSE. But I'm cooking dinner here, Papa. Pot roast.

MORDECHAI. Pot roast they got plenty at Fine and Schapiro. Also, it's kosher.

ROSE. I fix kosher, Papa. You know that. For you always, special. (*Mordechai puts on his hat and scarf.*)

MORDECHAI. I beg your pardon, *tuchter.* You can't make pot roast like Fine and Schapiro. (*Mordechai stands waiting near the front entranceway. Rose gets a coat, puts it on. Lusia gets her handbag.*) What's the matter, she got no coat?

LUSIA. Is good like this. *Tsu hais.* Too hot outside.

MORDECHAI. (*To Rose.*) Give her a coat. You got enough.

ROSE. I've tried, Papa. She won't. (*Mordechai hits floor with cane.*)

MORDECHAI. Get the coat! (*Rose leaves to get another coat. Mordechai considers for a moment, then decides to speak to Lusia.*) You know, I got a big family in Poland. The Greenspans was the only ones here before me. Mine mama and *taten* was both dead before I leave Poland. I wrote down the others, all I could remember, so I don't forget. (*He is taking a notebook from a pocket.*) Some, I find out what happens from this organization or that or from Greenspan, maybe. Some I don't know yet.

LUSIA. I got list like you. The same. (*Lusia takes out a similar notebook from her handbag. She and Mordechai move back into the living room. Rose returns with the extra coat. She sees that something is going on and hesitates in the background, ready to leave. She will slowly be drawn into the reading of the lists, although she does not want to hear them. The reading has a ritualistic quality. Mordechai opens his notebook, studies it. Lusia opens hers. She and Mordechai are on opposite sides of the room, both facing downstage. They read the lists slowly and quietly, as if checking an inventory. Mordechai takes out a fountain pen and makes notations according to Lusia's information.*)

MORDECHAI. Artur and Salek Elias, nephews. Sons *fun* Berta Weiss Elias.

LUSIA. Artur Elias, dead. Murdered, Maidanek concentration camp, nineteen and forty-two. Salek Elias, dead. Killed in battle, Warsaw, nineteen and forty-three, April.

MORDECHAI. Vladek Elias. Brother-in-law.

LUSIA. Vladek Elias. Murdered. Maidanek, nineteen and forty-two.

MORDECHAI. Berta Weiss Elias, sister.

LUSIA. Berta Weiss Elias. Murdered, Maidanek, nineteen and forty-two.

MORDECHAI. Zalmen Weiss, brother.

LUSIA. Zalmen Weiss, Esther Weiss, sons Motel and Ignacz Weiss, daughter Fela Weiss Friedman, grandchildren, Renia, Miriam, Moishe: murdered. All Auschwitz concentration camp, *fun* nineteen and forty-two until nineteen and forty-five. (*Mordechai sits. Lusia looks at him briefly, without expression, then continues reading.*) Son-in-law, Benek Friedman, reported in Palestine, nineteen hundred and forty-six.

MORDECHAI. Markus Weiss, brother.

LUSIA. Markus Weiss. No word. Last was seen, Chernov, nineteen and forty-one.

MORDECHAI. Pesha Weiss, sister.

LUSIA. Pesha Weiss. Murdered, Auschwitz, nineteen and forty-three.

MORDECHAI. Karol and Janka Eisenman, mother-in-law and father-in-law.

LUSIA. Karol and Janka Eisenman. Murdered. Belzek. Nineteen and forty-two.

MORDECHAI. (*Softly.*) Your mother, may she rest in peace, I know what happened—

ROSE. (*An outburst.*) But I don't! Why won't you tell me how she died, Papa? Lusia?

MORDECHAI. It's enough to know she died in such a place.

ROSE. And all the others. So many! Names you never told me, Papa. (*She sits. She is cold, even with her coat on.*)

MORDECHAI. They're dead.

LUSIA. *Ois gebarget.* Murdered. (*Pause.*)

MORDECHAI. And this they told me was no record. Shmuel Weiss and Minne Weiss, uncle and aunt.

LUSIA. Shmuel Weiss, no record. Minne Weiss, murdered, Chelmno, nineteen and forty-two.

MORDECHAI. Jakob Weiss and wife, cousins.

LUSIA. Jakob Weiss, murdered Treblinka, nineteen and forty-three. Maricia Weiss, murdered Birkenau, nineteen and forty-three. Daughters Gittel and Devorah Weiss, murdered, Birkenau, nineteen and forty-four.

MORDECHAI. (*Making a notation.*) For everything God does, there is a reason. (*He closes his book, puts it and pen in his pocket. He sits quietly, then notices that Lusia is still standing with her list open.*) Noch mer?*

LUSIA. Duvid Pechenik, husband to Lusia Weiss Pechenik, son-in-law to Mordechai Weiss, arrested, Chernov, Poland, nineteen hundred and forty. Sprinze Pechenik, daughter to Duvid Pechenik and Lusia Weiss Pechenik, *ainikl*—granddaughter—to Mordechai Weiss. Murdered. Auschwitz, nineteen hundred and forty-three. (*Lusia gently closes her book as lights fade to half. Mordechai and Rose remain motionless during the following scene, which takes place in Lusia's mind.*) Als vos Got tut.† He says there is a reason . . . Mama! (*Mama, her age the same as in the previous scene, enters, wiping her hands on her apron. Lusia continues facing downstage, looking at Mama, seeing her only in her mind's eye.*)

MAMA. *Es iz.*‡

LUSIA. There isn't! He says he knows, Mama. *Er vais!* He says he knows what happened to you. God's will.

MAMA. Your father never questions the will of God. And neither do I.

LUSIA. You're wrong! Even you, Mama!

*Even more?
†All that God does.
‡There is.

MAMA. You don't play with God. I say it, your father always said it.

LUSIA. But he can't really know what happened. Why does he pretend to?

MAMA. Maybe he thinks he knows. And what difference does it make?

LUSIA. He's so sure. And safe.

MAMA. You want him to have some pain?

LUSIA. Yes!

MAMA. (*Laughing a little, looking at Mordechai.*) I remember when I felt the same way. But maybe, now, he's had enough already.

LUSIA. I don't care!

MAMA. You want to hurt an old man.

LUSIA. Yes! This one. Yes.

MAMA. Your own father?

LUSIA. He's not my father. He can't be. I don't know him. We're strangers. I don't know where I am. Where am I, Mama?

MAMA. With your family. Your flesh and blood. All that's left. My baby. My Rayzel, my pretty, little girl. (*She looks at Mordechai.*) And your father, he was my husband.

LUSIA. I'm sorry, Mama, but—

MAMA. Never be foolish and you'll never be sorry.

LUSIA. Mama, Mama, I'm in a dream! I don't want to touch them.

MAMA. *Sha!* They might hear you. *Sha, shtil, mayn kind.**

LUSIA. (*Weakly, as a helpless child.*) Mama! What should I do? What should I do? I don't know what to do! *Ich vais nit vos tsu ton!* (*Pause. Mama puts a finger to her lips. The moment passes. The lights fade to black.*)

Scene 9

Later that evening. A loud blast of popular music on the radio. The lights come up in the living room. Lusia is seated on the sofa, reading a magazine. Rose is pacing.

ROSE. (*Urgently.*) . . . But I want you to tell me! Please, Lusia. How could you keep it from me? I have a right to know!

LUSIA. I got a right to study, listen the music, the words, so can talk more better. Get work, job. (*Rose runs and turns off the radio.*)

ROSE. That's not going to help you, Lusia. Talk with *me*. I'll help

*Hush, still, my child.

you. That'll be much better. But, please, you've got to tell me what happened. (*Lusia gets up and moves away to bedroom. Rose follows.*)

LUSIA. You seen that list, Rayzel. That's all it was. What it says on that paper. (*Lusia sits on bed, away from Rose, who continues to pace.*)

ROSE. Lists. Lists! Your list, Papa's list. Like taking inventory of dry goods. Then, all through dinner, not a word out of place. Not a tear. Not a sigh. Papa is stone. But I'm not a baby and I want to know what happened. I see pictures in the newspapers I can't believe. And in the newsreels. I couldn't look, but I wanted to see. Is that what it was really like? Was my mother in one of those pictures? Were you? You're my family, tell me! (*Lusia looks at Rose before she speaks.*)

LUSIA. I cannot talk it. About it. Is all of living and dying. Is too much from the . . . the *bainer* . . .

ROSE. (*Quietly.*) Bones.

LUSIA. The bones. The *hartz.* The *flaish.* I want not talk it no more. OK?

ROSE. (*Sitting on the bed.*) Not even about Mama?

LUSIA. About Mama I tell you this. . . . How was her *life.* Almost happy, only except for missing you. She was beautiful, skin like silk. Smooth and smells always from clean, like soap. And saying all the time things . . . words . . .

ROSE. Sayings.

LUSIA. Sayings to make things be better. She makes me laugh, and Hanna, my friend, too. She sings, not too good, like me. And cooks good, a lot, like you. She has head in dreams, has dreams in head, forever. Things, no matter how bad, be going better soon, says Mama. And just like Papa, whatever happens is the will of God.

ROSE. Even after—

LUSIA. Every day. The will of God. So that's Mama. What I remember. This I can tell you. (*Pause, while Rose considers something.*)

ROSE. (*Softly.*) Can't you get it off?

LUSIA. What?

ROSE. The number. The number on your arm.

LUSIA. Is forever. Get it off? No.

ROSE. How did they do it, Lusia? Did it hurt? What did you feel like when—

LUSIA. (*Going quickly into living room.*) Now pardon, please. I got to learn better English. (*Rose exits through bathroom doorway, distraught. Lusia turns on radio. When it warms up, a voice is in the middle of a* commercial. *She begins repeating the words on the radio. Lusia closes her eyes as the lights change to the fantasy glow.*)

Scene 10

In Lusia's memory, it is Chernov, Poland, 1939. The radio commercial changes to a lively Yiddish song.

DUVID. (*Offstage, calling lightly.*) Lusia. (*Duvid enters. Lusia runs to him and they begin dancing all over the stage. They are laughing.*)

LUSIA. *Cher oif! Ich ken nit otemen!** Enough, Duvid!

DUVID. (*Whirling Lusia even harder.*) *Shvahinker!* Weakling! Can't keep up?

LUSIA. (*Stopping, falling on sofa, out of breath.*) It's no use! You're right. I give up! You win, Duvid! You're in much better shape than I am!

DUVID. Condition, yes, I agree. Shape? Yours is better. It's my lungs. I'm running more now. They put Jews into a separate school, they help me build my strength. Twice a day now at twice the distance as before. And no more cigarettes. I take advantage of the rationing to improve my health.

LUSIA. A real opportunist.

DUVID. That's me.

LUSIA. You call too much attention to yourself with all this running. You could get to work five minutes later. Mr. Grubman understands about school. You're too noticeable. You stand out.

DUVID. It doesn't matter. No one can catch up with me.

LUSIA. No? (*Lusia lunges for Duvid, beginning a game of tag as frenetic as the dancing. It's unclear who is chasing whom. Finally, Duvid has Lusia cornered. He advances menacingly. She screams, laughing.*) No, Duvid, no! Mama will come in! What will she think?

DUVID. We're almost married. She'll encourage me.

LUSIA. No! Mama! Mama! Help! (*Duvid grabs Lusia and kisses her. Their embrace is innocent and chaste, somewhat awkward.*) I don't know if I can be married and still live here. With you and Mama. It seems indecent.

DUVID. She's used to me. She likes me. I like her. She used to give me cookies, cakes, handouts—all the time when I was a kid. So now

*I can't breathe!

I get you. Another handout. No difference. (*Lusia squeals and strikes out at Duvid. He grabs her again.*)

LUSIA. But Duvidl . . . in my room. And Mama right next door. It's not right. I won't be able to—

DUVID. To what?

LUSIA. (*Pushes Duvid away, then goes after him.*) I must be marrying you for your money since you have no brains.

DUVID. I'm marrying you for your mother's gefilte fish! You'd better watch out or I won't take you to America.

LUSIA. And Mama.

DUVID. And Mama. I won't take her either.

LUSIA. Anyway, between the Germans and the Russians, we're stuck.

DUVID. Leave it to me. (*Posing.*) With brains, brawn, and money, I'll lead the way.

LUSIA. (*Suddenly serious.*) You mean it, don't you.

DUVID. Of course I mean it. Together we can do anything. You'll see. Man and wife.

LUSIA. Man and wife. (*As the scene shifts from Lusia's memory to her fantasy of the future, they begin to dance romantically to a forties song playing in the background.*) Just like the old days.

DUVID. It hurts to think back.

LUSIA. We won't then. (*Pause. They are barely moving.*) Duvid.

DUVID. Yes?

LUSIA. Nothing. I like to say your name.

DUVID. Lusia. (*Lusia and Duvid stop dancing. Their embrace becomes more intense.*)

LUSIA. Wait, Duvid. My father. He'll be here any minute. And Rayzel. She's right in the bathroom there.

DUVID. So? We're married, you know.

LUSIA. I know, but still . . .

DUVID. But still? (*He laughs, teasing.*) Some things never change! (*Duvid continues to move in on Lusia, who is backing off.*)

LUSIA. (*Laughing.*) Stop it! Duvid! *Du gaist tsu shnel!** Nein! Papa! Rayzel! (*They are about to kiss again when Rose enters from the bathroom.*)

ROSE. Lusia! (*Lusia hears Rose, the music cuts off, radio comes back, and the lighting returns to normal. The sisters look at each other while Duvid recedes. Lusia is out of breath. Rose is puzzled and alarmed.*) What is it, Lusia? What are you doing? What happened?

*You're going too fast!

LUSIA. (*Also surprised.*) Rayzel? Oh, *mine shvester* . . . (*Looking about, bewildered, struggling with the language.*) I just am sitting here. Then I am remembering . . . something . . . (*Smiling gently, hopeful.*) that is gonna happen.

ACT II

Scene 1

Midday, the following Sunday. In the blackout, a regular thumping sound is heard, Mordechai counting with each thump. As the lights rise slowly, Mordechai is jumping back and forth over his cane, which is lying on the living room floor. He is encouraging Lusia to count with him. Lusia, looking less pale than in Act I, gets confused, is mostly silent. As the scene begins, the counting has reached "ninety-four." Rose enters from the kitchen to straighten chairs in the dinette and finish cleaning up after a meal. She is wearing a dish towel/apron. When she sees the scene in the living room, she stops, astonished.

MORDECHAI. Ninety-five, ninety-six, ninety-seven, ninety-eight—
ROSE. Papa!
MORDECHAI. (*Waving Rose off, not losing a beat.*) Sha! Ninety-nine, one hundred! (*Mordechai stops, breathes deeply, as if taking a bow, talks to Lusia, who only nods in response.*) Look. You see? I'm breathing like a teenager. In two months I'll be seventy. Also is teaching you how to count American. (*To Rose.*) I want she should know what a strong family she comes from. (*Mordechai turns back to Lusia, while Rose finishes tidying the dinette.*) Mine grandfather lived to a hundred two, still walking every day with a milk-wagon three miles. And he never missed in his life even one Sabbath in the *shul.* Finally, he died *fun* a frostbite that turned green. As it happened, he got frozen in the snow, with the milk coming up *fun* the cans, on Monday. He died just in time before sunset Friday and that's the first one he missed. This story it heard *fun* mine own mother, may she rest in peace, many times as a boy. So you know you're *fun* strong people. (*To Rose.*) You, too. Both of you. Even when I was born, on that same night, came soldiers on horses, cossacks, making trouble, setting fires. But I didn't cry and call attention. I didn't make even a peep.
ROSE. (*Coming over and sitting.*) Papa, you told me this before, didn't you? When I was little. I never heard you tell a story since then.
MORDECHAI. So now you heard.

ROSE. (*Enthusiastically.*) Tell another, Papa. From when you were a boy, about your family. We'd both like to hear it. Lusia? (*Lusia nods.*)

MORDECHAI. (*Abruptly, to Rose.*) Stories should only mean something. They should teach something, like Torah. If it's not teaching something, it's a waste of time to talk so much! I want she should know also how much respect this family got. (*To Lusia.*) When I first come here, I started as a stock boy, doing errands, no English. Now, Greenspan's an old man. Only seventy-two, but already an old man and I'm running the place. He, Greenspan, he calls me Morty, but no one else. Customers, salesgirls, everyone, "Good morning, Mr. Weiss" and "Let me speak to Mr. Weiss, he knows the answer." Look, I got even a business card. You see that? Mordechai Weiss. You understand? It's important you should know this. No matter how much you suffer, what you lose your family, you don't hardly know no English, you still can be a person with respect, which is worth more than all the tea in China. You understand? Your sister, she got it easier. American all the way. Nobody's gonna give her no trouble. You see that?

ROSE. Papa, I've had to work hard, too, and—

MORDECHAI. You got brains and health, that's what you're supposed to do! So don't tell me.

ROSE. I know it's not the same, but I never had anyone to help me with—

MORDECHAI. (*Hitting the floor with his cane.*) *Tuchter! Mit* God's *hilf,** you got brains and health you help yourself! This way you can live through anything. (*To Lusia.*) All right, *tuchter.* Get your hat and coat. We're going. (*He puts on his hat and stands up, ready to leave.*)

ROSE. Where, Papa? Lusia and I are planning to—

MORDECHAI. She comes with me to Brooklyn to meet Greenspan, to see the place I been living all these years! What would be her home if things work out and there's no Depression.

ROSE. Well, OK. I guess I should visit *Tanta* Perla, anyway.

MORDECHAI. No. I want she should come by herself. All of this, Brooklyn, Greenspan, you already know. Now it's her turn.

LUSIA. Papa, I want Rayzel should come.

MORDECHAI. Rayzel is staying here. She's got to do her tax.

LUSIA. I got to help her. (*Sits.*)

MORDECHAI. (*To Rose.*) Tell you sister.

*Help.

ROSE. He's right, Lusia. You go ahead. There's nothing you can help with. I've got things to do, business, from my job. I'll be better off by myself. And you'll get to see what might have been your home.

MORDECHAI. So go get your hat and coat. (*Mordechai waits in front hall while Lusia goes into bedroom. She returns carrying her pocketbook, no hat or coat.*) This is it again? No coat? (*To Rose.*) Get your sister a coat. (*Rose moves to do so, Lusia stops her.*)

LUSIA. (*Looking hard at Mordechai.*) I'm going with you like you want. I don't wear no coat. (*Mordechai, taken aback, looks from Lusia to Rose and back, then waves Lusia on ahead of him. To Rose.*) Is a good day Sunday to be home, no? (*Rose forces a smile and nods. Lusia exits. Mordechai starts to leave behind her.*)

ROSE. Bye, Papa.

MORDECHAI. (*Turning back.*) You made a good meal, Rayzel. (*He turns to leave again, stops.*) The fish was a little bit salty, but the eggs was good. (*He continues out.*)

ROSE. (*As he exits.*) Thanks, Papa. Bye.

MORDECHAI. Zei gezunt.* (*Rose goes into the dinette as if to clean some more, removes the dish towel from her waist, throws the towel onto the table, and goes into the living room, turns on the radio, picks up a magazine and tries to read. When the music comes on she waits a moment, listening, then turns it off. She tries to read again, finds herself staring at the page, not seeing the words. She closes the magazine, puts it down and, hesitantly, goes into the bedroom. She picks up the doll, looks at it, puts it down, and starts to leave. She changes her mind and touches Lusia's robe, which is on the foot of the bed. She slowly puts it on, looks in the mirror. Suddenly she hears something. It is the sound of a child crying softly. Frightened, she looks around.*)

ROSE. Who is it? Who's here? (*The child's voice occasionally calls* "Mama." *Rose speaks softly, unable to identify the source of the voice. She turns in the room.*) What's the matter? . . . How did you get in here? . . . Don't be afraid . . . Where are you? (*The sound has grown louder.*) Who are you? (*Rose catches herself in the "mirror" opposite the foot of the bed, turns toward the audience to see herself. At this moment, the weeping stops. She realizes that she is alone as she stares at her image in the mirror. She touches her dry eyes. Lights fade.*)

*Good-bye (literally: go good).

Scene 2

Tuesday afternoon. When lights rise, Lusia is in the living room, energetically cleaning with a brush and cloth. She is humming, on her knees. The lights shift to a glow. Facing downstage, she smiles as Hanna enters behind her.

LUSIA. Hanna.

HANNA. *Ken ich arayn kumen?**

LUSIA. (*Running to embrace her.*) Hanna! *Ch'ob gevart far dir!*† (*Hanna now looks Lusia's age and is dressed in outdated, secondhand clothes like hers.*)

HANNA. But your sister isn't home. Are you sure it's all right?

LUSIA. (*Leading Hanna by the hand. When she speaks, it is reminiscent of the first time Rose showed her the apartment.*) If she were here, she'd invite you in herself. You have to see everything. It's even got things we didn't know to dream about! Look here, look at this: carpet like a cloud. You could sleep on the floor. And what about this? This is a machine that makes it warm, like the middle of July, on the coldest winter day! (*Hanna exclaims over everything.*) And, Hanna, wait till you see the kitchen!

HANNA. Does it have a stove? A real one?

LUSIA. It runs on electricity, that's what you won't believe. (*Lusia runs into the kitchen.*)

HANNA. (*Looking after her.*) No!

LUSIA. (*Offstage.*) Yes! I mean it! And there's a machine that washes your clothes and then the dishes. Oh, it leaves a little egg sometimes, that you have to do over. But mostly it's like having a housemaid— five maids—to do the work. (*Lusia comes back into the dinette.*) And you put your garbage outside the back door and while you sleep, a man comes on an elevator and takes it away.

HANNA. There's something left to throw away?

LUSIA. Too much. You can't eat enough to use it up before it spoils.

HANNA. We used to dream of a piece of bread . . . (*She rubs the table top.*) Everything is so clean!

LUSIA. (*Back in the living room, turns to Hanna.*) Wait until you see the bathroom! Everything white and shiny. A bathtub big enough to swim in and water hot enough to boil an egg if you wanted to.

---

*Can I come in?

†I was waiting for you!

HANNA. Inside the house? (*Lusia nods. They laugh.*) And I can stay here?

LUSIA. Of course. Rose is out of town on business. You can have the bedroom—I'll show it to you in a minute—and I'll sleep here. It's where I'm used to. (*She poses on the sofa like Rose. They look at each other, then Lusia sits up and speaks softly.*) You know that whatever is mine is yours, Hanna.

HANNA. (*Arms held out to Lusia, who joins her.*) Whatever is mine is yours.

LUSIA. A half a potato.

HANNA. A quarter of a potato . . . A cup of barley-water soup.

LUSIA. A spoonful of soup. Half is yours.

HANNA. More than half sometimes.

LUSIA. Whoever needs it more.

HANNA. Whoever wants it less. (*Pause. The lights are beginning a slow change to cold blue.*)

LUSIA. You kept me alive.

HANNA. Your life was something to live for.

LUSIA. You were all I had left.

HANNA. You were everything. (*Pause. Their bodies are beginning to change, distort. They are clutching, rather than holding each other.*)

LUSIA. If you had no one you were dead . . .

HANNA. . . . much faster. If you had someone . . .

LUSIA. . . . you had to live so they would live. (*It is cold. A distant wind is blowing. Hanna and Lusia reach around each other even further, leaning on one another for physical support and warmth. Hanna breaks away, looks around.*)

HANNA. (*Whispering.*) Now follow me. Into the house. (*Hanna moves toward the bedroom. Lusia pulls back, frightened.*)

LUSIA. But we can't go in there! (*Both women are weak and cold. Hanna has the energy given by a fever.*)

HANNA. Yes we can!

LUSIA. No!

HANNA. But we're free!

LUSIA. I don't believe it.

HANNA. Liberated.

LUSIA. Liberated.

HANNA. He said it was all right. The Russian on his horse. He said the whole town belongs to us now.

LUSIA. (*Close to Hanna, outside the bedroom, whispering, terrified.*) But there might be someone in there.

HANNA. So what? Old women and babies only. They were left behind.

LUSIA. I wouldn't put my foot in a German house.

HANNA. It was a Polish house before they took it.

LUSIA. It's no good, Hanna. It had Nazis in it.

HANNA. We're free. We can go where we want to. We can take anything. Food. Clothes. Take back what they stole. He told us. The Russian on his horse. In Yiddish. Who would have guessed? In Yiddish.

LUSIA. But there's a grandmother in there, Hanna. And a little baby. We might frighten them.

HANNA. How can you say such a thing? Your mother wasn't frightened? (*As Hanna speaks, Lusia covers her ears, humming, to drown her out.*) Sprinze wasn't frightened on the way to the ovens? They took your sweet little girl. They took your mother. They took everything from us, but we can't take a warm coat or a piece of sausage from—

LUSIA. Stop! I don't want to hear! We can't be like them! We can't do what they did! And I don't want a warm coat. I want to be cold like the dead ones. I don't want—

HANNA. Shhh! See. She ran away. (*Leading Lusia into the bedroom. The wind stops.*) Took the baby out the window. Look. Lusia. It's empty. Come. There's nobody here. Look. A bowl of cereal. For the baby. Oatmeal. Still hot. And a sausage. Milk.

LUSIA. It will make you sick to eat all at once. Just take a little bit, Hanna! (*But Hanna is eating the imaginary food rapidly, insanely. Then she sees the doll. She picks it up and cradles it like a baby.*)

HANNA. This is for my baby.

LUSIA. It belongs to another child.

HANNA. It's for the future. For my baby.

LUSIA. You'd bring a child into this world? Anyway, we can't have children anymore.

HANNA. I can.

LUSIA. You can't, Hanna. I can't. We stopped our periods. We're not women anymore. We don't have women's bodies.

HANNA. We will. (*Lusia turns away from her.*) Eat. And get round. Soft. Clean. Bleed. (*She is weakening, having difficulty breathing, crumples on the bed. Lusia turns to her.*) Have babies. You and Duvid.

LUSIA. (*Moving to comfort Hanna.*) All right, Hanna. We'll have babies.

HANNA. (*Hugging the doll tightly.*) And me . . .

LUSIA. You with someone wonderful like Duvid.

HANNA. A handsome Russian soldier.

LUSIA. On a horse.

HANNA. Who, out of nowhere, speaks Yiddish.

LUSIA. (*Laughing.*) The horse?

HANNA. Even the horse speaks Yiddish. (*Hanna and Lusia both start laughing wildly until Hanna begins to cough. She weakens greatly.*)

LUSIA. Shh. Soon you'll be better. Now there'll be doctors and medicine.

HANNA. (*Giving Lusia the doll.*) I ate too much. You were right. But it's a good reason to be sick for a change. Overeating. What would your mama say? (*She rises with effort.*) Here, you take the doll.

LUSIA. But it's yours.

HANNA. You'll need it before I do. Don't even know the Russian's name yet. Let go of me. (*She pushes Lusia away.*) Hold the doll. Protect it. I'm going to throw up and I don't want to get it dirty. (*Lusia stands up as Hanna exits.*) Not dirty. Go away from me, Lusia. *Gai avek fun mir. Avek!* (*Lusia is standing alone, hugging the doll, as the lights return to normal. She looks at the doll, caresses it.*)

LUSIA. Hannele! Who can I laugh with now? (*Lusia quickly puts the doll down. She runs back to her cleaning, furiously. She sneezes.*)

Scene 3

She sneezes again. Rose enters from bathroom through bedroom with cleanser and rags on her way to kitchen.

ROSE. I wish you'd stop, Lusia, and take it easy. It doesn't need to be *that* clean.

LUSIA. I like to.

ROSE. I've never heard of anyone cleaning that way. I'm sure no one's ever done it in here before.

LUSIA. That's how come I . . . achoom?

ROSE. (*As she disappears into kitchen.*) Sneeze.

LUSIA. Sneeze. First time I use that word. Sneeze. For something to be too much clean is impossible. Anyway, if I live here, I do something to help.

ROSE. (*Coming into living room with dusting cloth.*) But you could stop for a little while and rest. If you will, I will, OK? You could get in the bathtub and soak all day. Go on. I know how you love that bubble bath. Sometimes I think you'll never come out.

LUSIA. I'm sorry. I'll try to be more faster.

ROSE. That's not what I meant. You can stay in as long as you like. Only I don't think you should always be working. Half the day at the immigrant office and here the rest of the time. You won't even come to the movies anymore. You deserve some peace. Outside of the bath.

LUSIA. (*A bit huffy.*) Peace I'll get when this all cleaned up. OK? (*Rose shrugs, goes back to her dusting and polishing with added energy. Lusia and Rose are both working furiously. Each begins singing to herself, Rose a popular song, Lusia a song in Yiddish, softly, not really aware that she is singing. It is the same song she hummed earlier to drown out Hanna. Rose, however, is aware of Lusia's song and listens to it as she continues her work. Then she is still, just watching her sister.*)

ROSE. That's pretty. (*Lusia stops singing, keeps working.*) No, don't stop. That sounded so nice. It reminds me of something. Lusia, it's one of those times I told you about. Did my—our—mother used to sing that song?

LUSIA. That song, no. But sing, yes, always when she's working in the house or cooking or sewing something. But not too good, same like me. Maybe this is what reminds you.

ROSE. No, you have a sweet voice. Sing some more. Teach me. I'd like to learn it. (*Pause.*)

LUSIA. This song is from the camps.

ROSE. (*Quickly.*) Oh, I'm sorry. (*She turns away.*)

LUSIA. (*Watching Rose.*) Rayzel. Rose. It don't matter. Is a good song. Happy. About how the world will be after war is over. Was a song then about future, yes? So now is a song about now. I teach you it. Come. (*Rose sits beside Lusia on the floor. Lusia sings, as a teacher.*)

> O, di velt vet verren shayna,
> libe greser, sine klayna

You know what this means?

ROSE. Some of it. Not every word.

LUSIA. It says the world will be beautiful. Love will get more and hate . . . (*She gestures.*)

ROSE. Less.

LUSIA. Less. And that's for everybody. Between women and between men and between one country and the other country. (*Lusia begins the song again. Rose joins in tentatively for the first two lines. When the verse is repeated she joins in again, singing more strongly.*)

LUSIA AND ROSE. (*Singing.*)

> O, di velt vet verren shayna,
> libe greser, sine klayna

tvishn froyen, tvishn mener,
tvishn land un land.

O, di velt vet verren shayna,
(*Lusia is singing more strongly, forgetting Rose*)
libe greser, sine klayna
tvishn froyen, tvishn mener,
(*Rose, watching Lusia, fades out and Lusia finishes alone*)
tvishn land un land.
(*Pause.*)

LUSIA. Enough for now. Is a longer song. Too much. Enough. Hanna used to sing with me.

ROSE. Is she a friend of yours? (*Lusia nods, returns to her energetic cleaning.*) From the war?

LUSIA. And from before. From children together.

ROSE. (*Treading carefully.*) Was she liberated with you? (*Lusia nods. Rose is relieved.*) You came through it all together?

LUSIA. Is why I live now. And Duvid.

ROSE. Well, where is she? We could bring her here, you know. You don't only have to be a family to sponsor someone. If the two of you went through it together and came out of it together . . .

LUSIA. Hanna was too sick. Tee . . . ty-phus, you know. She was all . . . nothing left of her. I say when I really look for first time in hospital, "But Hanna, we is bones, both of us, nothing but bones. We never be womens again." She say old saying, like Mama. Too sick hardly to talk, she says, "*Bainer on flaish iz do; flaish on bainer iz nito!*" (*She laughs.*) Farshtaist?

ROSE. I think so.

LUSIA. "Bones without meat you can have; meat without bones, is impossible." This way she makes jokes and was living only one more day. (*Rose turns away and goes off into kitchen.*) But she was free. And clean. And was thinking things for the future. (*Lusia goes back to her brushing. Rose returns shortly, with a full picnic basket.*)

ROSE. I know I can't get you to leave that spot, so I brought a picnic. (*Rose unwraps chicken legs, bread and cheese, etc. laying them on the cloth on the floor near Lusia.*)

LUSIA. For this I can stop.

ROSE. Your appetite is improving.

LUSIA. Mine sister is a good cook. An expert. (*Lusia and Rose eat heartily. Rose takes chocolate milk from basket and gives it to Lusia.*)

ROSE. With chocolate?

LUSIA. With chocolate. (*Enjoys drinking some.*) This chocolate in the milk you learn from your *Tanta* Perla, no?

ROSE. She used to do anything to get me to drink milk. Because she thought she should.

LUSIA. She seems like kind woman when I meet her. Like bird, like you say, but with hurt foot, hop . . . ? (*Rose nods*) . . . hopping to get seeds, to get a warm.

ROSE. Worm.

LUSIA. Worm. Warm. Worm. (*She considers.*) To get a worm to sing little bird song about bird troubles.

ROSE. You know her perfectly! That's just what she's like. More a sparrow than a hen. *Tanta* Perla could not hatch an egg.

LUSIA. In my house, your house, too, in Chernov, before the war, for long time we got chickens. Many. Eggs every day and some extra makes for more chickens for soup Mama makes delicious. In Brooklyn I see no one got chickens and much . . . hard where you walk, how you say this?

ROSE. Pavement. Sidewalks.

LUSIA. Much pavement sidewalks not good for to grow trees with fruit. We have in the summer baby apples.

ROSE. Crab apples.

LUSIA. And *barnes* . . . pears. Mama can make grow anything and then make for bread jelly, jam, all good, for whole year.

ROSE. That's something I never tasted homemade.

LUSIA. This we have even when trouble begins because is right by house. Until all Jewish got to move to one place. But before—how you say—married, . . . still childrens, me and Duvid, only fifteen, sixteen, we take—steal—from Mama the jam and bread and have . . . like this . . .

ROSE. A picnic.

LUSIA. By the river in woods. We feel so bad, like thief, so have to eat up all this jam, the whole bottle, with a spoon—

ROSE. To hide the evidence!

LUSIA. And is best pic-nic I ever have. (*Pause.*) Rayzel, yesterday in the morning a man came into immigrant office. Is very thin, much more than me. And teeth black and poor clothes, much worser than mine. He has list, he says, lots of names what happened last six years Poland, even from beginning of war, like time when Duvid been arrested. He kept list secret in camps and copied very neat, many pages, who died, who lived, who escaped, how, where. Of course, this

I want to see right away. The man says no, will not give list to nobody. Only will sell. For money.

ROSE. How awful!

LUSIA. No. He needs money for food, clothes, to live. This list is his work, his talent. He's not a bad man.

ROSE. Well, what happened? What did you do?

LUSIA. I can do nothing. I send him to a man more important. Today I'll see what happens. I think maybe Duvid is on this list.

ROSE. What makes you think so?

LUSIA. Is time for Duvid. Is already— (*The doorbell rings. Again. Then pounding on the door. Rose jumps up in panic.*)

ROSE. It's Papa! What's he doing here now? In the middle of the day! (*She calls.*) Papa? (*Rose is answered by more pounding. Tossing the cheese to Lusia.*) The cheese. Hide the cheese! I'm supposed to keep kosher. . . . Coming, Papa! (*Lusia starts to run off with the cheese as the pounding continues. She runs back; very serious.*)

LUSIA. But, Rayzel, is a sin to lie to a papa, no? (*Rose freezes, stares helplessly at Lusia. Suddenly.*) Di milch! (*Rose and Lusia are both frantic, grabbing the milk and other offending items. At the same time, they are beginning to laugh very hard. When Lusia is safely in the kitchen, and the remnants of the picnic are looking kosher on the floor, Rose goes to open the door. Mordechai enters behind her, wearing a hat but no scarf. It's a warm spring day. He carries a shoebox tied with a string.*)

MORDECHAI. It's nice. I got nothing better to do all day than to knock on a door. (*Lusia returns from kitchen. Both she and Rose are working to control their laughter. Seeing the picnic.*) What goes on here?

ROSE. A . . . picnic, Papa.

LUSIA. Rayzel just cleaned up the table so we been eating on the floor.

MORDECHAI. So, if I sweep the floor, maybe you'll eat on the table! (*This is too much. Rose and Lusia burst out laughing, holding onto each other to keep from falling. Mordechai is amazed at the success of his joke.*) Is good *shvesters* should laugh together. (*Rose and Lusia recover, aware for a moment of their physical closeness.*)

ROSE. I'm sorry, Papa. You want something? A drink, maybe? I've got some delicious chicken.

MORDECHAI. (*Putting down his hat and cane in the dinette.*) No, no. I got all I need. I want you two should clean up your picnic and come sit down. I'm on important business. (*During the next several lines of dialogue Rose and Lusia pick up and put away the picnic and cleaning things. Mordechai is arranging chairs around the dinette table.*)

ROSE. How come you left the store? You really surprised us.

MORDECHAI. Today they're doing inventory. For this, I can leave. For this, Greenspan can manage alone. He can count. He can write down numbers in a book. Especially when I got something more important.

ROSE. Does it have to do with that box? A surprise, maybe?

MORDECHAI. That's it. Exactly.

ROSE. Lusia, you see what your being here has done? Everything's topsy-turvy. Surprises in the middle of the week, yet. Papa taking off early. Amazing!

MORDECHAI. Enough, already. Sit. Both. (*Rose and Lusia sit. Mordechai, still standing, holds the box.*) This box is the most important thing in the world. In the universe, even, for us. In here is your family, your history, who and where you're coming from. It's proof who you are. (*He puts the box on the table.*) It's proof of people we'll never see no more, parts of them alive still, in you. And better yet, in your children, with God's help. Old pictures I had *fun* mine parents, *fun* aunts and uncles. Some I stopped showing you when you was little, Rayzel, always making you cry too much for your mother, may she rest in peace, or for Lushke, as you used to say.

ROSE. I don't remember that!

MORDECHAI. These I showed you again later when they was the same to you like pictures in your schoolbooks and they didn't make you cry no more.

ROSE. They were just faces. You *were*, Lusia, far away and different.

MORDECHAI. All these I got. I want Lusia and you should look at them together, remember together. Maybe like that it would mean more. All names and what year, what place, is written on the back. Anything you want to know you write down on a piece paper so you don't forget and next time I'll tell you what's what.

ROSE. We will, Papa.

MORDECHAI. Lusia? (*Lusia nods. Pause as Mordechai sits between his daughters. He includes Lusia, but is primarily speaking to Rose, presenting something to her.*) Some months ago came to see me a Polish woman. Nobility. A countess, a friend *fun* your mother—an employer—who your mother made beautiful dresses by hand and she, your mother, would give this rich woman sometimes a present, baked goods or fruit from her garden. (*Lusia looks stricken, turns away.*) This countess, of course, is not a Jew, but, still, a good woman. She came in person. She wouldn't take a chance to send something what it might get lost. In person, only, she wants to see me.

MAMA'S VOICE. *Ich blayb mit mayn kind . . . (Lusia pulls further away from the others. Mama enters the bedroom area slowly, as Mordechai speaks. She is older, in her late forties, moving around in the outer edges of the space. She carries a knapsack. Her head is covered by a scarf.)*

MORDECHAI. She never sat down, didn't take off her coat or take a glass tea. But she gave me a bundle *fun* your mother. *(Rose reaches for the box.)* Wait. *(Mordechai unties the package very slowly. Rose's attention is on the package, too. Unheard by the others, Lusia suddenly gets up, comes forward, paces as she talks to Mama, apart from her.)*

LUSIA. Mama! *Farvos bistu nit gegangen?** I told you to go!

MAMA. It was impossible.

LUSIA. But you would be here now! You'd be here with me and Rayzel and Papa. I told you to go! If only—

MAMA. If your grandma had a beard, she'd be your grandpa . . .

LUSIA. Don't do that. It's not funny. Don't be so stubborn!

MORDECHAI. Come, Lusia, sit. Stop pacing. It makes me so I can't think. *(Mama is signaling Lusia to hush. Lusia sits. Mordechai has the package opened. He puts the box aside and removes a smaller bundle wrapped in a head scarf identical to the one Mama is wearing. Lusia is frozen by it. The Voices begin quietly. Gently beginning to open the bundle.)* This is exactly how she gave it to me. I put it back the same so you could see. She didn't touch it from the way your mother first put it. *(Mama is sitting on the bed. In the dim, cold light, she opens the knapsack and removes an old candlestick, which she holds, barely moving.)* It was many years since I heard anything from *mine* wife. The first thing I found, in here, like this, was a letter for me. It was from over three years before. When I read it the worst already happened, but I didn't know yet. The countess carried this around the world until she came to America. Even if not Jewish, they knew to run from Hitler. Anyway, this from your mother she carried like a holy package, I couldn't believe it. The next is some pictures you never seen of your sister here when she graduated school and this is a wedding . . . *(Mordechai is passing the pictures to Rose, intending her to hand them on to Lusia. Lusia turns away, slowly gets up.)*

ROSE. Papa, can't we look at these later? I think it's hard for her. It's much too painful. *(Lusia is on her way to the bedroom. Voices fade.)*

MORDECHAI. *(Touching his head.)* All these pictures she's got here inside, already. This paper don't make the pain, believe me. *(Rose starts to follow Lusia. Mordechai holds her back. They continue to look*

*Why didn't you go?

quietly at photos while the scene in the bedroom continues. The lighting emphasis changes.)

LUSIA. Mama, you've got to go with her and get out of this horrible place!

MAMA. (*Repacking knapsack.*) Don't argue.

LUSIA. But she wants to protect you, to take a chance herself because she thinks so much of you.

MAMA. She's a wonderful woman.

LUSIA. Then go!

MAMA. All right. She said they have room for one more. You. But not the baby. Not Sprinze. You want to come, too?

LUSIA. How dare you! Don't be crazy, Mama!

MAMA. You stay with your child, I stay with my child.

LUSIA. But this is different. I'm not helpless like the baby. You have another daughter, too. You could be with Rayzel again. Finally. Mama. And Papa.

MAMA. When you have a grandchild, you have two children. Here where I am, I have two. There, where I may never arrive, is one I lost long ago. I won't take the chance of losing more.

LUSIA. But, Mama, then you had no choice. This time you do.

MAMA. It only looks like a choice. If God wanted us to be in America, you never would have caught scarlet fever. Your father would not have had such business troubles—

LUSIA. I'll never agree with you, never! About God.

MAMA. God doesn't care if you agree or not. He does what He does. God doesn't argue and God doesn't change His mind. Besides, maybe where they're sending us this time will be an improvement. In the country somewhere. At least not a ghetto. Trees, maybe, some flowers—

LUSIA. Mama, listen. Please! Anything the Nazis do will only be worse, never better. You go with the countess. I'm young. I'll do all right. I have the medicine for Sprinze. It puts her to sleep for two days so she won't cry. I'll carry her in my knapsack. Others have done it. They won't even know I have a baby.

MAMA. I stay with my child. (*She kisses Lusia on the forehead.*) . . . *Ich blayb mit mayn kind.*

ROSE. (*Standing and moving towards Lusia as lights return to normal in dinette and fade in bedroom.*) Lusia, look! (*Lusia, returning to reality, leaves the bedroom and meets Rose, who is holding a small silver spoon with a sealed letter and a scarf. Mama exits.*) Papa says this is my baby spoon! I used to eat with it. (*Lusia takes the spoon.*)

LUSIA. Sometimes I feed you with this.

ROSE. And a letter for me, from Mama! (*Rose is holding the letter out to Lusia. Lusia takes it, hands it back, with the spoon. She goes directly, angrily, to Mordechai.*)

LUSIA. How long ago this countess visits?

MORDECHAI. November, December, maybe.

LUSIA. Mama sends these things for Rayzel. Why you don't give them before?

MORDECHAI. Until I knew for certain—

LUSIA. And now you already know for a long time!

MORDECHAI. I was hoping we should all be a family again—

LUSIA. (*Overlapping.*) Is no more hoping! Mama's dead! We was supposed to come here! Was your promise. I want Rayzel should know this. (*To Rose.*) Mama was all ready we should wait. So we wait. Then comes a letter from your *Tanta* Perla. She's asking us why Papa won't take no money. Some group in Brooklyn is giving him the money so we could come and he should pay it back later. But Papa says no. He won't take from no one.

MORDECHAI. This you should understand. (*Pounding the table.*) Not to owe nothing! (*He rises.*)

ROSE. But, Papa!

MORDECHAI. What? I knew was coming the Depression? I knew the doors would be closed here? I had a crystal ball showed ten years ahead to Hitler? (*Pause.*) Every penny I made since went to bring them over myself! (*Rose is looking hard at Mordechai.*)

LUSIA. Then it don't matter no more. Is too late. (*To Mordechai.*) And now you don't want even to read to her what Mama is saying. Now you don't want even to touch something of Mama's. From shame. From shame!

MORDECHAI. (*Calmly, quietly.*) Rayzel, who you want should read your Mama's letter, me or your sister? Say only the truth. (*Rose holds out the letter to Lusia.*) It should be better a woman. *Tanta* Perla, maybe. (*Rose holds the letter out again. Lusia takes it, holding it away from herself. She moves slowly into the living room and sits down. Mordechai gets up, goes to get his hat and cane.*) Lusia, read the letter for your sister. I'll wait for you downstairs. When you're finished, you come. I got some new places we should leave word about your husband. (*Mordechai is almost out the door, remembers something. He comes back and removes a photograph from his vest pocket, shows it to Lusia and then Rose. Lusia closes her eyes.*)

ROSE. A pretty girl.

MORDECHAI. Age sixteen only.

ROSE. It's Mama, isn't it?

MORDECHAI. (*He nods.*) A shayna maidel. (*Mordechai puts the photo back into his pocket and leaves.*)

ROSE. (*After a moment, amazed, as she sits.*) He must keep that picture with him all the time.

LUSIA. (*Thrusting envelope to Rose.*) You open, please. Is your letter. (*Rose opens the envelope carefully.*)

ROSE. It's very fresh. Like it was just written.

LUSIA. Mama keeps the paper, I think, for a long time before she sends this letter. Was all ready for when someone comes like countess. I never seen her write nothing. (*Rose hands the open letter to Lusia, who hesitates, then smells the scent of the letter. Lusia can hardly speak.*) Is Mama. Before . . . (*She tries to give the letter back to Rose.*) Ich ken nit* . . . Ken nit! (*Rose keeps looking at her, waiting. Lusia breathes deeply, composes herself, then slowly sits apart from Rose, begins shakily, relaxes more as she feels and enjoys her recognition of Mama in the words. As she continues Rose stiffens, reacting almost politely, as someone at a tea party. There are no tears.*) Mayn tyereh tuchter, Rayzel . . .

Mine dearest daughter, Rayzel,

I'm not a learned woman. I wish I could be so I could say everything to you the right way. For a long time I have written and I know it could happen you don't get the letters. This one is meant by God's will to reach you. Maybe it is the last one for a time so I want to tell you everything how I feel.

If I could really be with you and put around you mine arms, it would be much better, but that is impossible. It cannot be. If I cannot hold you in mine arms, I hold you anyway in mine heart and this is true for every day in your life since you was born, if you was in Chernov, Poland, or Brooklyn, New York, America.

I want you should have your baby spoon. Your favorite, just your size and you could first feed yourself with it. Every day since you and Papa went away, I keep it in a pocket with me, to touch what you touch. I knew I would give it back to you before you were five years old and now look what happened! Well, who are we to question the plan from God? Now when you have this baby spoon, you must get a feeling from your mother. Sometime you will have a child to use it, too, and she will feel from her grandmother. Or, who knows, maybe the family will be together by then.

You would think I would have more to tell you besides this baby

*I cannot.

spoon; advice and so forth, but I can't think of anything more important right now. You can't put life on a piece paper. Or love. I am not a
smart person with writing down words, but I wish you understand
how I am feeling for you, mine pretty little girl.
Your only mother,
Liba Eisenman Weiss
Chernov, Poland, June four, nineteen hundred and forty-two.

(*Lusia and Rose sit silently for awhile, then Lusia puts the letter back in the
envelope, kisses it, and gives it to Rose.*)
ROSE. Thank you, Lusia. (*Silence again for a time, then Lusia stands
up.*)
LUSIA. Papa's waiting. (*Rose nods. Lusia gets her pocketbook. Rose gives
her the scarf in which everything was wrapped. Lusia leans over and kisses
Rose on the forehead. Lusia exits. Rose opens the letter again, tries to drink in
the scent. Rose clasps the letter and the spoon, which she is still holding, to
herself. She sounds at first like the child's voice she heard earlier.*)
ROSE. Mama. Mama! (*Now the sound that comes from her is a chant, an
intoning that is trying to make something happen. Each repetition becomes
more intense, almost angry.*) Mamamamamamamamamamamama. Mamamamamamamamamamama. Mamamamamamamamamamama! (*The
Voices are emerging out of Rose's call. She moves into the bedroom. She puts
down the letter and spoon. The Voices are continuous. She gets the pen from
the night table. Slowly and deliberately, as if she is carving, she draws a
number on her left forearm and stares at it. The sound of the Voices is a
comfort to her. As it becomes Mama's lullaby, she sits on the bed, arms
outstretched, welcoming it. She embraces the sound and herself, as the lights
dim. Slowly, she curls up on the bed as the Voices fade.*)

Scene 4

*Several hours later. Silence. The dim light continues. Lusia enters, excited,
puts down her bag.*

LUSIA. Rayzel? Rose? (*Lusia looks around; in the dinette, the kitchen
doorway, then goes into the bedroom. Seeing Rose turned away, asleep, Lusia
begins to talk with excitement as she turns on the bed lamp and sits on the
bed.*) Rayzel, you can't take no nap now! I got to tell you something.
Something good. Papa took me to the place I never been yet. (*Rose is
slowly awakening. She is groggy, confused.*) The woman there knows about
Duvid. I can tell. She don't say nothing, but—(*Rose begins to sit up*)
—is a smile in her eyes when we talk and she says will I be at home

so she can call me on telephone if—(*As Rose moves, Lusia suddenly sees the number on her arm. She cries out.*) Rayzel! (*She grabs Rose's arm, looks at the number, then at Rose.*) What you done to yourself? (*Lusia drops the arm and pulls back, horrified, not wanting to see.*) What you done? (*She stands away from Rose who, as a bewildered child, reaches out.*)

ROSE. Lushke. (*After a moment, Lusia rushes to the bed and takes Rose in her arms, cradling her, comforting her, stroking her hair.*)

LUSIA. Sha, shtil, mayn kind. Sha. Shtil. (*As Lusia is gently rocking Rose, Mama's scarf still on her head, the phone rings. The sisters slowly pull apart, not letting go of each other. Lusia is reaching for the phone as the lights fade to black.*)

Scene 5

An hour later. The radio is playing. Lights up in the living room. Lusia is alone, waiting, pacing, patting pillows, running to look in the mirror. With hands trembling, she turns off the radio, runs to the front door, returns at once, sits rigidly, waiting. There is a gentle knock at the door. She jumps, holds tightly to herself, remaining stiffly seated.

DUVID. (*Offstage.*) Lusia? Lusia, *ken ich arayn kumen?*

LUSIA. *Kum arayn.* [Then close the door behind you. (*If no door closing sound available.*)] (*Duvid enters, carrying a small suitcase. He is older, smaller, thinner than in Lusia's memory, dressed in an ill-fitting suit and hat. He, too, is frightened, unsure. Lusia does not look at him.*)

DUVID. S'ez ich,* Duvid. (*He stands back, puts down the case.*)

LUSIA. Duvid.

DUVID. Can't you look at me?

LUSIA. No, I can't.

DUVID. Why not?

LUSIA. I'm afraid. It's too much. You're real. It can't be.

DUVID. Look. See. (*Lusia slowly stands, turns, and faces him.*)

LUSIA. So thin! So much older! Lines. (*Duvid looks back at her silently.*)

DUVID. (*After a while.*) Can I take off my hat? (*Duvid removes his hat. Lusia takes it from him carefully, like a bomb that might explode, puts it down fast. She scrutinizes him.*) You're the same. (*Lusia shakes her head.*) The same.

LUSIA. A different person. A stranger.

DUVID. Lusia.

*It's I.

LUSIA. Six years.

DUVID. I knew where you were. Until the liberation. Then I lost you. But I knew you were alive.

LUSIA. I lost you from the beginning. Messages came, and word from people I didn't know, but they all said something different. So you disappeared. One said you died. Then I was sure you lived.

DUVID. I was in many places. I got moved.

LUSIA. Are you well?

DUVID. Getting stronger. You?

LUSIA. Healthy. Getting fat from my sister's cooking. (*Pause.*) There's too much! How to tell so much!

DUVID. I know everything. It was the same with me. (*He moves toward her.*) Lusia . . .

LUSIA. (*Turning away from him.*) I can't. (*He moves again.*) I can't! (*They are frozen in this impasse. From a distance, then growing louder and closer, is the sound of gentle, joyful music. Gradually the lights shift in mood and the fantasy glow rises, glowing throughout the apartment. There is a sound of laughter and merriment, a party, also coming closer. Mama, in a party dress, carries the old candlestick with a lighted candle in it, and a tray of honey cake. She puts these on the dinette table. She looks behind her.*)

MAMA. *Kum shoin,** Mordechai! (*Mordechai, wearing a flower in his lapel, enters with glasses of wine on a tray. Rose and Hanna are coming from the other side, laughing, admiring each other's finery. All but Rose speak accented English. Mama motions for Lusia to go to Duvid.*) Give your husband a hug, Lushke, then we'll have something to eat. (*Lusia looks at Duvid, then back at the festivities. Mordechai puts his tray on the dinette table.*)

MORDECHAI. First, a toast. Everybody take a glass. (*They all take glasses; there is an undercurrent of excitement.*) Let's say thanks to God for this happy occasion. With his blessing, will come soon a baby. May it not be long until the *bris.†* (*Silence while they all drink, then another burst of laughter. Hanna whirls past Lusia, who reaches for, but cannot touch her. Hanna giggles as she evades the touch.*)

HANNA. Look at this dress, Lusia, how it catch the light. Rayzel come with me to pick it out special for you and Duvid.

ROSE. (*Turning slowly, to Lusia.*) Tomorrow, if you want, we'll all go get one for you. OK, Papa?

MAMA. Your father says yes.

---

*Come on already.

†Circumcision ceremony observed when a boy is eight days old.

MORDECHAI. Why not? (*Rose runs and hugs Mama. Their embrace is slow and full, with a reach beyond reality. Mordechai continues after a while.*) Now, Liba, let go of Rayzel for a minute. I got something to show you. (*Mordechai begins to dance.*) Seventy years old and what condition, eh? A regular Fred Astaire. (*Invites Mama to dance.*) And here's my Ginger Rogers. (*The music swells into the foreground of the scene. Mordechai and Mama dance together in an old-fashioned way. The others enjoy. Mordechai becomes the beginning of a chain, leading Mama around Lusia and Duvid. Rose and Hanna add on. They all circle the couple smiling, with slow, slightly exaggerated movements. It is as if Lusia and Duvid were the pivot of a fantasy merry-go-round, the others circling in an attempt to pull them together. As the end of the chain passes, Lusia turns to Duvid. The others leave on tiptoe so as not to disturb them. Hanna and Rose look at Lusia and Duvid and giggle before they leave. Mama and Mordechai watch for a moment, his arm around her shoulders. They kiss happily, then remove their trays and steal away. As Mama is almost offstage, she and Lusia turn to each other. Mama again waves Lusia closer to Duvid, then she blows out the candle and is gone. The music comes to an end and the lighting returns to normal. Duvid and Lusia are standing as they were before the party began. They speak without accents again.*)

LUSIA. (*Dropping her "I can't" position.*) There's no one left but us.

DUVID. I know.

LUSIA. (*Turning to him.*) Duvid.

DUVID. What?

LUSIA. Your name. Duvid.

DUVID. Lushke! (*Lusia and Duvid embrace, not moving, clinging to each other. After a few moments, they lean back to look at one another.*)

LUSIA. I see her in you. Sprinze. And you never saw her at all. She was beautiful. (*Duvid moves away.*) She looked like you . . . (*Duvid sits on the sofa heavily, looking away. Lusia waits, then sits beside him. Trying to comfort.*) I was wrong, Duvid. There's more than you and me left. (*Duvid does not respond. After a while, Lusia continues in another tone.*) Do you speak any English, Duvid?

DUVID. A bissell.* Farvos?

LUSIA. *Mayn shvester Rayzel farshtait a bissel Yiddish, ober si red nor English.*† (*Continues in accented English.*) A hundred percent American, she is. I want we should speak English for Rayzel.

DUVID. This I can do. Slow, maybe.

*Little.

†But she only speaks English.

LUSIA. We practice a little, yes? (*Duvid nods. Lusia continues with great pride, taking Duvid's hands and speaking slowly so he will understand.*) Duvidl. Mine sister, when you call up on telephone, went in taxi, forget what time it is, all the way to Brooklyn where lives Papa. She's gonna bring him here personally, in person. *Farshtaist?*

DUVID. I understand.

LUSIA. So we sit here, wait.

DUVID. We got many yours . . . *years* yet for to talk. (*They both smile, almost laugh, when he gets through the sentence. A small echo of the old days.*)

LUSIA. So. In any minute now is coming a key in the door or they knock or ring the bell maybe. Then, Duvid—(*The doorbell rings. Lusia carefully lets go of Duvid's hands, smiling. She goes to the door. Duvid rises and waits. Lusia returns with Rose and Mordechai. The sisters stand together, arms about each other. Mordechai remains apart, uncertain.*) Duvid . . . I want you should meet . . . mine family. (*Rose and Lusia are watching Mordechai, who has not moved. He and Duvid observe each other from Mordechai's chosen distance. Rose motions Mordechai to come closer. He does, looking at his daughters. Rose nods, encouraging him. Mordechai moves slowly to Duvid, taking him by the shoulders as he did Lusia when first seeing her. He hesitates for a moment, then slides his arm around Duvid. The men embrace fully. Without turning, Mordechai lowers one arm and reaches out behind himself. Still holding tightly to Rose, Lusia steps forward and takes Mordechai's hand. Slowly, the lights fade to black.*)

Photograph by Gary Cohen

Sarah Blacher Cohen

CYNTHIA OZICK, in the foreword to her 1983 collection of essays, *Art and Ardor,* did not mention my name per se but said she was referring to me when she wrote:

> I have a conscientious and responsible friend, a professor and a scholar, and also a reputable literary critic; in her heart she is a secret playwright. She wants to make things up: characters, settings, dialogues, plots. So far she has not allowed herself to begin: she is too conscientious, too responsible. Instead, she concentrates, in sober prose, on literary and historical subjects. She knows that make-believe is frivolity. She will not permit herself a descent, however, alluring, into the region of the trivial. She is a writer of essays. (1988a, ix)

With the encouragement of my husband, Gary Cohen, I made that descent into the forbidden realm of make-believe where one lies to create the semblance of truth. From writing many solemn and respectful studies of humor in Jewish-American literature, I, as an English professor at the University at Albany, State University of New York, did an about-face and created my own irreverent comedy of character, ideas, situation, and language. I gave myself permission to discontinue being a sheltered critic, set in her ways, to become a vulnerable playwright, ready to revise and please many constituencies. In other words, I became that Jewish tailor willing to make the pants longer or shorter to please the customers.

The greatest catalyst to my creative energies was collaborating on the play *Schlemiel the First,* with Nobel Laureate Isaac Bashevis Singer. I shaped the structure of the play, fleshed out the characters, heightened the comedy of the scenes, wrote new dialogue, and pruned out anecdotal materials. In 1984 the play had a six-week run at New York's Jewish Repertory Theater.

In 1985 and 1986, ideas for my own play began percolating in my head during my daily physical therapy swims at the Albany Jewish Center. They came to a boil as I sat in the ladies locker room, that compressed chamber of life, and listened to scarred women speak openly about breast surgery, young nubile ones mutter narcissistic fears of growing old, and elderly women mourn the loss of family, friends, and vigor. Were we to meet each other outside in street clothes, we might never have talked beyond a cursory "hello." Yet, no matter what their public persona might reveal, people become vocal about their vulnerabilities when they shed the protection of their clothes. In those moments, some truth-telling takes place. The young pregnant women and the old-country menopausal ones told me their life stories in polished English and in fractured English. With their idiosyncratic personalities and unique physical impairments, they became for me the stuff of drama, quirky characters in search of an author.

What happens to these women in the ladies locker room? In what ways do these bared souls bare their souls? The play comically explores the connection among elderly, disabled, and young able-bodied women of different nationalities and religions. Through diverse, accented dialogue and varied levels of discourse, the play illustrates the intricate workings of the locker room as miniature United Nations, with its power plays, strained attempts at negotiation, inevitable compromises and capitulations. As it depicts their responses to minor catastrophes and major miracles, the play reveals how these women come to accept their flawed selves.

From a Jewish point of view, the locker room companions are, in the words of one reviewer, "a microcosm of Diaspora Jewry—East European, Central European and American. Susan's handicap places her in a doubly 'marginal' status. Jewish and disabled, she finds kinship as one who 'walks funny' with Sophie, who 'talks funny,' but who 'didn't have an accent' until she moved to America" (Cohen 1990, 7).

Although *The Ladies Locker Room* reveals the torment of youthful disability and old age, it is still a funhouse where the elderly create Jewish mirth to distract the disabled from their pain. The characters talk about the tragic parts of life; Sophie, in particular, engages her wit in the humor of verbal retrieval. Through her comic reformulations of the tearful, she succeeds in salvaging the antic from the anguished. Cynthia Ozick also commented on the play's humor of verbal retrieval. She wrote me: "You really dare to look the Medusa directly in the eye. You hide nothing. No cosmetics, no lies, instead the full range of mortal contingency and limitation. And all of it laced with quip and high jinks. Your *Ladies Locker Room* is a tragic place, a little hell. But your characters raise hell in that hell and make light of all our human bondage" (1988b).

The locker room is also a makeshift labor room where Sophie, the embodiment of the vibrant Yiddish past, motivates the disabled Jewish-American professor to help an able-bodied Gentile woman give birth to her first child. Thus, the locker room, with its overflow of affection and life-enhancing Jewish comedy, contributes to the symbolic rebirth and empowerment of the disabled.

Indeed, for Sally Chasnoff, the director of the Northwestern University production of the play, the "central issue of *The Ladies Locker Room* is disability, or rather the tension between 'dis-abled' and 'differently abled,' and how these perspectives do not simply influence but actually determine lives." The play compels us to look at "'disability' as a metaphor for the countless difficulties and limitations of living in the physical body for all of us, as well as a term for special bodily conditions. Are these 'disabilities' products of our psyches, 'just our imaginations,' or are they products of the culture into which we are born, and projected onto us until we finally accept them as our own, or refuse to do so any longer?" (1991).

For me, the play is not only about the disabled protagonist's acquiring a newfound agility and new self-respect; it is an expression of the multiple facets of myself. It contains the formative influences that shaped my identity: the unreserved Yiddish vitality of my Russian Jewish immigrant parents, who came to this country in 1921; the starched Gentile refinement of my Republican home town of Appleton, Wisconsin; and my rigorous English doctoral studies at Northwestern University. Here in the ladies locker room, which could be called "the theatrical bathhouse," the name given to the Yiddish theater, the eighty-some-year-old "Yiddish Dear Abby," Sophie Gold from Bialystok, modeled after Sophie Geller, who came to Albany in 1914, encounters the stilted English professor, Dr. Susan, and offers her a shtetl remedy for her defective feet and her depression. Prescribing liberal doses of optimism, Sophie, the Yiddish life force, whom Cynthia Ozick describes as the "deus ex machina and mentor and historian and explainer and continuer and sardonic merry angel," teaches Dr. Susan to experience "the victories of an imagination courageous enough for happiness." And these victories, waged and won in the ladies locker room, "hint or teach . . . that happiness is hard and muscular labor. (Like laughter!)" (1988b).

And so I, Sarah Blacher Cohen, professor of English, have given birth to my own literary baby, my fledgling play, *The Ladies Locker Room*. Like a good Jewish mother, I am loathe to let go of her to have a life independent of me. Will she thrive and prosper in the world? Will the world appreciate her special talents and view her as unique? Will it like her and seek out her company? I, who have been in control of her conception, want to be in control of her reception and ultimate fate. In my daydreams I want her to have instant recognition as a Masterpiece. I imagine stellar actors vying to play her roles. But as I discover some of her awkwardnesses, I realize, alas, that I am not a divine Thalia, effortlessly fashioning dazzling comedies. Rather I must accept myself as that earthbound Jewish tailor, arduously outfitting the baby, mending and remending her apparel to make her appear if not stunning, then at least presentable.

I continued to write about the bonding of women through comedy, but this time I cowrote, with Joanne Koch, a play with music, *Sophie, Totie and Belle,* about three gifted entertainers, Sophie Tucker, Totie Fields, and Belle Barth. These three innovative performers were funny, strong, and independent at a time when women weren't supposed to exhibit any of these traits. They were unkosher comediennes who broke tradition and flaunted taboos. Yet they made a remarkable contribution to American society. They were unique voices in the male world of comics. Together on stage in a quirky meeting in the afterlife, they share songs, anecdotes, routines, and self-discoveries. They compete, argue, and commiserate. Ultimately, they forge a close friendship before they do their last number—three women who have used humor to survive sexism, anti-Semitism, even ageism and, by so doing, have extended the boundaries of comedy.

This small musical, of three women and one man playing the significant other in their lives, has been very successful. It sold out its entire six-week run in Miami Beach in 1993 and played for another ten weeks in Boca Raton. It has been optioned for a tour in 1996 in New York, New Jersey, and Florida.

We also recently wrote a play with music on the life of Sophie Tucker, titled *Sophie Tucker: Red Hot Yiddishe Mama,* and a screenplay on the life of Belle Barth, titled *Belle.* We hope to entice Bette Midler, Roseanne, or Lainie Kazan to play the leading roles.

To appease my feelings of guilt for straying too far from the academic, in 1993 I cowrote *Saul Bellow's Stories on Stage,* sponsored by the New York State Writers Institute in Albany. With Nobel Laureate Saul Bellow's permission, I adapted his story "The Old System" and Joanne Koch adapted his story "A Silver Dish." The two one-act plays were chosen by the Streisand Festival and performed with Harold Gould the next year at the Gas Lamp Theatre in San Diego. As the author of a book on Bellow's humor, *Saul Bellow's Enigmatic Laughter,* I was able to recreate the ruefully comic memories of an aging scientist about his immigrant relatives living in Albany and Schenectady from 1910 to the 1950s. Although there are major family rifts over real estate transactions, there is ultimately mutual forgiveness and reaffirmation of affection between them so that the scientist, like Bellow's Herzog, can say: "My heart is attached with great power" to my immigrant family. "Here is a wider range of human feelings than I had ever again been able to find."

To reestablish my autonomy as a playwright without a collaborator, in 1994 I wrote my own play with music, *Molly Picon's Return Engagement.* This two-person play about Molly Picon and her scriptwriting husband, Jacob Kalich, is a musical revival of the spirited life and career of Molly, the diminutive but dazzling star of vaudeville, Yiddish theater, and film. It celebrates her meteoric rise to Broadway, Hollywood, London, and theaters around the world. Although Molly was hailed for her performances as the "Yiddish Helen Hayes" and a "bean-sized Bernhardt," in *Molly Picon's Return Engagement,* she is endearingly depicted in three phases of her life: as a young woman, as a married woman opposite her husband, and as a widow.

Molly Picon was particularly touched in 1946, when she was one of the first entertainers to visit the European camps for displaced persons. A woman came up to her with a little girl and said, "My child is two years old and she has never heard the sound of laughter." Jacob Kalich told Molly, "That's our job. Make them laugh!" Throughout her career Molly made them laugh. My *Molly Picon* play, in turn, has made them laugh in all the places it has appeared: the Modern Language Convention in Chicago, Toronto, Milwaukee, Syracuse, the Berkshires, the Catskills, Miami Beach, Boca Raton, Atlanta, Washington, D.C., Highland Park, Costa Mesa, Minneapolis, Cleveland, Albany. So, I, too, as a Jewish-American playwright, have been inspired by the comic muse and have attempted to transform the woeful into the whimsical or to seesaw between the two. Like Molly, I am committed to making people laugh.

The Ladies Locker Room by Sarah Blacher Cohen was sponsored by the New York State Writers Institute and the University at Albany's Disabled Student Services at the Lewis A. Swyer Theatre of the Empire Center, Albany, New York, on April 23 and April 24, 1994. The cast was as follows:

Lillian Lux*	John Whiteheade
Daphne A. Bladen	Martha Schmulback
Carolyn Rosenthal	Anneke Bull
Laure Jackson	Dan Ruge

Director: Frieda Scott Giles
Set Designer: Scott Dahl
Costumes: Sandy Davisson
Lighting: Paul Cowell
Sound: Christopher Pfeiffer
Props: Nathalie Lewis
Stage Managers: William Arthur Rennie and Alyssa Tullin

In April, 1989, the staged reading of *The Ladies Locker Room* was sponsored by the New York State Writers Institute. In June, 1990, *The Ladies Locker Room* received a Workshop Production at the Jewish Cultural Arts Center in St. Louis. In April, 1991, *The Ladies Locker Room* received a full stage production at Northwestern University.

The Ladies Locker Room
1989

Characters

SOPHIE, mideighties, amazingly fit for her age. Extremely gregarious and lovingly manipulative. She amuses most but annoys a few. She speaks with a pronounced Yiddish Eastern-European accent.

EMILY, early seventies, extremely fastidious about her grooming, rather judgmental about those who are not.

SUSAN, midthirties, a university English professor, suffers from a muscle-nerve disease that is mildly visible. She has a forced cheerfulness and sardonic wit.

*We wish to thank New York Actors Equity for permission to have Lillian Lux appear as a guest artist in the benefit performances for Disabled Student Services.

GRETA, early sixties, Viennese refugee, successful in real estate. Does not allow self-pity to interfere with her zest for life.

PEGGY, midtwenties, in an advanced stage of pregnancy. Rosy-cheeked and brimming with life, she is intent on doing what's best for her body and imminently future baby. She has read every manual on childbirth and reveres her obstetrician as a fount of wisdom. In the beginning she is obnoxiously narcissistic. (May be played by a woman of color.)

MOTHER, late fifties, long-suffering and overly protective. Beneath her solicitude is a strain of anger for being cursed with a disabled daughter.

CABDRIVER, short on intelligence, patience, and cash, is constantly hustling to get the best fare. Brutalized by the city, he has no time for the social amenities, no use for compassion.

ACTOR, a man in his late thirties, both the English nobleman lover of Queen Elizabeth in the play, *Elizabeth the Queen,* by Maxwell Anderson, and in real life the effete, narcissistic actor who plays the role of Essex.

BOTANIST, midthirties, a shy sensitive, intellectual scientist who adores Susan.

DOCTOR, a cold, professional man in his forties or fifties who views patients as objects, not human beings.

VOICE-OVER OF OBSTETRICIAN.

All of these male roles can be played by one versatile male actor. The Mother, the Cabdriver, the Actor, the Botanist, and the Doctor are not fully fleshed characters but voices in Susan's head. In an intimate thrust stage, these voice characters can appear on the periphery of the set or on the set itself, with a spotlight on them, and then they quickly disappear.

Setting

A Jewish Center locker room. A lounge area in the locker room decked out in comfortable hand-me-down furniture, including a rocking chair and a coffee table. Upstage are lockers with benches in front of them, a screen for changing and a full-length mirror.

Time

The very recent past.

ACT I

Susan, alone in the lounge area of the locker room, lifts heavy ankle weights and sings strains of "Havana Gilah" to help her bear the pain.

SUSAN. (*Sings with great effort, punctuated by labored sighs.*) Ha va na gi lah, Ha va na gi lah, Ha va na gi lah, Vi nis ma cho. (*Winded.*) Now the other leg. (*She unstraps the Velcro ankle weight from one leg and straps it onto the other one and resumes her singing.*) Bim bom, bim bim bim bom. Bim bom, bim, bim, bim bom.

SOPHIE. (*Enters from the swimming pool, hears Susan singing and joins in.*) Bim bom bim bim bim bom. *Alt und kalt.* Old and cold. You know my dear, I come swimming every day. If the bus don't pick me up, I walk here all the way from Myrtle Avenue. In summer and winter for forty-six years now. But I don't see you in the pool so much lately, Dr. Susan. I miss you when you're not here.

SUSAN. I've been busy with other things. (*Susan continues working with ankle weights.*)

SOPHIE. Busy with what?

SUSAN. I don't know. Just busy.

SOPHIE. Too busy to wash for me the back? The chlorine from the water, it stings and if you don't get it off, it hurts for a long time.

SUSAN. I can't just now, Sophie. I need to finish my hamstring exercises.

SOPHIE. Hamstrings is not kosher. In the Jewish Center you have to exercise with other people. Not all the time by yourself.

SUSAN. Sorry, Sophie.

SOPHIE. You want I should become a pickled herring from the chlorine?

SUSAN. Alright, Sophie, let me have the washcloth. (*She wipes Sophie's back with some difficulty.*) You know, too much chlorine can damage the tissue.

SOPHIE. Is that so! Then my tissue and me thank you.

SUSAN. Oh, dammit. I just dropped your clean washcloth.

SOPHIE. (*Reaching for it.*) It's okay. I'll get it.

SUSAN. (*Bending down laboriously.*) No, I'll pick it up.

SOPHIE. While you're down there, you can scrub the floor maybe.

SUSAN. (*Laughing.*) Well I could, but I don't do windows.

SOPHIE. So what kinda cleaning lady are you?

SUSAN. Lousy, but I still want that Good Housekeeping Seal of Approval.

MOTHER. (*A voice character in Susan's head.*) No, you cannot iron your own blouses. You put in more wrinkles than you take out. And I don't want to catch you practicing. You know you can't stand that long. Your sister'll do it for you. She's good at those things. She can do them just like that, but it's too hard for you. You get too exhausted. Even dusting. I have to go over whatever you do. You miss things. You leave spots. You got to rub real hard. You're just not strong enough, Susan.

SUSAN. (*Talks back to mother visible only to her.*) Couldn't I just try? There must be something I can do to please you.

SOPHIE. Dr. Susan! You want approval? You can rub a little Ben Gay on me. Here.

SUSAN. (*Unstraps her ankle weights and begins applying Ben Gay to Sophie's back.*) At your service, madame. Sophie, what a beautiful back you have.

SOPHIE. Not beautiful, *sexy!* Cause *five* men come to visit me every day.

SUSAN. Five? *Oy vey!*

SOPHIE. First, *Will Power* gets me up every morning and takes me to the *John.* Then, *Charley Horse* comes. After him, *Arthuritis* settles in and I go to sleep every night with *Ben Gay.* (*They laugh.*) So how about you? How many men do you see every day?

SUSAN. Mostly Charley Horse and Arthuritis.

SOPHIE. Come on, Dr. Susan, you must meet a lot of professional men. Doctors, lawyers, accountants.

SUSAN. There are no professional men in my life.

SOPHIE. So what about unprofessional? No butchers, bakers, plumbers? Sometimes they treat a girl better than those high class guys.

SUSAN. I swear. No butchers or bakers hiding under my bed. Not even a plumber.

SOPHIE. If you find one, he could fix a lotta things.

SUSAN. Sophie, let's change the subject.

SOPHIE. Alright. How about combing my hair? It always looks so beautiful when you do it.

PEGGY. (*Entering eating an apple.*) Is this the ladies locker room?

SOPHIE. It ain't the men's.

PEGGY. Oh I wouldn't care if it was. In California we have coed locker rooms.

SUSAN. Yes, of course, coed locker rooms.

PEGGY. But I've gotten used to what you have out here. My only problem is that the prenatal swim class was canceled at the Y. They're fixing the pool.

SOPHIE. Come on in, California. This pool works. Hello, my name is Sophie and this here is Dr. Susan from the university. What's your name, my dear?

PEGGY. I'm Peggy. Do they have water aerobics here?

SUSAN. No, but there's a hydroslimnastics class at one.

PEGGY. Oh, good. I can do my daily swim and still make the class. I always try my best to keep fit.

SUSAN. You seem to be succeeding.

SOPHIE. That's for sure. How long you been preggling?

SUSAN. Aren't you trespassing a bit on her privacy, Sophie?

SOPHIE. Somebody else was trespassing, not me. You got a husband?

PEGGY. Of course I do.

SOPHIE. What does he do for a living?

PEGGY. He's a lawyer.

SOPHIE. Oh, one of them high class guys.

SUSAN. Sophie!

PEGGY. He'll be a *high class father* too. Jim goes to all my natural childbirth classes with me. He's become an expert on the Lamaze method. He knows more about my pregnancy than I do. Do you have any children, Susan?

SUSAN. No, I don't.

PEGGY. You and your husband don't want any.

SUSAN. Actually, I'm not married.

PEGGY. Oh, well, just wait until you are. Having a child is really a wonderful experience.

SUSAN. I'm sure it is for some people. But being single doesn't rule out having children. Why, there are women who make more withdrawals at the sperm bank than they do at the cash station.

PEGGY. Thank goodness, Jim and I didn't need that. (*Slight pause.*)

SUSAN. Has it been a difficult pregnancy?

PEGGY. Difficult? What do you mean?

SUSAN. Well . . . you know . . . your legs. Has it been hard on your legs? And on your back?

PEGGY. No, not at all. But my doctor told me I was in very good shape to begin with.

SUSAN. I see . . .

PEGGY. Yes, I've always done aerobics and Nautilus and since I got pregnant, I've started swimming, so I'm in great shape. I'm as strong and flexible as ever.

SUSAN. Yes, I can see that . . .

PEGGY. Oh Susan, forgive me for asking. Is there something the matter with your legs? When I came in, you seemed to be walking funny.

SUSAN. (*Pained and then strainedly lying.*) I have some blisters on my heels. They'll go away.

PEGGY. Oh, good. As long as it's nothing serious. Well I'm off to my swim. (*Gets up to leave.*)

SUSAN. (*Slowly filling with anger.*) Would you mind moving some of your things from this bench and my locker? They're sort of in my way.

PEGGY. (*Starts to remove things from the locker.*) I'm sorry. I'll take my things to another locker. (*She rummages in the locker and picks up Susan's heavy orthopedic shoes and says with disgust*) Hey, what are these? An old lady must have left her orthopedic shoes in here by mistake. (*She drops them as they make a heavy thud.*)

SUSAN. (*Bends down to pick them up and painfully says*) Those shoes are mine. (*Angry.*) And now would you please leave this bench.

SOPHIE. That's okay. There's room for both of you.

PEGGY. Not much room. I'm due in a week and a half. See you later . . . (*She exits.*)

SUSAN. And she is still swimming . . .

SOPHIE. Now, would you comb my hair?

SUSAN. Sure. Glad to. But you come over here. You zoom around this place like the Twentieth Century Limited. Not a stalled freight car like me.

SOPHIE. Stalled? What are you talking? You're a busy lady. You teach, you travel, you give lectures, you write books, you . . .

SUSAN. Forget it, Sophie. I'm giving all that up.

SOPHIE. How come? Everybody respects you.

SUSAN. I don't respect me.

SOPHIE. You can always have a job in my college.

SUSAN. Sophie, I'm tired of everything. Even simple things—like just getting to the conferences, dealing with the cabdrivers. (*Spotlight on Cabdriver.*)

CABDRIVER. So this lady gets into my cab. I say, where to, lady? She says, "New York Hilton." That's only two blocks away, I say. "I know," she says, "just drive me there." Anything you say, lady. Just my luck—a two block fare, I say to myself. So I pull up to the hotel—as close as I can get. "But this is almost a block from the entrance to the hotel," she says. "I can't walk that far. You've got to drop me off at the entrance." But lady, I say, there's a line of cars ahead of me and I can't wait all day. I got other fares to pick up. "I'll pay you for your time," she says. Well, what am I supposed to say? Okay, okay, but next time, lady, take an ambulance!

SUSAN. (*To Cabdriver . . . angry and hurt . . .*) Drop dead, your jerk! Who needs your damn cab! (*Softly.*) I do. (*Spotlight off as Cabdriver disappears. Returns to Sophie.*) Cabdrivers can be so rude! Even when I said, "Up yours, mister," he didn't bat an eye. . . . But what am I gonna do? Walk?? (*Pause.*) You know, when I was a kid, the other kids threw snowballs at me because I *walked funny.*

SOPHIE. Some people don't like me because I *talk funny.* They say I talk with an accent. How is it before I came to America I didn't have no accent? And they don't like the way I look, the wrinkles, the white hair. Even my daughter wants to make me a blond so she won't have an old lady for a mother.

SUSAN. That's ridiculous! On a scale of one to ten, I'd say you're a nine and a half, Sophie.

SOPHIE. So what about the other half point? Just 'cause I'm old, people don't go out of their way for me. They're always too busy. But I tell them how young they look, and they should live to be my years. Sometimes I get a favor from that. I make friends with strangers one, two, three.

EMILY. (*Entering.*) Sophie, cover yourself up. How can you wear something like that in front of everybody? It's not right for a woman your age.

SOPHIE. And some friends I would like to make strangers. What're you doing here?

EMILY. I came to rehearse for the senior variety show. You know, you shouldn't walk around half naked. The little kids come through here.

SOPHIE. What I have is not so special to see.

EMILY. And Sophie, don't forget what I told you, put on your panties first, before you put on your pantyhose. Otherwise you'll get an infection. I know 'cause I read it in *Cosmopolitan.*

SOPHIE. Emily, maybe you got an extra blouse or sweater? I get so cold, like a tree without leaves.

EMILY. You shouldn't be a *schnorrer.* There's infections in hand-me-downs. Don't your children buy you clothes?

SOPHIE. They have other things to do with their money.

EMILY. But taking care of their mother is more important.

SOPHIE. I never see your daughter and son going out of their way for you.

EMILY. Thank God, I'm comfortably fixed. I don't need their help.

SOPHIE. How come they never see you in any of your senior variety shows?

EMILY. My son has an important job at the legislature and my daughter is a champion bridge player. They're busy all the time. They hardly see their own families so how can they take time for me? . . . But when a mother has to go begging, like you, that's shameful.

SOPHIE. If it don't bother me, why should it bother you? Instead of *schlepping* things to the rummage sale, people like to give them to me. I'm their rummage sale. Dr. Susan, maybe you got some outfits for me?

SUSAN. Sure. Come to my house and take what you want.

SOPHIE. Oh thank you. It's an honor to get used clothes from such a big professor, a doctor.

SUSAN. Yes, a doctor who fixes split infinitives and dangling modifiers. . . . Emily, that's a nice dress you're wearing.

EMILY. It's a Christian Dior. I went through every rack at Loehmann's until I found it. They had a couple more left. Why don't you hurry over and get one for yourself? A new dress makes you feel good.

SUSAN. No. No Christian Dior for me. (*Imitating Sophie.*) It's not kosher.

SOPHIE. You can pour salt over it. Then it'll be kosher.

SUSAN. Seriously, Emily, you really take good care of yourself.

EMILY. An older woman has to make the most of her looks. My daughter and her bridge players at the country club are very particular about their appearance. If I want to go with them, I have to be in style.

SOPHIE. You mean if you don't look good, they leave you home.

EMILY. That never happens.

SOPHIE. Maybe, if I get some stylish clothes from the rummage sale, they'll let *me* into the country club.

EMILY. Not the way you behave. You need better manners. You're always mixing in other people's conversations . . . but the country club isn't everything. As my mother used to say, "Too much leisure stiffens the helping hand." I see what happens to people who sit in the lobby waiting for someone to entertain them. They turn into a mushy stew from cooking on the stove too long.

SOPHIE. Just like my kasha. It sticks to the pot.

EMILY. Speaking of helping hands, did you know I was chairman of the Abigail fund-raising dinner and we made over one thousand dollars? We had Jerrold Pritzker's three-man band and Amy Leclair singing Richard Rodgers' songs. The girls loved it and gave the biggest pledges ever. It made me feel so good.

SOPHIE. Emily, you wanna feel good now? How 'bout using those helping hands to hook up my brassiere?

EMILY. I'm sorry, Sophie, I can't. My fingers are too stiff.

SUSAN. Too bad, Sophie. You're stuck with me.

SOPHIE. You got bigger things to think about than my brassiere.

SUSAN. Very funny, Sophie. You mean my hands can't do it either.

SOPHIE. Okay, you wanna hook it up? Hook it up!

SUSAN. At long last, I get to be a hooker. . . . (*Grunts, sighs!*) Damn these hooks! I give up. Sophie, you were right . . . can't do it.

EMILY. It's no tragedy, Dr. Susan. Come over here, Sophie. Do what I do. Fasten your brassiere in the front and then *twist* it around to the back. (*Emily demonstrates with an imaginary bra, then Sophie struggles with her own bra, which she puts on over her bathing smock.*)

SOPHIE. Okay, I'll try it but I may get it all twisted up. *Oy vey!*

EMILY. Sophie, are you doing what I told you?

SOPHIE. *Vey is mir!*

EMILY. Sophie, you can do it.

SOPHIE. *Oy,* my arm is stuck.

EMILY. How can that be?

SOPHIE. Now it's unstuck. . . . Oh, I done it. (*They applaud. Then Sophie changes behind the screen and comes out.*) You see, Dr. Susan, a good trick, you can do it this way too. It's good not to ask for help. Better to do for yourself and for other people.

EMILY. True. As my Aunt Rebecca used to say, "If you have a big pot of stewed prunes, share some with the most constipated. By giving more you're gaining more." . . . Sophie, where is your slip? You can't wear a dress without a slip. Everything will show through.

SOPHIE. So, it will show through. Is somebody looking?

EMILY. But Sophie, you have to be a lady.

SOPHIE. Says who? Lady is for rich, not poor. Me, I'm poor. In Bialystok, I had a piece bread and a piece herring for my supper. When I didn't, I'd sing the potato song and my stomach wouldn't hurt so much. "*Montag, Bulbas, Denstag, Bulbas and Shabbas, a kugele of Bulbas.*" I remember like it was yesterday.

EMILY. When my father died young, I used to sing to keep happy too. *He* was a cantor on the lower East Side and *I* became the soloist for the senior variety show. (*Emily sings.*) "Shine on, shine on harvest moon up in the sky. I ain't had no lovin' since January, February, June or July." Oh, I just love to sing.

SUSAN. I used to love singing too. Saturday mornings at the synagogue with the old men. (*Spotlight on Susan and Mother.*)

SUSAN. *Yismachu, b'malachuzecho,*
  Shomrai, Shomrai,
  Shomrai Shabbos
  V'korey Oneg Shabbos.

MOTHER. Don't sing at the top of your lungs. You're too loud for a girl. You're drowning out the men. And you're getting too old to sit with the men. Sit in the women's section and act like a lady. Try not to call attention to yourself . . . with those shoes. Whisper and tiptoe in during the service. Why can't you be like the other girls?

SUSAN. *V'tahere Libaynu. V'tahere Libaynu, V'tahere Libaynu, V'avdecho B'emet.*

MOTHER. Oh, there you go again! Didn't I tell you? Keep your voice down. You're embarrassing me. People are looking at you. (*Spotlight off Mother, who disappears.*)

EMILY. I didn't know you had such a pretty voice. You should sing more often.

SOPHIE. You can always sing with us girls whenever you want. Say Emily, what's your song this year for the seniors?

EMILY. I think I'll do "The Indian Love Call." You know the one Nelson Eddy and Jeanette McDonald used to sing? I'll be Jeanette and Sam Rabinowitz will be Nelson.

SOPHIE. Nelson Eddy and Jeanette McDonald? They don't sound like Indians to me. What kind of love do they make?

EMILY. They're musical comedy stars and this was their most romantic song. "When I'm calling you, hu, hu, hu, hu, hu, hu. Will you answer too, hu, hu, hu, hu, hu . . ."

SOPHIE. Since when is there an owl in the "Indian Love Call?"

EMILY. (*Continues with the song.*) "That means I offer my love to you, to be your own."

SOPHIE. Love can be beautiful in a song, but not always beautiful in life. It's like getting a crispy blintze on the outside, then finding hardly no cheese on the inside. But in the old days, people settled for the half-filled blintze.

SUSAN. Nowadays they prefer fancy crepes suzettes.

SOPHIE. So, without them *creplach suzettes,* I guess nobody's looked in your icebox for a long time. What do you do for that?

EMILY. Oh, Sophie!

SUSAN. You really want to know? When I was a teenager, I'd call men I didn't know on the phone.

SOPHIE. Hmmm! Sounds good. Tell us more, Dr. Susan.

EMILY. Yes, tell us.

SUSAN. Well, I'd call up some "tavern" and I'd say, "Can I speak to that handsome young guy sitting at the bar? . . . Yeah, Frank, right." Then I'd say, "Hi, Frank. You don't know me but I've been watching you for a long time. You're real strong-looking and sexy! I bet you're great in bed. . . . I can't wait to find out! . . . Tonight? Oh, uh, I'm afraid I'm busy, but let's connect. Soon. I'll call you." (*Sophie and Emily clap and hoot.*)

EMILY. "When I'm calling you, hu, hu, hu, hu, hu, hu . . ."

SOPHIE. Oooh! You naughty girl—"great in bed."

EMILY. Dr. Susan, I'm surprised at you.

SOPHIE. She was only talking, not doing.

EMILY. But you know, Dr. Susan, you can't fill up that icebox when you order on the phone. You have to shop in person.

SUSAN. Sometimes you don't want your "icebox" full.

SOPHIE. How can that be?

SUSAN. Well, you get used to the bare spaces. You don't like to feel crowded.

SOPHIE. You feel crowded now?

SUSAN. Yes, I do.

SOPHIE. You mean there's a man in your icebox and he don't work for Frigidaire?

SUSAN. Yes.

SOPHIE. So, what are you going to do with this man?

SUSAN. That's just it. I don't know.

EMILY. Who is he? What does he do?

SUSAN. He's a botanist.

SOPHIE. He's a what?

EMILY. A botanist. You know—he studies plants. Where did you meet him?

SUSAN. At the Botanical Garden. He was standing by a ficus . . .

SOPHIE. By a what?

SUSAN. A fig tree . . . with a fig leaf in front of him.

SOPHIE. So far so good. How long you known him?

SUSAN. Since last summer.

SOPHIE. Is he still wearing that fig leaf?

EMILY. Sophie, that's none of your business.

SOPHIE. Okay, so what do you do with him, this botanist with a fig leaf and no name?

SUSAN. Jonathan and I, well, we do all kinds of things. We go to lectures, concerts, and plays. We read aloud to each other. (*Spotlight on Botanist.*)

BOTANIST. Before I met you, my culture was horticulture. The only literature I liked was Joyce Kilmer's "Trees." But you introduced me to so many new works: *The Cherry Orchard, The Wind in the Willows, The Garden of Earthly Delights.* You gave me a new way of viewing nature that was wonderful. But you're even more wonderful.

SUSAN. (*To Botanist.*) I'm wonderful . . . (*soft laughter*) . . . I'm wonderful. . . . Do you really mean that? (*Spotlight off Botanist who disappears. Back to Sophie and Emily.*) The lectures and concerts are fine, but last week Jonathan invited me to the Botanists' Ball.

EMILY. Oh, that'll be lots of fun.

SUSAN. No, it'll be awful. I can't dance.

EMILY. We'll teach you. Come here, Sophie, and dance with me. We'll show Dr. Susan. I'll lead.

SOPHIE. No, I'll lead.

EMILY. We'll both lead. One two three, one two three. (*Emily sings the opening strains of "The Anniversary Song" and then hums the rest of the song.*) "Oh how we danced on the night we were wed . . ."

SOPHIE. Ouch, you squashed my bunion. Is that how they teach you to dance at the Country Club?

EMILY. I took rhumba, samba, and tango lessons and never once did I squash anyone's bunions. I got the Ginger Rogers award for best dancer . . . over 70. Dr. Susan, I'm sure I can help you. Come dance with me. I promise I won't step on you.

SOPHIE. I'm not so sure.

SUSAN. But I might step on you.

EMILY. Now relax, Dr. Susan, and we'll glide over the floor.

SUSAN. Schlep is more like it.

EMILY. Just relax. "Oh how we danced on the night we were wed . . ."

SUSAN. Oh my God, did I just step on you? Is that a bruise on your shin? I must have kicked you there.

EMILY. (*Lying.*) No, it's just a varicose vein I've always had. Let's try again. One two three, one two . . .

SUSAN. It's no use. I can't do it. I feel like a *klutz.*

SOPHIE. Take a little rest. Then you can try it again.

SUSAN. No, I've had it with dancing.

EMILY. You mean you're not going to the ball?

SUSAN. No. I'd rather be a shrinking violet at home than a wall-flower at the ball.

PEGGY. (*Entering from the pool.*) Excuse me, ladies. I forgot to bring my goggles. I need them to practice my underwater ballet pirouettes.

SUSAN. I'm sure the lap swimmers will appreciate that.

PEGGY. I sneak them in when they're not looking. I also pretend the pool is one gigantic womb where I perform a *pas de deux* with an imaginary partner. See you later. (*Peggy exits.*)

EMILY. Do you think that's sanitary?

SUSAN. Hey, maybe I should try an imaginary partner. I won't step on him and he won't step on me.

EMILY. I know, Dr. Susan, life *can* be disappointing. We can't always do what we want. I yearned to be a famous soprano, but instead I married Bernie, a gourmet caterer for Affairs Incorporated.

SOPHIE. And the singing?

EMILY. At the beginning—lots. We made beautiful music together in our little apartment in the Bronx. And Bernie brought home flowers and pâté and canapés and petit fours from all the receptions he ran. It was a party every night.

SOPHIE. But don't day-old food and day-old love get a little stale and soggy after a while?

EMILY. Some things stay fresh a long time. But then Bernie's father needed help with his tin can business in Albany. Overnight, no more gourmet. But I still decorated the shop on Pearl Street with the prettiest plastic azaleas. (*Sophie pantomimes decorating a shop with azaleas.*)

SUSAN. Then what happened?

EMILY. The worst. Bernie went to a tin can convention in Acapulco and died of appendicitis—at forty-nine yet. I never did become a famous soprano, but I can still sing "The Indian Love Call." (*She starts singing.*) "When I'm calling you, hu, hu, hu . . ."

SUSAN. That should make the seniors forget their troubles.

SOPHIE. *Oy,* troubles. Don't talk to me about troubles. Six weeks I was cooped up in a big ship coming alone from Bialystok. I weighed seventy-eight pounds when a cousin from Albany took me in. I had to beg in the streets. Later when they found me a man to marry, he didn't have no money neither. At restaurants, he bought me a glass tea and a pickle. He talked a lot and had plenty ideas on things he didn't know about. So he became a teacher.

SUSAN. Best definition of a teacher I've heard.

SOPHIE. But soon my husband got too nervous and became a paint-ner. Then before you could put in a spoonful of borscht and take it out, we had three babies. So I would go to bed later than him and get up before him, so we wouldn't have no more children. *Oy*, did we have troubles.

EMILY. But nobody likes to hear about other people's troubles. Better to smile and say everything's fine. That's what I do. At the variety show last year, I sang "Climb Every Mountain," you know, from *The Sound of Music.* People really liked it. They said it gave them courage to go on. (*She sings.*) "Climb every mountain."

SOPHIE. *Oy*, it makes me tired just listening to you climbing every mountain. Walking to the Center every day is enough for me.

EMILY. It's symbolic. Every mountain doesn't mean every mountain. It means facing every trouble and not running away from the pain. Say, Dr. Susan, you will be M.C. of this year's variety show again, won't you?

SUSAN. No. I don't think so.

EMILY. Come on, we're depending on you to tell us some of your jokes.

SUSAN. I can't.

EMILY. Then at least tell us one joke that we can use later.

SOPHIE. We need you to make us laugh.

EMILY. Please, Dr. Susan, keep us smiling.

SUSAN. All right, all right, already. Here goes: There was this rich old lady who went to her lawyer and said, (*in a British accent*) "I want to make out my will. When I die, I want to be cremated and have my ashes scattered on the first three floors of Bloomingdale's." "Why would you want to do that," said her lawyer. "Well," said the lady, "at least that way I can be certain my daughter will visit me once a week."

SOPHIE. You're a funny girl, Dr. Susan.

SUSAN. Yeah, I know, even when I'm not joking. In college I wanted so much to be a serious actress and finally I got to play Elizabeth the Queen! "Lord Essex, . . . Why could you not have loved me enough to give me your love and let me keep as I was?" (*Spotlight on Actor.*)

ACTOR. I'll tell you why. She ruined the play, that's why. We're right at the most dramatic moment. I'm just about to make my big exit and all of a sudden—bang—her kneecap pops and she's on the floor commanding me to pull down the curtain. What are you doing,

I say. Are you crazy? "Yes," she tells me, "I have delusions I'm a queen!" Queen? Ha! She's a goddamn joker.

SUSAN. (*To Actor.*) Then why isn't anybody laughing? . . . (*Spotlight off Actor, who disappears. Back to Sophie.*) Well, I was no queen when I spent a year in bed because of a screwed up knee operation. (*Pause.*) But the thought of never going on a stage again—that hurt worse.

SOPHIE. Why never? What about Sarah Heartburn?

EMILY. Bernhardt, Sophie!

SOPHIE. Yeah, her. She acted on wooden legs.

SUSAN. My legs felt wooden for a long time, but I didn't act again.

SOPHIE. Maybe you don't act on the stage no more, but you get a lot of attention from your students when you teach.

SUSAN. Yes, my captive audience. (*Suddenly brightening.*) But . . . you're right. They are a . . . great audience! From my desk chair, which is my thrust stage, I get to perform my favorite roles. I'm the Madwoman from Chaillot. (*In a French accent.*) "I have my dogs to feed and cats to pet." Or I'm Maura from *Riders to the Sea.* (*In an Irish accent.*) "They're all gone now. There isn't anything more the sea can do to me."

SOPHIE. I never knew you was part Irish.

SUSAN. Or if I want to be funny, I can be Lady Bracknell from *The Importance of Being Earnest.* (*In a British accent.*) "A man should know everything or nothing. Which do you know? I disapprove of anything which tampers with natural ignorance."

EMILY. Dr. Susan, you're making us laugh again.

SUSAN. I make my students laugh too. Especially when I play parts not supposed to be comic . . . like my rendition of Blanche Du Bois opposite a Brooklyn freshman as Stanley Kowalski. (*In a Southern accent.*) "Western Union? Yes! I—want to—Take down this message! 'In desperate, desperate circumstances! Help me! Caught in a trap. Caught in—' Oh!" My accent is so phoney that I start giggling and Tennessee Williams turns over in his grave.

SOPHIE. So all of you are having a good time together.

SUSAN. Yes, for a little while, I'm the class clown and I forget about my wooden legs. (*Greta enters.*)

GRETA. I hope you haven't forgotten about me.

SOPHIE. Not for a minute. Come in, Greta, come in. Welcome back to the locker room.

SUSAN. We haven't seen you in a while.

EMILY. Where have you been?

GRETA. Away on business.

SUSAN. Working on national and international mergers?

GRETA. I'm not at liberty to say. But my work has been high-leveled and high-powered with high-class men.

EMILY. You've had no time for volunteering then?

SOPHIE. You mean mixing into other people's affairs?

GRETA. (*Seductively.*) I have more affairs than I know what to do with.

EMILY. You must be away from your husband quite often.

GRETA. Yes, my work requires that I travel a great deal.

EMILY. I would never leave my husband for my work.

SOPHIE. But you never had a job.

EMILY. Thank goodness, I didn't need one. But if I had to work, my husband would always come first.

SUSAN. Freud says work and love are the two things that keep people happy.

GRETA. Yes, work and . . . (*seductively*) love! Say Sophie, have you been behaving yourself or have you been letting the boys get away with things?

SOPHIE. At my age, nothing much to do but behave. Do I have a choice?

GRETA. Sure you have a choice. You can be a sexy old lady or you can be a Jewish princess. While you're deciding, I'm going to grab my swim and you better grab your lunch.

SOPHIE. Lunch I can always have. If I don't eat with the seniors on time, I have an egg and a cold potato with me, just in case, for emergencies. . . . So Greta, how do you feel? Your new breasts look real nice. Before they were big like cantaloupes. Now they're smaller, like peaches.

EMILY. Sophie, don't refer to human anatomy as pieces of fruit.

SUSAN. Greta, how do you feel?

GRETA. Now that I'm through with the chemotherapy, I feel pretty good.

SUSAN. You are truly remarkable. Double mastectomy, reconstruction, chemo—and yet you carry your burden like it was a basket of chicken feathers.

GRETA. Well it may look like chicken feathers, but it feels more like a tub of dirty diapers. You know the old saying, "Life is like a baby's shirt, short in front and becocked in the back." . . . Still you go on. But there are some stains you cannot remove.

EMILY. When I scrub real hard, I can always get my undies clean.

SOPHIE. Greta's not talking about dirty bloomers, Emily!

GRETA. I wish it were that simple. I also try hard to get rid of the dark memories, the black thoughts. . . . Maybe that's why I travel so much and work all the time. So I won't have to think about the past.

SUSAN. I understand, Greta.

GRETA. Yet no matter how many profitable deals I make, or how many intriguing people I meet, I can't stop remembering.

SUSAN. How difficult for you.

GRETA. Yes. Mostly at night I . . . remember . . . I remember we were a well-to-do family in Austria, with a cook, a maid, a gardener.

SOPHIE. Did you dance those Viennese waltzes? Maybe you could teach Dr. Susan how to . . .

EMILY. She has a ball to go to.

SUSAN. Now Emily . . .

GRETA. (*Greta waltzes with herself around the room.*) Oh, yes, we waltzed around glittering ballrooms, in flowing gowns, with full or-chestra—until 1938, when Hitler stopped the music.

SUSAN. Then the Nazis played another tune.

GRETA. Yes. My husband and I were just married. Life was just beginning for us. But then Jews were not allowed to get degrees from Vienna University. We had to leave. We had no choice. We caught the first boat out and found ourselves in Africa. Seven long years. Strangers, broke, scared and alone. Somehow we had to make a living . . .

EMILY. But you weren't the only ones. A lot of people went through much worse.

GRETA. That's true. I was grateful to be alive then and I'm grateful to be alive now. I'm past sixty and people tell me I don't look my age, because my system produces extra hormones. But those hor-mones gave me the breast cancer. So go figure it. Nature gives you something extra to look young and then kills you with it.

EMILY. Why do you have to be so grim?

SUSAN. Greta has gallows humor.

GRETA. Better than begging for pity. There's a German saying, "*Baume wachsen nich in den Himmel.* Trees don't grow into heaven. They're cut down before they reach it." I accept the fact that I'm one of those trees, but while I'm here, I'm going to keep on growing and shake my leaves in the sunlight and you should do the same thing, Dr. Susan.

EMILY. There's nothing like a new dress to give you a lift.

SOPHIE. *Oy,* Emily. *Sha!*

SUSAN. I'm better at shaking than growing.

GRETA. You're missing the point. Life means doing both. What do you think, Sophie?

SOPHIE. I think you're right, Greta. But me?—I don't think I'm a tree. More like a bush. Closer to the ground. Thank God I'm not in the ground.

GRETA. Yes Sophie, thank God. Everyone is glad you're still with us.

EMILY. Speak for yourself, Greta.

GRETA. That's why we let you swim sideways across the pool when everyone else is swimming the length. We want you to be with us until you're a hundred and twenty. Listen, I better take my swim now or I'll never make it to my closing.

EMILY. I, too, must get to my rehearsal. They can't manage without me. But I don't charge for my services, like Greta. I sing for free. Bye bye. (*Emily sings the scales as she exits. Greta groans and waves goodbye as she exits in the opposite direction.*)

SOPHIE. Bye Greta. What's the matter with you, Dr. Susele? You don't laugh no more 'cause I swim sideways.

SUSAN. I don't know. . . . It's my feet. (*Sophie assumes the pose of an orthopedic specialist, sits down next to Susan, lifts her feet and puts them over her lap.*)

SOPHIE. Your feet are not so bad. Just a little crooked here and there and maybe a few sores.

SUSAN. Very crooked and a lot of sores.

SOPHIE. Now you listen to me. I'm going to tell you how to take care on your feet. A very big doctor from Russia showed me what to do. First, he said, you go *pishing* in the morning, you save it in a big white pot, then you soak your feet there for ten minutes. The healthy chemicals from the *pishing* go straight into the holes in the feet and heal all the sores. I do this myself three, four times a day. And when you're through soaking your feet, don't wipe 'em. Let 'em dry natural.

SUSAN. But, Sophie, don't your feet stink?

SOPHIE. No, it don't stink. Try it. It'll make your feet all better.

SUSAN. But Sophie, the doctor said my feet would get worse.

SOPHIE. Not true. Listen to my doctor, the biggest from Russia. He had three diplomas, five offices, six satchels and his great grandfather was doctor to the Tsar. The Tsar soaked his feet in the *pishing* and they were much better off.

SUSAN. Too bad the Tsar didn't soak his head in the *pishing,* then we'd all be better off.

SOPHIE. It's not only the feet, is it, Dr. Susan?

SUSAN. No. It's—I haven't been sleeping very well lately.

SOPHIE. Why? Because things with the botanist are growing too fast?

SUSAN. Sophie, you are amazing.

SOPHIE. So?

SUSAN. He wants me to get engaged!

SOPHIE. *Mazel Tov!* That's wonderful!

SUSAN. No, it's not, Sophie. It's not that simple.

SOPHIE. What do you mean?

SUSAN. Well, for one thing, he insists I meet his parents.

SOPHIE. So what's to be worried? Are they the king and queen from England?

SUSAN. No, they're Louis and Estelle Klein from Scarsdale.

SOPHIE. Scarsdale! Hu ha! And what do they do for a living, these Kleins?

SUSAN. His father's a business executive, his mother's an interior decorator, and I'm a nervous wreck.

SOPHIE. A nervous wreck? What are you talking about? You're an English professor.

SUSAN. My clothes don't fit. My shoes don't fit. Face it, Sophie—I don't fit. I can't meet them.

SOPHIE. You can do it. We'll help you. You've heard of a wedding rehearsal?

SUSAN. What do you mean? A meet-the-parents rehearsal?

SOPHIE. Why not? You wait here and I'll get Greta from the pool and Emily from her singing. I'll say we need them to conduct important business in the locker room. Meanwhile, we'll borrow one of Emily's outfits. She's got a whole wardrobe in her locker. (*She ruffles through Emily's clothes.*) Here's a pretty dress. Try it on.

SUSAN. (*Refuses the dress.*) But that's like shoplifting.

SOPHIE. No, it's locker-lifting. But I give you permission, since it's for a good cause. Let me help you on with it. (*She takes a robe, a towel, a scarf, whatever's lying around, and creates a comic outfit, which she haphazardly drapes over Susan.*)

SUSAN. Why it's an Albert Nipon, Emily's most high-fashioned dress.

SOPHIE. (*As she is exiting, she shouts back.*) That'll be perfect for Scarsdale. I'll go get the girls to help. Yoohoo Greta, yoohoo, Emily. Hurry! Hurry! (*Quickly thereafter, Sophie, Greta, and Emily enter.*)

GRETA. So what's the important business? I don't have much time.

EMILY. (*Rushes to her opened locker.*) What's all this about? Oh, my locker's been burglarized. Call the police. Call the FBI. My wardrobe's been stolen.

SOPHIE. Calm down. Nobody took nothing. Dr. Susan just borrowed one of your dresses. She's getting engaged! She needs your outfit to visit the parents in Scarsdale. She needs our help.

GRETA. We'll be happy to help. Just tell us what to do.

SOPHIE. Greta, you be Louis Klein, the Scarsdale big shot, and Emily, you be Estelle Klein, the fancy decorator. Then Dr. Susan can get some practice as the girlfriend guest.

GRETA. All right, let's begin. (*Greta assumes the airs of a stuffy business executive.*) Welcome to our home, Dr. Susan, or may I call you Susan?

SUSAN. Susan is fine.

GRETA. Well then, Susan, let me introduce you to my wife, Estelle. She's the leading interior decorator in Scarsdale and she's a designing woman too.

EMILY. Now Louis, you're embarrassing me. How delighted I am to meet you, Susan. That's an Albert Nipon dress you're wearing, isn't it? I have several of them myself. But how becoming that one is on you.

SUSAN. I'm glad you like it.

GRETA. You know I'm a major shareholder in the Albert Nipon dress company. Since I invested in it, it's become the Mercedes Benz of the garment industry.

EMILY. Oh, forgive me, Susan dear. I haven't asked you to sit down. Why don't you try that Louis Quatorze settee, and I'll go fix us some tea and crumpets.

SUSAN. Thank you.

GRETA. So, Susan, how long have you known our son?

SUSAN. A little under a year.

GRETA. It's about time somebody took that boy in hand. He still thinks plants are a man's best friend. We hope you change that.

SUSAN. You know, relationships are like plants. They don't spring up overnight. They need time to grow.

GRETA. But a little of the right fertilizer can speed things up. (*Emily enters and hands Susan a cup of water and a bagel.*)

EMILY. Here's your tea and crumpets, my dear.

SUSAN. Why, thank you, Mrs. Klein.

EMILY. Call me Estelle.

SUSAN. Estelle.

GRETA. You see, Susan, Estelle and I aren't getting any younger. We're hoping you two will provide us with some little grandbaby plants before we wilt ourselves, don't we, dear?

EMILY. Yes, dear. (*Susan knocks over teacup.*)

SUSAN. Oh, no. I've spilt my tea. This is stupid!

SOPHIE. *Oy vey.*

GRETA. Did I say something?

EMILY. Perhaps we went too far, Greta.

SOPHIE. No, you tried your best. You go back to what you were doing. I'll talk to her. (*Greta and Emily exit.*) It looks like Albert Nipon won't be going to any more country clubs.

SUSAN. No, I guess not.

SOPHIE. It's the dress that's stained, not you.

SUSAN. Come on, Sophie. Just look at me. I'm clumsy, I'm stoop-shouldered, I'm knock-kneed, I'm high-arched, I'm butter-fingered . . .

SOPHIE. So that's why the botanist wants to marry you? (*Spotlight on Botanist.*)

BOTANIST. I'm good at talking to plants, not to people. That's why I like being with you. I don't have to say much and you know what I mean. . . . You're so special. . . . You beautify my life. . . . Marry me.

SUSAN. (*To Botanist, she says in amazement.*) Marry you? (*Spotlight off Botanist, who disappears. Back to Sophie.*) He never says much. He just looks at me adoringly. But what I can't figure out is why anybody would want damaged goods.

SOPHIE. He doesn't see the damaged, just the good.

SUSAN. Then he doesn't see straight.

SOPHIE. But love is cross-eyed.

SUSAN. I'm not getting married.

SOPHIE. Oh, Dr. Susan, don't make up your mind so fast. Think it over. (*Spotlight on Mother.*)

MOTHER. I just don't think you should go looking for your own apartment just because you've got yourself a job. You know you're getting weaker every year. How will you be able to run an apartment all by yourself? It's better to be in other people's houses. Then you'll have someone to depend on when you can't manage. Now, I wish things didn't have to be that way. If I could be around forever, I wouldn't worry so much. For a mother to take care of her sick child is a responsibility she accepts, but for strangers it's a burden. A husband would be fine. But a husband expects a wife to wait on him, Susan, not the other way around. You know that.

SUSAN. (*To Mother, repeats.*) I know that. (*Spotlight off Mother, who disappears. Back to Sophie.*) No, I've thought it over. Marriage is not for me. I would always worry about being a burden.

SOPHIE. You know, my dear, carrying a load of worries is like wearing galoshes in the summer. You spend so much time waiting for the snow to fall that you don't enjoy the sunshine. Listen, ten years ago the doctor said I had a cancer in the rectum and he wanted to operate, but I wouldn't let him. By eating lentil soup, I healed myself and I'm still alive today. So you got to stop worrying the way I did. Throw those galoshes in the garbage. Sit in the sunshine instead. (*Peggy enters.*) So how was your swimming in the womb?

SUSAN. And your underwater pirouettes?

PEGGY. Wonderful! My doctor says that pregnancy is not a disease or an entrapment. It's a special period of blooming.

SUSAN. Just what we need, more plants.

PEGGY. I think it's more like bearing fruit.

SUSAN. Oh, God.

PEGGY. In fact, he says that having a baby is the glorious fruition of two people's love.

SOPHIE. Yeah, fruit, when I was preggling, my belly was big and heavy like a watermelon.

PEGGY. I don't feel that heavy. I only gained fifteen pounds.

SOPHIE. Only fifteen pounds!

SUSAN. You must be on a very strict diet.

PEGGY. Yes I am.

SUSAN. It's hard to be on a diet, don't you think? What do you do when you're tired or angry?

PEGGY. I never let myself get that way, so I've had no trouble following my diet. It's a high protein, low fat diet for pregnant women under thirty, designed especially by my doctor. It comes with this cassette, which I carry with me at all times. It's called "Shut Your Mouth" and when I get the urge to cheat, I just pop the tape in instead. Wanna hear?

SUSAN. Why not? I have everything to lose and nothing to gain.

VOICE-OVER OF OBSTETRICIAN. You are a powerhouse of determination. Your willpower is awesome. You are highly motivated to eat only small portions. Your strong resolve causes unwanted fat to melt away. You can mold your body into a sculpture of perfect proportion. All you must do is: Shut your mouth.

PEGGY. He makes it so simple, doesn't he?

SUSAN. Yes, simple.

SOPHIE. But what about the baby in you? Is she on a diet too?

PEGGY. Yes, in a sense, she—or he—is. My doctor says that fat fetuses become fat children. That's why he's having my baby learn good eating habits now.

SOPHIE. You call eating small meals in a lotta belly water good eating habits?

PEGGY. Not only good eating habits. Exercise is important for the baby's health too. And relaxation through visualization. That's kept both the baby and me in excellent shape. Now I have to warm up before my hydrotherapy, so if you're interested, I'll give you a demonstration.

SOPHIE. Sure. Go ahead.

SUSAN. Great.

VOICE-OVER OF OBSTETRICIAN. (*Peggy does exercises to illustrate the Voice-over.*) The same stream of life that runs through your veins night and day runs through the world and dances in rhythmic measure. It is the same life that is rocked in the ocean cradle of birth and death, in ebb and in flow. You feel your limbs made glorious by the touch of this world of life.

SUSAN. Do your limbs actually feel glorious when you do those exercises?

PEGGY. They sure do. Most times.

SUSAN. That seems hard to believe. But then you're in such good shape, nothing seems to bother you.

PEGGY. What'll bother me is if I don't get to that hydrotherapy class. Floating in the water has helped me adjust to the new, slower rhythms of my body and get in tune with my organic self. See you later. (*Peggy exits.*)

SUSAN. Organic self. What, is she a vegetable? (*Pause.*) No, she's alive. Full of potential. Her life is just beginning.

SOPHIE. And your life is ending?

SUSAN. Let's say it's an endless repetition of the same old bad habits.

SOPHIE. Then let's not talk that way. That's a bad habit. Why don't we start with some good habits, like eating lunch. How about if I share my cold potato and hard-boiled egg with you?

SUSAN. No, thanks, Sophie. I'm not hungry.

SOPHIE. Maybe you'd like some sardines? It's a tiny fish, but it gives you a lotta strength. I got a can of it in my pocketbook.

SUSAN. No, sardines won't help.

SOPHIE. How about if we call the botanist. He can water your plants.

SUSAN. It's too late for watering.

SOPHIE. Some fresh air then.

SUSAN. I'm too tired to do anything.

SOPHIE. So you'll take a little nap. I'll get you a glass hot milk. I'll sing you a lullaby. (*Hums "Raisins and Almonds."*)

SUSAN. Please, Sophie, no songs, no stories, no hard-boiled eggs, no more naps, no more plants!

SOPHIE. *Oy vey!* (*Sophie eats her egg and sighs.*)

ACT II

A half hour has passed. Susan is sitting on the couch with a stack of student papers on her lap. She skims through several of them and starts to crinkle one of them up.

SUSAN. These student papers get worse and worse! I've got to do something. Maybe if I use their lingo to discuss the books, they might understand them. (*Gets a devilish gleam in her eyes.*) Hey, I got it. From now on I'll call Hawthorne's *Scarlet Letter* the *Fuchsia Letter* 'cause it's filled with purple passion.

SOPHIE. Does passion have a color?

SUSAN. Oh, yes. The book's about this hot babe, Hester, who gets it on with this horny preacher in the woods, gets knocked up right away, and has this weirdo kid, Pearl, who can't keep her hands off her old lady's boobs.

SOPHIE. What kind of books they teaching in college?

SUSAN. Or how about this? Melville's *Moby Dick* is about the conflict between big fish and little fish, or . . . between a big dick and a tiny prick.

SOPHIE. Dr. Susan, how you talk!

SUSAN. But the essential question is: Am I my blubber's kippur? (*Laughs hysterically, turns sharply serious, throws down the whole batch of papers.*) . . . I can't stand it any more. . . . (*Sighs.*) I can't do it any more.

SOPHIE. (*Tramples across the papers.*) Dr. Susele, forget about the papers. Come on, get up. I'm going to make you into a new person. The first thing is: you gotta exercise the whole body. Look, see how I do it. I make believe I'm a Yiddish windmill and wave my arms from right to left. Next, I shake a blue hanky in the air to scare away the demons. After that, I make believe I'm a fancy goose and walk around raising my legs as high as I can. Then I do what no other old person in the Jewish Center can do. I stand on one foot, I lift my knee way up to my chin and give it a big kiss. (*Sophie does what she describes.*)

SUSAN. (*Smiling.*) Sophie, I thought you were supposed to explain the whole Torah while standing on one foot.

SOPHIE. That I can do also. My whole Torah is this: Take care on your own body, because nobody else will take care on it for you. That's why I am so strong. Also from stubbornness and from carrying heavy sacks of flour in the old country. I would *schlep* two bags at a time, twenty pounds each, fifteen miles to the bakery. I even had the strength left to dance the *Kozatchke* with them.

SUSAN. I have a hard time carrying my swimming bag.

SOPHIE. Stop already feeling sorry for yourself, Dr. Susan. Now you listen. I'm going to make you strong like an ox. Come here. Make like the Yiddish windmill and sway from right to left. (*Susan follows Sophie's directions.*)

SUSAN. Oh, I got mixed up. I'm going from left to right.

SOPHIE. Good. Getting mixed up is part of the therapy. Now shake the blue hanky in the air.

SUSAN. This feels silly. I feel like I'm waving goodbye from a ship.

SOPHIE. Then you're doing exactly right. Wave good-bye to all those demons and start sailing to a new life.

SUSAN. Bon voyage!

SOPHIE. Good! Now for something fancy. Walk like that goose I was telling you about. Stick out your chest, hold up your head and raise high your legs. I'll lead the way.

SUSAN. On a wild goose chase.

SOPHIE. *Sha!* Follow me.

SUSAN. All right. Here goes . . . (*Susan twists her ankle.*) Damn, my ankle. I can't do this. It's hard to be a wild goose when you're a lame duck, Sophie.

SOPHIE. Not a lame duck, just a tired duckele. You gotta get in shape. Here. Sit down for a minute. Rest a little. I'll give you a massage and take away all your hurts.

SUSAN. That's nice. . . . Where did you get your training?

SOPHIE. Making challahs in Bialystok. Rolling and squeezing the dough is like rubbing and pounding a person's body.

SUSAN. You promise I won't turn into a soft challah.

SOPHIE. I promise. But with all my pounding you might turn into a hard bialy.

SUSAN. Are you sure you want to do this? My back is ugly.

SOPHIE. Listen, you're a *shayna maidel*. You have a beautiful body, a pretty face, a healthy head of hair, and a little extra fat to keep you warm in winter. You should only take care of yourself. You'll be even more beautiful as you grow older.

SUSAN. I'd like to believe you, Sophie, but . . .

SOPHIE. No buts. You just gotta exercise.

SUSAN. In that case, I'll have another try at that wild goose chase.

SOPHIE. Good. Do you know the song, "*Di Grineh Kuzine?*"

SUSAN. Yeah, I know it.

SOPHIE. Then let's sing it as we do the goose step. It'll take your mind off your feet. (*Sophie marches and sings. Initially Susan faintly accompanies her. Then as she gets more caught up in the song, Susan becomes more animated and more coordinated in her walking. They sing together.*)

SOPHIE AND SUSAN.

> *Tzu mir is gekumen a kuzine,*
> *Sheyne vi gold is zi geven di grine,*
> *Bekelekh vi royte pomerantsn,*
> *Fiselekh vos betn zikh tsum tantsn,*
> *Bekelekh vi royte pomerantsn,*
> *Fiselekh vos betn zikh tsum tansyn.*

(*Greta enters from the pool during the singing.*)

GRETA. (*Applauding.*) Is this the Greenhorn Marching Band?

SUSAN. No, we're beautiful old country cousins whose cheeks are red as pomegranates and whose feet beg to dance.

SOPHIE. But you know what happened to *Di Grineh Kuzine* in America? She worked in a factory sixty hours a week for twenty cents an hour. The job made her sick. But, like me, she wouldn't take no welfare.

GRETA. But to make ends meet, she became a loose woman. You would never do that.

SOPHIE. No, after I married my Yossel, I always wore a corset.

GRETA. And *Di Grineh Kuzine* cursed the golden land for destroying her life.

SOPHIE. I also get mad on this country. Specially for the way they treat the seniors. Not like the Chinese who look up to their old relatives. But then I wouldn't want to live in China 'cause where could I get a good piece of gefilte fish?

PEGGY. (*Enters.*) Is this a deli or the Ladies Locker Room?

SUSAN. With your "Shut Your Mouth" tape, you don't have to worry. . . . How was your workout? Do you feel better?

PEGGY. No, I think I should do a few more relaxation exercises before I get dressed. I've been having these strange contractions. I guess they're what my doctor calls false labor pains. Do you mind if I lie on the couch?

SOPHIE. Go ahead. You'll warm the couch and bring good luck to infertile girls who sit on it. Greta, before you get dressed, I want you to meet a preggling girl who chants and blooms. Peggy, meet Greta, the Esther Williams of the Jewish Center swimming pool.

GRETA. Pleased to meet you, Peggy. But I'm a realtor, not a swimming star. So you're going to have a boy.

SOPHIE. What are you talking about? She's going to have a girl. Can't you see how round she is in the front? Boys have more pointed heads and they make the belly come to a peak.

GRETA. No, I'm sure it's going to be a boy. Look at the tilt of her lower back. Boys tend to kick harder and put pressure on the dorsal muscles. When I had my Freddie, I looked just like her.

SOPHIE. I tell you it's going to be a girl. Look how rosy her cheeks is, how pink her earlobes. When I had my Ruthie, I looked just like her.

SUSAN. Didn't your doctor test you to determine the sex of the baby?

PEGGY. No, he doesn't believe in intrusive tests. He's against anything that might interfere with the parents' process of bonding with the baby as an individual. He believes that the sex of the baby should be unimportant.

SOPHIE. *Oy,* that might be a problem for the baby when she grows up.

SUSAN. Don't mind Sophie. She's only teasing you.

PEGGY. I don't mind. (*She has a slight contraction.*) But now I really think I have to do my relaxation exercises. They help cultivate the inner rhythms of my unseen energy. I hope you don't mind if I play another tape. They're so soothing.

SOPHIE. Go ahead, we might learn something too.

VOICE-OVER OF OBSTETRICIAN. Contract your abdominal muscles as if you were squeezing an accordion and then feel the easy release as you open the folds. Feel your chest as a tightly wound ball of yarn and gradually unwind your skeins of muscle. (*A spotlight shines on Peggy as she follows the doctor's instructions.*)

GRETA. I wonder if he knits in his spare time. I know he can't mend straight.

VOICE-OVER OF OBSTETRICIAN. Contract your pelvic region. Lie on your side, curl up, clench your hands, press your lips together, hunch your shoulders and draw your knees up. Feel tightly encased within yourself.

SUSAN. Sounds more like a mummy than a mommy.

VOICE-OVER OF OBSTETRICIAN. Now imagine you are a peony on which the sun is shining. Gradually open yourself to its light. Let petal after petal unfurl, till you're completely open. Breathe in and out until you're sure that respiration is full and effortless. Make each breath longer and longer and longer.

PEGGY. That feels a little better. I think I'm going to try a shower. (*Exit Peggy.*)

SOPHIE. With his accordion and his peony, that guy talks about everything except how to have a baby.

SUSAN. That "guy" is a doctor.

SOPHIE. Doctor schmocter, he still don't know nothing about helping preggling women. In Bialystok we had a horse doctor who knew more than him.

SUSAN. That was good for the horses, but who did the women see?

SOPHIE. Bobeh Rivkeh, the midwife. I was her chief nurse when I was thirteen. We helped women who couldn't get preggling and those who could.

SUSAN. What did you do for the ones who couldn't?

SOPHIE. When I menstruated, Bobeh Rivkeh asked me to save some of my blood for her. She gave a little jar of it to the women who couldn't have no children and told them to keep it by the bed. Two months later, they got preggling.

SUSAN. That's amazing! Sophie, you could make a fortune with that remedy.

GRETA. Yah! Let's start a business! Fertility bloodmobiles all over the city—and I'll handle the leases.

SUSAN. Seriously, Sophie, tell me something. What about once the women got pregnant? Did Bobeh Rivkeh teach them how to take care of themselves?

SOPHIE. Yes, she told them to eat plenty eggs with oatmeal for breakfast, a whole herring and *kartoffel* soup for lunch, and a half chicken and *knaidlach* for supper. She said they gotta eat for two because the babies inside them have just as big an appetite as they do.

GRETA. I imagine those pregnant Bialystok ladies had extra big bellies.

SOPHIE. Thank God, they did. The fatter the better, not like that Peggy. Because the women got so big, the babies had so much room in their wombs that when it was time for them to be born, they just slid out. We was only there to catch them.

GRETA. In Vienna it wasn't that simple. We had Freudian-trained obstetricians. They would analyze the conflicts of the babies before they were born. The mother would lie on the couch and tell her dreams. If she dreamt she was making a speech and forgot to put on her clothes, the doctors said her baby would be an exhibitionist. If she dreamt she was being chased up steep mountains, they said her baby would be paranoid and hide under the crib. For this the women paid hundreds.

SOPHIE. Bobeh Rivkeh didn't charge much. Maybe a ruble and some pickled calves feet for a regular case. But in America when I had my first baby, the doctor was a regular thief. He made me stay in the hospital for two weeks and I had to pay fourteen dollars. That was more than a whole week's wages.

SUSAN. And then you had two more babies, didn't you?

SOPHIE. If you wanna know the truth, I would have had seven more babies, but I went to a doctor and he took care on it. In those days we had no protection. You went to bed and, bang, every Monday and Thursday you got preggling. We just couldn't have all those babies. We couldn't make a living. We was starving.

SUSAN. How awful for you.

SOPHIE. Yes, I wanted to keep those babies. But what could I do? I only wish Bobeh Rivkeh could have got rid of those babies for me. She would have poured pickle brine in my belly button, swung a rooster over my head, and sent for Lilith to take my baby. Instead I had to go to a butcher who charged too much.

GRETA. My sister got her abortion from the Nazis. They ripped out her baby and her insides too. And still she didn't escape the camps.

SOPHIE. We gotta stop talking about dead babies and be grateful for the living ones.

GRETA. Yes, I agree.

SUSAN. Okay, but let me ask you this. What if a woman isn't too old, isn't poor, isn't infertile, isn't victimized by the Nazis, and still she doesn't have children? What do you think?

GRETA. Well, what's the reason?

SUSAN. There could be several. Maybe she doesn't want children. She has her career.

GRETA. That's fine.

SOPHIE. Not true.

SUSAN. Or maybe she has a hereditary disease and her doctor convinced her not to have children. (*Spotlight on Doctor.*)

DOCTOR. Susan, I know you're only sixteen but I think we need to talk about this now in order to avoid future misunderstandings and disappointments. You're a pretty girl and I'm sure you must be looking forward to having a family some day, but I just don't think it would be ethical or fair of you to have children. As you know, your muscle-nerve disease is both hereditary and degenerative and, well, would you want your child to live your kind of life? Sure, you're alive but there are a lot of things you can't do and your condition will only get worse. It's your life, of course, and you can do what you want with it. But just remember. The percentages are not in your favor. You risk bringing a defective human being into the world.

SUSAN. (*To the memory.*) Maybe you're right. Maybe I am defective, maybe it would be immoral of me to reproduce myself. (*Spotlight off Doctor, who disappears. To Sophie and Greta.*) He said she was defective. He told her not to have any babies.

GRETA. Doctors, what do they know?

SUSAN. It wasn't just her doctor. It was her family, too. They agreed with the doctor. Especially her mother who felt the most pity . . . and the most guilt.

GRETA. Mothers, what do they know? Because I liked to talk to strangers and enjoyed selling them things, my mother said I would become a prostitute. But you see, I married a very respectable man and became an almost respectable woman.

SOPHIE. Yes, mothers, they try their best but they don't know everything. Mine wanted I shouldn't have a big mouth, but in Bialystok my sharp tongue kept people from taking advantage of me. And in America, my talking loud made people pay attention to me. So, my mother didn't know, just like this girl's mother didn't know.

SUSAN. This girl listened to her doctor and her mother. She chose not to have children.

SOPHIE. Barren—like Sarah in the Bible.

SUSAN. But God made Sarah barren. Not some doctor.

SOPHIE. Yeah, but then she got Isaac. Why couldn't this happen with the girl?

SUSAN. Because she avoids lasting relationships with men. She finds excuses to break up with them for fear they'll want a child with her. She's given up the thought of ever having her own baby. It's as if she performs her mental abortions on herself.

PEGGY. (*Offstage.*) Oh, my water's burst!

SUSAN. Oh, my God!

PEGGY. (*Still offstage.*) My water's burst! What shall I do?

SOPHIE. Don't worry. We're coming to help you.

SUSAN. We have to call an ambulance!

GRETA. I'll go to the desk!

SOPHIE. Wait. First we should make her comfortable on the couch.

PEGGY. (*Entering.*) What should I do? My doctor goes to New York City on Wednesdays and my husband is out of town trying a case.

SOPHIE. Don't worry. The baby is not here yet. When the water breaks, it's just a little shower to tell you she's coming.

SUSAN. As soon as you're comfortable, Greta's going to call an ambulance to take you to the hospital.

PEGGY. No, I don't want to go to the hospital. I want to go to the birthing center in Pittsfield. I know what to expect there.

GRETA. All right. We'll get an ambulance to take you to Pittsfield. (*Peggy has an extended contraction.*) Oh my God, oh my God, I'll go call now! Don't do anything until I come back! (*Greta runs out.*)

SOPHIE. She sounds like the baby's ready to come out—like the Bialystok women!

SUSAN. Pittsfield is over forty miles away. Can she get there in time?

SOPHIE. Never mind Pittsfield! The baby's coming before the ambulance gets here. Come on, we gotta help Peggy. I'll talk to her. Dr. Susan, you gotta be in charge.

SUSAN. Me in charge? What are you talking about?

SOPHIE. You're a doctor.

SUSAN. Sophie! I'm a college professor, not a doctor of medicine!

SOPHIE. But you're an educated lady. You know a lotta things.

SUSAN. I don't know the first thing about delivering babies—besides what I've read in the gynecologist's waiting room. You're the one who worked with Bobeh Rivkeh. You be in charge.

SOPHIE. That was a long time ago. I forgot everything. Maybe I'll remember some things when I see you. I'll be your chief nurse.

SUSAN. I can't even hook your bra! How am I supposed to help Peggy . . . with her great shape and perfect coordination?

SOPHIE. She's not so perfect now. She's hurting . . . and she's scared. She needs help.

SUSAN. And you really think I can help her?

SOPHIE. Positively.

SUSAN. But I'm not strong enough to deliver a baby.

SOPHIE. Don't worry. Peggy will deliver the baby. Do what you do when you organize those conferences. Let other people do the work.

GRETA. (*Entering.*) The ambulance is coming! Hold on. Stay calm!

SUSAN. (*Hesitating at first and then plunging into it.*) Okay . . . Uh, Greta, please go to the main lounge and bring some pillows, the hassock, and the afghan on the couch.

GRETA. What about my closing? I have to get to my closing.

SOPHIE. Greta, don't get so cockcited. Tell 'em you'll be a little late.

GRETA. I'm selling a very expensive house and getting a very large commission.

SUSAN. Greta, you're so efficient. Sophie and I . . . Peggy need your help.

GRETA. If I'm late, I'll lose the sale, but . . . all right. A beginning is more important than a closing! . . . I'll reschedule my appointment and return with the birthing equipment. (*Greta exits.*)

SUSAN. (*Shouts after her.*) Thank you, Greta. Now, Sophie, it's your turn. Please go to the laundry room for some towels and washcloths.

SOPHIE. Yes, Dr. Susan.

SUSAN. How are you doing, Peggy?

PEGGY. I learned in prenatal class that at this point I should be using psychoprophylaxis. Only now I forget what it means or how to do it.

SUSAN. You just relax now and everything will be fine. That's what psychoprophylaxis is.

SOPHIE. (*Returning with towels.*) No, prophylactery means you should put straps on your arms like the Orthodox Jewish men do, or does it mean you should clean your mouth with gargling? I forget which. Anyhow, with Dr. Susan taking care on you, you won't suffer.

PEGGY. But don't you think we should send for my doctor in New York?

SOPHIE. We don't have time for that. The baby's coming too quickly. But don't worry—Dr. Susan knows what to do. (*Reaction from Susan.*)

PEGGY. But at the birthing center in Pittsfield, they put you in a master bedroom with a four-poster bed. And you give birth in any position you want. (*Contraction.*) I'm scared about the pain.

SUSAN. Don't worry. You're in great shape.

SOPHIE. And you're in great hands. Look! Here comes your fancy bed right now. (*Greta enters carrying the pillows, afghan, hassock, and pots and pans, which rattle.*)

GRETA. I got it! I found it all!

SUSAN. Here, Peggy, let's get you up off that couch. Take my hand and sit in this rocking chair. Greta, put the extra pillows behind her back and cover her with this afghan.

GRETA. Is there anything else, Herr Dr. Susan?

SUSAN. Sorry, Greta. Guess I was taking my job as an organizer too seriously.

GRETA. That's all right. This is serious business.

SUSAN. Well then, how about getting a kettle of warm water from the kitchen? And a bowl of ice while you're at it.

GRETA. I'll try my best. (*She exits.*)

SOPHIE. (*Still holding her bundle.*) What should I do, Dr. Susan?

SUSAN. Why don't you pile the washcloths over here and I'll rock Peggy back and forth until she's all comfortable.

SOPHIE. Oh, that's nice, Dr. Susele—you have such a beautiful voice. Why don't you sing her a lullaby? You know the one, "*Shlof Mein Kind.*"

SUSAN. I haven't sung in such a long time. I'm not sure I can remember it. "*Mach tzu dein eigele, mein shayne faigele, Shlof mein kind, shlof. Mach tzu dein eigele, Mein shayne faigele, Shlof mein kind, shlof.*" That's a Yiddish lullaby my grandmother used to sing to me. Peggy probably didn't understand it.

SOPHIE. Then I'll sing an Irish lullaby: "Toura lura lura, Toura lura lay. Toura lura lura. Hush now, it'll go away."

PEGGY. Are you sure I can stand the pain?

SUSAN. Of course you can. You know, for all our medical technology, childbirth is just another physiological process.

GRETA. (*Returning with all the equipment.*) Yes, I'm sure cavewomen didn't use all this equipment.

PEGGY. Here comes another contraction.

SUSAN. Okay, then, stop rocking and breathe with it.

SOPHIE. As they say, relapse.

PEGGY. It's like a little fire inside me. I feel sparks.

SOPHIE. Don't worry. It's supposed to be like that. When I was giving birth, I felt even hotter, like a four-alarm fire.

EMILY. (*Entering.*) Is there a fire in here? Did somebody say there were sparks? Who is this woman? What is she doing clutching her stomach?

GRETA. She's having a baby.

EMILY. A baby? Here?

GRETA. Dr. Susan is in charge and Sophie is the head nurse.

EMILY. You can't be serious! What do they know from delivering babies?

GRETA. Sophie trained with the finest obstetrician, Bobeh Rivkeh, the midwife of Bialystok, and Dr. Susan's read some books.

EMILY. Are you all crazy? There are two lives at stake here. You can't entrust them to an old *yente* and a doctor of literature.

GRETA. We have no choice. The baby is coming fast and the ambulance isn't here yet.

EMILY. I'll call my grandnephew Mitchell. He's the most prominent obstetrician in town. He'll come right over.

SOPHIE. If he's so prominent, how come I never heard anybody but you talk about him?

EMILY. Why would you? How many babies have you had lately? (*To the others.*) When the girls have babies with my Mitchell, they never feel a thing. He uses all the latest drugs.

PEGGY. I don't want any drugs. They all have side effects. My doctor told me.

SOPHIE. Bobeh Rivkeh said the same thing. I bet your doctor traveled to Bialystok to learn from her.

EMILY. Highly unlikely. You know, my Mitchell is the consultant to the biggest baby doctors all over the world. I'm going to call him immediately.

SOPHIE. Thank you, we can manage by ourselves.

EMILY. Do as you like. But don't say I didn't warn you. (*She turns to leave.*) Oh, here it is! (*Picks up her scarf.*)

SOPHIE. Give me that scarf. (*She grabs it.*) We need it as a *schmatta* for the labor.

EMILY. A *schmatta!* It's my Perry Ellis scarf! It cost fifty-five dollars.

SOPHIE. Okay, then we'll use it for a headband for Peggy to keep her hair out of her eyes. So she can see her baby being born. You see, Emily, you, not your Mitchell, are good for something.

EMILY. Many people think so. They compliment me for my professional delivery of songs, not my amateur delivery of babies. I'm going to call an ambulance. (*She exits.*)

GRETA. I already did.

SOPHIE. Don't worry. Peggy's in good hands until the ambulance gets here.

PEGGY. I'm thirsty. I hate to be a bother, but could I have a drink?

SUSAN. It's no bother. But you're not supposed to drink anything now. It might make you throw up. I'll get you some ice to suck on.

GRETA. No, Dr. Susan, you stay by Peggy. I'll bring the ice. You mustn't get dehydrated now, Peggy.

PEGGY. Here it comes again. Oh, what was that verse from my tape? "Is it beyond thee to be glad with the gladness of this rhythm?

To be tossed and lost and broken in the whirl of this fearful joy?" Oh, shit!

SUSAN. Not like Wordsworth's "Our birth is but a sleep and a forgetting."

GRETA. Or like Schiller's "carried away in the cradle of the storm."

SOPHIE. What's this, college?—or are we getting a baby born?

PEGGY. Oh, Jesus!

GRETA. Relax, the way your doctor said you should, with the breathing exercises. Here, let me play some of his tape for you.

VOICE-OVER OF OBSTETRICIAN. Breathe in and breathe out until you're sure that respiration is full and effortless. Make each breath a little longer . . .

PEGGY. Oh, it's stopped, thank God.

SOPHIE. It's not going to be too long now, Dr. Susan. This labor is going very, very fast. Before you can say matzoh ball soup, she'll have a little matzoh ball of her own.

SUSAN. Sophie, what if the baby's in trouble? What if it's in a bad position or something?

SOPHIE. Well, I remember what Bobeh Rivkeh would do about that.

SUSAN. Peggy, lie down on the couch so Sophie can check you. Here, we'll help you. Are you comfortable?

PEGGY. I guess as comfortable as I can be.

SOPHIE. Let me first listen to your heart. (*Sophie puts her head to Peggy's chest and abdomen.*)

GRETA. Sophie, I didn't realize your hearing was so good.

SOPHIE. I hear what I want to hear. When they yell at me at the Center for taking a cup coffee that don't belong to me, that I don't hear. But the heartbeat of a young mother and her new baby, that I hear just fine. Now, Peggele darling, I'm going to feel your stomach a little to find out where the baby is swimming.

PEGGY. Is the baby okay? What about the umbilical cord?

SOPHIE. *Sha!* Everybody be quiet. I'll know in a minute. (*Puts on her glasses and carefully scrutinizes Peggy's abdomen and pelvic region. Then she takes her glasses off, waves her hands mystically in the air over the belly, eyes closed, in a trance, humming "Raisins and Almonds."*)

GRETA. Sophie, I didn't realize you could see so well.

SOPHIE. I see what I want to see. Umm. Uh-huh, uh-huh. Aha!

PEGGY. What is it? How does everything look?

SOPHIE. Everything looks perfect. Just the way it's supposed to look.

PEGGY. My back is really hurting.

SOPHIE. That's because your baby is getting ready to be born. Her head is pushing against your tailbone.

SUSAN. That's your coccyx, Peggy.

SOPHIE. Thank you, doctor. Now, Peggy, turn over on your side and the doctor will give you a little coccyxla rub.

SUSAN. Sophie, I don't think I can do that. Do you think my hands are strong enough?

SOPHIE. Dr. Susan, remember, it's just like making challahs. You roll the skin like you roll the dough. Here, use some of this cream that I rub in my skin after swimming.

SUSAN. (*Beginning to massage Peggy's lower back.*) Am I doing it correctly? Peggy, is this all right?

SOPHIE. Perfect. That's perfect.

PEGGY. (*Some relief.*) Mmmmm . . .

SUSAN. I think I'm getting the hang of it. (*Holds her hands in the air and looks at them with amazement.*) You know, my hands are stronger than I thought. I could make a dozen challahs!

PEGGY. Oh, that feels better. Thanks.

SUSAN. You're welcome. I'm happy to help you.

PEGGY. I'm really glad you're all here. I don't know what I'd do without you. Oooh—now I'm starting to shiver.

SUSAN. Sophie, let's unroll those towels and cover her up.

SOPHIE. Here, I'll do that. Greta, you take from my swimming satchel the pair of *gatges,* the long underwear I got there.

GRETA. But it's almost summer. What are you doing with winter underwear?

SOPHIE. Just in case, for emergencies. And this is an emergency.

GRETA. Oh, Sophie, when it comes to *schmattes,* we can always depend on you. (*Holds the* gatges *up for display.*) Now, what do I do with these?

SUSAN. Why don't you try putting the top of the underwear over her head and pull the bottoms up to her knees. Are you still cold, Peggy?

PEGGY. I'm getting warmer.

SOPHIE. Good. If I remember right, that means you're getting close to the time.

SUSAN. Greta, does your watch have a second hand?

GRETA. Yes, I'll time the contractions.

PEGGY. I feel like an enormous balloon is blowing up inside me. The pressure is incredible.

SOPHIE. As long as it don't carry you away, it's okay.

PEGGY. Now I'm too hot.

SOPHIE. That girl changes her mind a lot.

SUSAN. Okay, you can forget the *gatges,* pass me a cold washcloth. I'll sponge her off between contractions.

SOPHIE. We can do that. (*Sophie takes the underwear off Peggy, and Susan sponges Peggy with a washcloth, which Sophie wets for her.*)

PEGGY. Thank you, thank you. Oh, God, I'm gonna scream!

SUSAN. Let it out. You have to. Sheila Kitzinger says that in labor, the body is "like an orchestra responding to the conductor's baton." The contracting uterus is the conductor. It's running the show now.

SOPHIE. My body felt like an overworked *klezmer* band that didn't listen to nobody.

SUSAN. Greta, are you still timing those contractions?

GRETA. Yes, they're coming every two or three minutes. It's getting close.

SUSAN. (*Whispering to Sophie.*) Do you know what we do now?

SOPHIE. We gotta measure the opening. Now, Peggele, relax. This won't hurt.

SUSAN. But Sophie, how can you measure her? You don't have any instruments.

SOPHIE. (*Examining Peggy.*) Neither did Bobeh Rivkeh. And her measurements were never wrong. I learned from her that if the woman's opening is the size of a two-inch knish, the baby's ready to come out.

PEGGY. How much am I dilated?

SOPHIE. The same as a two-inch knish. Mamele, it's time now to start pushing the baby out into the world. Begin to push and breathe, push and breathe. (*Peggy obeys Sophie's command.*) Dr. Susan will put her arms around your shoulders and push and breathe to keep you company.

SUSAN. (*Pushing and breathing in unison with Peggy.*) Push and breathe! Push and breathe!

SOPHIE. Okay, time to get ready. Greta, go fill up the kettle with more warm water. This must be cold by now.

GRETA. Yes, Nurse Sophie, I'll be right back.

SOPHIE. Now girls, repeat after me. Push and pant. Push and pant. (*They follow her directions.*)

SUSAN. (*As Peggy pushes and pants.*) Push and pant. Push and pant.

PEGGY. Oh my God, I feel the baby's head trying to come out. Susan, don't leave me.

SUSAN. I'm here, Peggy. I'm here.

SOPHIE. Your opening is as big as three knishes now. The baby's head has plenty of room to come out now. Just a few more pushes and the little one's body will come out just as easy.

SUSAN. (*As Peggy pushes and pants.*) Push and pant. Push and pant.

PEGGY. Oh my God. Here it comes! Here it comes! It's beautiful. Just beautiful! (*Fast blackout.*) Dr. Susan, we did it! We did it! I can't believe it! We did it!

SUSAN. (*Radiantly holding the baby.*) This baby is a present from God!

SOPHIE. (*Looking adoringly at the baby.*) Boruch atoh, adoshem eloheynu melech hoolom, ha yatzer nes gadol.

SUSAN. Praised be thou O Lord our God, King of the Universe who has created a great miracle! Here, Peggy, here is your great miracle! (*Gently hands the baby to Peggy.*)

GRETA. (*Running in with a kettle of water.*) Sophie, was I right? Is it a boy or a girl?

SOPHIE. It's a girl, like I told you. When you live to be as old as I am, you know what you're talking about.

EMILY. (*Entering.*) The ambulance has just arrived. The men will be here any minute. Mitchell is waiting at the hospital.

SOPHIE. Very good—but why don't you look at the baby first? Isn't she beautiful?

EMILY. The baby? What baby?

SUSAN. Emily, meet the newest member of the Ladies Locker Room.

EMILY. My Mitchell won't approve. But isn't she sweet? I'll have to buy her some designer diapers.

PEGGY. My little darling! You know, we may name you Susan Sophie Greta Rivkeh. (*Baby coos spasmodically. Susan and Sophie walk arm-in-arm down to center stage with a glowing light bathing them.*)

SUSAN. "I'm one week old!" Like Ralph says in *Awake and Sing,* "I'm one week old."

SOPHIE. Forget about what books say. What do *you* say? How do *you* feel?

SUSAN. Well, I don't quite know. So much has happened.

SOPHIE. Well, maybe that girl you was talking about is not so helpless as you thought. Maybe she wouldn't be a burden to nobody.

SUSAN. Maybe not. But Sophie, changes don't happen that quickly.

SOPHIE. Well, at least the pot is on the stove, and it's starting to boil. Maybe she'll even let the botanist turn the heat up and not be afraid of getting burned.

SUSAN. Let's say she's willing to let the budding romance grow into something.

SOPHIE. And with the botanist, enjoy the sunshine.

SUSAN. Yes, enjoy the sunshine. (*Pause.*) Sophie, you're amazing.

SOPHIE. I know.

SUSAN. At your age, a successful midwife and a psychiatrist. How do you feel?

SOPHIE. Like it's a blessing from God—to be old yet to be young. To live to bring a new life into this universe.

SUSAN. And to bring new life into people's lives.

SOPHIE. Come, Dr. Susele, let's celebrate. Life, they say, is the biggest bargain. We get it from God for nothing.

SUSAN. For nothing? For everything!

SOPHIE. Yes, for everything! Come, Dr. Susele! Come Greta and Emily, let's sing and dance around Peggy and the baby. *"Siman tov, u mazel tov, u mazel tov v'siman tov / Siman tov, u mazel tov, u mazel tov v'siman tov / Siman tov, u mazel tov, u mazel tov v'siman tov, y'he la-a-a-nu / Y'he la nu, y'he la nu, u l'chol Yisrael / Y'he la nu, y'he la nu u l'chol Yisrael!"* (*If time and stamina permit, the entire song is repeated as Sophie and the women dance a spirited Hora around mother and child. Susan becomes the most agile she's ever been in her entire life.*)

Photograph by Beverly Orr

Lois Roisman

ONE CREATION MYTH claims that God created Adam and Lilith out of one mound of earth, cleaving straight down the middle, creating two equal creatures, male and female. Lilith and Adam together named things, shared responsibilities in the Garden, and neither dominated the other. Adam grew displeased with this arrangement, however, complaining to God that Lilith wouldn't let him dominate in any phase of their lives. God understood and expelled Lilith from the Garden, replacing her with Eve, who, as we all know, was created from Adam's rib. She was a more pleasing, malleable companion for Adam, more willing to submit to Adam's control and be an agreeable helpmate.

I am not the only woman of my generation who has claimed her Lilith. Many say that this is Lilith's time, and they worry that we have forgotten how to respect the joys of Eve. And therein lies the rub. "Either/or" is not the answer. For me, my challenge has become to reconcile the Eve that is me and the Lilith that is me into a cohesive unity. It is a constant negotiation, but one that has defined my life and energized my work.

It wasn't until I was fifty that I finally succeeded in reincarnating myself into a full-time writer of fiction. The Eve/Lilith struggle is now more of an ongoing discussion, but the myths are still significant concepts that reappear in my work and give me my voice. That voice, so long in the search, is fed by Jewish myth, culture, and circumstance.

I was born in Texas in 1938, the year of *Kristallnacht*. My generation has been given the task of preserving the remnants of memory of the lost European Jewish community, and of the Holocaust itself. It is a responsibility thrust on us by circumstance, but there it is. Although I am late in assuming my portion of the task, I now understand it as an important part of my voice.

At the same time, our focus on those sad tasks must not deprive us of the joys and wisdom of our culture. I have often felt that being Jewish meant supporting Israel and remembering the Holocaust, but for me, that was not enough. Judaism must be more than an old wall that we are holding up. In my quest for more, I have uncovered a rich vein of wisdom in Jewish mysticism and folklore, none of which was part of my early education. I believe this omission was a calculated one on the part of the early rabbinic schools, which always chose the rational over the nonrational. Now the Hasidic tales, the mysticism of the Kabbalah, and the legends hold the wisdom and the richness that feed me.

I write plays whenever the story fits the stage because I believe that a theater is a more felicitous place to be challenged by new ideas and to formulate or modify one's personal philosophy than, say, a synagogue or church. One always knows the punch line in a synagogue, whereas in good theater we must think it through with no parameters other than our own imagination. When the magic is present, the audience is the match, the play is the flint. In that sense I believe the theater has most value today when it serves its most primitive religious function. People are open to ideas in the theater that would seem stale or didactic if heard in the context of a religious institution.

I owe much to writers of other forms of literature, and I bow to Ozick, Singer, Bellow, and, of course, Rebbe Nachman of Bratslav, the rebbe who first fashioned tales of Hasidic values in the story forms of the secular culture.

The story of the exodus from Egypt is another theme that has captured my imagination for years, and I have explored it in children's and adult literature. The journey from slavery to exodus to wandering to redemption reflects life's journey, especially that of women and minorities. We must all struggle with our internal Egypts and find the strength to claim our freedom.

Scenes from a Seder is a play about five generations of Jewish women in twentieth-century America, as seen through the eyes of Elijah, a visitor at their seder tables. The evolution of these women requires that the culture evolve as well, creating an ongoing tension with consequences for the Passover seder and everyone at the table.

Children of the Exodus is a Passover play about children of different cultures who have made an exodus to a new land. In it, the stories of Native American, Cambodian, Irish, Jewish, African, and South American immigrants to America are woven into the story of the exodus from Egypt. *Leaving Egypt,* a children's book about two Haibiru children who must leave Egypt, explores the need to make difficult choices.

On the subject of Chanukah, I wrote *Chanukah Rapping,* a children's musical commissioned by Theatre J at the DC Jewish Community Center in Washington, D.C. A musical, it deals humorously with issues of greed and generosity, as well as exploring alternatives to violence in response to aggression.

I seem always to have a character in my plays who pierces the membrane between the real and the unknown, the visible and the invisible. Such a character lifts the action out of the everyday and gives it a broader perspective. The intrusion of a spirit from a previous, older Jewish culture onto a contemporary situation plays in my head and often turns into a play on paper. For me it is an interesting way to explore the ironies of this culture, and it adds a folkloric tone that I find satisfying.

I like to write with a comic edge; it lets me get away with more. I can almost feel the audience wanting to laugh, looking for something to laugh about. So I am happy to hear the laughter, hoping that later, on the way home or the next day, some idea will come back to them that will inform their lives.

Although I find didactic theater annoying and a preachy political play tedious, the truth is, I cannot seem to write a play without a message. I like to shine a light on a piece of life that needs attention, not always a spotlight because it is often too blinding, but enough light to bring a new awareness.

In *Nobody's Gilgul,* I play with the contrasts between Eve and Lilith in today's society. This is a time when an appreciation of Lilith is returning, modifying the attraction to Eve. In the play, I can value Eva's comfort in living within the restrictions of orthodox Judaism, even though it is not for me, and I can applaud Lily's tenacity and boldness as a woman living in a world where she can define her own boundaries. Both women are influenced by their advisors, Eva's rebbes who quote Talmud and folk wisdom and Lily's mentors, her hairdresser, her trainer, her manicurist, and her therapist, who advise her according to the wisdom of the day. None of the advisors are venal; they speak the wisdom they know. It is our perspective that gives it an edge.

Although the Eve versus Lilith struggle still exists inside me, I see it even more strongly in the lives of the next generation. It is a personal challenge that we must all address, tempering the boldness of Lilith with the discretion of Eve, the generosity of Eve with the self-centeredness (not always a negative quality) of Lilith. Both may now be present in the contemporary woman, but to make it happen harmoniously is a constant challenge. Will Eva and Lily work out their differences and live happily ever after? Probably not. Whose style will prevail? Lily's, I think . . . the prevailing society's. Our way of life is the most seductive in the world, and it has swallowed up many cultures to reach its present form. Eva was much more seduced by Lily's life than Lily by Eva's. And so it goes. When two species are thrown together geographically and can mate, they will, and the larger will consume the smaller. What else is new? We can hope that the smaller will flavor the larger and improve its texture. And we can hope that Eva will temper Lily and fill her emptiness.

I'm especially indebted to Ernie Joselovitz of the Playwrights Forum in Washington, D.C., for his encouragement and guidance. Larry Redmond and the cast of the first workshop at the Source Theatre helped me hear the play through talented and caring actors, a true gift to a playwright. The staffs of the Streisand Festival of New Jewish Plays and of the Utah Playfest were invaluable in shaping the final form of this play. Irene Fine and Sarah Blacher Cohen were my first contacts with a Jewish women's network and were instrumental in bringing *Nobody's Gilgul* to this anthology.

Nobody's Gilgul was first performed in workshop in 1993 at the Source Theatre's 13th Annual Washington Theatre Festival, Pat Murphy, producing artistic director, and Keith Parker, festival director. It was named Outstanding New Play of the Festival. The cast was as follows:

Emily Townley	Hugh Walthall
Sheira Venetianer	John Dow
Janet Antonelli	Irv Jacobs
Kerri E. Rambow	Tee Morris
Stan Kang	

Director: Larry Redmond

Nobody's Gilgul
1993

Characters

LILY GILBERT, a New York City attorney
EVA, a spirit from the shtetl
JUSTINE HEADRUP, Lily's therapist

DIANA, Lily's trainer
ERNESTO, Lily's hairdresser
MANICURIST, in Ernesto's shop
REBBE MOSHE, one of the Powers That Be
REBBE KITZEL, another of the Powers That Be
REBBE SHMUEL, yet another of the Powers That Be
CHAD LEWIS, Lily's fiancé
ADAM KAEDMON, public interest attorney

Scenes

The scenes move through Lily's life in New York City, alternating with scenes before the Gates of the Garden of Eden.

Time

The present. The day and night before Lily is scheduled to become Eva's gilgul.

ACT I

Scene 1

Stage left. In the office of psychotherapist, Justine Headrup, Lily is sitting in a recliner in her jogging clothes. Stage right, Eva is sitting outside the gates to the Garden of Eden watching a wall of television monitors, picking up bits of life on the screen, switching channels randomly. The following are offstage voices, coinciding with what Eva sees on the monitors.

NEW MOTHER ONE. Oh, Sam, isn't she adorable?

NEW FATHER ONE. Yeah.

NEW MOTHER ONE. But, she has Grandma Sarah's eyebrows.

NEW FATHER ONE. Yeah. Hey, there's always electrolysis. (*Eva switches channels.*)

NEW MOTHER TWO. Doc, she looks like she's a hundred years old and she's only been in the world five minutes!

NEW FATHER TWO. Like one of those dried apple dolls! (*Eva switches again.*)

NEW MOTHER THREE. But George, darling, she's doing that same thing with her nose that your great grandmother Rose did when she got off the boat at Ellis Island. That "I can smell it but I can't see it" thing she always did? (*Eva switches yet again. As Lily begins to speak, Eva focuses on her particular screen.*)

LILY. —so empty. Yes, I've got a man other women would die for, but I still feel, well, uninhabited. Like something's missing—inside me. But he *is* a great dancer!

HEADRUP. May I give you feedback?

LILY. Make it short.

HEADRUP. You seem to be basing a primary relationship on someone's facility to move rhythmically.

LILY. But all the good ones are married, aren't they? What choice do I have? I know you think I hate myself because I've fallen for a dead end. He just has this reluctance to bond. And I agree with him. I mean I know you think it's self-destructive, but so who am I going to date? I'm too selective for singles bars—well, alright, too old, but there's always something disappointing to find out about those guys. You talk and talk and then, aha, there it is—he has two kids at home, he lives with his mother, he can only do it if we're both wearing hula skirts. And right in the next office every day I've got this gorgeous hunk of a guy who can help me frame my interrogatories while simultaneously looking at me as though I'm lying naked in a tub full of bubbles. That's a choice? I can build a life on that.

HEADRUP. May I give you some feedback?

LILY. No. I'm not here for feedback.

HEADRUP. I had this crazy impression that you paid me one hundred dollars an hour to give you feedback.

LILY. I pay you one hundred dollars an hour to listen.

HEADRUP. To listen to you whine?

LILY. That's feedback.

HEADRUP. That's whining. You could buy a street person a meal and he'd listen to you for nothing. You pay me for feedback.

LILY. You despise me, don't you? I can feel your disgust wafting over me like exhaust fumes on Seventh Avenue. You don't respect me. I can feel it.

HEADRUP. Bullshit. What's wrong, Lily? There's something else.

LILY. Something happened at the office that—scared me.

HEADRUP. What happened?

LILY. Just listen, OK? No touchy-feely feedback. I'm not receptive.

HEADRUP. So tell me.

LILY. I was sitting in the conference room with the attorney for a group of people who've sued my client, Vertex Corporation, for allegedly polluting their water supply. And for the hundredth time, he's accusing me of—(*Kaedmon appears near the couch and they have the following exchange as if in a dream.*)

KAEDMON. —not turning over all the documents the court ordered. I know there are numerous memos written to the president of Vertex from the chief engineer, and you haven't given me one!

LILY. (*Sits up on couch.*) I don't know what you're talking about. For the hundredth time, Mr. Kaedmon, there are no memos between the chief engineer and the president of Vertex. If there were, you'd have received them.

KAEDMON. Oh, there are memos, Ms. Gilbert. There are a few decent people at Vertex who've confirmed their existence. You're obviously not in that category.

LILY. And what's that supposed to mean?

KAEDMON. You're obviously not in this to serve justice or seek truth. You're in it to protect your client, right or wrong, and support yourself in the manner to which you and your partners have become accustomed.

LILY. Some people think that lawyers are supposed to protect their client, Mr. Kaedmon, and I don't think it's appropriate that you attack me personally for following that philosophy.

KAEDMON. You corporate lawyers are something else. You drag these cases on for years so you can pay the rent, while little people like my clients suffer and sometimes even die because your client puts profit over corporate responsibility.

LILY. You holier-than-thou shmuck! Your clients smell a deep pocket and lunge for it. Vertex is supposed to roll over, right? That's what you call corporate responsibility. Your clients are inventing their ailments and you know it!

KAEDMON. Making up stillbirths? Making up cancers? Oh, please, Ms. Gilbert, that's a bit much even for a heartless person like you.

LILY. Heartless? I'm not heartless. I'm tough, but I'm not heartless.

KAEDMON. Don't you ever listen to that little voice inside you, about here, that tells you when you're on the wrong side? That what you're doing isn't right?

LILY. What little voice? I don't hear little voices, Mr. Kaedmon, and if I may give you some advice, you shouldn't go around bragging that you do.

KAEDMON. You really don't have one.

LILY. Have what? A voice? No, I really don't have one.

KAEDMON. A conscience. A soul. You're telling me the truth about that.

LILY. With all due respect, I don't believe that's relevant to the business at hand, Mr. Kaedmon.

KAEDMON. (*Points his finger.*) Fascinating. You have no soul. Where your soul should be, there's a dark, empty, silent place. With all due respect, you're empty, Ms. Gilbert. (*Exits.*)

HEADRUP. And how did that make you feel? (*Catches herself after a warning look from Lily.*) It just sounds like two lawyers getting down to business.

LILY. It was as if he'd looked inside me—through my skin into my center. I thought, "He's right. There's nothing there. I *am* empty. Where other people have feelings, I have—rebuttals."

HEADRUP. I don't buy that. I don't think you're empty at all. Maybe not in touch with all of your possibilities, but certainly not empty. I'm sure there's something there. We just have to keep looking.

LILY. (*Yelling.*) I'm telling you, I'M EMPTY! I'm so sick of your smarmy feel-good answers. I AM EMPTY! Believe me! There's no center in my middle. I've always known it, but I thought everyone was like that, until that son-of-a-bitch pointed his finger at me in the conference room and saw right through me. I know he was right. The bastard was right! There's no way to prove it, is there? I mean, you can measure heartbeats with an electrocardiogram and surmise that there's a heart in there doing its thing, but if you made an equivalent search for a beating soul, the line on my screen would be flat.

HEADRUP. We're coming to the end of our hour. This will be an interesting place to begin our next session.

LILY. Ah, the fifty minute friendship. You're good, Headrup. I almost forgot. Hold that emotion til next time! (*Backing off stage.*) But I can't wait! Don't you get it? (*Yelling.*) I'm empty! (*Lights.*)

Scene 2

Outside the gates of the Garden of Eden. Three rebbes rollerskate out through the gates in front of Eva; throughout the play, they never look directly at her or any other female.

EVA. Did you hear that? Did you hear it? She's empty. My great, great, great, great niece. She's empty and she knows it. I heard her.

REBBE MOSHE. Sh, sh, Evala. We heard.

EVA. So? It's a perfect match. She's my gilgul. Finally!

REBBE SHMUEL. It's not so simple. There are considerations.

EVA. What? She's family. She's empty. I'm ready. What?

REBBE KITZEL. Remember, Evala, patience is half of wisdom. Be wise for a change, little Evala. Let us consider.

EVA. Patience! I've been patient for two hundred years! This is my time! We've found my gilgul!

REBBE MOSHE. Sh, sh, Evala. We heard. We're thinking.

REBBE KITZEL. It's highly unusual. But perhaps a great opportunity, no?

REBBE SHMUEL. It's never been done so late—in the mature adult stage. I'm not optimistic.

EVA. She needs me. I need her.

REBBE KITZEL. Nothing reduces misfortune like patience, Evala.

REBBE MOSHE. And you've had your misfortunes, Evala, we know. But this will be your last chance.

EVA. I know it's my last chance. I'm ready. I know what I have to do and I'm ready.

REBBE MOSHE. So what do you have to do? Tell us again.

EVA. Keep the Shabbat, make a decent challah—

REBBE SHMUEL. (*Aside.*) Oy, your challahs!

EVA. —and go to the mikvah.

ALL REBBES. AND?

EVA. And find my Adam once again and have his child.

REBBES MOSHE AND KITZEL. AHHHHHH!

REBBE SHMUEL. AND?

EVA. And be silent when a woman should be silent.

REBBE KITZEL. You and your Adam have much to learn.

REBBE SHMUEL. Your Adam—Ehhhh, I am not optimistic. An old bear will never learn to dance.

EVA. Adam also is impatient with rules. I loved that about him especially.

REBBE KITZEL. Common sense is a gift; intelligence is an acquisition. Your Adam was not blessed with the gift of common sense.

REBBE SHMUEL. On the other hand, there are those who say that intelligence is a gift; common sense is an acquisition. Adam has yet to acquire common sense.

REBBE MOSHE. Again the argument. Always the argument!

EVA. (*Aside.*) And God opened the mouth of the ass.

REBBE MOSHE. What?

EVA. I'm ready to go. It's my destiny.

REBBE SHMUEL. This Lily won't like it. It's highly unusual to enter so late.

REBBE MOSHE. It usually happens at birth.

REBBE KITZEL. But she noticed. She is empty. She'll want to know, how could that happen?

REBBE MOSHE. Listen. It happens. We get distracted, we get a rush of new souls. It happens.

REBBE SHMUEL. She won't like it. She'll need some time to get used to Evala.

REBBE KITZEL. And Evala to her. Things are very different down there. It's been two hundred years. A few things have changed. I've been noticing.

EVA. Not so different. I've been watching the screens. Not so different. Well, maybe, around the edges. Anyway, I'm smart. You'll teach me.

REBBE MOSHE. Mmmmmmm. You'll slip into her life slowly, she'll get used to you. As her secretary. Yes. You'll make friends before the actual moment of union. Clever, no?

REBBE KITZEL. Yes, that's good. So when the moment comes, they'll already be friends and Evala can get on with her business.

EVA. What's a secretary?

REBBE MOSHE. This may be more difficult than we imagine. The language we can give you.

REBBE KITZEL. And some "minimum-office-skills," as they say down there. Typing is a fascinating form of communication.

REBBE SHMUEL. But the rest Lily will have to teach you herself, or you will learn from observation.

REBBE KITZEL. Or from experience. Best is from experience. You can't chew with someone else's teeth.

REBBE SHMUEL. But from your experiences so far, Evale, I'm not optimistic. (*The other rebbes and Eva mime these words as he says them.*)

EVA. Do you know why I'm optimistic? She knows she's empty. Not everyone down there knows.

REBBE MOSHE. Oh, she knows. We owe her a soul. It's our responsibility.

EVA. How long will I have before the moment?

REBBE SHMUEL. Ummmm, three days.

REBBE MOSHE. Good. Tuesday is a good day for new beginnings.

EVA. Three days? That's not enough time!

REBBE MOSHE. Evala. The whole universe was made in six.

REBBE SHMUEL. Time goes more slowly down there. Three days can be a long time.

EVA. If that's what must be, I'll do it! Teach me!

REBBE KITZEL. (*Tenderly.*) We'll miss our little Evala.

REBBE MOSHE. Pay attention this time. A good challah is worth the trouble.

REBBE SHMUEL. Ehhhh, I'm not—

REBBES MOSHE AND KITZEL. WE KNOW!

Scene 3

Chad Lewis downstage left on telephone to Mr. Dumpster offstage. Chad has in his hand a memo, which he peruses during this conversation.

DUMPSTER'S VOICE. Lewis, Vertex is very worried about this case. I get the sense that there may be something incriminating in the files. Have you checked all the paper we're turning over to the plaintiffs?

CHAD. Yes, sir, there's nothing there. I checked everything.

DUMPSTER. Kaedmon keeps insisting there's more.

CHAD. He's just guessing. Based on the information we've turned over, Vertex is clean.

DUMPSTER. Good. We wouldn't keep anything back, of course. Dumpster and Fuller never destroys evidence. Destroying evidence is a federal offense.

CHAD. Yes, sir. We'd never destroy evidence.

DUMPSTER. Now, if we inadvertently lost a memo, if it fell out of a file and slid under a bookcase that doesn't get moved 'cept every ten years or so, well, we can't be held responsible for chance happenings, not if we *thought* we'd turned over everything, now can we?

CHAD. I understand, sir. Dumpster and Fuller is not the sort of firm that intentionally withholds evidence.

DUMPSTER. Exactly. We have a reputation. Vertex is multinational, Lewis. Multinational. They mean a lot to this firm.

CHAD. I understand that, sir. We'll give them the representation they expect.

DUMPSTER. See that we do. You're doing a good job, Lewis. I won't forget it come partner time. (*Hangs up. Blackout.*)

Scene 4

Lily's office. Eva is at the typewriter outside her office; Lily is at her desk on the phone; while Lily talks, Eva examines the office machines, especially the fax.

LILY. I'll not sit here and let you slander me and my law firm with these comments, Kaedmon. You're going way beyond the bounds of propriety here.

KAEDMON. (*Speaking from a phone at stage's edge.*) I almost forgot. You're the one with the dark hole where a soul should be. You can't be held in contempt for aggressively representing your client, right? Well, Ms. Gilbert, pardon me if I personally hold you in contempt.

LILY. You bastard! I'll see you in court! (*Both slam down phone, Kaedmon exits; Lily goes to Eva's desk.*) Take a letter! No. A memo. To Mr. A. Kaedmon. From Ms. Lily Gilbert. This will caution you that if you persist in the slanderous accusation that this firm is withholding evidence on behalf of Vertex Corporation we will be forced to sue your firm for slander. My signature. Now who *are* you? (*Eva writes carefully, absorbed; Lily taps her shoulder.*) Who are you?

EVA. Oh, I'm Eva and I'm having a wonderful time. Ms. Baxter is out sick.

LILY. For how long?

EVA. Three days is all I can stay, so I'm sure she'll be better by then. But I'm having a fine time. This is a truly magical place. That fax machine is a miracle. I have a friend who'll love it.

LILY. I'm sure we're all tickled that you find the secretarial pool such a rich source of personal gratification. Now read me back that memo.

EVA. Yes, ma'am. To Mr. A. Kaedmon From Ms. Lily Gilbert. This will caution you that if you persist—

LILY. Make that Ms. Lillian Gilbert.

EVA. To Mr. A. Kaedmon from Ms. Lillian Gilbert. This will caution you that if you persist in the slanderous accusation that this firm is withholding evidence on behalf of Vertex Corporation we will be forced to sue your firm for slander my signature now who are you?

LILY. You'd better let me see that before you send it. I'll be in Mr. Dumpster's office. (*Lily exits, Eva begins typing. Fax comes in, she reads it, takes it into Lily's office. Chad enters.*)

CHAD. What are you doing here?

EVA. (*Frightened.*) Ms. Baxter's sick.

CHAD. Well, tell Lily I need to see her. How long are you here for?

EVA. Only three days. (*Leaves. Eva turns and sees Chad fold a piece of paper, put it in Lily's lawschool yearbook, and leave.*)

EVA. (*Under her breath.*) Cossack! (*Eva goes to the book, reads the piece of paper, replaces it; Lily enters.*)

LILY. What the hell are you doing?

EVA. Oh! Just dusting your books.

LILY. I'd rather you attended to that memo. The nerve of that holier-than-thou zealot. Thinks he's the only one with standards.

EVA. The Cossack came in to visit.

LILY. The Cossack?

EVA. He didn't leave his name. Blonde, tall, handsome. Barks.

LILY. Mr. Lewis?

EVA. He went back into that office next door. Ms. Gilbert, may I speak to you please?

LILY. Not now, Eva. In a minute. (*Lily exits into Chad's office; freeze. Eva steps over to rebbes.*)

REBBE MOSHE. Don't you think it's time you told her who you are, Evala?

REBBE SHMUEL. Three days isn't much time.

EVA. I know, I know. But she's very hot-tempered. I want her to be in a better mood. She hates this Mr. Kaedmon with whom she is having an argument. She says such things to him, Rebbes! You would not approve. Maybe when she comes out of visiting with Mr. Lewis. I think he's the one who looks at her like she's in bubbles.

REBBE SHMUEL. Oy vey! I told you this wouldn't work! Bubbles!

EVA. Don't worry about bubbles. Worry about my typing.

REBBE SHMUEL. The Talmud says that worry saps a man's strength.

REBBE KITZEL. That's why I'm telling you not to worry.

REBBE SHMUEL. Alright! So who's worrying?

REBBE MOSHE. You! You're worrying. You're in agony.

REBBE SHMUEL. The Perke Avot says we should never waste good agony.

EVA. You didn't tell me about a lot of things, Rebbes. For instance, this fax machine, did you know about it? It sends letters through space. Get a fax number for the Garden of Eden and I'll show you.

REBBE KITZEL. Actually, our equipment's a bit outdated. Who can keep up? One minute it's a typing instrument, then a computing machine, then they're sending letters through the air. Who can keep up? (*Eva sees Lily leave Chad's office; Lily is smiling and buttoning her blouse.*)

EVE. Oops! Gotta go! (*Eva returns to her desk.*) Can we talk now, Ms. Gilbert?

LILY. Certainly, Eva. (*They enter Lily's office and sit.*) What can I do for you?

EVA. I'm not who you think I am, Ms. Gilbert.

LILY. Of course you are, Eva. You're a temp who's never laid eyes on a fax machine and is surprised to see the letter she's typed appear out of the printer.

EVA. You noticed.

LILY. I'm keen that way.

EVA. My training was rather rushed, and on older equipment. But that's what I want to talk to you about.

LILY. Your outmoded equipment? Well, your clothes are a bit dated, but nothing a trip to Bloomie's wouldn't cure. The equipment underneath looks like it'll serve you quite well. Chad commented favorably on your equipment.

EVA. I don't want to talk about my equipment. I want to talk about your equipment, or your lack of equipment. You see, we heard you—we heard you crying—that you were empty.

LILY. (*Looks up from work.*) What? Who's "we"?

EVA. The Powers That Be. We heard you cry out that you were empty and the rebbes realized that they'd—well, that they'd overlooked you, and so here I am, to make you whole.

LILY. I don't know what you're talking about.

EVA. Of course you do. You were lying on a very strange chair, talking to a woman who wanted to give some food back to you but you weren't hungry, or it was too expensive, I didn't quite understand that part, but you didn't want it even though you did admit you were empty. How wise of you to know it wasn't your stomach that was empty.

LILY. Headrup? You've been talking to my shrink?

EVA. Is that the lady who wanted to feed you?

LILY. What else did she tell you?

EVA. She didn't tell me anything. She didn't need to. The way the Cossack can look at you as if you're naked under bubbles? That was very amusing, Lily, but forbidden, of course.

LILY. Who the hell are you?

EVA. The rebbes sent me. I've come to be your soul.

LILY. (*Rising.*) Right. And Madonna's a virgin. I know who you are. You're a spy for that bastard Kaedmon. I knew he was slippery but I never imagined he'd put a tail on me.

EVA. I'm not a tail, Lily. I'm a soul.

LILY. You think you can appeal to my conscience, is that it? Well, I have news for you and your boss. . . . I don't have the memo and I don't have a conscience.

EVA. You will, Lily, you will.

LILY. (*Starts moving Eva to door.*) Just get out. And tell Kaedmon he'll have to play with the cards that are on the table. I haven't got one up my sleeve and if I did, he'd never see it.

EVA. I don't play cards. But I can learn. I'm here to be your soul. I need to be your soul. I'm not finished.

LILY. Yes, you are finished! Get out! (*Freeze. Eva freezes, Lily steps out of action to Headrup, in her chair, stage left.*)

LILY. What the hell do you think you're up to, giving out privileged information about my sessions!

HEADRUP. I don't know what you're talking about. Though God knows you were yelling loud enough for anyone jogging in Central Park to pick you up on their earphones.

LILY. Not about the bubbles I wasn't yelling. Do you tape me?

HEADRUP. No, I do not tape you. What do you think I am, a fucking Freudian?

LILY. Then how did she know I'm empty?

HEADRUP. How do *you* know you're empty? (*Freeze. Eva steps to rebbes.*)

REBBE MOSHE. A genius you're not, Evala.

REBBE KITZEL. A specialist in human relationships you're not, Evala.

REBBE MOSHE. Patience, Evala. Patience is half of wisdom.

EVA. You can't expect me to change overnight. And it's more complicated. I mean, she loves a Cossack. As you know, I have my problem with Cossacks. Can you do anything about her attraction for the Cossack?

REBBE MOSHE. You must enter her as you find her, Evala. That's a condition of these late entries.

EVA. And she's very, well, bold. How can I be expected to correct my tendency to speak my mind in the body of a woman who seems to earn her living cursing at men?

REBBE SHMUEL. See? Already she wants to change her mind. I told you she couldn't do it. It's too much. I told you it would be too much.

REBBE KITZEL. Stop with the "I told you so" already. We've been together what? Eight, maybe nine hundred years. There's nothing you haven't told us so already. (*Rebbes make disparaging noises at one another as Eva speaks over their voices.*)

REBBE MOSHE. If I had a herring for every time you told us so I could feed everyone in Vilna!

REBBE SHMUEL. But I'm right! You just don't want to hear it! It's the truth I'm saying into your ears!

REBBE KITZEL. Oy, such a pain you're giving me in my *kishkes*. I can't stand it!

EVA. (*Hands to ears.*) I hate it when you argue! Forget it! I'll do it. Can you hear me? We only need to get used to one another. I said I'll do it! (*Voices fade away as Eva backs offstage; blackout.*)

Scene 5

Lily is at the gym, working out with her trainer, Diana; Eva, in a curly wig, is in a corner trying to blend in, but she's dressed strangely and has no clue about what to do; aerobics music blares.

DIANA. Burn, that's it! Push through it! That's great! Look at that body sweat. You're a fuckin' goddess, Lily!

LILY. (*Breathlessly.*) I don't know if it's worth it. I think my thighs are going to ignite.

DIANA. It's worth it! It's worth it! Didn't you tell me Chad loves your bod? You're doing it for Chad! You're doing it for Chad!

LILY. Yea. He told me just today (*puff*) he wants to have a baby (*puff*) with me, but he (*puff*) loves my body just the way it is, (*puff*) so he wants to have it in a surrogate, (*puff*) just use his sperm and my egg (*puff*).

DIANA. Gee, not many guys are that sensitive. Bend two three four! Deeper two three four! No pain, no gain! (*Freeze. Eva talks to rebbes.*)

EVA. Is that kosher?

REBBE MOSHE. We've been doing some research ever since her Chad first mentioned it.

REBBE SHMUEL. It's never been considered before. Not in the Talmud.

EVA. Will I get credit for the birth?

REBBE KITZEL. Maybe the Mishnah.

EVA. I know I must raise a child to the wedding canopy, but does it say that I must birth it? I'll need to know.

REBBE SHMUEL. I'm not optimistic.

REBBE MOSHE. We're thinking, Evala. We're thinking. On the one hand . . . (*Eva returns to gym and starts working out to music, sneaking closer and closer to Lily until she's next to her, in sync.*)

EVA. Hello!

LILY. What the hell are you doing here?

EVA. Burning. Is this hell?

LILY. You've got a lot of nerve, following me in here.

EVA. No pain, no gain. If that's not in the Talmud, it should be!

No pain, no gain. No pain, no gain. (*She continues jumping awkwardly to the beat.*)

LILY. I'll give you pain if you don't get out of here.

EVA. I just thought we could jump a little together, talk a bit, exchange recipes, you know. Get to know one another.

LILY. Get out of here or I'm calling the cops. I will not be harassed, do you hear me? OUT!

DIANA. I'll take care of her. She's not even a member. Members only, ma'am, and proper attire is required. (*Diana leads Eva out.*)

EVA. What? I'm covered! You call that proper? (*Points to Lily.*) Is this a proper way to treat a citizen of America! I have my bill of rights! (*Blackout.*)

Scene 6

Lily's apartment; door stage left; contemporary, with a modern kitchen at one end; door to bath on back wall so audience can see medicine cabinet; other door leads to a bedroom; Eva, in an outrageous wig and an apron, is trying all the appliances, running water, etc., expressing great wonder and delight, confusion and consternation.

EVA. Oy yoi yoi! You said things had changed, but this? (*Turns on hot water.*) So who's boiling this? (*Looks under sink. Opens refrigerator and shuffles things around.*) Oy yoi yoi! (*Leaves refrigerator open and turns to stove. Turns on burner, watches in amazement as it heats.*) So where's the wood? A wonder! (*Leaving stove on, she goes into bathroom, turns on light-switch, shrieks with amazement. Soon we hear a flush and another shriek. We can see her look in the mirror and react. Opening the cabinet door, she fumbles with everything, looking at the bottles and tubes. Finds box of tampons, opens box, reads directions, and expresses astonishment. She holds a tampon in her hand by the string and is examining it when the door opens and Lily walks into the living room.*)

LILY. What the hell? (*Lily runs into the kitchen area, closing and turning off appliances and water. She hears a flush and Eva's delighted laughter. Eva enters from the bathroom reverently holding the tampon.*) How did you get in here? (*Eva looks at Lily with surprise, then smiles and goes back to examining the tampon.*)

EVA. I'm the cleaning lady. Now this is truly a miracle. May I try one?

LILY. I said who are you? This is my apartment. How did you get in? Did you have some sort of tampon emergency or what? What do you want?

EVA. You're very wet. Did you just come from the *mikvah?* (*Lily begins to circle. Picks up a broom.*)

LILY. I know karate! And tai kwan do! You won't have a chance against me!

EVA. Your legs are showing. And your—(*touches her own nipples with her index fingers.*) That's not modest.

LILY. You're from the street, right? You live on the street and you came up here for a tampon. OK. It's a bad lesson for life, but take the tampon and leave. No trouble. Just don't do it again! OK? Just leave. Here! Here's some chocolate if you leave now. I really don't want to hurt you. (*Lily pushes box toward Eva, goes to the door, opens it and waits for Eva to leave.*)

EVA. Oh, thank you. I haven't had a sweet for a good two hundred years. (*Puts down tampon, opens a chocolate, relishes it.*) Ah, what a blessing! As sweet as the Sabbath. We had a peddler who came through Zemyock—Yitzhock the peddler—and he would stay with us on the Sabbath. He would always give me sweets.

LILY. Who are you? You sound familiar. (*Circles with broom.*)

EVA. I'm just the housekeeper. (*Starts to dust nervously with her apron.*)

LILY. (*Pokes Eva's wig off with the broom handle.*) YOU! In my apartment!

EVA. (*Points up, gesticulating throughout the scene with the tampon.*) They heard you crying, and I'm here. Be glad! Why aren't you glad!

LILY. I wasn't crying. But now I'm shouting. I'm shouting GET OUT OF MY LIFE BEFORE I HAVE YOU AND THAT SON OF A BITCH KAEDMON LOCKED UP!

EVA. Of course you were crying. You were on a funny chair, and you were crying that you were empty. They did a quick check, made the match, and here I am. Took some fast talking on my part, let me tell you, but in Zemyock that was my specialty.

LILY. (*Picking up bookend.*) Get up and get out! I don't know who you are and how you know what you know, but it's spooky and I don't like it. Just get out!

EVA. They warned me you might be hostile. Look, I can't give you references, but I'll tell you a little something, then you'll know. That business with your baby being born in another woman's womb, we'll have to talk about that. It's definitely not in the Mishnah!

LILY. How do you know that? (*Raises the broom.*) Did you bug Chad's office? Tell me! Now!

EVA. You just told your strainer (*puff, puff, Eva imitates Lily's exercises*) and I heard, because we're—well, tuned into you, you could say.

LILY. You mean you're bugging me. There's no way you could know that, except that you bugged Chad's office.

EVA. No, we heard you talking to your strainer. She remarked that you are a love goddess of—of a certain kind. We must discuss that later. No false gods, Lily. Forbidden you know. (*Freeze. Lily steps stage left where Headrup and Diana are sitting.*)

LILY. So how much did they pay you to put a microphone up your tights? How much?

DIANA. I have my integrity, Lil honey. The stories I could tell, but do I talk? Never!

LILY. But she knew everything we said! Somebody had to have told her and it wasn't me! That leaves you!

DIANA. Not necessarily.

HEADRUP. No, not necessarily. With those long distance bugging devices, people can follow you around and listen in on anything. Nothing is sacred anymore.

DIANA. But you have to have a bug on your person.

HEADRUP. Yes, on your person.

LILY. Where is it? (*Diana and Headrup shrug; Lily starts to frisk herself, then stops.*)

LILY. Wait a minute. She's small potatoes. I want the big guy! Nobody bugs me and gets away with it.

HEADRUP. And that Kaedmon guy really bugs you, as I recall.

DIANA. The key thing is to use your wits! You've got a sound mind in a sound body, so use it! Your wits against her wits! That's the way to deal with this Kaedmon fella, Lil hon.

HEADRUP. Don't lose it Lily. She's obviously trying to confuse you. It's your wits against her wits. (*Freeze. Lily steps back into apartment, more composed.*)

LILY. (*Takes a chocolate and offers another.*) So, who are these "we" people you say heard me crying?

EVA. Oh, the Powers That Be.

LILY. The powers that be. I see. And what do they think about what they heard?

EVA. They are naturally upset about the omission and they want it corrected.

LILY. What makes them so sure there was an omission?

EVA. Your cry. It was a prayer, really, and prayers travel great distances. You were crying for me. So here I am.

LILY. Yes, indeed. So here you are. What do you imagine I'm going to do? Hand you the memo and beg forgiveness?

EVA. Oh, you mean that memo? I've taken care of that. You don't have to worry about that.

LILY. There are no papers that Kaedmon doesn't have in his possession.

EVA. We can deal with that later. Look, I'm not just here because you cried. I need you as much as you need me! This is my last chance to recycle through earthlife so I can complete all of the good deeds, the *mitzvahs,* I need to enter the Garden of Eden. My previous stays were either interrupted or—unsatisfactory, sometimes both. So you don't need to feel grateful. it's not just for you. It's for me, too. I need you to be my gilgul.

LILY. Your what?

EVA. My gilgul . . . the human body that a dead person's soul passes into in order to continue living. To atone for sins committed in a previous incarnation. It's all right there in the Kabbalah. (*Lily looks confused.*) You don't know much, do you?

LILY. I thought I did.

EVA. In my case it's not so much sins as cleaning up loose ends, you know. Be glad we're not men. They have 613 rules to get right before they can sit in the Garden of Eden, so they're always recycling through, over and over. Most of them never get it right. Women just have a few things to get right, but the big one for me is to find my true mate again, my Adam, and have his child. So that's why you must be my gilgul.

LILY. I'm nobody's gilgul, sweetheart.

EVA. Well, that's what we're trying to correct. It was an oversight and we're trying to correct that. (*She takes another chocolate, then starts examining the tampon again.*) A miracle.

LILY. That's no miracle. It's just a tampon.

EVA. In Zemyock it would have been a miracle. You wouldn't believe what we had to—

LILY. NEVERMIND! Anyway, I never heard of Zemyock.

EVA. Oh? It's where your family comes from, on your mother's side. Didn't she tell you?

LILY. My mother doesn't know where her family came from. Last time I asked she just pointed toward the Atlantic Ocean.

EVA. Well then, I'll tell you both all about it. Maybe next Shabbat. We'll make a nice chicken, and kugel, and—

LILY. Hold it—What did you say your name was?

EVA. Eva Rochel.

LILY. But I think that's—

EVA. Your Hebrew name? Yes, they told me, that's why they think this is such a good match. You're named after your great grand-mother Eva who is named after me. Such a world now. One name's not enough, you have to have an English name, too. Do Gentiles have two names also? Do you know any Gentiles? Besides that Cossack?

LILY. You're a bizarre combination, do you know that? You're damn well-briefed about things you shouldn't know anything about, like who I'm named after, and you don't know squat about things that everybody else knows. Like that tampon.

EVA. A miracle!

LILY. Whoever you are, you're a cockleshell short of a full box of Godivas! But you're probably all Kaedmon could afford. Still, I'm calling security to get this on the record. (*Lily heads for the phone and starts to dial. Eva grabs the chocolates and the tampon, runs into bedroom offstage.*)

EVA. But we have business!

LILY. Hello? Get Security up here and call the police.

EVA. And we have a deadline. They're very serious about deadlines!

LILY. I've apprehended an intruder and I've got her cornered in the bedroom. Hurry, please. (*Lily slinks toward bedroom door with a broom. She kicks it open and discover that Eva isn't there.*) What the . . .? (*Lily goes off into bedroom and returns with candy wrappers, an empty box of tampons, and a pair of pantaloons.*) She's gone! And she took my pantyhose!

Scene 7

Eva appears at the Gates.

REBBE MOSHE. Evala! Eva Rochel!

REBBE SHMUEL. That wasn't a very good start, was it?

EVA. It was a very good start, really. I learned all about stoves, and refrigerators, and something called pantyhose, and . . . (*reaches into her pocket*) never mind.

REBBE SHMUEL. Your gilgul doesn't believe in you. We told you it would be difficult entering at this late date. We still have our doubts, Eva Rochel.

EVA. She'll learn to love it, she just needs time. I'm having a fine time. I'm going to love living in such modern times.

REBBE MOSHE. Umm. A worm in a jar of horseradish thinks he's in Paradise. She doesn't believe you. You're going to have to do better than just knowing her Hebrew name.

EVA. Like what? She's such a skeptic.

REBBE KITZEL. She learned that in law school. There are no miracles in law school.

EVA. Strange talk from someone who spent his time on earth studying the law day and night.

REBBE SHMUEL. Ah, we are too soon old and too late wise. You will have to use your wits. It's not for me to tell you how to do it. Carry your own lantern and—

EVA. I know, I know. I need not fear the dark. What if she still doesn't want me when the time comes?

REBBE MOSHE. Difficult. Very difficult.

EVA. Maybe if I didn't look so different.

REBBE KITZEL. What? You're clean. You're covered. What else?

EVA. Never mind. I'll work it out. (*Aside.*) "It's better to suffer in Hell with a wise man than to frolic in Paradise with a fool."

REBBE SHMUEL. What?

EVA. Nothing, nothing. I'll work it out. I could use a little more help. This isn't exactly a trip to the butcher's you know! (*Lights. End of scene*)

Scene 8

Lily is at Ernesto's, getting a haircut and manicure; Eva, in yet another wig, sweeps through a few times sweeping up hair and fingernail clippings, which she puts into her pocket, and disappears.)

ERNESTO. Next time you're in, love, we'll highlight—very subtly, you understand, only very subtly—around the face to give a sparkle to your eyes. You'll be amazed how a little highlighting will bring a sparkle to your eyes, love. And you shouldn't need a touchup for six months. Subtle, very subtle.

MANICURIST. I'm familiar with a horizontal method for putting a sparkle in the eyes that doesn't necessarily cost a hundred bucks. Of course it should be touched up, so to speak, more than once every six months. Maybe your eyes would sparkle more if you got a touchup more than once every six months, honey. (*Freeze. Eva steps to the Gates.*)

EVA. Please, somebody do something with these. (*Takes clippings from pocket, sets them on her chair by the Gates.*) The wrong person gets hold of these and—whew—I don't even want to think about it. (*Returns to scene.*)

LILY. —and she acted like she'd never seen a tampon before and said she hadn't had a piece of chocolate in two hundred years—ate the entire box of Godiva shells. Do you know how many grams of fat that was? I think I know whose payroll she's on, you know, but still it's very strange.

MANICURIST. I hear there are people who've never seen canned ravioli, if you can believe it. I mean, some people lead real sheltered lives. Even in this country, like in the South, you know?

ERNESTO. Right. Maybe she's just from the South, love.

LILY. She's not Southern.

MANICURIST. That cerise may not be you, Lily. Did you ever think about getting your colors done? I'll just bet cerise isn't one of your colors. Maybe she's from one of those farms in Minnesota where girls grow up and don't meet a guy until the traveling salesman shows up.

LILY. Will they come to my office? To do my colors. No, Minnesota girls would know about electric lights.

ERNESTO. The basic plan for you is to present an aura of competence, as a lawyer, with an undercurrent of sensuality, to keep the opposition off balance. Just a little distraction, but nothing obvious. The highlighting will make a huge difference. Maybe the swamp?

MANICURIST. Sienna swamp? Too much orange.

ERNESTO. Maybe this intruder is from the swamp. (*Eva sweeps through.*)

LILY. Who is that compulsive sweeper you've hired? You're getting your money's worth. (*Eva has been sweeping around chair; Lily notices her and gets more and more interested. As Ernesto and Manicurist end their comments, Lily stops Eva with a finger through her waistband.*)

ERNESTO. Just for today. Temp service sent her over. Talk about weird! You should have seen her when the first bleach job came out of the dryer. She screamed something about evil eyes and—

MANICURIST. Yea, and when I unrolled Mrs. Plimpton's permanent, she shrieked and started spitting all over the shop. You'd think she'd never seen a permanent before. I mean, it hadn't been combed out, but still, spitting!

LILY. Nice pantyhose.

EVA. Thank you. Excuse me. (*Lily pulls Eva's wig off.*)

LILY. AGAIN? YOU?

EVA. (*Speaking very quickly.*) No, it's not. Well, technically, yes, it's me. Listen, just a suggestion. You've got to stop leaving your hair with just anybody, and your fingernails. Do you know what can happen if fingernails get into the wrong hands?

LILY. IT'S HER!

EVA. And listen, I like the idea about the colors. We should definitely get our colors done. I'll ask the Powers That Be and maybe they can get us a deal—No? Gotta go! (*Eva runs off the scene; freeze. Eva visits rebbes.*)

EVA. I was thinking that if we got our colors done it would give us something to talk about, something in common, you know?

REBBE MOSHE. Your colors were done by experts.

REBBE KITZEL. Does a leopard change his stripes?

REBBE SHMUEL. Does a tiger change his spots?

REBBE MOSHE. Does a flower change from red to yellow? Well, sometimes, but only if it's part of the plan.

REBBE KITZEL. You are your own perfection as you were planned.

EVA. If I'm so perfect why do I have to keep recycling through earthlife?

REBBE SHMUEL. Ah, you want to return to the Garden of Eden?

EVA. I always thought I did, but there's a lot to be said for the life Lily's leading. Little miracles I could live with. But yes, yes of course, I want to return to Eden.

REBBE MOSHE. Then you must fulfill certain *mitzvahs.* Only then.

REBBE SHMUEL. Only then, Evala.

EVA. Well, what about highlighting my hair? Do you know anything about highlighting?

REBBE MOSHE. The clock is ticking, Evala. Earthtime.

REBBE KITZEL. And Evala?

EVA. Yes, Rebbe?

REBBE KITZEL. It arrived! (*Holds up large box.*)

EVA. Wonderful!

REBBE KITZEL. We'll stay in touch! (*Rebbes Moshe and Shmuel smack their heads. Lights, end of scene.*)

Scene 9

Inside a nightclub, Lily and Chad are sitting at a table; Eva, in yet another wig and dark glasses, is their waitress; music is soft rock.

LILY. I'm telling you, your office is bugged. Just trust me on this, will you?

CHAD. You're really getting paranoid, you know that? How long have I been practicing law? How long?

LILY. Ten years.

CHAD. And you've been practicing how long? How long?

LILY. Alright. Five years.

CHAD. That's fifteen years we've been practicing law, and in that period, how many times has one of us been bugged? How many times?

LILY. That we know of?

CHAD. That we know of.

LILY. None. But Chad, I'm telling you she knows things, things she could only know from bugging. How could she have known about our plans about the baby? There's no way. She's very opposed to it, by the way.

CHAD. What do you mean, she's-very-opposed-to-it-by-the-way? What's she got to do with your life that she's opposed to it?

LILY. Well, I'm not sure, but how I behave seems very important to her. Chad, you were telling me the truth about the memo Kaedmon keeps bringing up? I mean, you didn't destroy a memo, did you?

CHAD. I'm a Yale man, Lily. I don't destroy evidence. 'Nough said?

LILY. 'Nough said. (*They hold hands.*) About the baby, Chad, maybe it wouldn't be so bad to have it myself. I mean, in my own body. There's something kinda nice about the idea.

CHAD. But Lil, you can have it both ways. We can have a child with our genes, you can work the entire nine months in total comfort *and* you keep that beautiful body. We'll be helping to define contemporary lifestyles, integrating the latest in scientific breakthroughs into the daily lives of modern men and women. It sounds like a *People* cover story to me.

LILY. Yes, but Chad, I don't mind the idea of having a—

CHAD. Lil, I've told you before. Never do anything someone else can do for you. Your time is too valuable. You still want to make partner?

LILY. Yes, but if I carried the baby, I think maybe I wouldn't feel so empty.

CHAD. Lil, I pegged you from the start as a woman of her time, a woman who pushed the envelope. Maybe I was wrong.

LILY. No. You weren't wrong. Oh, Chad, let's dance. (*Lily and Chad do a very sensual dance to "Proud Mary"; Eva is startled; freeze. Eva steps out to talk to rebbes.*)

EVA. I can't live with that Cossack. How can I live with that Cossack? And what about Adam? How will I find him if I'm raising the Cossack's child? Adam could never accept that.

REBBE MOSHE. The fact remains that she cried out and you were there to answer.

EVA. I can't do it. It's impossible.

REBBE SHMUEL. The wheel has begun its roll, Evala.

REBBE KITZEL. It will happen. (*Eva steps back into scene, begins clearing glasses; Lily leaves for the restroom; freeze. Lily steps over to handlers who appear stage left.*)

LILY. I'm confused.

HEADRUP. We're all confused, Lily. But at least now we're confused together. I mean, now we have our sisters to talk it all over with.

DIANA. Think of us as your sisters, Lily.

LILY. Thanks. This idea of Chad's about having the baby in a surrogate has a lot to it. You know that's one of the things I love about Chad, the way he's so far ahead of the pack—a visionary really. He's always thinking ahead.

ERNESTO. So what's bothering you, love? We'll need to do the highlights before the *People* cover, but other than that, it's all do-able.

MANICURIST. And I'll give you a pedicure. When your feet feel right, everything feels right.

DIANA. I think she can't decide if she wants a child.

LILY. Maybe that's it. But I do want a baby, I really do. I think I'd like to do it the old-fashioned way, but I'm afraid Chad would be angry.

HEADRUP. And you don't want him angry?

LILY. I owe him so much. He's my mentor, really, and he does have good ideas.

HEADRUP. You already have a father, Lily, you're looking at a father for your *child* here, not for you.

LILY. Yes, of course you're right. Still, I do owe him so much. It's times like this when I feel that emptiness I talked about, Headrup. I can't find anything inside me to help me make these big decisions. Just a huge empty silence.

ERNESTO. Hey, love. We're here for you. You're doing great, love.

You're putting it all together, you're just too close to see the big picture.

LILY. Still, I wish I were certain that Chad really cared about me. (*Steps back into club, dance continues, this time back-to-back; Eva is clearing their table, Chad notices and steps over, leaving Lily dancing alone.*)

CHAD. Hey, don't take my drink. (*Looks her up and down.*) Nice jugs.

EVA. The Talmud says we must not look at the jug but at its contents.

CHAD. What?

EVA. For there are new jugs filled with old wine, and old ones in which there is not even new wine.

CHAD. You're not one for small talk, are you? I like that. Let's dance.

EVA. No, no I can't dance with you. It's against the rules.

CHAD. It's not against any rules. C'mon, you know you want to. (*Pulls her toward dance floor.*)

EVA. (*Struggling.*) No! No! I don't want to dance with you. I don't dance.

CHAD. Sure you do. Relax and let yourself go. You're a great lookin' gal, you know. I want to see your moves.

EVA. (*Screams*) NO! NO! Oh, please, NO! COSSACKS! (*Her wig and glasses fall off in the struggle; Lily sees what's happening and pulls Chad away from Eva; Eva continues shouting, out of control now; Lily tries to calm her as she guides her out of the club. Curtain, end of Act I.*)

ACT II

Scene 1

Lily and Eva are on a park bench.

LILY. You're really so scared of guys?

EVA. Just Cossacks.

LILY. Cossacks.

EVA. It's something that happened to me in a previous life . . . in Zemyock.

LILY. Previous life. I'm not into that.

EVA. I could have guessed.

LILY. I just don't believe all that. It's irrational.

EVA. Irrational. But you believe faxes?

LILY. Well, yes, I believe them.

EVA. And you believe telephones?

LILY. Well, yes, most of the time.

EVA. So why is it more difficult to believe that a human soul cycles through many lives in its journey to enlightenment? Faxes fly words across oceans and mountains in seconds, yet you believe in them without understanding; for this you require belief *and* understanding? Listen. Your mother is my great great grandmother Yentil still trying to make challah without burning it! Can't you see it? It should be so obvious.

LILY. How do you know my mother always burns the challah? How do you have that information? Who did you interview?

EVA. Everyone knows your mother burns the challah. She's been burning it for two hundred years. What is that? A secret? It's not so awful, nothing to be ashamed of, except that a woman's got to bake a decent challah if she's going to enter the Garden of Eden with her husband. And your Aunt Bessie? She and Uncle David lived in Zemyock; they sold wool to the rich Poles while their own families froze under straw, and now they sell Gore-Tex to mountain climbers. He was no student, let me tell you. She was so ashamed of him. She's back to learn to be respectful of men. Another bit of behavior women must learn. You and I will work on that one together. (*Freeze. Lily steps out stage left to her handlers.*)

LILY. Somebody's crazy here, and I'm beginning to think it's me.

DIANA. But dearie, she really shouldn't be afraid to dance. Great aerobics. You've gotta tell her that!

ERNESTO. Don't be mad at Chad, love. He was just drunk. These things happen. Forgive the little things and go on, that's my advice. Eyes on the prize and all that.

HEADRUP. Eva has a definite problem with Cossacks. See if she's willing to work on that.

LILY. You don't understand! I'm starting to believe her, and I'm scared outta my mind!

ERNESTO. Just don't let her talk you out of that man of yours. He's one in a million, I promise you. I hear a lot of tales in my line of work, and he's definitely one in a million!

MANICURIST. I'm sure when she has her colors done, she'll feel more together. (*Lily steps back to Eva.*)

LILY. Who in heaven's name are you?

EVA. It's a long story. It begins in the Garden of Eden and will end, with any luck at all, in the Garden of Eden. (*Lily sits next to Eva; rebbes skate in and gather to listen; handlers pull up chairs stage left.*)

LILY. Start somewhere in the middle, please. Maybe with the Cossack.

EVA. I had come back to Earth yet another time to find my Adam and try to bear a child with him. A woman can only enter the Garden of Eden at the feet of her mate, and my luck with men in my lives hasn't been very good, I'm warning you. And with your Cossack, it doesn't look too good for this trip either. It took me I don't know how many lives before I finally found my true mate, my Adam. We'd think about each other all the time, when he was studying Torah or saying his prayers, when I was lighting the Sabbath candles or walking to the synagogue. We were always in each other's thoughts. Two sparks of a single soul.

LILY. Sounds good to me.

EVA. Not for a scholar. Nothing must interfere with his studies. But Adam wouldn't concentrate. If it wasn't thoughts of me distracting him, it was thoughts of revolution, of reforming the social order. You won't tell anyone—he read forbidden books. We had been taught—if someone throws stones at you, throw back bread. Our people were always so afraid. When the soldiers would come into our village and make mischief, the old people would say "sh, sh, they'll be gone soon." If you protest, only something worse will happen. Adam couldn't stand that. But always, the next day after the soldiers, some Poles would pass through our streets and pat our children on the head, and our elders would say, "You see, everything is fine again." But Adam said we shouldn't think that the lion is smiling when he bares his teeth; it is only waiting to devour. Then, one night, a few months after our wedding, the Cossacks raided our village. They were drunk and angry, blaming us for the death of some horses. Two of them broke into the house moments before Adam returned from the synagogue. By the time he arrived, it was over, and I was dead. Poor Adam went crazy and tried to fight back, but they killed him, too. The lion devoured us both. So you see, we need another lifetime to get our *mitzvahs* in order.

LILY. Don't you get some credit for difficult circumstances?

EVA. Not in this century.

LILY. But why me? I'm not convinced that I'm the gilgul for you, Eva.

EVA. When you cried, the rebbes realized that they'd skipped over you when you were born. Sometimes they get distracted arguing some fine point of law, you know? And they skip someone. They're very adorable, really, but they get *fashimled,* you know what I mean?

So they seem to have let you get by, empty. Some people are empty and don't know it. But you noticed, so the Rebbes believe they have an obligation to correct their oversight.

LILY. That's the omission you were talking about? My soul? Not a memo?

EVA. What's with you and memos? What *is* a memo? I've been waiting around for two hundred years for a member of my family to need me. We've had an excess of souls this century looking for their new gilguls; so it's been a long wait. Everytime it looked like there was a spot for me, someone else had priority. I was running out of patience, which is something else I've got to correct. Forget memos.

LILY. So the gig is that you enter my body and drive it from the inside like one of those floats in a Macy's parade, right? (*Eva shrugs assent.*) And just what will our agenda be?

EVA. We—I mean, you—will keep the Sabbath, make challah, and go to the *mikvah*. Then of course we'll—

LILY. Wait a minute, that last thing you mentioned—the mik— mik?

EVA. The *mikvah?* It's the ritual bath. You really don't know anything, do you? We'll go there to clean ourselves after our monthly period. Although with these little miracles that should go pretty fast.

LILY. We've got little individual *mikvahs* that come to *us* now. Remind me to tell you about them. Your rebbes'll love 'em.

EVA. I don't know. The rebbes are very strict about the *mikvah*. I don't think your little ones will count. They're very strict about the *mikvah*.

LILY. I'll bet they are. You and I may have some trouble with that one.

EVA. My most important task is to find my Adam and raise our child. In all my lives, I've yet to raise a child, and that's a requirement.

LILY. For Eden.

EVA. For Eden.

LILY. Well, I'm working on that—with Chad.

EVA. With the Cossack. I know. Listen, you should know, I've tried to stop it, this merger. I can't make a life with your Chad person. But the rebbes won't listen; they say we have to do it. The wheel is rolling.

LILY. And when is this grand merger supposed to occur?

EVA. Tomorrow night.

LILY. Tomorrow night? But that's tomorrow night!

EVA. Yes.

LILY. So in twenty-four hours I'm going to turn into a little Jewish housewife who lights her Sabbath candles, makes challah, goes to that *mikvah* place, and finds her brilliant Torah scholar to make a baby with so she can sit at his feet forever—and ever—and ever, while he studies Torah into eternity. Did I get it right?

EVA. Basically.

LILY. Surely you know that I have no intention of leading the life you describe.

EVA. And there's the part about keeping my mouth shut.

LILY. I don't remember you mentioning that one.

EVA. I'm afraid I've had trouble over the years with authority figures . . . my husbands, my rebbes, my fathers. "A never-silent bell," that's what they called me. I like arguing with rabbis, and when Adam and I made love, it was very difficult for me to stay quiet. Only Adam didn't seem to mind so much. Still, it's written that a woman must be quiet and submissive to her husband. Oh dear.

LILY. Oh dear is right. I'm a lawyer, a litigator. You know that? I'm paid to argue forcefully with men. Your rebbes know that?

EVA. They know you're a liquidator.

LILY. Li-ti-ga-tor!

EVA. Whatever. But they say we must work it out.

LILY. Not to be rude, but I had other plans for my mouth other than to keep it shut for the rest of my life.

EVA. And I had no plans to spend this next life arguing points of law with men as if I were their equal as a scholar. That's definitely not the road to Eden.

LILY. This can't happen. I'll lose my edge.

EVA. This cannot happen. I'll get an edge.

LILY. And what about Chad? He'll never stand for it.

EVA. He's still a factor? After what he did to me in there?

LILY. He was just drunk. We have to choose our battles, we can't get mad at every little thing. I read that in *Cosmopolitan.*

EVA. Once you explain it all to Chad, I'm sure he'll realize that it's best for all concerned if he found himself a nice Polish girl.

LILY. Never! Look, neither of us thinks this is a good idea. You've got to let me talk to the Powers That Be. They've got to change their minds!

EVA. HA! You don't know Rebbes. They argue, and they think, well, maybe yes, maybe no, but they don't change their minds.

LILY. I could change their minds. I was moot court.

EVA. So what are you going to do? Sue them? Go sue them! (*Freeze.*)

REBBE SHMUEL. So can she sue us?

REBBE MOSHE. On what grounds? We're on solid Kabbalistic ground here. Rabbi Luria himself has said this is kosher.

REBBE KITZEL. Invasion of privacy.

REBBE MOSHE. Invasion of what?

REBBE KITZEL. Privacy.

REBBE MOSHE. It's been added to the Talmud? What?

REBBE SHMUEL. Invasion, shmasion. What's that her business? Now, dereliction of duty, maybe.

REBBE MOSHE. We did overlook her.

REBBE KITZEL. But we're trying to repair the damages.

REBBE SHMUEL. So what then? Time off for good behavior? (*Freeze. Stage left, Lily's handlers.*)

DIANA. So explain to me—Lily gets the outside and Eva gets the inside, right? I mean, am I gonna have a whole new body to deal with here? This Eva's an ectomorph, and they're the worst. I was just gettin' some definition with Lily.

ERNESTO. Definitely it's Lily on the outside. She was just finding her look. I mean, Fifth Avenue marries Wall Street! What this shtetl chick's gonna do I don't know. I think she's going to compromise the total package.

MANICURIST. Yea, she looks like the type with ragged cuticles.

HEADRUP. I'm intrigued. This could make my reputation if they let me write it up in the *Journal of Unfounded Medicine.*

REBBE MOSHE. No writing up!

REBBE KITZEL. Definitely no writing up!

HEADRUP. (*To herself.*) Yes, I owe it to science to write about this. The Gilgul Phenomenon. It's a breakthrough.

REBBE SHMUEL. A breakthrough! Thousands of years we've been matching gilguls with souls and she's announcing a breakthrough!

REBBE MOSHE. Go figure!

REBBE SHMUEL. Maybe *we* could sue! (*End of scene.*)

Scene 2

Lily's office; Kaedmon storms in.

LILY. You can't come in here.

KAEDMON. I can understand your reluctance to talk. I have here a copy of the nonexistent memo that you knew nothing about, the—

EVA. Adam?

KAEDMON. Do I know you?

EVA. I'm Eva! Eva!

KAEDMON. How do you do. (*Turns back to Lily.*) So drop the pretense. It's time to talk serious settlement, no more dirty tricks. Your client is going to do right by my people.

EVA. But Adam, it's me. I'm here.

LILY. You're telling me that you worked for him after all?

KAEDMON. Excuse me, but I never saw her before in my life.

LILY. Oh, really? Who's pretending now? Are you going to tell me you didn't hire this lunatic to break into my apartment, trail me all over town, eavesdrop on my private conversations, my *therapy* sessions, for God's sake, collect my fingernails, can you believe it? and steal my pantyhose? Are you going to deny that?

KAEDMON. Ms. Gilbert, if I wanted to get into your pantyhose, I'd be much more direct. And, for the record, I don't.

LILY. Really, Mr. Kaedmon, you strain credulity. At least Eva admits the relationship.

KAEDMON. I don't think you heard me. On my fax machine, not thirty minutes ago, what should come singing over the wires but a copy of a memo to the president of Vertex Corporation from its chief engineer warning that the deposits into the Eden Rock landfill exceeded safe levels by a factor of one hundred because said landfill leaked like a sieve, and do you want to know the date of this memo? Eight years before they did a damned thing about it! Eight years! Do you know how many neighborhood children died of leukemia in those eight years? Do you know how many women in a six-block radius lost babies in utero in those eight years? How many men developed mysterious systemic diseases from which they never recovered? Do you want to know how many? Because I know. I've talked to everyone who lives or ever lived within ten blocks of that death-trap, and I know them all. Every last one of them. Eight years, Ms. Gilbert, eight long years.

LILY. Let me see that fax.

KAEDMON. What a gameplayer you are. Sure you can see it. Then a little gasp, and "I've never laid eyes on this. It's a fake." Spare me.

LILY. (*Reads.*) I've never laid eyes on this. It's a fake. I would have known if it existed.

KAEDMON. Oh, it exists. And you owe me the original.

LILY. I'm telling you, I don't have the original. But I'm interested in who sent you that fax. (*Looks at Eva.*)

EVA. Not me. I didn't do it.

LILY. Why do I think you did?

EVA. If what he says is true, I wish I had. But I didn't. I sent it to—

LILY. You sent this memo to someone?

EVA. (*Pause.*) I sent it to the rebbes.

KAEDMON. Who in hell are the rebels? An underground environmental group?

EVA. The rebbes. They're hardly in hell.

LILY. They're little men who dance around on the head of a pin inside her pin head! You can stop with the games, you two. Eva, it's more than a little unprofessional to fabricate a memo just because you can't find the one you were hired to find. You could go to jail for this.

EVA. It isn't fabricated. I found it.

LILY. Where?

EVA. In your lawschool yearbook. The Cossack.

LILY. Mr. Kaedmon, we'll discuss this again at 8 P.M. Here. I'll have this all sorted out by then and we'll decide how to proceed.

KAEDMON. I'll be here, and no more games, Ms. Gilbert. These folks have suffered too long. (*Kaedmon exits.*)

EVA. What if I told you that Chad planted that memo in your office? You wouldn't believe that, would you?

LILY. Absolutely not! We have an understanding, Chad and I.

EVA. I thought so.

LILY. And if there were a memo—and I'm not saying there is— and it was found in this office—Chad cares about me. I can't say he loves me, that might overstate it, but we have a sufficiently strong bond that he would never do anything to undercut my credibility as an attorney. We share the same ambitions.

EVA. Why don't you look in the yearbook, Lily.

LILY. (*Goes to bookshelf, picks out yearbook, memo falls out.*) Why would he do that? Why?

EVA. You're both under consideration for partner, is that correct?

LILY. So what? Chad's been a great help to me—he's like a mentor.

EVA. And how many partners will they choose this year, Lily?

LILY. One.

EVA. I'm sorry. Look Lily, if I could arrange it, would you like to meet with my Powers That Be?

LILY. Your controllers?

EVA. My Powers That Be.

LILY. Higher up than Kaedmon?

EVA. Much higher up than Kaedmon.

LILY. I'd be very interested in that.

EVA. I'll see what I can do. (*Lights, end of scene.*)

Scene 3

Eva, Lily, and rebbes are stage right, next to the wall of monitors.

LILY. Holy shit! Am I drugged?

EVA. Rebbes?

REBBE MOSHE. This is not permitted!

EVA. She must speak to the Powers That Be. It's the only way to make it happen.

REBBE SHMUEL. It will happen. No earthbound creature has power here.

LILY. And yet you've done me an injustice.

REBBE KITZEL. One which we fully intend to rectify.

REBBE SHMUEL. With no help from you.

LILY. I didn't ask for your help.

EVA. Yes. You asked. You just won't believe I'm the answer.

LILY. Not *this* answer, for sure.

REBBE MOSHE. And now you are asking that we ignore our mistake. We have responsibility.

LILY. Listen, I'm the wrong gilgul for Eva. We don't match up, you know? I've been raised to speak up and speak out. I was raised to have balls! I've got 'em! And I'm proud of 'em!

EVA. This you learned at mute court?

LILY. And this *mikvah* business. Where have you been for the last few hundred years? You're so repulsed by our bodily functions that you create these bizarre rituals to avoid having to deal with them? Things are different now. Women won't allow that kind of disrespect.

EVA. Lily, there's much more to the *mikvah* than that. You don't know what you're—

LILY. And let me explain something else. I love my body. I love sex. I want men to enjoy my body, whether we're married or not. I want to enjoy men's bodies, whether or not they're my husband. Does that make me a whore? (*Rebbes nod.*) You've acknowledged in your writings that sex is a wonderful gift. Well, now, on earth, in my culture, we agree, and we've worked the baby thing out so that we can have great sex without all those rules she's still trying to get right. And I like to make noises when I'm doing it!

REBBES. She's Lilith! (*Spit, spit, spit.*) Avert the Evil Eye!

LILY. And let me tell you something else. When I'm not in the mood, I'm not in the mood!

REBBES. (*Spit, spit, spit.*) Avert the Evil Eye!

LILY. And this business of sitting at the feet of my beloved for eternity while he studies Torah and has all the fun . . . what the Hell am *I* supposed to be doing? Shining his shoes? I can't even turn the pages, according to you, because I'm not supposed to touch the sacred books. Well, Eternity's a helluva long time. I want assurances that I can study at his side, *if* I have a husband, and *if* we choose to study.

EVA. (*In despair.*) I don't think we'll ever have to face that issue now. But it is true, my rebbes, that you are always telling me that if I carry my own lantern I need never fear the dark, but you want me to live by the light of someone else's lantern, even in Eternity. That is very worrisome.

LILY. And about Chad. My Cossack of choice. It's true, he hasn't yet agreed to marry me, but we do intend to have a child together. We're bonded. Eva seems to have a primary aversion to him. It cannot be resolved.

EVA. That's correct. Chad must go. Adam and I must get on with our lives together.

LILY. I might add that I know her Adam and I find him reprehensible. We could never make a life together.

REBBE KITZEL. This mate of your choice. Is he the one who looks at you through bubbles?

LILY. The same.

REBBE SHMUEL. Forbidden.

REBBE MOSHE. Bubbles interfere with study.

LILY. (*Notices the multiscreen wall.*) What's that?

EVA. That's how we heard you. We see everything from here.

LILY. Everything.

REBBE SHMUEL. Unfortunately.

LILY. You invaded my God-damned privacy!

REBBE MOSHE. Do not take His name in vain!

LILY. *His* name? *His* name?

REBBE MOSHE. (*Pause.*) Alright. *Its* name.

EVA. (*Pause.*) *Its* name? *Its* name?

REBBE KITZEL. (*Shrugs.*) The longer a blind man lives, the more he sees.

EVA. Did you hear that? You made them change their minds.

LILY. You're surprised?

EVA. You challenged them and they changed their minds.

LILY. They blinked. Yes! But now, this screen has got to go. (*Goes to screen and looks for cord; she receives a big electrical shock that bolts her out of the scene. Lights, end of scene.*)

Scene 4

Eva, in despair, walks stage left and sits with Lily's handlers. Each handler begins to comfort her, combing hair, buffing nails, rubbing feet, holding hands.

EVA. My rebbes are very angry with me. They look like harmless nebishes, but when you make them angry . . . (*Holds hands above head sharply.*) And my Adam doesn't even recognize me. Of course, that's how it's supposed to be.

HEADRUP. Full of repressed anger. Typical male behavior.

ERNESTO. Gave her the frizzies for sure.

MANICURIST. What did you soak these hands in, honey? Bleach?

EVA. Lily was so wrong about the *mikvah*. It wasn't like that at all. I was taught that I belonged to my husband for two weeks, and to God for two weeks. It was forbidden for me to touch any man when—when I belonged to God. I couldn't even hand Adam his cup. I'd put it at his place on the kitchen table and he would pick it up from there. We slept in separate beds, of course. When my time was over and I went to the *mikvah*, I was so happy at the thought of lying with Adam that night. The water was cool on my body. I could feel Adam's touch, his kisses wherever the water licked me. Walking home from the *mikvah* someone would always call out, "Make twins tonight, Eva." Of course, I couldn't *tell* Adam I was ready for him, not with words; that was forbidden. But at dinner, after he'd sat down at his place and said the blessings, I would hand him his cup. And he would look at me and my cheeks would burn.

DIANA. Listen, Eva. If you're gonna be part of this scene, you gotta let go, loosen up, learn to boogie. Here, I'll teach ya! (*Starts to dance with Eva.*)

HEADRUP. You know, you have some problems yourself that could do with a little attention.

EVA. Tell me about it. I've been trying to deal with them for a few hundred years now and this is the mess I'm into.

HEADRUP. Nothing personal, but you're a very repressed personality. Lily is a perfectly normal, representative woman of her time. Oh, her sails could use a little adjusting, but whose couldn't? She's just confused. She overstated it when she said she was empty, and you jumped in where you aren't needed, or wanted. I'm perfectly capable of getting her through this little crisis without outside consultation. Now, if you want to work on your Cossack phobia, I have openings at 1:30 on Monday, Wednesday, and Fridays.

EVA. (*Stops dancing.*) Will you be my rebbes?

ERNESTO. Sure kid. Just make an appointment at the front desk.

MANICURIST. Make sure I'm available, too.

DIANA. Sure. You can have the timeslot with Lily. Two for one discount. You just need some definition is all. No hard edges, that's your problem.

HEADRUP. I'll be your best friend, for $100 an hour.

EVA. $100 an hour?

HEADRUP. Well, I only have my masters. If I were a fucking Freudian, I'd get $150.

EVA. You're all very kind, but I still feel a little lost. (*Lights, end of scene.*)

Scene 5

Lily's office; Chad is seated, Lily paces.

LILY. So he came barging in with this fax of a very incriminating memo—I mean, if he were looking for the perfect memo to seal his case, that would have been it! Vertex knew for eight years and did nothing!

CHAD. But Lily, you told me there was no memo!

LILY. No, Chad, you told me. Where did it come from, Chad?

CHAD. Lily, I never saw a memo. If I had, you can be certain I would have turned it over. I'm a Yale man, Lily, and Yale men don't—

LILY. —destroy evidence? But obviously they do plant it in their alleged beloved's office, don't they? Don't they? That's within the code?

CHAD. I didn't send that memo to Kaedmon. I swear!

LILY. I believe you. What I don't understand is why you hid it in my office. Chad, we were going to have a child together! Was I getting too good, is that it? Making you nervous?

CHAD. Lily you've got to separate business from your personal life. Believe me, Lily, this was nothing personal; it was just a defensive measure. I never anticipated really using it against you. You know how you keep a $100 bill in the lining of your wallet?

LILY. For an emergency?

CHAD. Exactly. Just in case. For a rainy day!

LILY. But you were going to rain on me, Chad. Your Lily.

CHAD. (*Seductively.*) Lilys need rain, too.

LILY. You were protecting your future. And I wasn't part of it. God, I'm blind. I don't have what it takes to play in this game.

CHAD. Lily, you're taking this too personally. Now pull yourself together and help me work out some damage control. I suggest that we—

LILY. Do you know what's wrong with you, Chad? You're empty! Where other people have a little voice inside them telling them right from wrong, you have a balance sheet.

CHAD. Oh, really, Lily. Don't be—

LILY. Where other people have a soul, you're hollow.

CHAD. But Lily, Vertex is our biggest client! We've got to—

LILY. Get out, Chad. I've got things to do and very little time to do them in.

CHAD. Listen, I was wrong to even think about double-crossing you, Lily. I never would have done it when push came to shove. You know you're very special to me, Lily. Why, if you want to have our baby in your own womb, well, it might slow down your making partner, but—yea, I think you *should* have the baby yourself. (*Fax begins to buzz. Lily retrieves it, reads silently, smiles, then points a finger at Chad and says forcefully:*)

LILY. May you spend your life shearing your cows and milking your sheep! OUT! (*Chad exits. Lights, end of scene.*)

Scene 6

Lily's office, 8 P.M.; Kaedmon is waiting; looks at his watch as Eva enters.

KAEDMON. She's late.

EVA. It's been a difficult day.

KAEDMON. You mean, thanks to me?

EVA. No, actually, I would say due to circumstances beyond our control.

KAEDMON. Withholding evidence is very controlling.

EVA. We'd better not talk about that. (*She sits down on the floor next to his chair.*)

KAEDMON. Don't you want a chair? What are you doing on the floor?

EVA. It's been a hard day for me, too. I'm comfortable here, thank you.

KAEDMON. Sit up here. Don't sit on the floor. (*Eva moves to chair next to him.*) So your boss wants to talk settlement.

EVA. You don't sound convinced.

KAEDMON. I don't trust her to begin with, and when she segued into talk about settlement so fast, well, I'm suspicious. She'll probably make some sneaky proposal to buy off my clients, but won't begin to deal with the problems of cleanup. We have to think of the future, too, not just the people who've already suffered. She's going to have to deal with that upfront or no deal.

EVA. Sounds like you've been deceived before.

KAEDMON. You bet.

EVA. I had a friend once who said we shouldn't think the lion is smiling when he bares his teeth. (*Freeze. Eva starts to speak again to Kaedmon; a force draws her out of the scene to confront the rebbes.*)

REBBE MOSHE. (*Wagging finger.*) No words, Evala.

REBBE SHMUEL. Words are forbidden, Evala.

EVA. But Rebbes, we are taught that when you want someone you love to look in, you must open the curtain.

REBBE KITZEL. This is a special case, Evala. You can't open the curtain between earthlife and the beyond. You did it once with Lily, and you saw what happened.

REBBE MOSHE. This involves destiny. It is beyond earth time.

REBBE SHMUEL. Remember we are also taught that if it is a man's destiny to drown, he can drown in a glass of water. You can take hope from that.

EVA. But Lily's going to do something evil and he'll hate her more than any other person on earth in the morning. If I could only get him to leave, not meet with her until tomorrow when I've merged with her, then I can see that she does the right thing and he and I, I mean he and Lily, might at least be speaking to one another. But if they meet tonight, there won't be any tomorrow for me and my Adam, and I'll have lost my last opportunity.

REBBE MOSHE. It must not be. The rules are the rules.

EVA. There are exceptions.

REBBE MOSHE. No exceptions.

EVA. An exception casts light on a rule. *Numbers Rabbah.*

REBBE SHMUEL. No exceptions.

REBBE KITZEL. You must have faith, Evala.

EVA. I've had only faith for too long. We have only the day and hour in which we stand and tomorrow is a new world. You taught me that. I believe it.

REBBE SHMUEL. Don't be foolish Evala. This is your last chance.

EVA. And don't call me Evala. My name is Eva. (*Freeze. Eva returns to Lily's office and resumes place next to Kaedmon.*)

KAEDMON. Did we go to high school together? Peace Corps? Jamaica Plains rent strike? You're so familiar.

EVA. Adam, Mr. Kaedmon, I don't think Lily's coming. Maybe you should leave now and wait for Lily to call you tomorrow. I'm sure she's just been accosted by brigands or run over by a wagon or—

KAEDMON. A wagon? Run over by a wagon? (*Fax starts running.*) What's that sound? Somebody's sending in a fax—maybe you'd better get it.

EVA. Yes, I'd better get it. (*Goes to fax, reads incoming message, looks up, shakes her head, turns abruptly and returns to office.*) Nothing important. Just some very oppressive, controlling sorts who think they can make the laws without the consent of the governed. That's un-American, right?

KAEDMON. Right. Sounds like one of the firm's clients. Out to make their fortunes on the backs of the poor.

EVA. I like what you do. I think you're on the right side.

KAEDMON. Thanks. My parents would prefer that I practice law in a firm like this. But I have to believe in what I do.

EVA. No common sense?

KAEDMON. (*Laughs.*) That's just what my parents say.

EVA. The Rabbi of Kotzk said that one man buys himself a fur coat in winter, and another buys kindling. The first wants to keep only himself warm, the second wants to keep others warm, too.

KAEDMON. Yes, that's right. (*Fax begins again.*) There it goes again. (*Eva returns to fax, reads another short message, looks up, shakes head, returns.*)

EVA. It's Lily. She can't make it tonight, so you'd better leave.

KAEDMON. Why would she fax instead of calling? (*Lily enters, drunk. Reads fax, enters office. Eva looks away.*)

LILY. Ah, Mr. Kad! Sorry I'm late. Couldn't be helped. This has been one of those days that one never forgets. No matter how hard one tries.

KAEDMON. (*Gets up.*) Looks like you've been trying pretty hard.

LILY. I've been saying goodbye to the feast of my former life, dish by dish, savoring it bite by bite, before I go on what you might call a very restricted diet.

KAEDMON. Sounds grim.

LILY. I have no doubt that it will be.

EVA. Lily, you're in no condition to negotiate anything with Mr. Kaedmon. Your judgment is clouded. Don't you think you should wait until tomorrow?

LILY. Funny you should mention that. Someone just sent me a fax that said "When liquor goes in, judgment goes out." Do you know who sent that? No, Mr. Kad, I think we can do business this very day and hour. Monkey business, ha ha.

EVA. Lily, please, you're going to be so sorry if you do this.

LILY. Eva, if we're going to be—friends, you'll have to stay out of my business life. There's no place for you and what you represent in my business life.

KAEDMON. Eva, if Ms. Gilbert wants to negotiate, let's go at it. (*Sits down and slaps hands on desk, obviously enjoying himself. Lily sits down and slaps hands on desk as well.*)

LILY. Ah, that reminds me. 'Scuse me a minute. Just a God damn little minute. (*Retrieves memo from yearbook, puts it in her blouse.*) Mr. Kad, there comes a time in the life of every thinking woman, even those unburdened by conscience (*looks at Eva*), when one must review one's life and, weighing it in the balance, find it to be less weighty than one had heretofore pretended.

KAEDMON. I hear ya.

LILY. And when one finds that one has been putting one's thumb on the scale, so to speak, it is incumbent upon one to take one's thumb off of the scale and put it in one's mouth.

KAEDMON. You've lost me.

LILY. Which is to say, to speak the truth. Which is to say, to quit one's firm, which is to say, to dump one's boyfriend, which is to say, to hand over the Vertex memo to you and hope I never lay eyes on your cocky, holier-than-thou face again. (*Unfolds the memo and lays it in front of him.*) Now if you'll excuse me, I have to clean out my desk before midnight. (*Lays back in chair and passes out.*)

KAEDMON. (*Looks at memo.*) Well, I'll be damned.

EVA. I sincerely hope not, Mr. Kaedmon.

KAEDMON. Please call me Adam.

EVA. Adam.

KAEDMON. Did she really quit the firm, and dump her boyfriend?

EVA. It would seem so.

KAEDMON. Over this memo?

EVA. It would seem so.

KAEDMON. You just never know, do you? People can fool you. What will she do now?

EVA. Tomorrow's a whole new world, isn't it?

KAEDMON. And you? What will you do?

EVA. Oh, I'll— (*Fax begins.*) I'll just disappear.

KAEDMON. (*Goes to fax machine.*) "When you fight with the rabbis, don't make peace with the bartender." Who's sending these things?

EVA. Oh, just the Powers That Be. I'll take care of it. (*Pulls out the plug and steers Kaedmon to door.*)

KAEDMON. But I want to see you again. I think I need to see you again.

EVA. I'll be around. Look for me in the most unlikely place, and I'll be there. I'll be looking for you, too. (*She escorts him to the door and closes it. Lights, end of scene.*)

Scene 7

Eva and Lily are sitting back to back at the front of the stage, drinking tea. All handlers and rebbes are watching from left and right.

LILY. So tell me something. Who is this Lilith? (*Spit, spit.*)

EVA. Avert the Evil Eye! (*Spit.*) She was the first Adam's first wife. They were the two equal halves of the first human creature. But they had terrible fights, especially because when they made love she wanted to be on top. Do you understand what I'm saying? (*Lily nods.*) She was thrown out of the Garden to live with the demons, and she's caused trouble ever since. You don't want to know.

LILY. Sounds like a woman whose time has finally come. Chad might have liked her. I can't stop thinking about Chad and what a dope I was.

EVA. In Zemyock, the older women used to say there were four kinds of men. What's mine is mine and what's thine is thine; what's mine is mine and what's thine is mine; what's thine is thine and what's mine is thine; and what's thine is mine and what's mine is thine. Chad was definitely a what's mine is mine and what's thine is mine kind of person. Who can make a life with a what's mine is mine and what's thine is mine? Not even Lilith. (*Spit.*)

LILY. (*Spit, spit.*) Yea, but where do you find the kind that—that last kind?

EVA. The what's thine is mine and what's mine is thine kind? I think we can find one.

LILY. Together?

EVA. Together. (*Freeze.*)

DIANA. I'm confused.

HEADRUP. Mmmmmm. They just need to get out of their heads and trust their radar, now that they'll have some.

ERNESTO. I hope she'll still want the highlighting. She'll need it more than ever.

DIANA. Maybe we can get to work on those glutes now that she's out of a desk job.

MANICURIST. They'll never agree on a nail polish.

HEADRUP. I can't wait for Lily's next session. I wonder if she'll be phobic to Cossacks. My guess is it's something you never outgrow. (*Freeze. Back to Lily and Eva.*)

EVA. We'll work it out. Haven't you noticed that Jews are always talking to themselves? They're negotiating with their gilguls, that's all.

LILY. We've got a lot of negotiating to do.

EVA. Tell me about it. I don't see how I'll ever work things out inside a gilgul like you. My luck. I'm supposed to be learning to keep my mouth shut inside a foul-mouthed barrister. No disrespect.

LILY. And I'm being retrofitted with a medieval feminine consciousness who thinks that silence is golden. Listen up. Even the rebbes can change, remember? Think about it this way. Maybe what's a sin in one generation is a virtue in another. I would venture to say that the biggest sin for my generation of women is silence, and the greatest compliment you could give me is to call me a never-silent bell. (*Eva and Lily begin a back and forth bell-like motion as the toll of a bell marking midnight peels.*)

EVA AND LILY. Ding, dong, ding, dong! (*Freeze.*)

REBBE MOSHE. Stop with the ding donging already! Such an ache in the head I'm getting!

REBBE KITZEL. They like each other.

REBBE SHMUEL. Too much. I'm still not optimistic.

REBBE MOSHE. What's that supposed to mean?

REBBE SHMUEL. We'll lose her.

REBBE KITZEL. What we'll lose her? What are you moaning about now?

REBBE SHMUEL. When there are no fences we lose them, and there are no fences in America. We'll lose her. Such a nice girl, our Evala.

REBBE KITZEL. She's over two hundred years old. What do you mean, "girl"?

REBBE SHMUEL. Alright, "woman." So shoot me. (*Freeze. Bells resume.*)

LILY. Oh, my God, this is really going to happen! I'm not ready.

EVA. You won't even remember me in the morning. Or my rebbes.

LILY. I'm willing to forget the rebbes, but listen, go easy on the Godivas, will ya? I don't metabolize.

EVA. Sure. I can't wait to try your little *mikvahs*. And Lily?

LILY. Yes?

EVA. Will you teach me that movement you were doing on the dance floor? It's very beautiful.

LILY. I'm not sure it's you, Eva.

EVA. Try me.

LILY. Eva, will I really have a—a soul now?

EVA. Yes, Lily, you'll really have a soul.

LILY. A little voice about here (*Touches chest*) where the silence used to be?

EVA. I'll be there, Lily.

LILY. Eva, I can't make any promises about Adam. You know that.

EVA. I know that. But the next time you see him, promise me you'll at least speak to him.

LILY. Alright. I'll at least speak to him.

EVA. Maybe even—hand him a cup of tea?

LILY. He can hand *me* a cup of tea!

EVA. I'm sure that's forbidden.

LILY AND EVA. (*To one another.*) You still don't know anything, do you? (*Lights out, both disappear. Curtain.*)

Photograph by Joseph Bly

Barbara Kahn

I WAS BORN AND RAISED in Camden, New Jersey. My maternal grandparents, Joseph and Pearl Litwin, emigrated from Ananyev in the Ukraine as young marrieds, along with all of Joe's family. They settled in Mt. Laurel, New Jersey, proprietors of a small general store with living quarters attached, where I spent the first three years of my life. Pearl died when I was just a few years old, but I remember my grandfather, called Pop, as a vigorous and funny man. Long after I could see how he did it, I pretended to be astonished at Pop's one and only magic trick. I knew he did not really find that coin behind my ear, but I trusted it would always end up in my hand for me to keep.

My paternal grandfather was Louis Kahanofsky, a blacksmith-turned-ironworker, who left a town near Kiev with his oldest daughter to establish residency in the United States and send for my grandmother Shifra and the four other children. However, World War I, the Russian revolution and civil war, and changes in U.S. immigration laws kept the family separated for a number of years. Shifra managed to survive with her children, reaching safety in Cuba and finally reuniting with her husband and daughter in Philadelphia. Louis died before my parents met, and Shifra never learned to speak English, so I knew only the simplest outline of their lives. I was always thrilled, however, when the family drove to Philadelphia, and my father would point out a large building with an ornate iron gate and proudly proclaim, "Your grandfather made that gate."

Every Wednesday night we would visit Bubbah in her rented rooms in a house on Poplar Street in West Philadelphia. My most vivid memory of those visits is waiting what we thought was long enough before my sisters, my brother, and I started pestering our parents, "Can we go home yet?" It would be many years before I learned the extent of the suffering that my grandmother and her children had endured and of her extraordinary accomplishment in getting them all safely out of Europe. Once when still in Russia, they were betrayed by a local villager while hiding during a pogrom and were put before a firing squad. They were saved at the last moment by an officer who arrived on horseback and decided to let them go. Shifra was a real-life Mother Courage. I think of her whenever I see Brecht's play. That is why it has always been one of my favorites.

My father spoke little of his harrowing childhood except to impress upon his children the good fortune we had to be in America, with its many opportunities. Although his formal schooling had been limited by circumstance, he was an avid learner and instilled in us an unshakable respect for knowledge. Determined that we would all go to college, he worked long hours in his grocery store in Hainesport, New Jersey, in order to provide for his family. I started working weekends with my father when I was about eight years old. I was proud when he let me wait on customers and taught me to total the sales on the back of brown paper bags. My father also taught me a respect for people. He operated his store with unwavering honesty. Unlike some other shopkeepers, he never cheated the Puerto Rican migrant laborers who worked the nearby farms every summer or the day laborers who came from Philadelphia on ancient yellow buses to pick the fruit and vegetables. I loved to see the smiles and handshakes and genuine goodwill between my father and his customers. And he always included me in that goodwill. He was a gentle boss, and a gentle father. And he lived long enough to attend the four bachelor's degree and one of the three graduate degree ceremonies of his children.

My mother, Esther, was a full partner with her husband. She worked during much of their marriage, setting an example for us. She taught us the value of every human being, especially our own value. "As long as you tell me that you did your best, whatever you accomplish is good enough" was her philosophy. A high school dropout because of a family crisis, she went back to night school in later years to get her diploma.

With these grandparents and parents as role models, my siblings and I learned early on a compassion for those less fortunate that influenced our life choices as adults. Joyce is a high school guidance counselor, Phyllis and Larry are social workers, and I work in the theater.

I cannot remember a time when I did not want to be an actor, but I waited until I was ten years old to tell my parents. I read every book about the theater in the East Camden Public Library, borrowing my sister's adult library card until I was old enough to get my own. My Aunt Bea, a regular theatergoer, took me to see my first play—a pre-Broadway tryout in nearby Philadelphia. Eventually, I started taking the bus across the bridge on my own after school to hang around the stage doors. I wanted to meet the famous actors with whom I hoped I would someday be working. I set up interviews with some of them, ostensibly to play the tapes for my school drama club. Julie Harris, Robert Preston, and George Grizzard were among those who were nice enough to meet with and encourage a child's visions. While in high school, I spent a summer in the Temple University Summer Theatre Program, getting my first taste of working in the theater. This was followed by a year's free study with Bob Sickinger at the Philadelphia Theatre Workshop Foundation, thanks to a theater-loving philanthropist named H. B. Lutz. I went on to receive a B.A. degree in Theater Arts from Adelphi University. While a student, I performed Off-Off Broadway, creating roles in plays by Tom Eyen, Ted Harris, and others and working with directors such as Ron Link and Robert Dahdah.

After college, I continued my professional study with director Arthur Storch. Arthur helped me blend my previous training and experience with his ideas into a solid method of creating a character. After a series of scenes in Arthur's class resulted in grueling critique of my work, I confronted him. He had been so harsh, had I done something to offend him? He said no, but that he expected more of me because I had the imagination of a writer—I had written a play, after all. (I had collaborated with Ray Hagen on the book for a musical that had been produced at the famous LaMaMa E.T.C.) Like my mother, Arthur would not allow me to settle for less than my best. That was the first time I thought of myself as a playwright as well as an actor, although it would take a few more years for me to write a full-length play on my own. In the meantime, I added directing to my credits, including a trip to London to direct *Nijinsky's Journal* at the National Theatre. Then, during a dry spell in acting work, I recalled Arthur's words and decided to write a play with, of course, a part for myself—*Hell's Kitchen Has A Tub In It*. Though I did not appear in the first production, I directed it and learned to love playwriting separately from my love of acting. I continued writing plays, expressing my experiences, my political and social consciousness, and my Jewish heritage. Thanks to artistic director Crystal Field, my plays have had a home at Theater for the New City in New York for the past three years with both readings and full productions. I co-founded Sisters On Stage, a nonprofit organization to mentor lesbian playwrights. I am a member of the Women Playwrights Collective and Village Playwrights, two peer groups where playwrights can test material at various stages of development, and of the Dramatists Guild. I was a recipient of the 1995 Torch of Hope Award for life-time achievement in playwriting, presented by the Barbara Barondess Theatre Lab Foundation, following honorees such as Terrence McNally, John Guare, and A. R. Gurney.

Beginning each new play is truly an adventure. As I wrote in a monologue called *The Weaver:* "I am a weaver of tales. I can create great adventures, terrible tragedies, tales of romance, seduction and passion. And all of my stories are true, if you want them to be. . . . I can create wonderful characters, so that even when I am hungry or cold, I am never, never alone, and I am always, always loved."

Many things provoke or inspire me; I try not to write the same play twice. *Hell's Kitchen Has A Tub In It* is a semiautobiographical romantic comedy about the subculture of the "creative poor"—aspiring actors and writers—who live among the working poor in the Hell's Kitchen neighborhood of New York City. The tenement apartment setting has the significance of a character in the play. In later plays, I again expropriated bits of my own experiences to give to my characters.

After my father's funeral during a February snowstorm, the rabbi was on the phone in my parents' house pleading with strangers to dig out of their driveways because he needed a *minyan.* I counted twenty-two people in the living room, including my mother, sisters, aunts, and other female relatives and family friends. I told the rabbi that if he counted two women as one man, he could start the service. He was not amused. But then neither was I. My rage remained until I wrote *Unorthodox Behavior,* a drama set in a Russian village in 1913, about the tragedy that results when a young woman attempts to say kaddish for her father. Here, as in my other plays, I express my sense of justice and impatience with bigotry, however grounded in religious tradition. Unwilling to exercise my power as playwright to stack the deck for my own views, I present the rabbi not as a villain it would be easy to hate, but as a kind and compassionate man who believes as fervently in his own sense of right and wrong as the

character Simi believes in hers. *Unorthodox Behavior* has been described as "a little Yentl, a little Antigone and the rest Barbara
Kahn." Pearl Gluck of *Tikkun Magazine* said, "We were completely
impressed. Coming from an Orthodox background, we have not seen
something with as much sensitivity as this . . . and with so much
charm and such warmth."

I carefully research all my plays. For *Whither Thou Goest,* the sequel
to *Unorthodox Behavior,* I spent hours in the Buttenweiser Library of
the 92nd St. YM-YWHA reading the records of the original Home
for Immigrant Girls. Unlike many other immigrant plays, my play
evokes the plight of single women alone in a new country and at the
mercy of both those who despise them and those who mean them
well. In the play, two women, one a poor Jewish immigrant and the
other a wealthy American "do-gooder," overcome the barriers between them only to find those barriers put back in place by the
society around them. More than just a romantic drama, *Whither Thou
Goest* deals with issues of class and culture, homophobia, assimilation,
and differences in religious beliefs, issues that divided the Jewish
community in the early twentieth century and that continue to di-
vide us.

Through my sister Phyllis, a human rights activist with Amnesty
International, I met former prisoners of conscience. Phyllis's work
and their stories inspired me to write *Pen Pals,* a play set in twenty-
first-century America when the religious right has taken over the
government and turned their bigotry into law. I wanted to show that
when democracy dies, there are no fences left to sit on. Monica, a
workaholic archaeologist, cannot or will not see the political changes
around her until her own arrest for simply muttering an obscenity to
a policeman. In prison and tortured, Monica refuses to denounce
others in order to gain her freedom and get back to her precious
work. And, once again, I give voice to the opposition. Gabrielle is a
warm, loving person who was raised to believe in the Faith In America Party, accepting their euphemisms as fact.

While working in London, I was given a play about the nine-
teenth-century French writer George Sand. It was not a very good
play and after workshopping it in New York, I abandoned it, and
with Colleen Curtis, the actress who had played Sand, wrote *The
Forgotten Truths.* Rather than continue the myths about George
Sand—one man in the audience had called her a "star-fucker" because of her relationships with Chopin, DeMusset, and others—we

wanted to find the truth. Sand herself wrote, "All I want is for people to question the accepted lies and call out for the forgotten truths." We showed her as the celebrity she was in her own time.

Seating Arrangements started as a one-scene, one-act play about a woman despondent about her lover walking out who encounters a gregarious younger woman in a train station. The play was produced several times, and people kept asking what happened next. I kept writing more scenes, the two women got together, the ex-lover came back, and the play finally became a full-length lesbian romantic comedy called *Seating and Other Arrangements*. The play is a very traditional comedy about two women in love, with all the joy and angst and need to compromise that is part of any human relationship.

I create the characters in my plays and then they tell me what is going to happen to them. They determine the style of play—comedy or drama, contemporary or period piece—and they determine the form—monologue, one-act, or full-length play. My plays are *always* about conflicts, about overcoming adversity of different levels of significance and about commitment to truth and historical accuracy. Like the archaeologist in *Pen Pals,* I want to capture the people and places of our past and present so they will not be lost to the future. With fundamentalists of all religions assuming the power to define other people and the work they create, I am determined to reclaim the definition of my life. Members of the religious right, with their presumptions and arrogant claims to the words "family" and "values" and "Judeo-Christian," do not know me or my family, and they have no right to link my Jewish heritage with their form of Christianity. I refuse to tailor my work to fit the current political fashion.

My life in the theater has been governed by a passion for justice and for quality. I am an actor, a director, and a playwright. Portraying human truth is what gives me pleasure as an actor. Directing with integrity and detail is what I bring to other actors and playwrights. Preserving the truth is the essence of why I write plays.

The first scene of *Whither Thou Goest* was presented at Theater for the New City, New York, on February 27, 1995. The play was then presented by Calico Productions as a staged reading at Common Basis Theatre on July 30, 1995, directed by the playwright, with the following cast:

Jackie S. Freemen   Douglas E. Huston
Jolie Dechev   Matt Collins
Cassie Angley

Whither Thou Goest
1995

Dedicated to Aaron Libson, my cousin and friend.

Characters

SAMANTHA LASSER (called Simi, pronounced Simmy), born Cyma Lozawick. Russian Jewish immigrant in the United States for eight years. Former student, now part-time staff member at the Hannah Lavanburg Home. She has a slight trace of accent, mostly in inflection and syntax. Midtwenties.

RACHEL, resident student at the home. In the United States for about a year, she still has a pronounced Russian accent. Teenager.

CHARLOTTE LOBELL, American Jew descended from early immigrants. Midtwenties.

RICHARD LOBELL, Charlotte's father. Founder of a successful publishing house. Midfifties.

Scene

The Hanna Lavanburg Home for Immigrant Girls at 319 East Seventeenth Street (Second Avenue); Simi's room in a rooming house. New York City.

Time

1922

ACT ONE

Scene 1

An office in the Hanna Lavanburg Home for Immigrant Girls. Simi is doing paperwork at a desk. Rachel enters, carrying as many hatboxes as she can hold at one time. She puts them down on and around Simi's desk.

SIMI. Rachel!

RACHEL. I not finished. There are lot more boxes. They all by the front door, and no one can come in or go out.

SIMI. You can't put them in here. You're blocking all the files. What is this, anyway?

RACHEL. Hats!

SIMI. Where did they come from?

RACHEL. They come from Russek's. There are so many. Enough for all of us I think.

SIMI. Who brought them here?

RACHEL. The wagon from Russek's.

SIMI. Who sent the wagon from Russek's?

RACHEL. There was driver. He unload all the boxes by the door, and he let me sign paper.

SIMI. You signed the receipt? Rachel, you are supposed to come to someone in charge for things like that.

RACHEL. But I know how to sign my name in English.

SIMI. Just because you can sign your name does not make you in charge here. And just because you can sign your name does not mean you should do it because someone asks you to. Your name belongs to you. Don't give it away like a piece of penny candy.

RACHEL. Will I get in trouble? Will Miss Sommerfeld send me away? I sorry, Simi. I not mean to do anything wrong. Maybe if I go to the man from Russek's he give me my name back. But I not know how to go there by myself. Will you go with me? Please.

SIMI. Stop acting like a child, Rachel.

RACHEL. Maybe I go there alone. I try. I find the man. (*Hugging Simi from behind.*) Just don't be mad at me, please.

SIMI. (*Giving in.*) All right. Forget the man. (*Simi tries to go back to her paperwork.*)

RACHEL. I glad you not mad with me. (*Rachel squeezes Simi harder.*)

SIMI. What's done is done. (*Simi pulls loose from Rachel.*)

RACHEL. *Vos zoln mir ton mit de ale* boxes?* (*Rachel sits on Simi's desk.*)

SIMI. In English, Rachel. Always in English. And sit properly. In a chair. (*Simi goes back to her paperwork.*)

RACHEL. (*Doesn't like being ignored.*) What shall I do with the rest of the boxes? (*Charlotte enters.*)

CHARLOTTE. Oh, good, here are the rest. Did you count them? There should be five dozen hats in all.

SIMI. Five dozen? Really? You don't say? And who are you that you walk in here without a hello or a name even, and you know all about the hats?

---

*What shall we do with the rest of the boxes?

CHARLOTTE. I'm sorry. I'm not usually so rude. I'm Charlotte Lobell. And you are?

SIMI. I'm the person in charge here today.

RACHEL. (*Interrupting.*) She Samantha Lasser. She not really in charge. She part-time teacher here—I mean tutor—I think that's the word. Isn't it, Simi? Miss Sommerfeld ask her to work in here today.

SIMI. Rachel, you talk too much.

RACHEL. (*Emphatically.*) But you not in charge.

CHARLOTTE. Miss Lasser . . . Where is Miss Sommerfeld?

SIMI. She's not here.

CHARLOTTE. Is she upstairs with new arrivals or is she out?

SIMI. Why should that concern you where Miss Sommerfeld is? It's not your business, excuse me for saying so.

CHARLOTTE. Look, Miss Lasser, I came here to make sure the hats were delivered. I'm sorry that offends you.

SIMI. Miss Sommerfeld is not here. Miss Meyerberg is not here. *I* am in charge—Rachel, don't say another word—and I don't remember anything about any hats.

CHARLOTTE. Of course, you wouldn't remember. They're a surprise.

RACHEL. They are a wonderful surprise. Aren't they, Simi?

CHARLOTTE. The Young Jewish Ladies' Benevolent Society, I'm this year's charity chairwoman, decided that the Hanna Lavanburg Home for Immigrant Girls would be the recipient of this month's fundraising. It's been over two years since we did anything for you girls.

RACHEL. (*Leaning over the desk between them.*) I think that's nice. It's a real *mitzvah*,* isn't it, Simi?

SIMI. Rachel, get off the desk. And go find Bertha. The two of you must have some work to do. Practice writing in English something else besides your name.

RACHEL. Oh, you two want to talk. Okay.

SIMI. Not "okay." Proper English.

RACHEL. Okay. I mean, all right, Simi. Oh, Miss Lobell, thank you for the hats. Would it be okay, I mean all right, if Bertha and I open some of the boxes just to see what they look like?

CHARLOTTE. Of course, dear, they belong to you girls. It's "okay" with me.

SIMI. Rachel, don't touch the boxes.

RACHEL. But there still some more to bring in.

*Good deed.

SIMI. Leave them for now. They're going back. And close the door behind you. (*Rachel exits.*)

SIMI. Now, Miss Lobell, you'll take a seat, and we'll talk about hats.

CHARLOTTE. Pardon me for saying this, but you could be a little nicer to Rachel.

SIMI. So maybe you'll make her next month's project. Save her from the big bad bully at the Lavanburg Home.

CHARLOTTE. That's not what I meant. She was excited about the hats. What was the harm in letting the girls open the boxes and even try them on?

SIMI. The harm, Miss Lobell, is in the girls accepting handouts from people who decide for them what they need or don't need. They need to learn control of their own lives. They don't need hats. They need schooling and jobs and most of all, they need to think for themselves.

CHARLOTTE. I'm sure you're right about all those things, Miss Lasser. But people also need pleasure in their lives. There is pleasure in knowing that others care.

SIMI. I think you are mistaken in who is getting the pleasure. You sit in your meetings, drink a little illegal sherry, am I right? Or maybe some light wine? And you feel good about yourselves. You call the department store on the telephone, and they send hats to the poor needy immigrant girls down on Second Avenue. You can relax for another month. You can party and shop and go to the opera and not have to do another good deed for thirty days more. Whose pleasure are we really talking about, Miss Lobell?

CHARLOTTE. You think because you sit behind that desk for one day that you can be another Julia Sommerfeld? That you have the right or even the capability to criticize me and my friends? Let me tell you who we are. Three years ago my friend Beatrice worked day after day at Mount Sinai Hospital bathing patients with influenza and changing their dirty linen until she fell ill herself. My friend Willa ran away from home in 1917 so she could join the ambulance corps and go to France. I could go on, but I won't. You don't know me or my friends. You can think about us whatever you please, Miss Lasser. I really don't care. You are a presumptuous arrogant snob.

SIMI. Now we get to the truth—how you really feel about us here.

CHARLOTTE. No, it's how I feel about you. Only you. (*Rachel enters. She is wearing a hat.*)

RACHEL. I sorry, Simi. I could not help it. All those boxes. So I peek. And this was the first I opened—the only one, I promise. And it fits me perfectly. I look like a real American. Bertha says I look like I from Paris. She been to Paris.

CHARLOTTE. You look beautiful. Look how the color highlights your eyes.

RACHEL. It does?

CHARLOTTE. You have excellent taste, Rachel.

RACHEL. Thank you. (*Turning to Simi.*) Look, Simi, look. Do you see how it show my eyes?

SIMI. I see.

RACHEL. Maybe I could wear it once to the Welcome House social on Sunday night. Then I give it back.

CHARLOTTE. You don't have to give it back. It's yours. No one else would look so good in it. (*Simi gives Rachel a look.*)

RACHEL. But Simi said we have to give the hats back.

CHARLOTTE. We'll see about that. Even so, that hat will be a personal gift from me to you. When is your birthday?

SIMI. Her birthday is not until next April.

RACHEL. It is on the twelfth of April. So far away.

CHARLOTTE. Well, my birthday is in two weeks. So consider it your gift to me. (*Rachel smiles at Charlotte, then looks at Simi, puzzled.*)

RACHEL. I no understand.

CHARLOTTE. It will make me very happy—give me pleasure—to know that you have such a beautiful hat that you enjoy. The pleasure is in giving, isn't it, Miss Lasser?

SIMI. That's enough. Rachel, the hat is beautiful. But you are beautiful with or without that hat. So now you'll give it back.

RACHEL. No.

SIMI. You're telling me no?!

RACHEL. You not Miss Sommerfeld or Miss Meyerberg. You not my mother. You have no right to tell me what to do. The hat is mine. Miss Lobell give it to me *personally*, so now it is mine. No matter what you say.

SIMI. So, wear it well, Miss French Lady. You can wear it maybe when Miss Lobell and her friends invite you to tea.

RACHEL. Simi, please.

SIMI. Don't Simi please.

CHARLOTTE. What is your point, Miss Lasser?

SIMI. Rachel, you don't need gifts from rich ladies who think they are better than you because they were born here and speak perfect English and have more money than they know how to spend.

RACHEL. She is better than me. But someday I speak English good and I make money, too. I want to be just like her.

SIMI. Listen to yourself. Look at yourself. You can't be what you are not. Use your brain, Libby.

RACHEL. I not Libby! You always call me that.

SIMI. You're right. I'm sorry.

CHARLOTTE. Who is Libby?

RACHEL. That's Simi's little sister back in Russia. They not get along so well . . .

SIMI. Rachel!

RACHEL. That's what you said. (*To Charlotte.*) Sometimes when I make her angry, she forget and call me Libby. She says I just as annoying and . . .

SIMI. (*Interrupting.*) Rachel, that's not anyone's business. Teaching you English is dangerous . . . (*Simi turns away from Rachel, goes back to her paperwork.*)

RACHEL. (*Hugging Simi.*) Simi, please don't be angry.

SIMI. (*Embarrassed.*) Rachel, stop this, so maybe I can breathe a little.

CHARLOTTE. Rachel, I think Miss Lasser is angry with me, not with you. Why don't you go show the hat to your friends, and let them pick out the ones they want. Miss Lasser and I will finish our argument.

RACHEL. Okay.

CHARLOTTE. (*Smiling.*) Okay. (*Rachel looks at Simi who doesn't look at her. Disappointed, she exits.*)

CHARLOTTE. I've changed my mind. I'll be going, too. I'm sure that someone who is in charge of this office for one day is not in charge of the Home and does not have the authority to turn away any charitable gift. Tell Miss Sommerfeld I was here. I'll be back soon to meet with her. (*Charlotte exits. Simi, feeling alone, tries to go back to work. Unable to concentrate, she looks at the boxes for a time, then goes to them and opens them. She removes a hat, puts it on and tries to see herself in the reflection from a glass-covered photograph on the wall. Charlotte reenters unnoticed and watches Simi for a moment.*)

CHARLOTTE. Surely, Miss Lasser, somewhere in the Lavanburg Home there must be a mirror.

SIMI. What are you doing back here?

CHARLOTTE. I'm not spying on you.

SIMI. No?

CHARLOTTE. I came back to see if we might declare an armistice or, at the least, a truce?

SIMI. We're not at war.

CHARLOTTE. No, we're not. I'm not your enemy. I'm not even your friend yet, but we could work on that.

SIMI. On which? Being enemies or being friends?

CHARLOTTE. Well, we could get to know each other first and see what the possibilities are. You made some assumptions about me. I mean, we made assumptions about each other. We started off badly. Let's try again, shall we?

SIMI. Is it important to you?

CHARLOTTE. It might be . . . Yes.

SIMI. So, what do we do?

CHARLOTTE. Let's schedule a meeting to talk about the school here—the girls, what they want and need.

SIMI. And after all the talk, what then?

CHARLOTTE. We'll see what can be done to help. Together. But first, put that hat away, please. It doesn't suit you at all. (*Charlotte looks through boxes for another hat.*)

CHARLOTTE. There's another one somewhere here that's much better for you.

SIMI. So now you'll decide what hat is for me?

CHARLOTTE. All right. I'll show it to you and *you* decide.

SIMI. That's right, Miss Lobell.

CHARLOTTE. Charlotte . . .

SIMI. Charlotte. This is *my* head and . . .

CHARLOTTE. It's a very fine head . . .

SIMI. Thank you. . . . And I will decide what hat will go on this very fine head.

CHARLOTTE. You're absolutely right. (*Charlotte takes another hat from box.*) So long as it's green or brown and something simple in design so it won't detract from your hair. (*Holding out hat to Simi.*) You have beautiful hair. (*Simi, surprised and embarrassed, smiles shyly at Charlotte and reaches for the hat as lights go down.*)

Scene 2

Several weeks later. Morning. The Home. Simi is doing paperwork. Rachel is sitting on her desk.

RACHEL. I want to go with you, Simi, please.

SIMI. Rachel, don't sit like that. And tuck in your blouse.

RACHEL. (*Jumping off desk.*) Let me go with you. Please.

SIMI. (*Teasing.*) What happens if you go with me to Ellis Island, and it's the same runner as last year and he sees you? And he remembers you?—(*Melodramatically, imitating a "villain" twirling his mustache.*) "Oh, there's that little girl that got away from me. Not this time. No sirree! This time she's mine!"

RACHEL. But you be there, Simi.

SIMI. And while I'm busy saving you again from *this* runner, suppose there's *another* runner who gets *another* little Rachel in his trap. That would be your fault.

RACHEL. I take care of myself, I promise. Just let me go with you.

SIMI. And what happens if there is a new immigration officer there in charge and he sees you and says, "Who made such a mistake last year and let that little Rachel get in. Fire him immediately and send her back to Lithuania."

RACHEL. I not come from Lithuania, Simi, you know that.

SIMI. *I* know that, but if *he* doesn't, you'd better take a map of Lithuania with you.

RACHEL. *Ikh vil geyn mit dir. . . . Gey nit on mir.**

SIMI. In English.

RACHEL. I just want to go with you today.

SIMI. No, Rachel, not today.

RACHEL. You would let Charlotte go with you, if she wanted to.

SIMI. Maybe I would.

RACHEL. But she can't help you like I can. She can't speak Yiddish or Russian or Polish.

SIMI. Charlotte speaks French.

RACHEL. You see—*she* can't help you. Jews do not speak French.

SIMI. Charlotte is Jewish.

RACHEL. She does not act like a Jew should act.

SIMI. So now all Jews should act the same? Where is it written that God doesn't let Jews speak French? Tell me that. No, don't tell me. Tell the Jews who live in France. And didn't you say that Bertha was in Paris once?

RACHEL. That is not the same thing.

SIMI. Ohhh . . . it's different because we're talking about Bertha. I thought you liked Charlotte.

RACHEL. I never said . . .

SIMI. (*Insisting.*) You like Charlotte. You like her. She gave you that

---

*I want to go with you. . . . Don't go without me.

hat that you wore every day, day after day, until Miss Sommerfeld told you, "Enough is enough." Now you don't wear it at all.

RACHEL. I not like it anymore. It's an ugly hat. It does not suit me at all. Mrs. Rabinowich told me.

SIMI. Mrs. Rabinowich who last week you told me will always be a *greene** even if she is in America for a hundred years? You don't listen to yourself talk. Now, find something to do somewhere else, please. Finish your story about the trip to the museum. It was very good, what you started.

RACHEL. I finish it tomorrow.

SIMI. I have work to do before I go.

RACHEL. Why can't I stay? You only come here one day a week, and then you spend all the day with Charlotte.

SIMI. Charlotte is working here now, you know that. We're working together to help the Home.

RACHEL. (*Hugging Simi.*) I not get to see you at all.

SIMI. You see me now, Rachel. (*Breaking the hug.*)

RACHEL. You not like me anymore. You only like Charlotte.

SIMI. Stop acting like a child.

RACHEL. I not a child. You like Charlotte better than you like me. She is beautiful and she smart and she can speak French. Well, I can learn to speak French, too. I can if I want to. If you want me to.

SIMI. Nobody wants you to learn French. Only English. And proper English. Like you do in your stories. And if you don't sit like a lady and fix your clothes, Miss Sommerfeld will make you study the class about deportment again instead of the second writing class. And this time, she will get no argument from me. (*Charlotte enters.*)

CHARLOTTE. Hello, you two. Rachel, how are you? I brought the film star magazines that you and Bertha asked for.

RACHEL. Bertha ask you, not me. I not want them.

SIMI. Rachel, be nice.

RACHEL. No. I not have to be nice. I can be . . . not nice. (*Rachel gives Charlotte a dirty look and runs out.*)

CHARLOTTE. What's wrong with Rachel?

SIMI. She thinks I like you better than I like her.

CHARLOTTE. Do you?

SIMI. (*Ignoring Charlotte's question.*) Rachel needs to be with friends her own age, not with me.

*Unassimilated immigrant.

CHARLOTTE. She just wants to know that you care about her. (*Changing the subject.*) So, how are you today?

SIMI. She knows I care. For a whole year now, she knows. It was I who rescued her from the runners.

CHARLOTTE. The runners?

SIMI. They work for the factory owners. They go to Ellis Island and look for young women who arrive alone with no one to meet them. Or they work with the agents in Europe who sell false names to people without relatives here. They pretend to be the cousin or brother, so immigration will release the girl, and the girls end up instead in the sweatshops working like slaves or worse even.

CHARLOTTE. That's terrible. Someone should stop them.

SIMI. Someone does. That's what *we* do.

CHARLOTTE. How do you do that?

SIMI. We go to Ellis Island to rescue the girls. Or sometimes immigration sends the girls to us if they see it in time. As a matter of fact, Frieda, who was supposed to go to Ellis Island today, has to see about a new job instead, so I'm going in her place. We can't have a long meeting.

CHARLOTTE. How much time do we have?

SIMI. I need to be there by 12:30, no later. And I have to finish this other work besides.

CHARLOTTE. That's not much time for us.

SIMI. Then let's get to work.

CHARLOTTE. I could go with you to Ellis Island.

SIMI. Not you, too.

CHARLOTTE. Is Rachel going with you?

SIMI. One time on Ellis Island was enough for her. One day last year, when it was my turn to go to Ellis Island, there was little Rachel, all alone, standing by the gate, her papers clutched in one hand, a cloth bag in the other—a real greene. Just then, I spotted the runner. I knew his face from other times. We call him Valentino because he's handsome like an actor. He turned to Rachel, removed his hat and bowed. She gave him the most radiant smile, and I started screaming in English, in Yiddish, in Russian, "Leave my cousin alone! *Loz mayn shvesterkind tsu ru! Ostav'te kuzinu v pokoye!*" He ran away, and there stood Rachel, looking at me like I was a madwoman.

CHARLOTTE. What a glorious sight you must have been. Coming to the rescue of the young maiden.

SIMI. Rachel's an orphan since very young. Her parents left some money for her care and her future. She used the money to buy a sponsor from an agent in Bremen. The little that was left is for a dowry.

CHARLOTTE. And you, did you have to buy a sponsor?

SIMI. Oh, yes. Somewhere in America is my cousin Malka's husband, who came here many years ago and never sent for her or wrote to her even. Besides that, I have no family here.

CHARLOTTE. You were very brave.

SIMI. Courage is easy to find when you can't turn back, when there is only one direction you can go.

CHARLOTTE. I don't understand.

SIMI. For people who are alone and desperate, there is always someone offering a better life for the right price. But Rachel is truly brave. What she went through and still to have such love of life and find so much enjoyment.

CHARLOTTE. If I were like Rachel, all alone on Ellis Island, would you rescue me?

SIMI. Definitely not. Sewing all day, everyday, in a sweatshop might do you good, I think.

CHARLOTTE. I'm serious, Simi.

SIMI. That is not a serious question, Charlotte. You are not alone and you are not poor.

CHARLOTTE. So what would it take for me to get more of your attention?

SIMI. All of a sudden, today everyone wants my attention.

CHARLOTTE. You didn't answer my question.

SIMI. What's to answer? Everyday except Thursday and *Shabbas*, I work at the studio. Thursday, I'm here and you see me. *Shabbas*, I go to shul and then, believe me, I rest. More than that, there need to be more hours in the day or days in the week. Unless you come to the studio and pay Mr. Rosen to take your photograph. Then, maybe, you get to watch me hold the light for him, and the photograph turns out badly because you're not paying attention. That leaves Saturday, if I decide not to rest one week.

CHARLOTTE. Every Saturday, I go to temple with my father, and then he has guests for dinner. He needs me to be his hostess. He insists. I'm sorry.

SIMI. So, it's settled. Thursday it is and only Thursday. I think, Charlotte, you will survive. Now, please, we have work to do.

CHARLOTTE. I brought the catalogue of books my father publishes. We can go over the lists and see which ones they can use here.

SIMI. It's very kind of your father to give us the books.

CHARLOTTE. He doesn't know yet.

SIMI. Charlotte!

CHARLOTTE. He'll do it. He's very generous. He donates to a lot of places. He always has.

SIMI. You have to ask him first.

CHARLOTTE. I'll ask him when we know which books we want.

SIMI. That is not the proper way to do things.

CHARLOTTE. It's all right. He won't mind. This is nothing for you to get so upset about.

SIMI. I don't like when you decide for other people what they will do.

CHARLOTTE. He's my father. I know what he's like.

SIMI. You don't know me.

CHARLOTTE. You're right, I don't. But I'm trying.

SIMI. Don't try so hard. (*Simi glares at Charlotte.*)

CHARLOTTE. (*Feigned contriteness.*) I'm sorry . . . (*Pause.*) Simi, I said I'm sorry.

SIMI. If you would ask people first before you decide things for them, it would not be necessary to ask forgiveness after.

CHARLOTTE. (*Self-mocking.*) You're right. You're absolutely right. I'm a terrible person. But I apologized. (*She gets no response.*) If you won't accept my apology, then what? . . . I know—I should be tarred and feathered. . . . No, I should be stoned. Stoning would definitely be appropriate. I'm sure Rachel would be glad to help you do it.

SIMI. (*Visibly upset.*) You make jokes about things that are not funny. Not to me. I want you to go now.

CHARLOTTE. (*Puzzled and concerned.*) No. Tell me why you're so upset. I'm not leaving. Not like this. What happened to you?

SIMI. Nothing happened.

CHARLOTTE. Something happened. Was it in Russia?

SIMI. It's not your business.

CHARLOTTE. You're my friend. I want to know all about you.

SIMI. (*Pulling herself together.*) Nothing happened, Charlotte. It's all right.

CHARLOTTE. No, it's not. I won't leave until things are right between us. Whatever it takes.

SIMI. Charlotte, please.

CHARLOTTE. No! I won't move from this spot until it's settled between us. I won't.

SIMI. It's getting late. I have to leave soon anyway.

CHARLOTTE. I won't let you leave until I know I'm forgiven. No matter how long it takes.

SIMI. You are as stubborn as Rachel.

CHARLOTTE. You forgive her when she makes you angry.

SIMI. So, I forgive you.

CHARLOTTE. Are you sure?

SIMI. Yes, I'm sure.

CHARLOTTE. What do you forgive me for?

SIMI. For . . . I don't know. I don't remember. (*Simi realizes the absurdity of their argument and laughs.*)

CHARLOTTE. (*Teasing.*) Prove it to me that you forgive me.

SIMI. What do you mean?

CHARLOTTE. Do something so I know that I am truly forgiven.

SIMI. (*Pause, thinking.*) All right, what you can do, if you like, is go with me today to Ellis Island.

CHARLOTTE. I'd love to go with you.

SIMI. But this is not a game. You do what I say when we get there. Don't make your own rules.

CHARLOTTE. We'll take my car.

SIMI. (*Laughing.*) I can hear all the greeners when they see it. "Such a big motorcar! Like in the films. Ayyy! What a country! America is truly paved with gold."

CHARLOTTE. (*Laughing.*) Let's go.

SIMI. First I need to find Rachel and tell her. She's angry because she wanted to go, too.

CHARLOTTE. You can see her tonight. We'll come back here and take her and Bertha for a drive.

SIMI. Not tonight. Tonight I have to help develop the photographs from the whole week. Mr. Rosen is letting me work extra to pay for my own camera.

CHARLOTTE. Then I'll take Rachel and Bertha. Maybe I can convince Rachel I'm not so bad after all.

SIMI. When Rachel decides something, it's hard to change her.

CHARLOTTE. She's very much like you, you know. More than you realize. Finish your work while I find her, and I'll meet you outside in the car in . . . say, twenty minutes? Leonard has the car on Nineteenth Street. (*Charlotte exits.*)

SIMI. (*To herself.*) Rachel is not like me at all. She could never do the terrible things I've done to survive, *Got zol mir moykhl zayn! Zolst mir fargebn! Ikh veys ikh hob gezindikt.** Charlotte is not the one who needs forgiveness. (*Rachel enters, overhears the above.*)

---

*God, forgive me! Forgive me! I know I have sinned.

RACHEL. *Vos redst du? Farvos shlogst du zikh aleyn?**

SIMI. Rachel! You frightened me.

RACHEL. *Du bist*† a wonderful person. A good person. The best.

SIMI. Thank you, my friend.

RACHEL. Are you all right?

SIMI. Yes, I am all right. Charlotte is looking for you.

RACHEL. So? She can find me. I am right here. With you. (*Simi looks down at papers on her desk, spots something and reads it.*)

SIMI. Look at this, Rachel. (*Rachel sits on arm of Simi's chair and puts her arm around Simi's shoulders.*)

SIMI. (*Pointing at the paper and laughing.*) "former resident Miss Nastassia Smith from Moldavia" . . . Look—Smith from Moldavia! . . . "needs a reference to be sent to Pittsburgh that she is honest and a hard worker." (*Lights go down.*)

Scene 3

Several weeks later. Early Thursday morning. Simi's room in a rooming house. There is a single bed, a night table with a lamp, a wooden chair, and an armoire. There is a wooden waste basket on the floor. Simi is getting dressed. There is a knock on the door. She opens the door. Charlotte is standing in the doorway.

SIMI. (*Surprised and nervous.*) What are you doing here? We're supposed to meet at the Home.

CHARLOTTE. It's a beautiful day. I thought we might take my car and drive to the country instead.

SIMI. The country?

CHARLOTTE. To Long Island. We can see trees and flowers and watch the sunset over the ocean.

SIMI. We're supposed to meet at the Home.

CHARLOTTE. You said that already. May I come in?

SIMI. No. We're supposed . . . (*Catching herself.*)

CHARLOTTE. I can't come in?

SIMI. No. You were not invited here.

CHARLOTTE. So, invite me now.

SIMI. No.

CHARLOTTE. How can you be angry on such a glorious day? The

---

*What are you saying? Why are you flogging yourself?

†You are.

sun is waiting for us. There is a light breeze. I'll bet the ocean is as blue as the sky. Let's see if I'm right.

SIMI. I had enough ocean in my life. All the way from Bremen to New York. Even if you told me the ocean was purple with yellow dots, I don't care to see it again. So go to the Home, and I'll be there at ten o'clock, and we will have our meeting as usual.

CHARLOTTE. As usual is boring.

SIMI. I didn't know I was obliged to entertain you. Excuse me that I'm not amusing enough to hold your attention, Miss Lobell. Does the ocean maybe dance and sing and tell you jokes?

CHARLOTTE. Oh, Simi, you don't bore me. You fascinate me. I want to show you how beautiful the day can be. To share it with you. Why are you turning my offer into some insidious plot to bring a little pleasure into your life?

SIMI. What that means, I don't care to know.

CHARLOTTE. What word didn't you understand—insidious or pleasure? (*Charlotte goes into the room and sits.*)

SIMI. (*Angry.*) You were not invited to my room.

CHARLOTTE. (*Looking around.*) So *this* is where you live?

SIMI. Finish your thought, Charlotte. This is where you live—in this slum, this hell hole . . .

CHARLOTTE. I didn't say that, and I didn't think it either. It's clean and comfortable and private. That's what matters.

SIMI. Could *you* live here? In one room? Could you get up each morning and hold your bladder while you dress to go down the hall to the common toilet? I don't think so. Or maybe you could hire someone to do it for you. They say money can buy anything.

CHARLOTTE. You know it can't.

SIMI. That's right. You're a smart lady. Rich and smart, too. Any man would be grateful to have you.

CHARLOTTE. Simi, what is going on with you?

SIMI. I'm taking notice of you, making an observation. Charlotte Lobell, intelligent and fully uh . . . (*hunting for the word*) . . . assimilated . . . heiress. But with all the proper pity for the rest of us Jews who were not so fortunate to be born in America and have a wealthy father and grandfather. Why haven't you married, Miss Lobell? You're quite a catch.

CHARLOTTE. Why do *you* care?

SIMI. I don't care. You can marry a Rockefeller and count each other's money for the rest of your lives. I don't care at all.

CHARLOTTE. I thought we settled these differences when we first met. You know it doesn't matter to me where you live or how much money you have. It's you I care about. And I think you care about me. I feel it. We've become very close, haven't we?

SIMI. I don't want to talk about this.

CHARLOTTE. I do. I'm not embarrassed to say it. I feel very close to you. Like a true friend. I need you. I want you to need me.

SIMI. You have everything you need. You don't need me, too.

CHARLOTTE. But I do. I think about you a lot, you know. All week, I wait for Thursday. Three more days until Thursday . . . two more days . . . tomorrow. Fridays are the worst. On Fridays, I think about a whole week of waiting for next Thursday.

SIMI. I'm not somebody you should think about all the time. So, I want you to stop. Think about someone else, if you have to. Not me.

CHARLOTTE. I don't want to think about anyone else. I love thinking about you. Even when you argue with me or when you give me that look.

SIMI. What look?

CHARLOTTE. That one! You just did it. You look at me like I'm not real, not a real person, like you're deciding whether or not to make me disappear.

SIMI. I can't make anyone disappear.

CHARLOTTE. I didn't mean that literally . . .

SIMI. (*Doesn't know the word.*) What does that mean?

CHARLOTTE. It's the way you make me feel sometimes. Like I don't exist for you. If I went away, it would have absolutely no significance in your life. I want you to miss me.

SIMI. So go away, and I'll miss you. Is that what you want?

CHARLOTTE. Dammit! Don't pretend you don't know what I'm talking about.

SIMI. I do know what you mean, Charlotte. You don't have to say it. I don't want you to say it. I can't feel that way, and you shouldn't either. It's not right.

CHARLOTTE. But what if you do? Can you turn off the feelings? And why should you?

SIMI. I told you. It isn't right. Not in this world. Not before God.

CHARLOTTE. You believe in God?

SIMI. You don't believe?

CHARLOTTE. No.

SIMI. But you go to shul every Saturday with your father. You said.

CHARLOTTE. He insists. My great-grandfather helped establish

Temple Emanu-El. My father is on the board. It's important to him that we two represent our family at the temple. It doesn't matter whether I believe or not.

SIMI. I don't understand you.

CHARLOTTE. To tell you the truth, Simi, I don't think often enough about God to believe or not to believe. It's not important to me whether God exists or not.

SIMI. It's more important than you know, Charlotte.

CHARLOTTE. Why?

SIMI. I have done things in my life . . . I need to believe that there is a loving forgiving God. That I can atone for my sins.

CHARLOTTE. God has nothing to do with forgiveness.

SIMI. Charlotte!

CHARLOTTE. What could you have done that was so terrible?

SIMI. I knew what was right in God's eyes when everyone else said otherwise.

CHARLOTTE. You were very brave.

SIMI. I was very stubborn. I gave up my family, my home, everything because I believe in God.

CHARLOTTE. Tell me about your home. Your family. Before. When you were a child. Tell me about Libby.

SIMI. No. Samantha Lasser was born on Ellis Island. Cyma Lozawick died crossing the ocean.

CHARLOTTE. Cyma is a beautiful name. For a beautiful woman. You asked why I never married. I could ask you the same.

SIMI. I left Russia because I couldn't be obedient to any man, to every man. Why would I give up everything for that, then come here and sell myself to a man? I could have married Itzak Gerson in Russia and still have my family.

CHARLOTTE. Who was Itzak Gerson?

SIMI. The rabbi's son. We were betrothed.

CHARLOTTE. Did you love him?

SIMI. I didn't even like him very much.

CHARLOTTE. He loved you. I'm sure he did.

SIMI. He hated me at the end. He joined the others against me.

CHARLOTTE. (*Intrigued.*) Why?

SIMI. When my father died, may he rest in peace, I thought Sherstagrad was ready for a very learned and pious scholar who also happened to be a woman to take her father's place with the men in the shul.

CHARLOTTE. And?

SIMI. And nothing. They were not ready. Very far from ready, as a matter of fact.

CHARLOTTE. What happened?

SIMI. (*Reluctantly.*) There was trouble.

CHARLOTTE. What kind of trouble?

SIMI. (*Matter-of-factly.*) I insisted. They refused. Things happened.

CHARLOTTE. What things?

SIMI. Never mind, Charlotte.

CHARLOTTE. Your family. Were they against you, too?

SIMI. Libby and I didn't get along so well about many things, but always, I think, there was love. She said she wanted to join me in my protest, but I knew she was afraid and in the end, I did it alone. When I had to leave Sherstagrad, my cousin Malka gave me the money. Her savings for a new sewing machine. Eight years now and no news, no letters. So every week I write to them, I send money when I can, and I pretend that I still have a family. Besides that, I'm very lucky to be here.

CHARLOTTE. I'm glad you're here.

SIMI. Here there is reformed where there are no curtains, no upstairs for us to hide in shame before God for being women. Here there are also Itzaks, but I don't have to obey them. Or marry them even.

CHARLOTTE. Is it only the obedience that bothers you? I used to look at all the wonderful young women in my life and watch them marry, one by one. Each time it seemed like another loss to me. I didn't want to lose myself that way. I don't want to lose you.

SIMI. I'm glad you didn't.

CHARLOTTE. Are you?

SIMI. (*Embarrassed.*) I said it, didn't I?

CHARLOTTE. So, will you invite me to your room?

SIMI. I don't understand. You are already in my room.

CHARLOTTE. I know, but I want it to be legal. I mean, I want you to make it right. I need it to be all right with you.

SIMI. So, you're here, and it's all right. How is that?

CHARLOTTE. It's fine for now, Simi. Thank you.

SIMI. You're welcome, Charlotte.

CHARLOTTE. (*Smiling.*) I'm welcome? That sounds even better than all right.

SIMI. You play with words. Sometimes I think you're playing with me. Laughing at me.

CHARLOTTE. Never. But I wish I could make *you* laugh, make you happy just once.

SIMI. I'm very happy. I'm happy that you are my friend. I'm even happy that you need me. And I will make every effort to need you, too. As a matter of fact, I need you right now. You can help me decide which of my two dresses to wear to go to Long Island.

CHARLOTTE. (*Smiling.*) What you're wearing looks wonderful.

SIMI. I've never been to Long Island. What exactly does someone do there?

CHARLOTTE. They do what two people who enjoy each other's company do when they want to be alone together outdoors. They tell the driver to leave them in the park or at a beautiful spot by the sea, and he goes away for awhile. A long while. Maybe even all day. And after the sun goes down and the night air begins to get chilly, he returns with the car. The two people get in and take the blanket that's always in the car. They put it around themselves and get warm and think about the perfect day all the way back to the city . . .

SIMI. We can go by the studio, so I can take my camera with us. We can take photographs, if you like.

CHARLOTTE. I'd like that very much. We can have a picnic.

SIMI. What is that—a picnic?

CHARLOTTE. It's a picnic. You know. Oh . . . I forget sometimes that you don't know everything. You speak English so well.

SIMI. I do know everything. I just don't know it all in one language. So, you see, I do need you. (*They exit as lights go down.*)

Scene 4

Simi's room. Evening, the same day. Charlotte and Simi enter, Charlotte carrying a cloth napkin that is folded like a sack to hold objects. Simi puts down her camera and wooden tripod and lights the lamp. Charlotte goes to the bed, opens napkin to spread seashells on the bed.

CHARLOTTE. Bring the light closer so we can see what we have. (*Simi brings lamp closer, sits on bed with Charlotte.*)

SIMI. Such colors and shapes. They're beautiful, Charlotte. (*Holding up a seashell.*) Look how the light catches this one.

CHARLOTTE. They'll stay beautiful for a long time if you keep them in water in a jar or bottle.

SIMI. Tomorrow, I'll get a bottle from the pickle man. I'll put the seashells together for Rachel.

CHARLOTTE. You're not keeping them yourself? To remember today?

SIMI. I'll remember with or without the seashells. Last week Rachel looked at me like we were in Russia, and I was a Cossack who wanted to gobble her up and throw her in the Volga. Maybe she won't be so angry with me when I give her such a beautiful gift.

CHARLOTTE. What did you do?

SIMI. (*Indignant.*) I did nothing to her. It's in *her* head that I'm mean to her.

CHARLOTTE. I don't mean what did you do to make her angry. I mean did you do anything afterward to make her feel better?

SIMI. I told her that my cousin Malka still has lines on her . . . (*pointing to forehead, doesn't know the exact word*) . . . head?

CHARLOTTE. Forehead.

SIMI. Thank you . . . Malka still has lines on her forehead from always being angry with Libby, and she should be careful. No man wants to marry a woman with so many lines on her forehead.

CHARLOTTE. Simi, you didn't. What did she say?

SIMI. She ran out of the room. Rachel will get over this. She'll forget it next week when I give her the seashells.

CHARLOTTE. That's enough about Rachel. Today belongs to us. No one else.

SIMI. It was a beautiful day. Thank you.

CHARLOTTE. I loved watching you in the sunshine. And when the sun set and you made the fire for us. I could see the flames reflected in your eyes.

SIMI. Don't, please, Charlotte. Just say goodnight. It's late. Leonard is waiting.

CHARLOTTE. No, he isn't. I told him to take the car. And I gave him some extra money to go out—wherever chauffeurs go for fun. We have plenty of time.

SIMI. Charlotte, no!

CHARLOTTE. It's done. I'm your guest tonight. All yours.

SIMI. (*Irate.*) Without asking me? *Du bist a chutzpenik!**

CHARLOTTE. If you're going to be angry, it will take me too long to

---

*You have some nerve.

make it up with you, and then it'll be morning before we know it. That's not fair, Simi. We'll be wasting all that time. We had a wonderful day, didn't we? Don't spoil it now.

SIMI. You can't stay here. Where will you sleep?

CHARLOTTE. We can sleep here. Together. Like this. We'll just hold each other. Like close friends. We are close friends, aren't we?

SIMI. I don't like that you didn't ask.

CHARLOTTE. So, I'll ask. Miss Lasser, dear friend, would you let me, no, would you do something in return for your friend who took you to see the ocean today? And prepared a picnic? Would you give her the pleasure of keeping you company tonight?

SIMI. I don't know what to say.

CHARLOTTE. Don't say. Let's put the shells away first. (*Charlotte puts shells back in napkin, ties it, and puts it on the night table.*) Come here. (*Simi moves closer. Charlotte holds her.*) Like this.

SIMI. It feels strange.

CHARLOTTE. No one ever held you before?

SIMI. My father embraced me many times, and Malka. Libby never let anyone touch her, not even Papa.

CHARLOTTE. It won't feel so strange after awhile. It'll feel safe and loving. (*Pause.*) Do you know what I like most about you?

SIMI. No.

CHARLOTTE. Everything you do, you do completely, fully. Nothing part way, once you make up your mind.

SIMI. So it's not my charm you like? Maybe I should go to one of those schools you told me about.

CHARLOTTE. Finishing school?

SIMI. Yes, to the finishing school. I still don't understand why it's called with such a name.

CHARLOTTE. Don't you dare go to a place like that. They're full of women who would take one look at you, and I would never see you again.

SIMI. Don't be silly, Charlotte.

CHARLOTTE. Do you have sand from the beach in your stockings?

SIMI. I have in my blouse where it's tucked in. (*Charlotte gets out of bed, removes her stockings.*

CHARLOTTE. I'm just going to shake out the sand in the wastebasket. (*She shakes her stockings.*) Take off your blouse, and I'll shake it out for you. (*Simi removes her blouse, Charlotte takes it and shakes it over the wastebasket.*)

SIMI. Give it back now, Charlotte. (*Gently, but insistent.*) Charlotte, my blouse.

CHARLOTTE. Don't put it on again, Simi. (*She puts it over back of chair.*) I'll take mine off, too. (*She takes hers off, puts it over chair, gets back on bed.*) It's cooler like this. (*She rubs Simi's arm.*) Your skin is still soft and warm.

SIMI. This frightens me.

CHARLOTTE. Why? There's nothing here to hurt you. There's just the two of us and what we feel for each other. Close friends.

SIMI. I don't know, Charlotte.

CHARLOTTE. How does it feel when I touch you like this?

SIMI. It's a very good feeling, but . . .

CHARLOTTE. No "buts." That's what I like least about you.

SIMI. I don't understand.

CHARLOTTE. You always add a "but" to everything. There are always two sides to everything with you. Tonight, no "buts." And only one side. Our side.

SIMI. (*Sitting up, indignantly.*) I don't do that!

CHARLOTTE. (*Trying to take back her words.*) Never mind, Simi.

SIMI. Why do you say that I always do that? I don't. I don't do that.

CHARLOTTE. (*Exasperated.*) I'm sorry I said it. All right?

SIMI. All right, but I don't like that you said it. (*Charlotte starts to laugh.*)

SIMI. What?

CHARLOTTE. What you just said. You just did it again. (*Imitating Simi.*) All right, (*exaggerating*) but I don't like that you said it.

SIMI. No!

CHARLOTTE. You did! (*Still laughing.*)

SIMI. I didn't. (*Starting to laugh.*)

CHARLOTTE. Come back here.

SIMI. I should turn out the light.

CHARLOTTE. Not yet. In a little while. (*Charlotte caresses Simi's arm, lifts it to her mouth, begins to lightly kiss her arm. Simi watches her. Charlotte puts Simi's arm down, touches her shoulder, her neck, her face. She leans over Simi, kissing each place she has touched. Simi begins to respond. She touches Charlotte's cheek, lifts her chin. As they kiss, they explore each other's body with their hands. The lights go down.*)

ACT TWO

Scene 1

Early the following morning. Simi is asleep. Charlotte, almost dressed, watches her for a moment, then checks the time on her watch. She hurries to finish dressing as Simi wakes up.

SIMI. Charlotte?

CHARLOTTE. Go back to sleep. I have to leave.

SIMI. You said you would stay until morning.

CHARLOTTE. It is morning, and I have to leave. Now. I have to be home by seven A.M., before breakfast.

SIMI. We could have breakfast together.

CHARLOTTE. I have breakfast with my father.

SIMI. So today you'll have breakfast with me. I would like that very much, Charlotte.

CHARLOTTE. I can't.

SIMI. Today is different. It's special for us.

CHARLOTTE. I told you. I always have breakfast with my father.

SIMI. Your father sees you every day. He can spare you for one breakfast with me. He is a nice man. I could see it in the photograph you showed me in the newspaper, in the eyes. The camera sees that, you know.

CHARLOTTE. I told you no!

SIMI. (*Trying to cover her hurt feelings.*) So it's no. (*Pause.*) Hand me my robe, please. It's inside the closet. (*Charlotte gets Simi's robe, holds it out to her to put on.*)

CHARLOTTE. Here, Simi. (*Simi slips into robe, ties it, and turns to face Charlotte.*)

SIMI. Just "here." Not even a good morning, Simi. Or "how are you feeling this morning, Simi?" Just, "here, Simi."

CHARLOTTE. (*Contrite.*) I'm sorry. Good morning, Simi, how are you feeling this morning? Thank you for last night. With all my heart. (*Charlotte kisses Simi.*)

SIMI. Thank you. (*Gently pushes Charlotte away and sits on bed.*) Now go if you have to. I won't be greedy. (*Charlotte looks at her watch again, realizes it has stopped.*)

CHARLOTTE. Damn! I forgot to wind it last night. What time is it? (*Simi looks at her own watch.*)

SIMI. Well, if your father is waiting for you still, his tea is already cold by now. It is just after eight o'clock. I'll dress, and we can stop by the breakfast wagon on Third Avenue before I go to the studio at nine o'clock.

CHARLOTTE. (*Frightened.*) It's too late. I have to go home right away.

SIMI. Is breakfast with me so terrible? After last night, I could maybe have a smile?

CHARLOTTE. (*Distraught.*) I need to use the bathroom.

SIMI. You know where it is. (*Charlotte starts to leave.*)

SIMI. Take the paper with you.

CHARLOTTE. I forgot. (*Charlotte takes paper from night table and exits quickly. Simi takes her clothing from closet, preparing to dress. Her back is to the door. A few moments later the door opens. Mr. Lobell enters.*)

SIMI. Charlotte? (*She turns around, sees Mr. Lobell.*)

MR. LOBELL. Where is she? Where is my daughter?

SIMI. (*Surprised.*) Mr. Lobell? Excuse me, please, but this is my room, and I am not dressed. You may wait for Charlotte in the hall.

MR. LOBELL. Where is she?

SIMI. She will be right back. She is down the hall. Now, please excuse me.

MR. LOBELL. You will not be giving me or anyone else orders, Miss Lasser. You are already in plenty of trouble. (*Charlotte enters during the following.*) You may be able to convince my daughter to follow you for one night, but we will see who is in charge now.

CHARLOTTE. Father, please, it's not what you think. I swear.

MR. LOBELL. Leonard has the car in front. Go there and wait for me.

CHARLOTTE. I can explain everything. (*Mr. Lobell turns away from Charlotte. She touches his arm. He turns and slaps her across the face. Simi reaches under the bed pillow for a knife.*)

SIMI. Touch her again, and I'll kill you. (*Mr. Lobell steps back.*)

CHARLOTTE. Simi! No!

SIMI. (*Enraged.*) There are two men dead in a forest near Shepetovka who also thought a woman was their property to slap around.

MR. LOBELL. (*To Charlotte.*) Go to the car. Now!

CHARLOTTE. (*Clutching her father.*) She doesn't mean it, she doesn't. Please, Father. Nothing happened. I swear. Simi, tell him. Nothing happened.

MR. LOBELL. (*Trying to push her away.*) You will leave now, Charlotte. Now, or I will have her thrown out of this country back to whatever dirt village she came from.

CHARLOTTE. No, please. She didn't do anything.

MR. LOBELL. Always, it comes to this. This is the last time, Charlotte. Go to the car.

CHARLOTTE. What are you going to do?

MR. LOBELL. What I always do. Miss Lasser and I will have a talk.

SIMI. We have nothing to talk about. You are the one who will leave my room. Not Charlotte.

MR. LOBELL. Always the same, isn't it, Charlotte? The threats, the bravado, and, finally, the negotiations. Tell your friend how many times we've had this scene.

SIMI. You're lying. (*Furious, lapsing into Yiddish.*) *Du kenst lign tif in d'erd.**

MR. LOBELL. Perhaps she believes she's the first. They usually do.

CHARLOTTE. (*To her father.*) Don't do this, please.

SIMI. Charlotte, tell me. (*Charlotte looks at Simi, starts to cry. She can't speak. Simi lowers the knife and turns away.*)

MR. LOBELL. Now, will you go?

CHARLOTTE. Simi, what should I do?

SIMI. (*Angry.*) Why do you ask *me* what to do?

CHARLOTTE. Don't believe him, Simi.

SIMI. Both of you leave.

CHARLOTTE. Tell me to stay with you.

SIMI. I can't do that, Charlotte.

CHARLOTTE. It could work out. I'll get a job.

SIMI. And what? You'll forget you have a father? We'll live here together happily. In this room or another just like it? You'll learn to do without? I think not, Charlotte.

MR. LOBELL. Maybe you're smarter than I thought, Miss Lasser. Charlotte tried that once. I doubt she mentioned that to you. I cut her off, of course. Tell Miss Lasser how long your arrangement lasted with Miss Frankel before you came to your senses.

CHARLOTTE. (*Going to Simi.*) Simi, that was different. I swear.

MR. LOBELL. They are all different, Charlotte. But they always end the same way. Every time, you promise me no more. And every time you break my heart again.

CHARLOTTE. Simi, please. (*Simi turns away from her.*)

MR. LOBELL. You would destroy our family, our name, throw it away for something like this in a place like this. You are my life. Why do you hate me so much?

*May you lie deep in the bowels of the earth.

CHARLOTTE. I don't hate you. . . . Father, I don't hate you.

MR. LOBELL. I have only you. Everything is for you. Always. (*Charlotte goes to her father, embraces him. He stiffens.*)

CHARLOTTE. Father, I don't hate you. (*Charlotte takes his hand, kisses it. Mr. Lobell kisses her on the forehead.*)

MR. LOBELL. (*Emphatically.*) Wait in the car. Tell Leonard I won't be long.

CHARLOTTE. Simi? (*Simi doesn't answer.*) I'm sorry. (*Charlotte exits.*)

MR. LOBELL. You can put your weapon away. I am not a Russian peasant. (*Simi puts knife on night table. Mr. Lobell sits in chair.*)

MR. LOBELL. Now, Miss Lasser, how much do you want to leave my daughter alone? She will probably try to see you again. I don't want that to happen. You may not believe this, and I don't care whether you do or not, but I love my daughter very much. And she does love me, you know. It would only have been a matter of time before she decided to come home. And then it would have been much more difficult for *you*. I'm willing to pay you for your cooperation. (*Simi is silent.*) Surely, Miss Lasser, living like this, you've dreamed of something better?

SIMI. You are the businessman, Mr. Lobell. How much is Charlotte worth? You start the bargaining. (*Simi sits on the edge of the bed.*)

MR. LOBELL. All right. Let's make this easy, shall we? Avoid the police, the immigration service. We'll make our deal quickly, I'll leave, and you can get on with your life. In some other city, of course.

SIMI. (*Defeated.*) Of course.

MR. LOBELL. Name your price. Within reason. I have a great deal of money. I do not enjoy giving it away like this.

SIMI. All right. Charlotte's beauty, which is apparent to all, is not so important to me. Shall we say $1000 for her beauty? Her mind, which is no doubt *less* important to you, is worth a great deal to me, at least twice as much. Her heart I find it impossible to price. (*Mr. Lobell writes a figure on a piece of paper, shows it to Simi.*)

MR. LOBELL. Will this be enough, Miss Lasser?

SIMI. Oh, yes, it will do very well. You will make the check payable to the Hanna Lavanburg Home for Immigrant Girls. When they tell me the money has come through, I'll leave New York. Are we agreed?

MR. LOBELL. You surprise me, Miss Lasser. But, as you wish. The Home will have a bank draught tomorrow morning. You have until Monday to leave. Three days should be sufficient to make your plans. You will not see my daughter again. Or communicate with her in any way. And you will not discuss this arrangement with anyone. Understood?

SIMI. Yes, understood, Mr. Lobell. Now, this is still my home, and you will leave my home, please, while it is still mine to decide. (*Mr. Lobell folds the paper, puts it in his pocket, takes his hat, and exits. Simi picks up the knife, looks at it for a moment, and puts it back under her pillow. Standing very still, she looks at the bed as the lights go down.*)

Scene 2

The following Monday morning. Simi's room. She is folding the bed linen. There is a knock at the door. Simi opens the door. Rachel is standing there.

SIMI. Rachel. You can't come here. I can't talk to you now. Go away.

RACHEL. No. It's a free country.

SIMI. You should be in class.

RACHEL. Miss Sommerfeld said I must not ever talk to you again. She said you were not going to work at the Home anymore, and I should stay away from you.

SIMI. Good advice.

RACHEL. She would not tell me why. But I know. It's Charlotte's fault.

SIMI. I won't talk about it.

RACHEL. Everything was okay before Charlotte. I hate her.

SIMI. No you don't. My cousin Malka used to say that the Jews are hated by so many people, that it's important for us not to hate each other.

RACHEL. Charlotte hurt you. I know she did.

SIMI. She couldn't help it. We can't help who we are, who our fathers are.

RACHEL. I would never hurt you, Simi.

SIMI. Maybe not.

RACHEL. I wouldn't. I am not like Charlotte.

SIMI. No, you are not. But please, Rachel, try to forgive her. I'm trying, but I can't do it with you here talking about it. So go now, please.

RACHEL. I do not want to go. Let me stay with you.

SIMI. You already missed your morning classes. (*Teasing.*) You don't want to miss lunch. That would be a terrible thing.

RACHEL. I not care about that. What about you, Simi?

SIMI. Me? I'll survive, with or without lunch today.

RACHEL. Stop making fun. I am frightened for you.

SIMI. Don't be. This is not the first town I was forced to leave. But, I promise you, it will be the last.

RACHEL. You are leaving New York? No, Simi.

SIMI. It's not a choice for me.

RACHEL. Why?

SIMI. Never mind why. It's very complicated.

RACHEL. I will understand. I not stupid.

SIMI. No, you're not stupid, Rachel, but I don't want to talk about it.

RACHEL. It's Charlotte's fault. I know it's Charlotte's fault.

SIMI. Not that again.

RACHEL. How can you leave? You have a job, and the Home . . . and . . . how can you leave it all?

SIMI. It's settled. Mr. Rosen is letting me take my camera. I can pay him the rest later, he said, whenever I have it to send him. There are still some very nice people in the world.

RACHEL. You see? You not have to leave. You have friends here. I am your friend.

SIMI. Rachel, I made a bargain. With the devil himself, I think.

RACHEL. I do not understand. Tell me what happened.

SIMI. No.

RACHEL. Tell me.

SIMI. I said no!

RACHEL. Miss Sommerfeld would not tell me either, but some of the girls were whispering.

SIMI. That's what girls do, Rachel, to make life seem exciting and more mysterious than it really is.

RACHEL. What they were whispering about—is it true?

SIMI. I don't know. I wasn't there to hear their whispers, and I don't care.

RACHEL. No, you only care about Charlotte.

SIMI. (*Angry.*) What does it matter to anyone who or what I care about?

RACHEL. It matter to me. You not care about me at all—only Charlotte. You were going to leave New York without one thought about me.

SIMI. Never, Rachel. You are very important to me.

RACHEL. I do not believe you.

SIMI. Look. There on the table. (*Pointing to bottle of seashells in water.*)

That's for you. From me. Mr. Rosen was going to give it to you after I left. You see I did think of you. Very much.

RACHEL. (*Grabbing Simi, holding tight.*) Then stay here. Stay with me. I need you here. There is no one else I care about like you. *Loz mir nit iber aleyn! Gey nit on mir! Blab de mit mir!**

SIMI. (*Trying to remove Rachel's arms.*) Leaving is very hard. Don't make it harder for me.

RACHEL. I won't let you leave. *Loz mir nit iber aleyn! Gey nit on mir!*

SIMI. (*Pushing her away.*) It's already settled.

RACHEL. Then I am going with you.

SIMI. Don't be silly, Rachel. You can't go with me.

RACHEL. Yes I can. It's a free country. I can go anywhere I please.

SIMI. This country is not as free as you think it is.

RACHEL. I am going with you.

SIMI. Just like that? I don't even know where I'm going.

RACHEL. I don't care. We both came to America alone. It would be good to leave here together. I know it would. We can go anywhere we want. Be together. Just the two of us. I would never hurt you. And I would not let anyone else ever hurt you again. Don't go without me. Please, Simi. I don't want to stay here without you.

SIMI. (*Distraught.*) Rachel, the whispers you heard. They could be true.

RACHEL. (*Softly.*) I know.

SIMI. (*Shocked.*) You know? What do you know about such things?

RACHEL. From the first. I saw how Charlotte felt about you. That she wanted you . . . that way. Like Frieda's friend Jake wants her. Like he looks at Frieda. Like . . .

SIMI. You saw that? (*Ironically.*) And you didn't say anything to me?

RACHEL. Do you feel the same way . . . that way . . . about Charlotte?

SIMI. That's a very big question. The truth is, I don't know. I know I feel sad, very sad. I did not think about such things before Charlotte. But, always, Rachel, I felt different. So it must be that God made me to be different. (*Pleading.*) And if he made others like me, then where were they? (*Bitterly.*) They were not in Sherstagrad, that much I am certain of. So, I decided that for someone like me . . . that I would be alone in my life. That it must be God's plan. And I made myself believe that until I met Charlotte.

*Don't go without me! Don't leave me alone! Stay with me.

RACHEL. What happened?

SIMI. For the first time in my life, she made me feel that being different was a good thing. That I could be different and maybe not be alone. Rachel, the way she looked at me and touched me . . .

RACHEL. She hurt you.

SIMI. Before the hurt . . . I tried to pray God to stop the feelings, but I didn't want them to stop. And then I didn't think about God at all. (*Simi turns toward Rachel. Rachel moves to hold her.*)

RACHEL. (*Comforting.*) It will be better soon. I promise. I make it better.

SIMI. I shouldn't talk about this with you. It's not right.

RACHEL. I am not a child. I am as old as you were when you came to America. And I been here a whole year now.

SIMI. I'm sorry. You're right. You are a woman—a very dear young woman. I'm very proud that you're my friend.

RACHEL. You are?

SIMI. Oh, yes. Every week when I write to Malka and Libby, I write about you. "Today Rachel read aloud to the class a whole chapter from *David Copperfield* . . . and not one mistake." "On Thursday, Rachel read to me a story she wrote about her grandmother in Odessa. It was so beautiful, it made me cry."

RACHEL. I did not know that you wrote about me in your letters.

SIMI. Especially about your stories. Your wonderful stories.

RACHEL. Really? You never said.

SIMI. Oh, yes. And your kindness and laughter. . . . But never yet an answer from them. The war, the revolution—I don't know if I have a family. That pain stays with you always. This with Charlotte, I'll get over. (*Determined.*) I'll make myself forget this pain.

RACHEL. Let me help you.

SIMI. There's nothing you can do.

RACHEL. I can help you.

SIMI. It would be easy for me to say to come with me, my dear friend, so I will not have to miss you every day of my life, like all the others I left behind. But I will not do that. You deserve better. Only good things, you deserve. Not following around someone like me. If you want to help me, then stay here and do good things with your life. Be happy.

RACHEL. (*Delighted at Simi's admission.*) You want me to go with you. You do.

SIMI. I can't let you go with me.

RACHEL. I am going with you. I insist.

SIMI. I don't know where I'm going, and already in your mind your bags are packed.

RACHEL. We will go to a new place. We came from a very old country. We will go somewhere truly new.

SIMI. You need to finish school, find a job, a husband . . .

RACHEL. America is so big. Surely, in such a big country, somewhere they need a photographer, don't you think? And I will help you. I know I can. (*Rachel continues talking about all their possibilities as the lights go down.*)

Scene 3

Optional: while the set is being changed, slides of photographs are projected on screen in front. They start with a New York train station and show photos of people and places heading west from New York—Pennsylvania farms and farmers, midwestern cornfields, the Mississippi, etc., ending with scenes of the West, such as ranch life and Indian reservations. During the slides, the sound of a train changes to sound of a cattle drive and then horses running. After last slide, screen is removed.

The following year. A summer morning. Lights come up on Simi's photography studio in Shoshoni, Wyoming, near the Wind River Indian Reservation, home of the Shoshone and Arapahoe tribes. Sleeping quarters are upstairs; the studio doubles as a living room; the darkroom is offstage left. In the studio are various props and furniture and backdrops for photographs. Rachel enters, dressed in blue jeans, denim shirt, and cowboy boots. She is very dusty and dirty. She goes to door of darkroom and knocks, very excited.

SIMI. (*Offstage.*) Not yet. Don't come in yet.

RACHEL. Hurry, Simi.

SIMI. The photos take their own time to finish. (*Rachel is impatient. She goes to the props and plays with them, arranging imaginary photo settings and posing in them. Simi finally enters.*)

SIMI. Rachel, look at you. And look at the floor. Did you leave any dirt on the ground?

RACHEL. I need to practice for next week. You know that. I want to be the best rider of all in the Cheyenne Frontier Days parade.

SIMI. Did you find out yet if they will let you ride?

RACHEL. I don't care. I am not going to ride in the wagons with the other women. Did you see what those old dresses look like? I am going to ride on my horse. I can ride as good as the men. Bareback, even, if I want to. Leela White Wing's brother is teaching me. I want you to be proud of me.

SIMI. I am proud of you. Always.

RACHEL. Then give me a hug.

SIMI. When I want to hug something that smells like a horse, I'll go to the stable. Take a bath first. (*Rachel puts on ten-gallon hat, sits in one of the settings.*)

RACHEL. Take my picture. With my hat.

SIMI. Not in the settings, with all that dirt. Rachel. Please. I never saw anyone who wants her picture taken as much as you do.

RACHEL. When you have your moving picture camera, you can make a movie with me and the horses. Like Tom Mix, only with me. We can make the movie on the reservation. I know they would let us. And I already know the story. I'll tell you. It's a very exciting story.

SIMI. You told me that story.

RACHEL. It's different this time. I changed a lot.

SIMI. I have more photos to develop, and you should finish the story for the paper. So we can get the money.

RACHEL. Oh, that. That's almost done. Let me tell you about the movie. Listen, Simi. I'm riding down into the canyon, I hear a baby cry. I don't know if it's an Indian or a white baby, but . . .

SIMI. No one will know it's a baby at all. You can't hear a baby cry in a movie—Indian or not.

RACHEL. (*Caught off guard.*) I know that.

SIMI. You have to show the baby.

RACHEL. I know, I figure that out later. Anyway, while I ride toward the sound of the baby, in the distance there is a wagon with two people in front, dressed all in black, very mysterious, riding away from the sound of the baby. I don't see them . . .

SIMI. And who are these riders?

RACHEL. They're Jews—from Cheyenne—a man and a woman.

SIMI. That's good—you put Jews in your movie. Where are they going?

RACHEL. They are on their way to Montana.

SIMI. That's very interesting, too.

RACHEL. Thank you. What they didn't know is that when they stopped to rest their horse, the baby climbed out of the wagon.

SIMI. Didn't they hear the baby cry?

RACHEL. They rode too far away before the baby started to cry. So I find the baby, just as some Shoshonis come upon us.

SIMI. No! Are they going to take the baby?

RACHEL. This is not like the other movies that lie about the Indians. This is my movie. I tell the truth.

SIMI. Rachel, you know I didn't mean it like that. Leela told me how it was for the Shoshonis before the reservation. They were hunted and chased. Just like the pogroms in Russia.

RACHEL. my movie will be different from the others.

SIMI. Good. So you found the baby. What happens next?

RACHEL. One of the Indians takes the baby, wraps it in his blanket and holds it out for me to take. There is a title on the screen: "Caring comes in many colors." But I *give* the baby to the Indians to care for, while I follow the tracks to find the baby's family.

SIMI. You didn't have that before in the story, either. It's very good.

RACHEL. I didn't write the details of the rest yet, but I know it in my head. The captain of the soldiers in Fort Washakie hears from a merchant who was doing business there that on the reservation is a white baby. The captain thinks that the Indians must have stolen the baby. He doesn't really know what the Shoshonis are like. He is like so many people in Wyoming.

SIMI. He thinks about the Indians the way some people think about Jews back in New York or in Russia. My cousin Malka said that people treat us differently, then they hate us for not being like they are.

RACHEL. Always in town people talk about the Indians. That they are stupid and lazy and not proper, because they don't speak English so well or they look so different.

SIMI. Did you put that in the movie?

RACHEL. I did . . . like this—The captain gets a group of soldiers to ride to the reservation. There's a title that says something like: "Knowing your neighbor brings peace, ignorance brings destruction." The captain doesn't know that it's really the white soldiers who steal Shoshoni babies. When they get to the reservation, they find that the baby is being cared for very well, but they don't believe the Indians found the baby.

SIMI. They are Indians, so they must have stolen the baby.

RACHEL. They surround the Indians, then you see me riding up with the wagon behind me, with two very happy parents. The title there is: "A tragedy postponed." (*Sound of doorbell. Rachel goes to open the door.*)

SIMI. Don't you go to the door like that.

RACHEL. Everyone sees me like this all the time. No one cares.

SIMI. I care. People already talk about us. I'll get the door.

RACHEL. I'm already almost there. (*She goes offstage to open the door.*)

RACHEL. (*Offstage.*) Ayyy! Simi!

SIMI. (*Calling out.*) What is it? (*Rachel returns, holding something behind her back.*)

SIMI. Who was at the door?

RACHEL. Mr. Jackson.

SIMI. Where is he?

RACHEL. He couldn't stay. He brought something on his way home for lunch.

SIMI. So, what did he bring you from the post office? Is it your story about the boat from Hamburg? Did they buy it? Tell me.

RACHEL. (*Smiling.*) Yes, it's from the post office, but it's not for me.

SIMI. Then what? I don't understand. Stop looking at me like that. Tell me what it is.

RACHEL. (*Grinning.*) It's for you. A letter.

SIMI. Don't joke about such a thing. It's not funny.

RACHEL. No, it's not funny at all. It's wonderful. You have a letter.

SIMI. I don't believe you.

RACHEL. It's true.

SIMI. Well, where is the letter?

RACHEL. (*Holding it up.*) Here, Simi, here! (*Simi stares at the envelope, sees where it's from. Excited, she grabs Rachel, kissing her all over her face.*)

SIMI. The letter! Give me the letter. (*Simi takes the letter, struggles to open it. She is too excited and gives it to Rachel.*)

SIMI. Here. You open it. (*Rachel starts to open the letter.*)

SIMI. Hurry.

RACHEL. I'm hurrying. There. Look, photos, too.

SIMI. (*Taking them from Rachel.*) It's Malka and Libby and (*turns over photo*) Libby's family. Look, a daughter. Named Rebecca for my grandmother. (*Unfolds the letter, reads.*) They got only one letter from me. All those letters and they only got one. They got some of the money I sent. That's good. At least they got one of the letters with money in it. Libby's husband is a teacher. Like my father. Wait. (*Reads some more.*) But now there are no Jewish schools—so he teaches reading and writing and philosophy. Libby works also. She is the bookkeeper for the farm cooperative in Sherstagrad. (*Looking at Rachel.*) Rachel, she's a bookkeeper. That's a very important job.

RACHEL. It is. She must be smart like her sister.

SIMI. (*Returning to the letter.*) Rebecca already reads and writes. (*Looking at photograph.*) Look, she's beautiful.

RACHEL. (*Leaning over Simi from behind, her arms around her.*) She looks like her aunt in America.

SIMI. You think so?

RACHEL. Oh, yes. See, the eyes and the hair and around the mouth.

SIMI. We must take more pictures to send them.

RACHEL. Definitely. (*Kisses Simi on the cheek.*) Finish reading your letter while I take a bath, and you can tell me all about it at lunch.

SIMI. (*Caught up in the letter.*) Malka made all the clothes they're wearing in the photos. By hand. But now she will get her sewing machine. They are going to live together now. In Papa's house.

RACHEL. I'll be back in a little while. (*She starts to exit to upstairs quarters.*)

SIMI. Rachel.

RACHEL. What?

SIMI. Come here. (*Rachel comes back.*) Give me a hug before you go.

RACHEL. I'm just going upstairs to take a bath.

SIMI. When did you ever turn down a hug?

RACHEL. I am so dirty.

SIMI. It's good Shoshoni dirt. (*They embrace.*) From a real cowgirl who just happens to be from Russia. Who next week will ride her horse in the parade, we will see to that—no matter what they say— and I will take pictures of her to send to Russia.

RACHEL. (*Kisses Simi.*) I love to see you so happy. Today is a special day. We must remember the date. (*Simi embraces Rachel, kisses her on the cheek, then on the mouth. Rachel starts to respond. Simi pulls away.*)

SIMI. Forgive me.

RACHEL. You don't know everything, Simi, not about me . . .

SIMI. So what's to know that I don't already know?

RACHEL. I am not Charlotte . . .

SIMI. I know you're not Charlotte. I'm sorry.

RACHEL. Simi, don't be sorry. Be quiet, please.

SIMI. I will. Please. Go on.

RACHEL. Charlotte hurt you. And I am sorry for that. But I am not sorry that maybe you . . . felt toward Charlotte . . . toward a woman . . . like you would toward a . . . a man.

SIMI. Rachel!

RACHEL. There, I said it. And I won't take it back.

SIMI. Rachel!

RACHEL. Now you know. (*Simi looks at Rachel, stunned. Rachel kisses Simi.*)

SIMI. (*Smiling.*) This is not happening!

RACHEL. It's happening, Simi. (*Simi stares at Rachel, whose smile turns to laughter. Simi slowly smiles back at her and joins in the laughter.*)

SIMI. (*Shaking her head.*) God, in his infinite wisdom, would not let this happen . . .

RACHEL. He would, Simi. I think he already has. I'll be back soon. Very soon.

SIMI. Just one more thing. Remember to take off your boots in the bath. The hat maybe you could wear, but the boots will make mud in the bathwater. (*They kiss again, briefly.*)

SIMI. *Kimt geshvindt, mayn tireh.**

RACHEL. In English. Always in English. (*Rachel puts on the ten-gallon hat and smiles at Simi. Simi smiles in return and goes back to reading her letter. Touched by Simi's happiness, Rachel watches her briefly then turns to go upstairs as lights go down.*)

END OF PLAY

*Come back quickly, my dear.

Photograph by Nik

Hindi Brooks

I WAS RAISED AS A JEW by tradition, culture, and gastronomy. My only entry to religious Judaism was when I went to my Bubby's and Zaidy's Orthodox synagogue on the High Holidays to wish them *Gut Yom Tov,* before I went home and changed into play clothes. My life as a "practicing" Jew came with my entry into Labor Zionism at age thirteen, when I joined Hashomer Hatzair and started training to live on a Kibbutz. My contribution to the organization was mostly in the form of articles for its publications and in playlets I wrote for our holiday and Oneg Shabbat sessions and our various protest meetings.

I left Hashomer Hatzair, but not Zionism, because writing became more important to me than kibbutz life. I didn't get to Israel until 1967, as a tourist.

My mother says that she knew I'd be a writer when I was three years old and that my incessant babbling was merely poetry the rest of the family couldn't understand. I knew it when I was eight and joined the *Detroit News* Young Writers Club. The paper printed stories, poems, and drawings done by children aged eight to fifteen. It rewarded the top contributors with books or magazine subscriptions, tours of the newspaper's plant, and lunch with the reporters. When I won, I chose *Gone With the Wind* for my prize and spent that summer acting out Scarlet and Rhett with my best friend.

At Wayne University (it became Wayne State later), I was published in *College Poets* and worked on the school newspaper. Then I left Detroit for Los Angeles, hoping to become a screenwriter. I had just turned twenty. I supported myself as a classified ad saleswoman for a local throwaway paper where, for no extra pay, I was allowed to write articles and do reviews. More important, I became involved in local small theaters. I wrote one-acts—some Jewish oriented, some avant garde, some both. A production of my plays titled *Would Hindi*

Brooks Lie to You? brought this from one reviewer: "Hindi Brooks does lie to you—and beautifully."

There was no money involved in the theaters, but I decided to quit my job, live on unemployment, and write my plays. My boyfriend, Manny Kleinmuntz, a struggling actor, afraid that I'd starve, decided to go to work as a high school drama teacher so that he could support me. We were married in 1951.

My first full-length play, *The Illustrious Uncle*, ran for nine months at the Circle Theatre in Hollywood, in 1957. The director, star Anne Revere, and three of the other actors involved were victims of the infamous HUAC, House Un-American Activities Committee. The rest of the cast were ingenues, and the play was almost stalled because their agents didn't want them associated with blacklisted actors. *The Illustrious Uncle* was a comedy about a Brooklyn Jewish family and the chaos created when the husband's lie that he was related to a famous anthropologist catches up to him. It has had several productions, among them a long run at Nomads Theatre, formerly associated with the University of Judaism in Los Angeles.

I followed that play with *Color Scheme*, about racial prejudice in a college, and the sit-ins in which I had participated at Wayne. *Color Scheme* took second place in a contest sponsored by *Back Stage Magazine* but was never produced.

I was having more luck with the one-acts, getting them produced in little theaters and having some of them published. But all of that didn't pay the bills, and Manny's teaching salary didn't pay all of them either. So when an agent saw one of my plays, told me she loved the way I wrote, but I should write something she could sell, I wrote a screenplay. It was *Boiler Room*, written first as a play. *Boiler Room* dealt with the machinations of telephone soliciting in classified advertising, taken from my years in the field. It had won second place (again second place!) in the Neil Simon (now the Julie Harris) Beverly Hills Theatre Guild contest, but had never been produced. I turned it into a screenplay, my agent sold it to CBS as a Movie of the Week, and I was catapulted into television.

Fourteen years of television movies and dramatic series convinced me I wasn't going to solve any world problems in that medium. But it did give us—Manny, me, and, by now, our two children—the bankroll so that I could go back to theater. And Manny could quit teaching and go back into his own career.

There were more productions of short plays, more awards, more being published, and none of them giving me the satisfaction of having really reached beyond myself. I wanted to write meaningful plays, I wanted to recapture my childhood dream of changing the world for the better with my words. And, maybe now that I was an adult and more realistic, I wanted to make a name for myself.

My next play was a comedy. *The Whole Half* wouldn't change anything, but it did make a point about senior citizens being live, vital people needing and capable of love. And it did deal with the ability of people of disparate backgrounds to function together. He's an immigrant retired Jewish plumber; she's the sixth-generation Wasp widow of a doctor.

I needed to get away from everything—family, friends, the telephone—so I spent a month at the Virginia Center for the Creative Arts. The moment I was accepted, I went blank. For most of the trip to the colony I flagellated myself for not having an idea in my head, for thinking that I was or ever could be a serious writer. I was ready to turn around in Philadelphia, where I was to change planes from the jet to a little propeller-driven toy, to get to Sweet Briar, Virginia. As I bent over in the tiny plane's low-ceilinged aisle, the idea for *Happily . . . Even After* popped into my head. I started writing on a yellow pad, right there in the plane. At VCCA, I told the driver to drop my suitcase in my room, but drive me and my computer to my studio. And I kept writing. Two weeks later I had a first draft. I express mailed it to Manny, and he sent it right back with a few suggestions. The final draft doesn't differ too much from the original. It was the most exhilarating writing experience I have ever had.

In *Happily . . . Even After* a dead woman, about to be buried, gets out of her casket to confront her husband, who had left her for a younger woman and has now come to pay his respects. She refuses to be buried until she finds out what went wrong. In the play, the couple play themselves from their youthful meeting until the present, using only minor onstage costume changes and their attitudes to show the passage of years.

What Are Mothers For? was written after an argument I had with my mother. I thought . . . what would we say to each other if we could really talk? The result was a two-character play in which a mother and a daughter, trapped together for a day at the beach with nowhere else to go, finally come to terms with each other and resume the love they thought they'd lost. The San Diego Repertory Theatre showed *Mothers* to a local actress, Bryna Weiss, to see if she was interested. She was, but they never produced the play. Instead, Bryna approached me to write a one-woman play she could perform for

Jewish audiences. The result was *Lily*. In Israel, during the Gulf War, Lily tells a documentary filmmaker about her life from the Holocaust to the present, because she wants to use her story as a plea for peace. Bryna has performed *Lily* internationally in theaters as well as for organizations and festivals.

The Night the War Came Home comes closest of all my plays to the goal I had set for myself—to write something that made a difference. It was probably the security I felt, both financially and in my status as a writer, that allowed me to revitalize that goal.

I was a young teen when the 1943 Detroit race riot broke out. We were in the middle of World War II, Detroit auto factories were producing war materials, and the newspapers and newsreels kept us in a constant state of anxiety. The tension between white and black southerners, who came to Detroit to work in the plants and live and go to school together for the first time, only intensified that anxiety. The riot made it explode.

Since then every racial uprising, anywhere in the world, has brought back many painful memories. The 1992 riot in my home city, Los Angeles, brought it all to a head. I watched it on television and read about it in the papers. I was frightened as it extended beyond the African-American areas and into the "safety" of the middle- and upper-class, mostly white, sections of the city. I deplored how it would set back any progress we had made in racial relations so far.

I went back to the first riot, my memories of it and my research into it. I remembered all my parents' stories of how they lived as persecuted Jews in Poland, and how they barely escaped. How they worried about my brother in the navy. How they related to their multiracial neighbors and customers. I pumped my relatives for more details. I relived hiding in our home, afraid to go out, and my parents' reversal about my having multiracial friends. I grilled my husband for his experiences escaping Germany in 1938 and returning as an American soldier during World War II. Much of the character of Nate in the play is based on that information.

And I came up with *The Night the War Came Home*. The play is not really about my family, but they are at the core of much of it and of its ambiance. We did live upstairs from the store in the early years; my brother was on a ship somewhere in the Far East; and I was already a rebel.

But this play is not an autobiography. It's my own plea for racial understanding, and for an end to racial conflict. It investigates the differences and the similarities of the Jewish and African-American experience. It deals with the relationships and the hostilities between them. The play also looks at the after-effects of war and violence, and how they continue to color lives long afterward. It studies the young and the old, their concerns, their fears, their love lives.

It's drama laced with humor. The characters have a real and frightening experience during that first night of the riot. They wait, trapped by the riot in the store and home of the Kaufman family. Their fear unleashes hidden and not-so-hidden feelings. They fight their own private war among themselves and with the chaos on the streets outside. But they're able to laugh at themselves, and to find love, romance, and honor in the midst of it all.

The Night the War Came Home won the Mildred and Albert Panowski Award at Northern Michigan University and was produced by their Forest Roberts Theatre. I spent twelve beautiful summer days in Marquette, listening to the play being read each night and honing it each day. Sandwiched between the writing, I lectured each day to university theater classes.

I returned in that frosty winter for the final rehearsals and the production. This time Manny, who had played the part of Nate in early workshop readings, was with me. The entire experience was a heady one: luncheons with the city officials; cocktail parties with the university's theater arts staff; question and answer sessions after each of the five performances.

The Night the War Came Home was directed by Dr. James L. Rapport and performed by a cast of students and alumni of the university. Dr. James Panowski, producer, head of the Theatre Arts Department, and a walking encyclopedia of theater, kept the chaos to a minimum.

Manny now acts in film, television, and theater. He is still my first and best critic, performs in workshop readings of my plays, and appears in some of them. Our children have followed in our footsteps. Joshua is an actor living in New York. Nomi, who lives in Santa Monica, is a fiction writer and book editor.

I continue to churn out plays—long ones, short ones—and articles on writing. I teach playwriting at UCLA and am writing a how-to book on the craft. My latest play, *Eyes of the Beholder,* is another plea, this one against censorship.

I'm very proud to be listed in *Who's Who of American Women* and *Who's Who of American Film*—and to be published by Syracuse University Press.

The Night the War Came Home was developed at The Playwrights

Group (TPG) in Los Angeles. For the workshop production in 1992, the cast was as follows:

Manny Kleinmuntz	Sara Davis
Darlene Kardon	Hill Harper
David Kaufman	Richard Barboza
Karen Reed	

Director: Iris Merlis

The Night the War Came Home
A Drama In Two Acts
1992

I dedicate this play to my husband, Manny Kleinmuntz, and children, Joshua and Nomi.

Characters

NATE, the father, 60
ESTHER, the mother, 59
DANNY, their son, 25
REVA, their daughter, 20
THE VISITORS (black):
   CHRIS, 24, an army MP
   JOYCE, the store's employee, 20
   LEON, the looter, 21
OFF-STAGE VOICES:
   RADIO ANNOUNCER
   BLACK RIOTERS
   WHITE RIOTERS

Scene

Paris Imports, an accessory store in downtown Detroit, Michigan; the office, alcove, and secret room adjoining it.

Time

June 21, 1943
Act I, Scene 1—11:45 P.M.
Act I, Scene 2—Several minutes later
Act II, Scene 1—A moment before the end of Act I
Act II, Scene 2—Just before dawn, June 22

ACT I

Scene 1

Paris Imports is a small women's accessories store. The store itself covers the entire upstage area. The upstage wall is the front of the store: two glass windows with a glass door in the center. A hanging bell tinkles when the door is opened. Blackout shades on the windows and door keep us from seeing through to the sidewalk and street outside. The shelves are stocked with hats, purses, gloves, and hosiery. Some are arranged as displays in the windows.

Downstage, and a level lower than the store are the office and an alcove, the walls separating them from each other and from the store are indicated by open frames, and usable door frames. Covering most of downstage right is the office, separated from the store by an open doorway. This doorway is the only entrance from the store to the upstage rooms. The office is cluttered with a desk, chairs, unfiled papers, garment boxes, etc., spread over everything. On the desk, in addition to all the papers, are a phone and a desk lamp. A safe is secreted in the partition wall behind the desk. A door on the office stage right leads to a storeroom. A door on the office stage left leads to the alcove.

Downstage left: the alcove, barely large enough for a narrow cot and the narrow stairway leading upstairs. There's a door at the top of the stairs which, when open, reveals an entry into the family living quarters.

On the stage left wall of the alcove, behind the cot, is a secret door, hidden in the wall. The door leads to a secret room, which will be visible in Act II. It contains a double-decker bunk.

Note: Throughout the play, on and off, we can hear the muffled riot sounds from outside, sometimes closer, sometimes farther away. Gunshots, scuffling, yelling, glass breaking, etc. They are pervasive characters in the play, injecting themselves into everyone, into everything else that happens.

At rise: It's 11:45 P.M., June 21, 1943. The stage is almost dark. Thin streams of light from the street peek around the shades on the store windows and door, barely lighting the store. The office is dimly lit by a night light near the floor. 1940s music is heard on the radio in the upstairs room. It's cut off abruptly by:

RADIO ANNOUNCER. We interrupt this program to bring you a special announcement. The outbreak which started last night on or near the Belle Isle Bridge has developed into the worst rioting Detroit has ever experienced. More than fifty Detroit police, called to the bridge, have been unable to stop the spread of the violence. Governor Kelly has proclaimed a state of modified Marshall Law. Anyone without official business must be off the streets before the 10 P.M. curfew. No alcoholic beverages—(*Someone pounds on the front door. The radio is clicked off. Nate opens the upstairs door, spilling light into the alcove, and takes a step down. Esther is right behind him. They're both in robes.*)

NATE. Reva?

ESTHER. It's not Reva. She'd use her key. Don't go down!

NATE. I told you we should take the gun up.

ESTHER. They won't come up.

NATE. Because I'll get the gun and I won't let them up. (*There's a gunshot, quite close. Esther pulls Nate back up a step.*)

ESTHER. Nate, don't go down!

NATE. I think they're gone.

ESTHER. What are they doing outside anyway? The radio said curfew after ten.

NATE. You think they listen to the radio if it's not loud music?

ESTHER. There's no music, only announcers.

NATE. So they shut it off. (*Another shot, closer.*)

ESTHER. Don't go down!

NATE. I'll get the gun later. (*Esther pulls him back upstairs, closes the upstairs door, and the light is cut off. Muffled, from the upstairs room, the radio is clicked on.*)

RADIO ANNOUNCER. . . . rumors range from an argument between sailors and Negro picnickers last night on the Belle Isle Bridge, to a Negro man assaulting a white woman, to a white man assaulting a Negro woman. . . . Most persistent is the rumor that a colored baby was thrown off the bridge during a confrontation there. Other unverified reports hint that the entire riot was planned, with incidents occurring at the same time throughout . . . (*At the same time, in the store, a key unlocks the front door. The bell tinkles. Joyce hurries in and locks the door behind her. The upstairs door is opened again. Nate and Esther look out.*)

NATE. Reva?

JOYCE. It's me, Mr. Kaufman.

ESTHER. Joycy? (*Nate and Esther hurry downstairs as Joyce goes into the alcove. Overlapping at first:*)

NATE. Joycy, what are you doing here?

JOYCE. I came to take you and—

ESTHER. Is your mama all right?

JOYCE. Yes, I took her out of—

NATE. You shouldn't be outside now.

JOYCE. I know, but I had to—

ESTHER. It's curfew.

JOYCE. I know that, Mrs. Kaufman, but—

NATE. You could get hurt.

ESTHER. Don't go back out there, Joycy. Stay here tonight, on the cot.

JOYCE. Mama's waiting in the car. I'm taking her to my aunt in Livonia.

NATE. Smart. That's smart.

JOYCE. There's room for you guys there, too.

NATE. That's not smart.

JOYCE. You're not safe here, Mr. Kaufman.

NATE. And if I go, the store's not safe.

ESTHER. Joycy, that's very nice of you, but we can't go.

JOYCE. I can't leave you here.

ESTHER. Reva's not home yet. Joycy, do you know where she went?

JOYCE. No, I don't . . . She didn't . . . she doesn't . . . Okay, look. I'll get Mama safe, then I'll come back for you, and we'll go look for Reva.

NATE. I'm not leaving the store.

ESTHER. Go, Joycy. You look for her. We'll be okay, here.

JOYCE. But—

ESTHER. And I don't think we'll open up tomorrow, so you don't need to come to work.

JOYCE. Mrs. Kaufman, I can't just leave—

NATE. And if you do find Reva, tell her if she doesn't come home right now, either they'll kill her or I will.

JOYCE. Oh, Mr. Kaufman—

ESTHER. Or better yet, take her with you, and let us know.

JOYCE. Okay . . . But—

ESTHER. Go, go.

JOYCE. And you all stay upstairs.

NATE. Don't worry about us. Go. Go, Bubbela, I'll lock the door. (*Joyce and Nate go through the store. Joyce exits and Nate locks the door. He returns to the alcove, where Esther had been watching.*)

NATE. Why didn't she take her mama out hours ago?

ESTHER. Because she's stubborn. Like someone else I know.

NATE. You want to leave without Reva?

ESTHER. (*Realizing he's right.*) . . . Come upstairs. (*They start upstairs. As they reach the top Nate remembers something and starts to go down.*)

ESTHER. Where are you going?

NATE. I'm getting the gun. (*Another close gunshot.*)

ESTHER. Not now.

NATE. (*At the same time.*) Later. (*Esther pulls him into the upstairs room and closes the door. The light is cut off.*)

RADIO ANNOUNCER. . . . fighting has now spread beyond the black-populated area of Paradise Valley, bounded by Jefferson, John R, East Grand Boulevard, and Russell. Stores throughout downtown have been broken into and vandalized and cars have been set on fire. Unofficial and unverified reports have listed at least two deaths and thirty beating victims who have been taken to area hospitals. We repeat, these statistic are unverified . . . (*At the same time, the front door is opened a crack and the bell tinkles briefly before a hand reaches in and stops the sound. Upstairs, the radio is turned off. In the store, a shadowy male figure slips in and closes the door quietly. The upstairs door is opened again. Nate and Esther look down, relieved.*)

NATE. Reva's home.

ESTHER. Come upstairs, Reva. Don't go down, Nate. She'll come up. Hurry, Revela.

NATE. And bring the gun. (*There's no answer. The figure doesn't move. Nate takes a step down.*)

NATE. (*Continued, calling.*) Reva? . . . (*Whispering to Esther.*) It's not Reva!

ESTHER. (*Whispering.*) It's somebody.

NATE. (*Calling.*) . . . Is somebody there?

ESTHER. (*Whispering.*) Maybe Joyce came back.

NATE. (*Calling.*) Joycy? Is that you?

ESTHER. (*Whispering.*) Maybe the bell didn't tinkle.

NATE. (*Calling.*) Something else tinkled?

ESTHER. (*Whispering.*) Outside?

NATE. (*Calling.*) Outside? (*Whispering.*) Of course, outside. . . . (*Takes a step down, then a step up.*) Or . . . maybe inside? (*Pulls Esther up a step, then stops.*) So where's Reva?

ESTHER. Probably still at school. (*Realizing, horrified.*) Nate! . . . You think they're fighting there? At Wayne?

NATE. (*Cynically.*) At a college? At an institute of higher learning? They probably started there.

ESTHER. The radio said Belle Isle. On the bridge.

NATE. You think the radio knows everything?

ESTHER. So probably they're nowhere near Wayne. . . . You think Reva is still there?

NATE. Do I know where she is? Ever?

ESTHER. I'm calling the police. (*Esther hurries downstairs, through the alcove and into the office—with Nate right behind her, as:*)

NATE. You already tried to call them. You couldn't get through.

ESTHER. They can't still be busy. (*Dials, hangs up.*) Busy.

NATE. And even if you could get through, you think police would come here in the middle of a riot? (*The riot sounds come closer. Shots ring, very close. Nate hurries upstairs, Esther follows and closes the door. Upstairs, the radio is clicked on.*)

RADIO ANNOUNCER. . . . Valley's largest night spot, Wilson's Forest Club, seven hundred colored people have poured into the street and are attacking whites. At the Roxy Theatre on Woodward, whites have left the show and are dragging coloreds from their cars. In a broadcast earlier today, Mayor Jeffries asked for Michigan State troops but they were not available. Federal troops from the 728th Military Police Battalion in Fort Custer have been on alert since early this morning, but Governor Kelly's request for their help was not placed in the proper form so it must be sent through again. In a news conference this morning, the mayor stated that the only people to benefit from the rioting were the Nazis and the Japs who will welcome this . . . (*At the same time: the figure in the store moves into the office. The night light reveals Danny, in an oversized, brand new topcoat. It covers a dirty and rumpled uniform—U.S. Army Infantry, PFC. Quietly, he pulls the desk away from the partition, and reveals the safe in the wall. He dials the combination, opens the safe, takes a wad of money out, and pockets it. He looks into the desk drawers, doesn't find what he wants. He goes into the alcove, opens the table drawer, finds a note pad and pencil. He writes a hurried note, takes it to the safe, puts it in, and closes the safe. He goes back to the alcove, to replace the pencil and pad. Before he can, the radio suddenly crackles and goes off. Esther opens the upstairs door and starts downstairs. In the alcove: Danny retreats under the cot.*)

NATE. Esther, don't go down!

ESTHER. I have to find out if everyone's radio stopped playing.

NATE. If ours stopped, everyone's stopped.

ESTHER. But we have to know what's happening.

NATE. Maybe we're better off we don't know.

ESTHER. You maybe. Not me. (*Gunshots. Close.*)

ESTHER. Later.

NATE. (*At the same time.*) Not now. (*Just then the front door is rattled. Outside voices shout:*)

FIRST BLACK RIOTER. Kick it in.

SECOND BLACK RIOTER. Get a rock! (*In the alcove: Nate and Esther freeze on the steps. Outside:*)

FIRST BLACK RIOTER. Forget it. This other one's open. (*Then footsteps running away.*)

NATE. They're gone.

ESTHER. Nate, don't go down.

NATE. I have to get the gun.

ESTHER. You won't get the gun. You'll get killed.

NATE. They'll steal everything.

ESTHER. Better they should steal our lives? (*Nate is about to argue, but there's a round of gunshots. That gets him.*)

NATE. You're right. (*He pushes her ahead of him up the stairs and closes the door. In the alcove: Danny emerges from under the cot and starts toward the office. Seeing that the table drawer is open, he shoves it closed—with a loud scrape. He freezes as: Nate opens the upstairs door. Esther is right behind him.*)

ESTHER. Let them have the gun.

NATE. And when Reva comes home . . . ?

ESTHER. (*A take, realizing.*) . . . I'm coming with you. (*Danny retreats under the cot. Nate and Esther tiptoe fearfully down the stairs, Esther first. They whisper:*)

NATE. I should go first. I'm the man.

ESTHER. He'll shoot a man before he shoots a woman.

NATE. Them? Ha! (*He squeezes beside her and they continue downstairs and to the office door. Nate opens the office door and peeks in. They're still whispering.*)

ESTHER. What do you see?

NATE. Sha! (*Nate takes a step into the office. Waits. Esther takes a step. Waits. They repeat: his step; her step. Outside: a closer gunshot. In the office Nate drops to the floor. Esther screams.*)

NATE. (*Whispering.*) Sha!

ESTHER. (*Aloud.*) You're not shot?

NATE. Sha or I will be. (*He gets up and starts toward the desk. Both whisper:*)

ESTHER. Where are you going?

NATE. The gun.

ESTHER. I'll get it.

NATE. No. Let me.

ESTHER. (*Aloud.*) They won't shoot a woman.

NATE. (*Whispering.*) Unless she's shreiing.

ESTHER. (*Whispering.*) I'm not shreiing. Besides, nobody is in here anyway. (*A moment. They stop whispering.*)

ESTHER. See? (*Nate gestures "wait," creeps hesitantly to the storeroom and looks around. Gingerly, Esther gets the pistol out of its desk drawer. Nate turns off the storeroom light and closes the door.*)

NATE. Nothing. (*Esther, startled, points the pistol at him.*)

NATE. (*Continued.*) What are you doing? (*Takes it from her and pockets it.*) Come upstairs before you kill someone. (*He grabs her hand and pulls her toward the stairs. Esther pulls free.*)

ESTHER. I'm not going upstairs until Reva goes upstairs with me.

NATE. Reva is probably out there organizing it.

ESTHER. Oy! (*She starts into the store. Nate stops her.*)

NATE. Or maybe she'll be smart for a change, she won't come near it.

ESTHER. But where would she go? (*Off Nate's shrug, he doesn't know.*) We have to find out. (*Sits at the desk.*) We have to call everyone and find out. (*She turns on the desk lamp, opens an address book, and picks up the phone. Nate turns off the lamp.*)

NATE. Are you *mishugah?** Turn off the light!

ESTHER. I can't see the numbers in the book.

NATE. You know the numbers by heart.

ESTHER. (*Turning on the lamp and dialing—by heart.*) But I can't see them.

NATE. You can't get through.

ESTHER. I can try. (*She dials, listens, hangs up.*)

NATE. I told you. Busy.

ESTHER. Stop making me nervous, Nate. Go lock the front door.

NATE. I locked it before.

ESTHER. Now lock it after. After the gunman. (*She's right. Nate goes warily into the store. He tries to see into the dark corners as he heads for the front door. In the office Esther talks on the phone.*)

ESTHER. Naomi, thanks God, I got through. I'm sorry to bother you so late, but—Yes, our radio, too, just now . . . I heard, someone threw a baby over the bridge. . . . No, my radio said it was a colored baby. . . . A white baby? . . . Oy! . . . Naomi, is Reva there? . . . You have any idea where . . . ? I'll call there. (*She hangs up. Nate checks the front door, and calls:*)

NATE. Esther, it's unlocked!

ESTHER. (*Dialing, calling to him.*) So lock it.

NATE. What if he's still inside?

ESTHER. What if he's not? (*Nate starts to lock the door, but sees something outside. He flattens against the door jamb and peeks out around the shade. Outside the rioting noises are closer. In the office:*)

ESTHER. (*To phone.*) This is Esther Kaufman, is Reva . . . ? Yes, I

*Crazy.

heard. A baby . . . It wasn't a baby? . . . Who said it was the Jews' fault? . . . Listen, right now I don't care what that *kholabria** Coughlin says, I'm worried about Reva. (*A gunshot, very close. A woman screams. In the store, Nate drops the shade back into place. In the office:*)

ESTHER. (*Continuing, reacting to the shot.*) Oh, my God! (*She hangs up and starts toward the store, but Nate comes into the office, stunned.*)

ESTHER. (*Continuing.*) What was that?

NATE. He shot her.

ESTHER. Reva?!

NATE. No.

ESTHER. Joyce?!

NATE. No. Some woman. He shot her.

ESTHER. Oy! . . . Is she all right?

NATE. I don't know. She fell down . . . and she didn't move.

ESTHER. Didn't somebody help her?

NATE. No. (*Esther starts for the store. Nate holds her back.*)

NATE. (*Continuing.*) And neither are you.

ESTHER. Nate . . . we have to do something.

NATE. . . . She was running away from him.

ESTHER. We can't just sit here and wait for . . . for . . .

NATE. She was begging him . . . and he shot her.

ESTHER. (*Picking up the phone.*) I'm calling the police.

NATE. Esther, he was the police.

ESTHER. (*Hesitates, surprised, then:*) He was a bad police. I'm calling a good one.

NATE. A good one! (*They don't notice Danny stand and step to the open doorway.*)

DANNY. Put the phone down, Ma. (*Nate and Esther freeze. Then:*)

NATE. Danny?!

ESTHER. You're home! (*Esther envelops him in a bear hug. Nate is off in his own story. Overlapping:*)

NATE. Do you know what just happened out there?

ESTHER. Did anyone attack you?

DANNY. No, Ma, I'm okay.

ESTHER. What kind of a uniform did they give you? It doesn't even fit.

NATE. Did you see?

ESTHER. (*Taking off Danny's coat and throwing it over a chair.*) Take it off, I'll fix it.

---

*Cholera. In usage, a terrible person.

NATE. The cops—a cop—shot a woman in the back.

ESTHER. Look how dirty you are.

NATE. She wasn't doing nothing.

ESTHER. You got a furlough?

DANNY. No, Ma . . .

NATE. But it's her own fault.

ESTHER. Some time to get a furlough.

NATE. She shouldn't be here.

ESTHER. In the middle of a riot.

DANNY. Listen to me—

NATE. She was probably stealing something.

ESTHER. Did you see Reva anywhere?

DANNY. No. Please—

NATE. I knew something would happen.

ESTHER. I tried to call her friends but nobody knows where she is.

NATE. When they started coming from the south, *schvartzehs,** whites, all together . . .

DANNY. Ma, I have to tell you—

ESTHER. You think we should go out and look for her?

NATE. . . . And when they started moving in the neighborhood together . . .

ESTHER. Danny, you know where she goes. Maybe if we spread out—

NATE. . . . I said there would be trouble. They don't like it so close together, the *farshtunkina** South people . . .

ESTHER. Nate, you take the car, and—

NATE. . . . but did anyone listen to me?! (*That stops the others, but just for a moment:*)

ESTHER. I'll go by all her girlfriends. Danny, you go by all her boyfriends—

DANNY. Ma, I don't have time now!

NATE. When, then? After a hundred women get killed?

DANNY. Pa, I have to go.

NATE. (*On the verge of hysteria.*) Just like Warsaw. Nobody listened.

DANNY. Ma, don't let him start on Warsaw now. (*Esther holds Nate's face so that he has to look at her.*)

ESTHER. Nate, It's not Warsaw.

NATE. It's Warsaw. All over again.

---

*Dark persons. In usage, a derogatory term for African Americans.
*Stinking.

ESTHER. It's America, Nate.

NATE. We have to hide, Esther.

ESTHER. We have to look for Reva.

NATE. Look where? Wayne? Downtown? And while we're looking, they shoot us and when she gets home we're not here? We're not nowhere?

ESTHER. Nobody's going to shoot you.

NATE. And they'll take us . . . and they'll . . . they'll . . .

ESTHER. Nobody's going to do nothing to us. . . . (*Leading Nate toward the alcove, gesturing to Danny to follow.*) All right. We won't go out. We'll stay here. We'll take Danny upstairs and he'll take a bath and put on clean clothes . . .

DANNY. No, Ma—

ESTHER. (*Riding over that.*) And I'll fix the coat. And Reva will come home, and we'll move her in with us. And Danny can sleep in her room, in a real bed. Come, Danny.

DANNY. I'm not staying.

ESTHER. Call the army. Tell them there's a riot, you can't get back.

NATE. No, he should go back.

ESTHER. What kind of an army gives a furlough for two minutes, anyway?

NATE. He'll be safe by the army. They can't break into the army.

DANNY. Pa, I'm not going back there. (*That stops them. They try to absorb this.*)

NATE. They're sending you to Fort Custer already? Basic training is over already?

DANNY. They didn't assign me to Fort Custer.

ESTHER. Where, then? To a hospital in another state? They told you Fort Custer. How far away?

NATE. . . . To a hospital in Europe?

DANNY. Yeah, in Europe. But not to a hospital.

ESTHER. But . . . you signed up to be a . . . a . . . a medic.

NATE. You're going to be medic on the front!

DANNY. Yeah, Pa, on the front. No, Pa, I'm not going to be a medic.

ESTHER. I don't understand.

DANNY. (*Showing them the insignia on his arm.*) Look at the uniform.

ESTHER. That's not your uniform. You had that little snake thing.

NATE. You're in the infantry?

ESTHER. You're not in the infantry.

DANNY. Yes, I am.

ESTHER. But you told them you don't believe in it. You're halfway through medical school. They promised.

DANNY. Yeah. The recruiter promised. My captain had other ideas. (*Imitating a "redneck."*) "I'm recommending you for the infantry, Jewboy. The Nazis and the Japs need all the help they can get killing off you Kikes."

ESTHER. Oh, my God!

NATE. He deserted!

ESTHER. No!

DANNY. The army deserted me.

NATE. There's a war—

DANNY. Which I don't believe in.

NATE. They're killing Jews—

DANNY. And we're killing everyone else.

NATE. You agreed—

DANNY. I had a God-damned deferment to finish med school, Pa, and you made me enlist!

NATE. I made you? (*To Esther.*) He agreed.

DANNY. I didn't agree, Pa. You twisted my arm.

ESTHER. And he told them . . . he said only if he didn't have to kill anyone.

NATE. My son is a traitor.

ESTHER. He's not a traitor! He's a pacifist.

NATE. Another word for coward.

ESTHER. Who are you to talk . . . ? (*Which devastates Nate. Esther could bite her tongue. She turns to Danny.*)

ESTHER. (*Continuing.*) Tell Pa, Darling. Tell him you're not a coward.

DANNY. . . . Pa, you know what I did when they announced my unit was going over? I shit in my pants.

ESTHER. You know what Pa did when the Polish army wanted him?

NATE. Esther, don't!

ESTHER. So it runs in the family.

NATE. Esther, why . . . ?

ESTHER. Because this is our son. And he's in trouble. And we have to help him.

NATE. But you didn't have to—

ESTHER. I'm sorry, Nate. Danny—

DANNY. I have to go.

ESTHER. No! Come upstairs. Until morning. We'll talk in the morning.

DANNY. I have to get out of here before—

ESTHER. Nobody will be looking for you now, in all that . . . (*Finishes the sentence by indicating "outside."*)

NATE. Why did you come here, Mr. Pacifist? You thought we'd hide you?

ESTHER. We are hiding him.

DANNY. I didn't want you to hear about it from the army.

NATE. So you came to tell us in person. By sneaking in and out without waking us up.

DANNY. I was . . . I was just about to wake you up.

NATE. By banging the furniture around?

DANNY. I was . . . It was dark. I bumped into . . .

ESTHER. Nate, enough!

NATE. It's not enough. I want to know the truth.

DANNY. I . . . I was going to leave you a note.

NATE. Saying what? "Dear Folks, I'm a traitor and a coward, and let Hitler have America, too."

ESTHER. Stop it, Nate! He's not the enemy!

NATE. What then? The ally?

ESTHER. He's our son. Finished! Now, everybody. Upstairs.

NATE. I'm not hiding traitors!

ESTHER. I'm not turning in my son!

NATE. He has to stop the Nazis before they come here!

ESTHER. They're not going to come here!

DANNY. Please, Pa, I can't do it.

ESTHER. (*Tenderly.*) This is not Poland, Nate. This is America. We're safe here.

NATE. Safe? . . . He shot her in the back. A policeman. In the back. (*Outside someone rattles the doorknob. In the office Danny freezes. Esther turns off the light. Nate takes the pistol from his pocket.*)

DANNY. They're here.

ESTHER. No!

DANNY. Don't let them in.

ESTHER. (*Seeing the pistol.*) Nate, what are you doing?

NATE. They're not going to shoot me.

ESTHER. Put that away! It might be Reva!

DANNY. I'm not going back. (*Nate goes into the store.*)

ESTHER. Nate, come away from there. Danny, you don't have to go back. I won't let you go back.

NATE. This time, I'll shoot them, first. (*In the store a key is inserted into the lock. Nate aims the pistol toward the door. In the office Esther pushes Danny into the alcove, closes the door, and stands guard in front of it. In the alcove Danny tries to hear through the door. In the store the front door is opened. The bell tinkles. Reva's hand comes in to stop it. Then, just a silhouette, she enters and indicates to someone outside to wait.*)

NATE. . . . Reva?

REVA. You are still here. Are you okay, Pa?

NATE. (*Cynically.*) Just hunky-dory.

REVA. Is Ma okay?

NATE. She's okay. She's right here.

REVA. Is Joycy still here?

NATE. No, she's looking for you. Are you okay?

REVA. Yes, Pa. Someone's here with me. Is Ma decent? (*Nate goes to the office door to whisper to Esther.*)

NATE. Someone's with her. (*Esther takes the gun from Nate, pockets it and whispers:*)

ESTHER. Go to them.

NATE. What are you going to do?

ESTHER. Go. Talk to them out there. And don't say a word about Danny.

NATE. I'm coming in there, Reva. We got to talk.

REVA. We don't have time to talk, Pa. We have to get you out of here.

ESTHER. (*Whispering.*) And don't fight with her! (*Esther goes into the alcove. Nate goes back into the store.*)

NATE. Don't fight with me, Reva. (*In the alcove: Esther moves the cot away from the wall, digs her fingers under the floor in that wall, and opens a hidden door.*)

ESTHER. Come, Danny. Come in here.

DANNY. What is this?

ESTHER. Sha. I'll explain later. (*Esther takes him out through the secret door. A moment later, she re-enters alone, closes the secret door, and shoves the cot back in front of it. In the store at the same time, Nate stalls Reva with:*)

NATE. So . . . who's with you?

REVA. A . . . he drove me here.

NATE. Oh . . . (*Calling out the front door.*) Thank you, thank you, Mister. . . . We were so worried about you, Revela.

REVA. I knew you would be. I tried to call.

NATE. And you're okay?

REVA. Yeah, Pa. I'm fine.

NATE. So who is this drove you?

REVA. Pa . . . let's go into the office and I'll explain—

NATE. Where were you, Revela? Why didn't you come home when it first started? Why didn't you call? Do you know what you did to your mother?

REVA. I can only answer one question at a time, Pa.

NATE. Please, Reva. This is no time for your smart answers.

REVA. Okay. I was at school. I tried to call but the lines were all busy. And the buses weren't running. And then I ran into my . . . him. This . . . man . . . Chris. Is Ma all right? Are you?

NATE. All right? Surrounded by crazy *schvartzehs?*

REVA. Please don't use that word, Pa.

NATE. Crazy black people, then.

REVA. And they're not crazy.

NATE. And we're sick with worry over you, and you're out wherever.

REVA. At school.

NATE. In the middle of the night?

REVA. I had an evening class, and then I couldn't get here—

NATE. We called all your friends.

REVA. I asked you not to do that, Pa.

NATE. And I asked you not to . . . do . . . all the things you do.

REVA. Pa, we don't have time for that now. We have to get you and Ma out of here.

NATE. (*Calling out the front door.*) And you, too, Mister. Thank you for bringing my daughter home. You'd better go home yourself before the cops or the crazy *schvartzehs* kill you.

REVA. Pa, please!

NATE. Okay. Before the nice, friendly, don't want to hurt nobody *schvartzehs* kill you. (*Esther appears in the office doorway.*)

ESTHER. Nate, stop teasing. She doesn't like the word. Come inside, Reva. Both of you. (*Reva pulls someone inside. The shadowy figure of a man. Chris.*)

ESTHER. (*Continuing.*) Are you all right? Did you get hurt? Either one of you? Let me take a look. (*Esther turns on the store light. Now Chris can be seen. He's African-American, and in the uniform of an army MP, complete with holstered pistol. Black out.*)

Scene 2

Note: The rioting and the reactions to it continue throughout this scene. At rise: It's several minutes later. The store light has been turned off. In the alcove, Esther comes downstairs. She carries two trays nested together. They hold a teapot, lemon, sugar, five glasses and spoons, and a plate of cookies. She sets the trays down on a step and separates them. She pours tea into a glass, adds a spoon of sugar, puts it on the smaller tray, and adds several cookies. She hesitates, takes the pistol from her pocket, studies it, almost puts it back, then puts it on the small tray. Then, quietly, carefully, she moves the cot from the wall, opens the secret door, takes the smaller tray and goes into the secret room. A moment later, she comes out, puts the cot back in place, and picks up the larger tray.

In the office at the same time: The overhead fixture is on. Nate grows more and more nervous as he stalls Reva and Chris, waiting for Esther to come back.

NATE. The radio said the army couldn't come yet, because the governor didn't ask the right way.

REVA. And we can't wait for them, Pa.

CHRIS. Mr. Kaufman, we really have to get out now.

NATE. So, they sent military police instead?

CHRIS. Well, I—

REVA. (*Stopping him.*) Pa, you can read it in the *Free Press* tomorrow.

CHRIS. I'll go hurry Mrs. Kaufman.

NATE. Wait! . . . Did they . . . Is . . . Did they attack Lardner's?

REVA. Every window is broken.

NATE. Who did it? The Schv . . . (*a glance at Chris, then*) . . . white people?

CHRIS. Everyone is doing it, Mr. Kaufman. Whites and Negroes.

REVA. Mostly whites.

NATE. And they took everything?

CHRIS. Couches, chairs, lamps. Mr. Kaufman—

NATE. And Mackay's?

REVA. Hammers, chisels, pliers . . .

NATE. Anything they can use for weapons. (*With a look to Chris.*) Both. Negroes and whites. (*To Reva.*) How about the bakery? Did they attack the bakery?

REVA. You want it itemized? You're not safe here. Ma's not safe.

CHRIS. You have to get out, Mr. Kaufman, before it's too late.

NATE. That's right. You'd better get out before it's too late.

REVA. He's helping us get out.

NATE. And that's very nice of him. Mr.—Chris, thank you for bringing my daughter home. I'd like to give you a little something for your trouble but—

REVA. Pa!

NATE. I'm sorry, Reva. I put all the money away when everything started. (*To Chris.*) If you leave me your address—

REVA. He doesn't want to be paid!

CHRIS. Mr. Kaufman, all hell is breaking loose out there.

NATE. No, no, it's by the Schv—Negroes . . . in Paradise Valley.

REVA. Does that sound like it's in Paradise Valley?

NATE. The radio said most of it is there.

REVA. You didn't listen long enough.

NATE. Because it stopped playing.

REVA. Pa, what are you doing?

NATE. I'm staying here to protect my property.

REVA. Well, I'm going to protect my mother. (*She starts toward the alcove door. Nate blocks her.*)

NATE. How? By taking her out there? Into that . . . that . . . pogrom?

CHRIS. My car is right outside.

NATE. You better move it before someone burns it.

REVA. I don't understand you.

NATE. So we're even. (*To Chris.*) Since she's a little girl, I never understood her.

REVA. Pa—

NATE. We don't have to run, Revela. It'll stop.

CHRIS. After they bang enough colored heads together.

NATE. They aren't that crazy about Jewish heads either. (*Reva starts for the alcove door again. Again Nate blocks her. He looks past her to Chris.*)

NATE. (*Continuing.*) So, Chris, you got some idea what started it all? One reporter said one thing, the next reporter something else . . .

CHRIS. We'll tell you all about it in the car.

NATE. And then nobody said nothing. Did I tell you it stopped playing, the radio?

REVA. Pa, you want to stay here, stay. I'm getting Ma out. (*She tries to get around Nate, but he keeps blocking her.*)

NATE. They said in the paper there would be trouble. All those South people.

REVA. Pa, move.

NATE. They're not used to it. Those . . . different races.

REVA. Move, Pa.

NATE. Living together. Working together in war plants.

REVA. Pa, move!

NATE. You're from the South?

REVA. I'd better get some money. Chris, you get my mother.

NATE. No! Don't go in there!

REVA. Why? Are you hiding something?

NATE. I . . . I don't want you should wake Mama up.

REVA. She is up.

NATE. Before. Now she went to bed.

CHRIS. She can't go to bed.

NATE. (*His "polite" veneer cracking.*) Don't tell me where my wife can go!

CHRIS. (*His "polite" veneer cracking.*) Hey, if you don't want my help—

REVA. (*Calming Chris with a touch.*) Chris, Pa, please. We're all friends here.

NATE. . . . I'm sorry. I apologize. I'm nervous.

CHRIS. I know. We all are.

NATE. It's this . . . all the . . . out there . . . (*a take, realizing*) Friends? . . . You just ran into him—He's your friend?

REVA. From school.

NATE. Oh, from school. (*Esther enters from the alcove, with the tray. She puts it on the desk.*)

ESTHER. I couldn't find the sugar, that's why I took so long.

NATE. Esther, they went to school together.

ESTHER. That's nice. Look, I found a half a lemon, too.

NATE. (*Pointedly.*) That's why he's here. They're friends.

ESTHER. I heard. (*To Chris.*) The cookies are a little old, but—

NATE. So he didn't come on . . . (*To Chris.*) You didn't come on army business, right?

ESTHER. (*Catching on.*) The army didn't send you?

CHRIS. No . . .

NATE. So . . . what are you doing here?

REVA. Ma, I'll tell you all about it in the car.

ESTHER. Would you like some tea, Captain?

CHRIS. I'm a sergeant, Ma'am.

ESTHER. (*Pouring tea into a glass.*) Sergeant is nice, too.

REVA. Ma, forget the tea.

ESTHER. I shouldn't offer tea to a friend? (*Reva is exasperated. Chris calms her.*)

CHRIS. It's okay, Reev. Let's have the tea first.

NATE. So . . . you're . . . good friends, Reva? You and him?

REVA. He has a name, Pa. Chris Harrison.

ESTHER. (*To Chris.*) How many sugars, Sergeant Harrison?

CHRIS. One. And please, call me Chris.

NATE. Chris . . . you were friends with Reva . . . in school? Or after school?

CHRIS. Both.

NATE. . . . Both . . . like . . . clubs . . . parties . . . ?

REVA. Because we were in the same major, Pa.

NATE. (*As a put-down.*) You took socialism, too?

CHRIS. Socialism?

REVA. He means sociology.

CHRIS. Oh, you thought . . . It's not the same thing, Mr. Kaufman. Socialism is—

REVA. He knows, Chris. He's just being sarcastic.

ESTHER. (*To Chris.*) Lemon?

CHRIS. Do you have any milk?

ESTHER. No, I'm sorry. I'm fresh out.

NATE. Milk? In tea? You're from England?

REVA. His mother went to school there.

ESTHER. College?

CHRIS. Oxford.

ESTHER. Isn't that nice, Nate? (*Serving Chris his tea.*) Here, drink up, Chris. (*To Nate, almost accusing.*) His mother's parents sent her to Oxford College.

NATE. We should have sent our daughter to Central High School.

CHRIS. Couple of us there, too.

REVA. Chris . . .

ESTHER. Tea, Nate?

NATE. Not with milk.

ESTHER. We don't have any milk.

NATE. Even if we did have. (*Esther prepares Nate's tea, with lemon and three sugar cubes.*)

ESTHER. It was very brave of you, Serg—Chris, to bring Reva home in the middle of all this.

CHRIS. Well, that's what you do for friends.

NATE. You bring her from peace to war.

REVA. To help you get out of here.

ESTHER. So he should rest now. Put up his feet, take off the gun

. . . (*She gestures to the desk. Chris puts the pistol on the desk. Nate and Esther exchange a look of relief.*)

ESTHER. (*Continuing.*) Now, doesn't that feel better? (*Esther hands Nate his tea. He holds it, but doesn't drink.*)

ESTHER. (*Continuing.*) So, Chris, where are you stationed? Nearby?

CHRIS. Fort Custer.

NATE. (*Almost spilling the tea.*) In Michigan, Fort Custer?

CHRIS. That's the one.

ESTHER. But . . . they didn't send you here? For the riot?

CHRIS. No, they're sending the white battalions.

REVA. (*Cynically.*) That's the American way.

NATE. Then . . . why aren't you there? In Fort Custer?

ESTHER. Drink your tea, Nate.

NATE. (*Handing the glass to Esther.*) I don't want it. (*To Chris*) Why are you here?

REVA. To see if his family is okay.

ESTHER. They're in Paradise Valley, your family?

CHRIS. Palmer Park.

NATE. They're moving in Palmer Park, now?

ESTHER. (*Gesturing Nate to stop it and offering his tea to Reva.*) They're fighting there, too?

CHRIS. Not yet.

REVA. I don't want any tea, Ma. Let's go.

ESTHER. Then they're all right?

CHRIS. Yes. I took them out to our cottage at Walled Lake.

NATE. (*To Esther.*) They're in Walled Lake, too.

ESTHER. So, if they're all right, then shouldn't you go back to camp?

REVA. He's on furlough.

CHRIS. Don't lie for me, Reev. (*To Nate and Esther.*) I'm not on furlough.

ESTHER. Then . . . why . . . ?

CHRIS. We all wanted to come home, the Negroes from Detroit, to help our families. But they wouldn't give us leave, so I just . . . took off.

ESTHER. But won't you get in trouble?

CHRIS. I already am.

REVA. Chris, don't . . .

ESTHER. Oh . . . you're AWOL!

NATE. He's a traitor.

REVA. He's not a traitor! They wouldn't let him help his family!

NATE. And his family is okay. So what is he doing here?

CHRIS. (*Really beginning to lose his cool.*) I'm beginning to wonder about that myself.

REVA. He's my best friend, that's what he's doing here.

NATE. Now he's your best friend?!

ESTHER. (*Sipping Nate's tea.*) I don't know how you drink this so sweet, Nate.

NATE. What does that mean, exactly? Best friend?

REVA. It means you shouldn't treat him like dirt.

NATE. (*Ignoring her, to Chris.*) My daughter doesn't have best friends, traitors. (*Chris puts his glass down and stands up.*)

CHRIS. You coming with me, Reev?

ESTHER. No! Nate, what are you doing? He's her friend.

NATE. She doesn't need such friends.

REVA. He's not a traitor!

CHRIS. That's not it, Reev. (*To Nate.*) It's because I'm Negro. Right?

NATE. (*Ineffectually.*) It's . . . both.

REVA. Pa, I'm surprised at you. You never objected to my other Negro friends. You never objected to Joyce being my friend.

NATE. She's a girl. (*To Esther.*) And this is a man. And he should— (*to Chris*)—He should be best friends with a *shvartzeh* girl and . . . stay with his own kind . . . and . . . and leave my daughter alone. (*Outside: a round of gunshots, very close, and voices yelling incoherently. In the office everyone freezes, except Chris, who grabs his pistol. When it's quiet, he puts it back in its holster.*)

REVA. Okay, that's it. We've got to go. Now.

CHRIS. No, they're too close. We're safer inside.

REVA. Yeah . . . I guess you're right.

NATE. (*To Esther.*) Now she agrees. Because he says so. (*To Chris.*) So, thank you, traitor. And good-bye.

REVA. It's not safe for him out there, either. He's staying right here.

ESTHER. But he can't stay here.

REVA. Ma . . . ? You, too?

CHRIS. So much for your broadminded mother.

ESTHER. No, no. You don't understand . . . there's no room.

REVA. He can sleep in the alcove. (*To Chris.*) It's Danny's room. It's not too uncomfortable.

ESTHER. It is too uncomfortable. He's too big for the cot.

NATE. We don't need to explain. He can't stay. Finished.

REVA. If you kick Chris out, Pa, you kick me out, too. (*Outside: the front door is rattled. Voices shout:*)

FIRST BLACK RIOTER. Break it.

SECOND BLACK RIOTER. Here's a rock. (*In the office Chris bolts for the store.*)

REVA. Chris!

NATE. He's going to let them in!

ESTHER. Reva, stay here! (*Esther holds Reva back. In the store Chris unlocks the door, and steps halfway outside.*)

CHRIS. Hey, Brother, back off.

FIRST BLACK RIOTER. There's kikes in there, man!

CHRIS. They're gone. It's mine. Back off.

FIRST BLACK RIOTER. After I get mine.

CHRIS. Does the pistol make it any clearer?

FIRST BLACK RIOTER. Oh, big man got a little rod.

CHRIS. You want to see the rest of my arsenal, inside?

SECOND BLACK RIOTER. Come on, let's go. There's nothing but hats in there anyway. (*Offstage, a white mob approaches. Ad libs:*)

FIRST WHITE RIOTER. There's some more niggers.

SECOND WHITE RIOTER. Let's get 'em.

SECOND BLACK RIOTER. (*His voice fading off.*) Come on, let's get the hell out of here. (*They run off, the black mob, followed by the white one.*)

FIRST WHITE RIOTER. They're going through the alley!

SECOND WHITE RIOTER. Don't let them get away! (*The rioting will move farther away now. Chris comes inside, locks the door, and returns to the office. In the office Reva leaps into his arms.*)

REVA. Chris. Are you okay? (*Realizing they've exposed the truth, they pull away from each other.*)

REVA. He . . . chased them away.

CHRIS. The white mob did. (*Over her head, to Nate.*) There'll be others. You'd all better stay upstairs until morning. You'll be safer there.

REVA. You, too.

CHRIS. I'll stay downstairs . . . on guard. (*He gestures to Reva, "one thing at a time."*)

REVA. . . . I'll get some bedding for you.

ESTHER. Wait, Reva, let me help you. (*Esther casts a warning glance at Nate, and follows Reva into the alcove. Nate and Chris glare at each other, in a standoff. In the alcove: Esther holds Reva back from the stairs.*)

ESTHER. Wait, I want to talk to you.

REVA. You don't understand, do you, Ma? He's my boyfriend. (*Starts upstairs, comes back down.*) Or maybe you do understand. Maybe that's why you want him to go out there and get killed. (*Goes upstairs.*)

ESTHER. I don't want him to get killed. (*Esther looks after Reva, then at the secret door, unsure what to do. She goes upstairs.*)

ESTHER. (*Continuing.*) Reva, wait. (*Esther exits upstairs and closes the door. In the office:*)

NATE. What is that about? All that hugging?

CHRIS. She was glad I wasn't hurt.

NATE. She could see that, she didn't need to hug.

CHRIS. Mr. Kaufman, we'd better call a truce.

NATE. You should have gone when I told you to.

CHRIS. (*Looking into the store.*) If there's anything important out there, you might want to put it in the safe.

NATE. You stay away from my safe.

CHRIS. Hey, man, I don't give a shit if they take your whole damn store.

NATE. My store is none of your business.

CHRIS. That's fine with me. (*It's another standoff. Then:*) The goods'll be safer back here, but . . . it's none of my business. (*A moment, then Nate starts into the store, but hesitates at the doorway.*)

NATE. . . . You might as well make yourself useful. (*Chris goes into the store and gathers some hats. Nate looks into the alcove, then at the secret door, then upstairs. Chris enters from the store, with the hats.*)

CHRIS. Where do you want them?

NATE. (*Hurriedly closing the alcove door.*) In there. (*He opens the storeroom door and turns on the light. Chris goes into the storeroom, then as he comes out without the hats:*)

CHRIS. I didn't offer to do this alone, Massa.

NATE. I didn't ask you to. (*As they go back and forth, taking merchandise from the store to the storeroom:*)

NATE. How come Reva never mentioned you?

CHRIS. She didn't think you'd understand. Correction. She knew it.

NATE. When?

CHRIS. When she knew it?

NATE. When did you meet her?

CHRIS. Two years ago.

NATE. When she first went to Wayne?

CHRIS. The first day.

NATE. I knew she shouldn't go there.

CHRIS. It's a good school.

NATE. For her, it's a waste of time.

CHRIS. Because men don't want educated women.

NATE. You agree?

CHRIS. No. Reva said you felt that way.

NATE. Am I wrong?

CHRIS. Yes.

NATE. What do you know?

CHRIS. I know Reva's an intelligent woman.

NATE. An intelligent woman sticks to her own kind.

CHRIS. And inherits the store her brother doesn't want.

NATE. Anything she didn't tell you about the family?

CHRIS. Mr. Kaufman, Reva wants more out of life.

NATE. She doesn't know what she wants.

CHRIS. She doesn't want to run this store.

NATE. And social worker in the slums is better? Going around by all the winos and the bums, and being paid *bupkas** for it is better?

CHRIS. We can get the winos off the bottle. And get jobs for the bums. And—and . . . I don't know what the hell *bupkas* are.

NATE. That's the problem! (*Chris goes back to moving merchandise. A moment, then Nate joins him. In the alcove Reva carries linens downstairs. Esther is right behind her. Reva makes up the cot as:*)

ESTHER. You should have told us.

REVA. So you could break us up?

ESTHER. No . . . maybe . . . Oy, Revela, we had such plans for you.

REVA. Run the store. Then marry someone who'll run it for me.

ESTHER. And take care of you.

REVA. I don't need anyone to take care of me, Ma. I need an education.

ESTHER. You can have that, too.

REVA. Then why do I have to pay my own way?

ESTHER. You know how bad we were doing before the war.

REVA. You paid for Danny to go.

ESTHER. It's different. He's a boy.

REVA. And . . . (*imitating Nate*) men don't marry college girls. College girls become old maids.

ESTHER. I never said that.

REVA. Pa did.

ESTHER. He was making a joke.

*Goat droppings. In usage, worthless or penniless.

REVA. Uh-uh. He was saying I'd better not do anything to hurt his precious store.

ESTHER. It supports you, Reva. Don't you forget that. The precious store feeds you and clothes you—

REVA. And makes a slave out of you.

ESTHER. I'm not a slave. I'm a . . . an owner. And I love this store as much as Pa does.

REVA. You love living upstairs from it, in a couple of tiny rooms?

ESTHER. Better than I loved living in one room behind the store. This room. You don't remember that, do you?

REVA. I remember it. And I remember bathing in a wash basin. In the water you and Pa and Danny already used.

ESTHER. So where do they bathe in the slums? In a golden bathtub?

REVA. Oh, Ma.

ESTHER. Revela, why go to worse, when we're going to better? The store is doing good now. We could even move away from upstairs. To Dexter Blvd, maybe. And even take a vacation in Florida next winter. You always wanted to go to Florida.

REVA. You want to go to Florida. And live on Dexter. And work in the store. I don't want any of that.

ESTHER. You want security?

REVA. Ma, there's no such thing as security. When the war's over, the plants will shut down. Nobody will be able to buy hats and gloves—

ESTHER. I'm not talking hats and gloves—

REVA. Just because Danny's not in a combat unit and . . . and Pa's suddenly going to Paris to buy merchandise . . . it's not all . . . Pa keeps saying everything is hunky-dory. Listen outside, Ma. There's no such thing as hunky-dory. (*Esther sinks onto a step. Reva continues making up the cot. In the office Chris and Nate keep moving merchandise from the store through the office and into storeroom.*)

CHRIS. Reva said you immigrated from Poland. In 1915. During the first war.

NATE. (*Cynically, indicating the street.*) A lot good it did.

CHRIS. Didn't you have to serve in the Polish army?

NATE. No, they . . . I was . . . I didn't run away.

CHRIS. Okay.

NATE. I wanted to live in America. And not send my daughter to the slums.

CHRIS. Which are in America.

NATE. Not her America! (*In the alcove:*)

ESTHER. Revela, you know why Pa went to Europe?

REVA. On a buying trip. In the middle of a war, he decides to really buy . . . (*cynically*) Paris Imports. (*Imitating Nate.*) "Don't worry. I'm an American citizen. There are no Nazis in Paris. Everything will be hunky-dory."

ESTHER. He didn't go to Paris. He went to Warsaw.

REVA. Warsaw? How did he get into Warsaw in the middle of a war?

ESTHER. His American passport and a few dollars to a few people, he got in.

REVA. But why would he go to Poland for French merchandise?

ESTHER. He didn't go for merchandise. He went to get his father out.

REVA. But . . . then why didn't he?

ESTHER. Stubbornness. It runs in the family. His father said it would all blow over. The Nazis would be kicked out of Poland.

REVA. And he wouldn't leave?

ESTHER. And if your father wasn't an American citizen . . . (*shudders the rest of the sentence.*)

REVA. . . . What happened to his father? (*Off Esther's shrug—she doesn't know*) Why didn't you tell me?

ESTHER. So you shouldn't worry. Pa didn't want you to worry. You see how he tries to protect you?

REVA. Control me.

ESTHER. He doesn't want to control you.

REVA. Just like he controls you.

ESTHER. Oy, Revela, don't start that again.

REVA. Ma, didn't you ever want anything more than this?

ESTHER. You're such a *narish** child.

REVA. I'm not a child. And it's not foolish to have dreams.

ESTHER. When you have two kids to raise and a husband who needs your support, you give up dreaming.

REVA. Well, I won't. Ever. Chris needs a pillow. (*Reva goes upstairs. Esther sinks into remembered dreams. Nate and Chris are still moving merchandise.*)

CHRIS. You know what my dad said when I signed up?

NATE. Don't go to the slums?

CHRIS. He said I was too young to join the army. But Mom said it was my duty as an American citizen, and they needed colored men who were trained.

---

*Foolish.

NATE. Trained in what? Socialism?

CHRIS. ROTC. All through high school. I took a lot of needling about that at the Cass-Warren Grill.

NATE. That bunch of anarchists?

CHRIS. Because I thought a black man could get anywhere in the army.

NATE. You didn't get anywhere? You're a sergeant.

CHRIS. Mr. Kaufman, I sailed through OCS. I learned to speak Japanese like a damned native. I was supposed to go overseas as an intelligence officer. But here I am, stateside, a sergeant, in a Negro unit, arresting Negro soldiers. That's not what I enlisted for. (*In the alcove Reva comes downstairs with a pillow. Esther shifts on the step to make room for her.*)

REVA. What was your dream, Ma?

ESTHER. I forgot.

REVA. Did you want to . . . be a doctor? A lawyer?

ESTHER. Don't be *mishugah*.

REVA. An artist? You wanted to paint? . . . sing? . . . be a movie star?

ESTHER. I was very good.

REVA. . . . At what? . . . When?

ESTHER. In school. I played Portia. (*Emoting.*) "If to do were as easy to know what were good to do . . ."

REVA. You wanted to go on the stage?!

ESTHER. (*Shrugging it off.*) And before that I wanted to dance. And before that I wanted to write poetry.

REVA. You should have.

ESTHER. I couldn't afford a typewriter. Revela, this is no time for such silly—

REVA. Did Pa have any dreams?

ESTHER. To get his family out of Poland. To have a good store. . . . At least he got the store.

REVA. (*Imitating Nate.*) "And I'm not turning it over to strangers."

ESTHER. And you can't understand how much it means to him? How hard he had to work?

REVA. I understand that he's the only one of us who's gotten his dream. At the expense of the rest of us.

ESTHER. What expense? Danny didn't go to medical school? You didn't go to Wayne?

REVA. You didn't become an actress.

ESTHER. You know my most important dream? To live out my life with the man I love.

REVA. Me, too, Ma. That's my most important dream.

ESTHER. But couldn't it be with someone else? Someone . . .

REVA. Jewish. (*And off Esther's nod.*) And not Negro. Ma, I love him.

ESTHER. You're twenty years old. Look around a little first.

REVA. I've looked.

ESTHER. Where? At that Cass-Warren place?

REVA. At Junior Hadassah. At Young Judea. I don't want to spend my life discussing clothes and boys, and whether or not to date a guy who doesn't have his own car.

ESTHER. What do you and your . . . Chris discuss? How the Jews have all the money? How they killed Jesus?

REVA. Did you hear him do that?

ESTHER. Give him time.

REVA. Give him a chance! (*In frustration, she plops down on the cot, making it hit the door to the secret room.*)

ESTHER. Don't!

REVA. What?

ESTHER. . . . Don't put your shoes on the blanket.

REVA. (*Amused.*) Oh, Ma . . .

ESTHER. Ah, what does it matter. Put your shoes wherever you want. Try to get some rest.

REVA. No, you rest, Ma. (*She gets up and prods Esther onto the cot.*)

ESTHER. But you're tired.

REVA. (*Sprawling across the steps.*) I'll be okay here. I learned how to do this during a sit-in at school.

ESTHER. That's what you're learning in college? (*They almost laugh. Then Esther turns to the secret room door and touches it, as if to secure it. Reva lies back, thinking. In the office Nate and Chris, loaded with merchandise, are crossing from the store to the storeroom.*)

NATE. Tell me something.

CHRIS. Yeah?

NATE. What do they do to them? The army. To the trait . . . to the men who desert?

CHRIS. Well, when there's a war on . . .

NATE. But if a man has a good reason . . .

CHRIS. Reasons don't count in a war. If they catch you, they use a bullet they were saving for the enemy, and you're dead. (*Nate drops his load.*)

CHRIS. (*Continuing and picking up Nate's load.*) I'll finish up. You'd better rest.

NATE. I don't need to rest. (*But he sinks into a chair, numb. Chris carries the load into the storeroom. As he returns:*)

NATE. (*Continued.*) What happens if they don't catch you? Catch the deserters?

CHRIS. They stay out of the stockade . . . and alive.

NATE. But what about . . . can they go back to . . . everything? After the war?

CHRIS. Like social work, you mean.

NATE. Social work. Lawyer work. Medicine work. Any work.

CHRIS. I don't know. Guess it's a good thing I'm going back, huh? (*Nate sits back, more worried. Chris keeps working. In the alcove Esther isn't really asleep. She whispers:*)

ESTHER. Reva? Are you asleep?

REVA. No, Ma.

ESTHER. Sleep, sleep.

REVA. I can't. What do you want?

ESTHER. I don't hate him. Your friend, Chris. But we have enough troubles of our own. We don't need his troubles, too.

REVA. I'm not asking you to—

ESTHER. And you don't need them. Let him fight his own fights.

REVA. Ma, it's one fight. We're all in the same fight. Don't you know that?

ESTHER. What am I, a dummkopf? Of course, I know. But I'm not going to win it by myself. And neither are you.

REVA. But maybe together, we can.

ESTHER. . . . Let me put that another way. (*Reva almost laughs. She kneels at the cot, and puts her head on Esther's chest.*)

REVA. Oh, Ma, I love you.

ESTHER. Then don't break my heart.

REVA. Don't ask me to break mine. (*A moment. Then they go into each other's arms and hold on tightly. In the office Chris enters and plops, tiredly, onto a chair.*)

CHRIS. I'm bushed.

NATE. . . . Supposing you did desert . . . what would you do then?

CHRIS. I'd say I was Spencer Tracy with a deep tan. And have one hell of a good time until they shoot me.

NATE. You can joke about a thing like that?

CHRIS. What's better? To cry?

NATE. That's a Jewish joke.

CHRIS. Works for me, too. (*Looks into the teapot.*) Want some cold tea? (*Nate gestures "no." Chris pours tea for himself and drinks it as:*)

NATE. What if, while you're deserting—(*Off Chris's look.*) What if while someone else is deserting, he does something . . . like . . . like a real hero? Would they forgive him? Give him a medal or something?

CHRIS. Maybe. Unless he's a *schvartzeh*. Why are you asking me all these questions?

NATE. I . . . I'm worried about you.

CHRIS. Sure you are.

NATE. But, listen, you'll go back and they'll shake a finger at you and it'll be over.

CHRIS. From your mouth to God's ear.

NATE. Where did you—? (*Off Chris's look.*) From Reva.

CHRIS. Okay. Now it's my turn. Can't you understand that Reva doesn't want to be a—a businesswoman?

NATE. What's wrong with business? What are you, some kind of communist?

CHRIS. A realist.

NATE. A realist doesn't waste his life with winos and bums.

CHRIS. A realist knows that someone has to help them.

NATE. How old are you? Twenty? Twenty-one?

CHRIS. I'm an old man. Twenty-three.

NATE. And you think you know everything?

CHRIS. I know I've got to try to do something.

NATE. By taking my daughter into all the . . . with all the . . .

CHRIS. I'm not taking her. We're doing it together.

NATE. Sure, together you can get . . . shot at . . . killed.

CHRIS. I would never let anyone hurt Reva.

NATE. And neither would I. If I had to break both her legs.

CHRIS. You won't put a finger on her.

NATE. You're telling me what I can do with my daughter?

CHRIS. I'm telling you nobody's going to hurt Reva while I'm around.

NATE. Only you can do that, right?

CHRIS. Mr. Kaufman—

NATE. I want a decent life for my daughter.

CHRIS. So do I. For my wife.

NATE. Listen, you. I don't like you for her friend. Don't even joke about anything else.

CHRIS. We're married. (*Then, off Nate's shock.*) Reva and I are married. (*A moment. Then suddenly, Nate wails:*)

NATE. Esther! (*Esther and Reva bolt into the office.*)

ESTHER. What is it?

REVA. Are you all right, Pa?

NATE. They're married. (*Esther looks to Reva. Reva questions Chris with a look. He gestures an "I had to tell him." Reva turns back to Esther.*)

ESTHER. No . . . no . . .

REVA. Yes, Ma. (*A beat as it soaks in. Then Esther turns on Chris, beating on his chest and wailing. Chris and Reva try to stop her. Nate tears at his shirt as if in mourning. His wailing wells up to match Esther's. Through it all, overlapping, and growing louder:*)

ESTHER. No! No! It's not true.

REVA. Ma, please. Pa, don't.

NATE. How could you do this to me?

CHRIS. Mr. Kaufman, Mrs. Kaufman, please. (*It grows louder, ad lib, until it sounds as if the rioting has broken into the store. Suddenly, in the alcove, the secret door bursts open, overturning the cot. Danny leaps out of the secret room, waving the pistol. He bursts into the office. Danny points the pistol—not wanting to shoot—not knowing where to shoot. Everyone is standing too close together. All of them staring back at him. Chris draws his pistol.*)

REVA. Danny?! (*Overlapping:*)

DANNY. I'm not going back.

REVA. Back where?

ESTHER. No, Danny, he's not here for you!

DANNY. (*To Chris.*) You're not taking me back there.

REVA. What are you doing?

NATE. Danny, don't—

CHRIS. Drop it.

ESTHER. Give me the gun, Danny.

DANNY. No, I won't go back. I won't.

NATE. He's not here to arrest you.

CHRIS. (*Putting his pistol on the desk.*) Look, Man. I'm putting down my gun.

DANNY. No, it's a trick . . .

ESTHER. He's with Reva, Danny.

DANNY. Stay away, Ma.

NATE. (*Pulling Esther back.*) He's crazy. (*There is loud shuffling and angry voices outside. We can't make out who is there, and what the words are, but the argument is: a male voice making demands and a female voice resisting them. It continues under: in the office: Danny, more crazed now, waves the pistol between the store and the office. Everyone else is now frightened, both by Danny and the threat outside. Overlapping:*)

REVA. Looters!

DANNY. I'm not going with them.

NATE. It's a pogrom.

ESTHER. No, Nate!

CHRIS. (*Starting toward the store.*) I'll get rid of them.

DANNY. Stay away from me. (*Chris backs off.*)

NATE. It's Warsaw.

ESTHER. No, no, Nate, it's not the police.

CHRIS. If you'll let me get my gun—(*He tries to pass Danny, to pick up his pistol, but Danny waves him back.*)

DANNY. Don't touch it.

CHRIS. They're not MPs. They're looters.

DANNY. They're not getting me. (*The outside voices grow more threatening.*)

REVA. (*Grabbing Esther's and Nate's arms.*) Go upstairs.

NATE. No, we'll be trapped.

CHRIS. You, too, Danny. Go upstairs. I'll handle them.

DANNY. Yeah, I know what you'll do.

REVA. Please, Ma—

ESTHER. No, not upstairs. Danny, come with us. Back inside the room.

REVA. What room?

NATE. No!

ESTHER. Nate, it's not a secret any more.

NATE. But we built it for . . . later.

ESTHER. For now, Nate. For an emergency. For now. (*A moment . . . and Nate gives in with a nod. He lets Esther lead him toward the alcove.*)

ESTHER. (*Continuing.*) Come, Danny. They won't get you in there.

DANNY. No . . . they'll know. (*Indicating Chris.*) He knows.

REVA. He's my husband. (*As Danny reacts to that, the front door is rattled. Esther pushes Reva and Nate toward the alcove.*)

ESTHER. Hurry. Danny, come.

DANNY. You married a soldier? An MP?

REVA. But he's not—

CHRIS. We'll explain later. Get them out of here, Reev. (*Reva goes with Nate and Esther through the alcove and into the secret room. Reva looks about, puzzled. She, too, wasn't aware that it existed. The secret door is pulled shut behind them. In the office Chris and Danny are alone. Chris closes the door to the alcove. In the store the door is being kicked in.*)

DANNY. It's a lie. You're lying.

CHRIS. Danny, I know you don't want to use that gun.

DANNY. Stay away from me. (*He backs into the store, just as the front door is kicked open. Leon shoves Joyce in. Overlapping:*)

JOYCE. Let me go!

LEON. Get the hell in there. (*Danny whirls on them. Leon sees the pistol and stops short.*)

DANNY. (*Screaming.*) I'm not going back! (*He points the pistol. Chris runs toward the store, but before he can get there, Leon leaps at Danny. They scuffle and there's a shot. Black out.*)

ACT II

Scene 1

Note: The rioting and the reactions to it continue throughout this scene. At rise: A moment before the end of the last scene. (Repeated from Act I, Scene 2.) Esther, Nate, and Reva are in the secret room. Chris is in the alcove. Danny backs into the store, just as the front door is kicked open. Leon shoves Joyce in. Overlapping:

JOYCE. Let me go!

LEON. Get the hell in there. (*Danny whirls on them. Leon sees the pistol and stops short.*)

DANNY. (*Screaming.*) I'm not going back! (*He points the pistol. Chris runs toward the store, but before he can get there, Leon leaps at Danny. They scuffle and there's a shot. End of repeat from Act I, Scene 2. As Joyce, Danny, and Chris watch in horror, Leon jerks backwards then sinks slowly to the floor. He's been shot in the shoulder. In the secret room Reva, Nate, and Esther react to the shot. Overlapping:*)

REVA. Chris!

ESTHER AND NATE. Danny! (*In the store.*)

JOYCE. Leon?! (*Numbly, Danny backs away. Chris and Joyce kneel beside Leon. Reva and Esther run through the alcove and the office, toward the store. Nate starts to follow them, but suddenly he gasps, clasps a hand to his buttocks, and backs away.*)

JOYCE. Help! Mrs. Kaufman! Reva! Help him! (*In the secret room.*)

NATE. (*A whisper.*) Esther . . . (*No response. He sinks to the floor. In the store:*)

CHRIS. Brother? Can you hear me?

LEON. What the fuck happened? (*Reva and Esther don't see Danny . . . or Leon's face.*)

ESTHER. Danny! (*She pushes at the others to get through.*)

REVA. What happened?

JOYCE. (*Stunned, to Danny.*) You shot him. (*Reva and Esther follow Joyce's look.*)

REVA. Danny . . . ?

ESTHER. You're alive! (*Esther tries to hug Danny, he backs away.*)

DANNY. . . . I shot him. (*Now Reva and Esther are aware that the pistol is still in Danny's hand.*)

REVA. We'd better call a doctor. (*Reva hurries into the office. Esther takes the pistol from Danny and puts it on a shelf. In the office Reva goes to the desk and dials the phone. In the secret room: Nate can see through the two open doors to the office. He watches Reva and sinks more into himself. In the three areas, overlapping:*)

ESTHER. No, Danny would never do such a thing.

REVA. (*Into phone.*) We need a doctor here. A man's been shot.

JOYCE. You killed him!

DANNY. No! . . . I didn't mean . . . the gun . . . it . . . the gun.

REVA. (*Into phone.*) How long?

CHRIS. He's not dead.

REVA. (*Into phone.*) We can't wait. He may be dying! (*Leon groans. Esther tries again to hug Danny.*)

REVA. (*Into phone.*) I know there's a riot on!

ESTHER. Hear that, Danny? He's alive. You didn't kill him.

REVA. (*Into phone.*) 1512 Michigan Ave.

JOYCE. Leon? Talk to me, Leon. (*Leon coughs.*)

ESTHER. Leon . . . ?! Leon Thompson? (*Joyce starts to pick Leon's head up.*)

REVA. (*Into phone.*) It's a store. Paris Imports.

DANNY. (*Still numb but by rote.*) Don't move him! (*Joyce puts Leon's head down.*)

ESTHER. Be careful!

REVA. (*Into phone.*) Please, hurry. (*She hangs up and goes back into the store.*)

ESTHER. Did you get a doctor?

REVA. They said it might take a few hours.

JOYCE. A few hours?!

CHRIS. (*To Danny.*) Can he wait that long?

DANNY. I don't . . . it depends where the bullet . . . I shot him!

ESTHER. No, it was an accident.

DANNY. (*Trying to accept that.*) It was an accident . . . He came at me . . . He was trying to—

JOYCE. He was trying not to get shot.

REVA. Or trying to steal something.

CHRIS. That's not important now.

REVA. Joycy . . . you weren't with him, were you?

JOYCE. Sure. I came back here with him to rob you.

REVA. Well, I didn't mean . . .

ESTHER. Please, Reva, she came back to help us.

JOYCE. He grabbed me and pulled me in here. (*To Danny.*) You saw it.

DANNY. (*Not hearing her.*) He came at me . . . I thought . . . (*Leon groans.*)

CHRIS. Danny!

DANNY. It was an accident!

CHRIS. You'd better look at him.

DANNY. Look . . . no . . . I . . . can't . . .

ESTHER. Go, Danny, darling. You can make him better.

JOYCE. Help him, Danny!

DANNY. I . . . can't . . . I . . .

CHRIS. (*Harsh.*) You're supposed to be a doctor, do something!

DANNY. I'm not a doctor!

CHRIS. Didn't they teach you anything in med school?

REVA. Don't yell at him! Can't you see how he feels?

CHRIS. I see that a man could die, and he's the only one who can help him. (*Reva and Chris are stunned at having quarreled. The moment is broken as Leon groans.*)

LEON. Oh, shit.

ESTHER. He's talking! See, Danny, he's not going to die. You can save him. (*She propels Danny to Leon. Danny just now realizes:*)

DANNY. Leon?

LEON. (*Snidely.*) Hi, Danny.

DANNY. It's Leon . . .

REVA. (*To Chris.*) We grew up together.

CHRIS. (*To Danny.*) Then get off your ass and help him.

REVA. He will! (*To Danny.*) You're the only one who can.

JOYCE. Please. (*Leon groans.*)

ESTHER. Fix him up, Danny.

LEON. Yeah . . . finish the job. (*Slowly, unsure, Danny tears Leon's shirt from the wound and begins the examination.*)

CHRIS. Can you see the bullet?

DANNY. No . . . it's too deep.

LEON. (*Howling in pain.*) Hey, lay off!

JOYCE. Can you get it out?

DANNY. I don't have the . . . I need something to; . . . a probe . . . Ma, where's the first aid kit?

ESTHER. I'll get it. (*The others gather around Danny. Esther hurries through the office and into the alcove. As Esther starts for the stairs, Nate whispers from the secret room:)*

NATE. Esther.

ESTHER. *(Seeing him through the open door.)* Nate . . . ?

NATE. *(Whispering.)* Close the door! *(Esther is torn, then she closes the secret room door almost all the way, hurries back into the office, and calls to the store:)*

ESTHER. Reva, go get the first aid kit. *(Esther hurries back through the alcove, into the secret room, closing the door behind her. In the store Reva looks toward Esther.)*

REVA. I'm helping . . . Ma?

DANNY. Where's the kit?

REVA. I'll get it. *(She goes through the office and the alcove, looking for Esther. In the alcove {Reva} and the secret room {Esther and Nate}:)*

REVA. Ma, where are you?

ESTHER. Nate? Are you okay?

NATE. Sha. Someone's out there.

REVA. *(Hurrying upstairs.)* Ma?

ESTHER. It's all right. She's gone. *(In the store {Danny, Chris, Joyce, and Leon} and the secret room {Esther and Nate} overlapping: Leon groans.)*

JOYCE. Don't hurt him.

ESTHER. Did you see what happened?

DANNY. I'm trying not to.

NATE. Do you think she saw?

ESTHER. *(About Leon.)* We all saw. It was terrible.

LEON. I'll bet.

CHRIS. Shut up, man.

NATE. I'm so ashamed.

ESTHER. It's my fault. I gave him the gun.

NATE. Esther . . .

ESTHER. And yours, Nate. You sent him to—

NATE. Help me.

ESTHER. *(Realizes what's wrong, then gently.)* Oh! . . . Oh, Nate . . . *(She goes to him, but he pulls back, shamed.)*

LEON. It hurts.

DANNY. Maybe he should be on a bed.

JOYCE. The cot. Inside. *(They all pick Leon up and carry him into the office. In the office {Danny, Chris, Joyce, and Leon} and the secret room {Esther and Nate}, overlapping:)*

NATE. This is the first time it happened since Poland.

ESTHER. It's the first time you were so afraid. *(Leon groans.)*

JOYCE. Be careful! (*They move more slowly toward the alcove.*)

NATE. You really think nobody saw?

ESTHER. Nate, darling. A man could be dying out there. Nobody cares if you make dirty in your pants.

NATE. Sha! Don't say it! (*Leon howls in pain.*)

CHRIS. We're almost there. (*They carry Leon into the alcove. In the alcove {Danny, Chris, Joyce, and Leon} and the secret room {Esther and Nate}, overlapping:*)

NATE. (*Whispering.*) Someone's coming. (*Reva comes downstairs with the first aid kit.*)

REVA. I don't know where Ma went.

NATE. (*Whispering.*) Don't tell her.

ESTHER. (*Losing patience.*) Nobody cares, Nate!

DANNY. Give me the kit. (*Reva hands it to Danny. He opens it and searches through it.*)

NATE. You ran out and left me sitting here in . . . you didn't help me.

REVA. How is he?

JOYCE. (*Harshly.*) How do you think he is?

ESTHER. I was in the store. Trying to help Danny.

REVA. (*Hurt.*) I just asked.

NATE. Danny was shot?!

ESTHER. He shot someone.

NATE. . . . Danny? . . . He shot . . . ? Who?

ESTHER. A boy from the neighborhood.

NATE. Not so loud.

CHRIS. Can you use anything in there?

DANNY. I think so. (*He takes some tweezers out of the kit.*)

NATE. Was he stealing from us?

ESTHER. Nate, stop it. He could be dying! (*Danny tries to probe for the bullet. Leon screams in pain.*)

ESTHER. (*Starting to go.*) They need help.

NATE. Don't leave me, Esther. (*She stays.*)

CHRIS. He's bleeding more.

DANNY. Get something . . . towels. (*Reva races back upstairs.*)

CHRIS. (*To Danny.*) What if you don't get it out?

DANNY. I don't know.

JOYCE. He'll die?

DANNY. I . . . I don't know.

LEON. (*Slipping in and out of consciousness now.*) He don't know much, does he?

JOYCE. Can't you do anything for him?

ESTHER. (*Starting out again.*) I have to do something.

DANNY. I don't know what to do.

NATE. Why did you give him the gun? (*Reva runs downstairs with a load of towels, just as:*)

JOYCE. You knew what to do with a gun in your hand! (*Danny runs into the office.*)

ESTHER. Why did you send him where he learned how to use it? (*But she stays.*)

REVA. (*Turning on Joyce.*) He didn't mean to shoot Leon.

JOYCE. But he did it. (*Reva runs into the office and embraces a shaking Danny. In the office {Reva and Danny}; in the alcove {Chris, Joyce, and Leon}; in the secret room {Esther and Nate}, overlapping:*)

NATE. Please, Esther. Don't leave me here alone.

CHRIS. (*To Joyce.*) Why the hell don't you shut up?

JOYCE. Why the hell don't you go fight Nazis or someone? (*Chris goes into the office and watches:*)

DANNY. I can't help him.

REVA. But you tried.

DANNY. I shot him, Reev. (*In the office {Reva, Danny, and Chris}; in the alcove {Leon and Joyce}; in the secret room {Esther and Nate}. Reva rocks Danny. Nate, sobbing, rocks himself. Esther holds him.*)

ESTHER. I won't leave you, Nate.

LEON. (*Half-waking.*) . . . Where . . . ?

JOYCE. You're safe.

LEON. . . . Joyce?

JOYCE. Yeah, it's me.

LEON. What the fuck are you doing here?

JOYCE. Waiting for a doctor.

LEON. (*Tries to laugh, coughs.*) What'd you do? Tell him it was for a nigger?

NATE. Who was it, the boy from the neighborhood?

ESTHER. Leon Thompson.

NATE. The jailbird?

ESTHER. Enough, Nate!

NATE. It's not the first time he stole from us.

ESTHER. It's the first time Danny shot someone.

DANNY. He's going to die.

REVA. No, no, Danny.

CHRIS. Yes! Unless you get back in there and keep him alive.

REVA. Chris!

CHRIS. Stop lying to him, Reev.

REVA. Stop punishing him. It was an accident. (*She rocks Danny, but it doesn't help. Disgusted, Chris moves away from them.*)

LEON. Who's the nigger with the stripes? Your boyfriend?

JOYCE. Yeah, sure.

LEON. That's what you'd like, ain't it?

JOYCE. I'd like you to shut your mouth, so's I won't have to do it for you. (*Leon groans.*)

JOYCE. (*Continued, gently.*) You dumbass fool.

NATE. I didn't know he would use it like this.

ESTHER. No, you just sent him to learn how.

NATE. He signed up himself.

ESTHER. For you. So he could be a hero, for you.

DANNY. Reva . . .

REVA. I'm here.

DANNY. It was an accident. Wasn't it?

CHRIS. Not according to you pacifists.

REVA. Chris! Stop it!

CHRIS. According to you, the minute you put a gun in someone's hand—

REVA. What are you doing?

CHRIS. Going stir crazy. With a lot of help from your brother.

REVA. Danny, don't listen to him.

NATE. That's not why—

ESTHER. When will you stop punishing yourself?

REVA. Go back in there and try to help Leon.

DANNY. There's nothing more I can do. We have to wait for . . . I can't, Reev. . . . I'm not . . . I'll never be a doctor.

REVA. (*Without conviction.*) You will, Danny. (*To Chris.*) Tell him.

CHRIS. . . . The hell he will. (*Chris goes into the store. Reva starts after him, but stays to help a shaking Danny instead.*)

ESTHER. You weren't a coward, Nate. The way the Polish army treated Jewish soldiers, you had a right not to go.

NATE. Please, Esther, stop.

LEON. It's your fault.

JOYCE. Mine?

LEON. You could've reformed me, you wasn't so uppity.

JOYCE. That what you're going to tell the judge?

LEON. Or the coroner.

JOYCE. (*Covering compassion.*) You'd try anything to get in my pants, wouldn't you?

LEON. Almost. (*She laughs, he tries to. It causes a coughing spasm. Reva, Danny, and Chris hear that.*)

REVA. Danny . . . ?

DANNY. I don't know what else to do for him. (*Chris enters from the store.*)

CHRIS. I'll go. (*In the alcove, {Joyce and Leon}; in the office {Reva and Danny}; in the secret room {Esther and Nate}. As Chris enters the alcove, he questions Joyce with a look, "How's he doing?" Joyce shakes her head, "not good."*)

CHRIS. Hold on, man.

LEON. I ain't One-A no more, so no use trying to draft me. (*And he has another coughing spasm.*)

ESTHER. And you went back, Nate. You tried to get your Papa out.

NATE. I should have stayed and protected him.

ESTHER. And leave me here to face this alone?

NATE. And now, you're not facing it alone?

DANNY. You really married to him? To an MP?

REVA. He signed up to be a translator.

DANNY. Then they fucked him up, too.

NATE. You would be better off if I never left Poland in the first place.

ESTHER. And I would leave there without you?

LEON. How come you're not over there getting killed?

CHRIS. It's a long story.

LEON. A short one. They give a nigger too many stripes.

NATE. You'd be better off if you never met me.

ESTHER. So how would I have Reva and Danny?

DANNY. You ever hold a gun, Reev?

REVA. No.

DANNY. I did.

REVA. That BB gun Pa gave you? That was an accident.

DANNY. You know what's scariest about it?

REVA. You didn't mean to do it.

DANNY. It feels . . . it makes you feel . . . so . . . powerful.

LEON. And you were dumb enough to think it meant something.

CHRIS. Not as dumb as you, fool.

JOYCE. Leave him alone.

NATE. Maybe you'd be better off without them, too.

ESTHER. Bite your tongue!

DANNY. It's like . . . like why I wanted to go into medicine.

REVA. To help people.

DANNY. To . . . have power over life and death.

LEON. What's dumb is coming anywheres near a shithole you ain't stuck in.

CHRIS. My wife's parents are.

JOYCE. . . . You and Reva? You're married?

LEON. No shit?

NATE. One marries a *schvartzeh* . . . and the other is a deserter.

LEON. Now, that's dumb.

REVA. Over life. You wanted power over life.

DANNY. Death is a part of life.

REVA. Stop talking like that. That's not you.

DANNY. Isn't it?

ESTHER. (*Angry again.*) He's not a deserter! And he's not a coward!

CHRIS. It's caring about someone besides yourself. But you wouldn't know about that.

ESTHER. Would a coward be out there trying to protect us?

DANNY. They both give you that power.

REVA. I don't want to hear any more.

DANNY. Medicine . . . and guns.

REVA. You know what, Danny? You belong in the army!

ESTHER. Would a coward come here in the middle of a riot? (*Reva marches into the alcove.*)

LEON. Hey, Reva. How is it fucking a nigger?

CHRIS. You son of a bitch! (*Chris goes at Leon. Joyce holds him back.*)

REVA. He should have killed you! (*Chris tries to calm her but she pushes him off and goes back into the office.*)

JOYCE. (*Accusing Leon.*) Now that was dumb. (*Chris follows Reva into the office. As he enters:*)

REVA. What were you doing? Discussing our sex life?

CHRIS. Better than telling a man he should die. (*Chris goes back into the store. Now each of them—Danny, Reva, Chris—is and feels alone.*)

NATE. But why did he run away from the army?

ESTHER. Why did you make him go in the army?

NATE. Enough . . . Esther!

DANNY. Reev, what should I do?

REVA. I don't know.

DANNY. I can't go back to camp.

REVA. If you don't . . . Deserters can't become doctors.

DANNY. Murderers can't, either.

LEON. They think they're something special.

JOYCE. And you're jealous.

LEON. And you ain't?

JOYCE. We're talking about you. You want his uniform and his ofay* woman.

LEON. Damned right.

JOYCE. Well, they don't put a uniform on an ex-con. And no woman would have you.

LEON. If the kike hadn't of shot me, I'd had any woman I want.

JOYCE. With a few dollars stolen from an old man.

LEON. Might even've got you.

JOYCE. I'd kill you first.

NATE. You don't know what it was like . . . hiding in a corner in a dark closet . . .

ESTHER. I knew . . . every time I came to bring you food.

DANNY. I didn't want to desert. But when the captain said . . . I had to.

LEON. They won't let me in the army. In the war plants. It ain't fair.

NATE. You think I liked it you had to do that? And . . . and take out my dirt . . .

ESTHER. You think I liked they wanted to use you like an animal?

LEON. I'm tired of being outside looking at them having it all.

DANNY. The way he looked at me. Like he wanted to kill me himself.

NATE. Every time I heard steps I thought if it's not you, I'll stuff a coat in my mouth and choke myself.

DANNY. I thought I was going to die, right in front of him.

LEON. I gotta right to some of it.

NATE. I would have killed myself before I let them take me.

DANNY. If I'd had a gun . . .

LEON. And if I get a chance like tonight, then I gotta take it.

DANNY. But I didn't. I couldn't do anything.

NATE. And was it worth it, Esther?

DANNY. So I said "Yes, Sir," and I saluted. And I ran.

LEON. 'Cause I'm not no animal. And I ain't going to go on living like one.

NATE. Is it any better here? (*The lights dim slowly to black.*)

---

*African-American derogatory slang for a Caucasian person.

Scene 2

Note: The rioting has quieted down to intermittent yelling, glass breaking, shots, etc. As the scene and morning progress, the rioting sounds will grow in intensity. At rise: Just before dawn. Each room will be lit independently for its first scene, leaving the others dim. But at rise all four rooms are lit to half. There are four tableaus of despair: each of the seven people alone, disconnected by the events of the night before, physically and emotionally. In the secret room Esther sleeps on the lower bunk, Nate, in clean pants, on the upper one. In the alcove Leon sleeps on the cot, Joyce sits on the stairs, nodding off, trying to stay awake. In the office Danny sleeps in the easy chair. Reva sleeps on the desk chair, her head on the desk. In the store Chris sits on the floor, leaning on a shelf, trying to sleep. Lights dim down in the office, alcove, and store. Lights come up to full in the secret room:)

NATE. Esther? You sleeping?

ESTHER. *(Forcing herself to wake up.)* No, I'm awake.

NATE. . . . I'm sorry.

ESTHER. No, I am. I had no right to talk to you like that.

NATE. . . . You had a right. *(A moment, then.)* Esther, you sleeping now?

ESTHER. No.

NATE. I was thinking, if we get out of this alive . . .

ESTHER. Sha. We will.

NATE. When we get out of this . . .

ESTHER. What?

NATE. . . . I don't know.

ESTHER. I know. We sell the store and we move to Dexter Blvd.

NATE. Ten years too late.

ESTHER. Don't talk past. Talk future.

NATE. What future? For who? Our *schvartzeh* grandchildren?

ESTHER. For us. We deserve a little pleasure.

NATE. Then forget Dexter. Florida.

ESTHER. Florida . . . Miami Beach.

NATE. . . . Yeah . . . Facing the water.

ESTHER. No kitchen. We'll eat out.

NATE. Three times a day.

ESTHER. Why not?

NATE. Why not? *(Falling asleep.)* Steak every night. And wine.

ESTHER. One glass. Well, maybe two.

NATE. Why not? *(Esther gets up, sees that Nate's asleep, and touches him gently.)*

ESTHER. Because, my darling, it's too late. There's nothing left to sell. . . . There's no one left to give it to . . . (*She sits down on her bunk, resigned. Lights dim down on the secret room. Lights come up on the office. Reva turns in her sleep, and almost loses her balance. That wakes her. She looks around, disoriented at first, then remembers what happened. She gets up, looks at the sleeping Danny, looks into the alcove, sees Leon and Joyce sleeping. She goes into the store. Lights dim down on the office. Lights come up on the store. Seeing Chris, Reva hesitates. How to get over last night's fight? She doesn't know. She turns to go back to the office.*)

CHRIS. I'm awake.

REVA. . . . Me, too. (*He pats the floor beside him. Thankfully, Reva hurries to sit beside him.*)

REVA. That was our first fight.

CHRIS. I'm sorry.

REVA. Me, too! (*She cuddles in his arms.*)

CHRIS. There'll be others.

REVA. Oh, no! Chris, promise me—

CHRIS. Everyone fights, Revela. And we have more to fight about than most of them.

REVA. You called me Revela.

CHRIS. How'd it sound coming from me?

REVA. Natural.

CHRIS. It won't be natural, Revela. Or easy.

REVA. Well, maybe not at first.

CHRIS. But, I love you.

REVA. You know I love you, Chrisala.

CHRIS. Chrisala?

REVA. No, that doesn't sound natural.

CHRIS. Then what's the Jewish equivalent?

REVA. Uh . . . I don't think there is one!

CHRIS. I hope that's not an omen.

REVA. Wait. You could use Khaim.

CHRIS. Kh . . . Kh . . . I can't pronounce it.

REVA. But I love hearing you try. (*They kiss. The first gunshot of the morning freezes them in their embrace.*)

CHRIS. It's okay. I'm here.

REVA. Hold me tighter. (*He does. Then, to lighten the mood:*)

CHRIS. You're giving my chest two permanent dents. (*She laughs. They relax.*)

REVA. It's my brand.

CHRIS. See why I chose you?

REVA. It was because I'm white.

CHRIS. If that was it, I'd go all the way and pick a blond.

REVA. You know why I chose you?

CHRIS. Because it's chic at Wayne to be with a Negro.

REVA. Only if he's a musician.

CHRIS. Well, I can strum a bit of ukulele. (*She laughs as he strums her from stomach to mouth, and they kiss again.*)

REVA. Chris . . . what are you going to do about Danny? You wouldn't . . . arrest him, would you?

CHRIS. I can just see it. A black AWOL bringing in a white deserter. They wouldn't know which one of us to shoot first.

REVA. That's not funny.

CHRIS. What's better? To cry? (*They laugh again, this time wryly. Lights dim down on the store. Lights come up on the alcove. Leon groans with a sharp pain. Joyce wakes and goes to him. Leon will have more pain, more trouble speaking now.*)

JOYCE. I'm here, Leon.

LEON. (*Disoriented.*) . . . Joyce? What're you doing here?

JOYCE. Taking care of you.

LEON. Oh . . . yeah . . . the store. . . . The doctor come?

JOYCE. Not yet.

LEON. Should of told them it was for one of the kikes.

JOYCE. Damn it, Leon. Cut it out.

LEON. You know your trouble, girl? You been with them too long. You think you're one of them.

JOYCE. No, I think you're a dumb schmuck.

LEON. (*As if he scored a point.*) See?

JOYCE. And Jewish words aren't the only thing I learned from them.

LEON. You learned if you kiss their asses, they let you come in and sweep up their shit for them.

JOYCE. You jealous?

LEON. Hell, no. I'd never brown-nose them.

JOYCE. Which is why you keep asking them for a job.

LEON. And you know why they won't give it to me?

JOYCE. Because they caught you stealing a box of stockings.

LEON. Nylon stockings. For you.

JOYCE. You thought I'd accept stolen nylons from you. You must have been crazy.

LEON. No, I was mad.

JOYCE. Mad also means crazy.

LEON. You think you're smart, don't you?

JOYCE. Hell of a lot smarter than you. (*Leon starts to cough.*)

JOYCE. (*Continued.*) I'd better get help.

LEON. No, stay here. I want to tell you something.

JOYCE. Don't talk.

LEON. I was jealous. Not when we was kids. Not when we all played together . . . me and you and them. Danny and Reva.

JOYCE. We grew up.

LEON. (*Falling asleep.*) But you're still with them. And I'm . . . Joyce, if I get out of this one . . . can I play with you guys again?

JOYCE. . . . Sure, Leon.

LEON. Maybe you'd even be my woman?

JOYCE. (*To calm him, but doesn't mean it.*) . . . Sure . . .

LEON. Damn, I wish I had witnesses . . . (*And he's asleep. Lights dim down in the alcove. Lights come full in the secret room. Esther has dozed off. Nate startles, wakes, realizing:*)

NATE. We can't do it, Esther. It's too late.

ESTHER. It's early. Go back to sleep.

NATE. There's nothing left to sell.

ESTHER. There's a whole storeroom full of merchandise.

NATE. And who do we sell it to? Who's going to walk through all the bricks and the . . . broken glass . . . and . . . the . . . the blood?

ESTHER. Listen, a good broom, a little soap and everything will be hunky-dory again.

NATE. Hunky-dory! It was never hunky-dory.

ESTHER. Nate, go to sleep, we'll talk in the morning.

NATE. It is morning. In my head. Suddenly, the light beams. You know what we got, Esther? In this store? We got borscht.

ESTHER. We got $523 in the bank, and $96 in the safe.

NATE. And I forgot what it was for.

ESTHER. For Florida.

NATE. The store wasn't for the store. It was for us. For you, me, the kids.

ESTHER. And it was very good for all of us.

NATE. Good?! Look what it did to us. Danny is . . . Reva is . . . And I'm . . . a stupid old man.

ESTHER. You're a very clever man.

NATE. And you, Esther. Look at you.

ESTHER. Sure, after last night—

NATE. You were a beautiful young woman.

ESTHER. Well, after twenty-six years—

NATE. Twenty-six years you stood out there twelve hours a day, six days a week.

ESTHER. I sat down once in a while.

NATE. Stop making jokes, Esther. It's no time for jokes.

ESTHER. It's the best time for jokes.

NATE. I ruined our lives. I ruined your life.

ESTHER. Nate Kaufman, without you I wouldn't have a life.

NATE. Without me, you'd be . . .

ESTHER. Who? Marlene Dietrich?

NATE. (*Beginning to relax.*) Why not?

ESTHER. If I was Marlene Dietrich, what would I want with you? I'd get Clark Gable.

NATE. With his ears? (*They laugh but it's a half-cry. Lights dim down in the secret room. Lights come up to full in the store. Reva and Chris are still in each other's arms. More peaceful now.*)

REVA. When I was fifteen, I decided there were three things I want in a man. You were the first one who had all three.

CHRIS. Looks.

REVA. Kindness, intelligence, and a sense of humor . . . and looks.

CHRIS. That's four.

REVA. The last one's a bonus.

CHRIS. You know why I fell for you?

REVA. I had all four?

CHRIS. Five. You make me horny. (*They embrace, laugh. Gunshots, closer than before. Lights up on all the rooms. In the alcove Leon starts screaming. Joyce doesn't know what to do. Simultaneously, reacting to that: in the secret room Esther gets up and helps Nate down from the top bunk. In the office Danny startles in his sleep, thrashes, mumbles incoherently. Lights dim down in the store as Chris and Reva hurry into the office. They see what Danny is doing. They don't know who to help—Danny or Leon.*)

JOYCE. Someone! Help!

REVA. (*To Chris.*) Stay with Danny. (*She runs into the alcove, just as Nate and Esther open the door to the secret room.*)

ESTHER. I'll help him, Joycy. (*Closer gunshots.*)

REVA. No, Ma, stay in there. (*She pushes Nate and Esther back into the secret room, where they wait, afraid and helpless. In the office Chris tries to comfort Danny. Reva closes the door and stays in the alcove. Overlapping:*)

JOYCE. (*Snidely, to Reva.*) Where's the . . . "doctor"?

DANNY. (*In his sleep.*) No! . . . Don't! . . .

REVA. There's nothing else he can do.

NATE. We should do something.

JOYCE. Somebody has to do something!

CHRIS. It's okay, Danny. It's just a dream.

ESTHER. She said to wait here. (*Leon falls asleep.*)

REVA. Shh. He's asleep. (*Danny quiets down. Chris falls into the desk chair, exhausted.*)

ESTHER. It's quiet now.

NATE. (*Listens, she's right.*) He must be asleep.

ESTHER. Yes, sure. Come, Nate, we should try to sleep, too. (*They get into their bunks, but are wide awake. During the following, they'll fall asleep. Lights dim down in all but the alcove. Reva touches Leon's head.*)

REVA. He's hot.

JOYCE. Where the hell's the real doctor?

REVA. We're on their list.

JOYCE. Where? At the bottom? (*A glass window breaks in the distance. In the office, Danny jolts awake, and sits up, afraid.*)

DANNY. What was that?

CHRIS. It's a mile away. Go back to sleep. (*Danny shakes his head "no," but in a moment, he drops off. In the alcove:*)

REVA. Are you okay?

JOYCE. (*Shrugs, then suddenly blurts.*) Why didn't you tell me you were married?

REVA. I was about to tell everyone. But there was a bigger news story out there.

JOYCE. How long ago?

REVA. A week. It took time to get up the nerve.

JOYCE. To tell me?

REVA. My folks.

JOYCE. I'm asking about me. How come you didn't tell me?

REVA. Joycy? What's going on?

JOYCE. You couldn't understand.

REVA. Hey, this is your friend, Reev, here.

JOYCE. Still?

REVA. Well, you don't drop people you were born with.

JOYCE. We weren't born together.

REVA. Same hospital. Same time.

JOYCE. Different floors. (*The tension eases a bit.*)

REVA. Yeah. The floor of the admitting office. You were in such a hurry to get here.

JOYCE. That's 'cause I didn't know what I was getting into. (*Leon groans. Both women lean close to him.*)

JOYCE. (*Continued.*) I'm here, Leon.

LEON. It hurts.

REVA. An ambulance is on the way.

LEON. (*Trying to get up.*) Cops?

REVA. No. Lie still.

LEON. Am I going to die?

REVA. No, you're not going to die.

LEON. Joycy?

JOYCE. . . . Of course not.

LEON. I'm scared. (*Joyce holds him. And he quiets down. He's half awake during the following.*)

LEON. (*Continuing.*) I didn't want to hurt your folks, Reev.

REVA. I know.

LEON. But somebody was going to take the stuff. (*Obviously, Reva disapproves.*)

JOYCE. You don't understand that, do you?

REVA. No, I don't.

JOYCE. You won't make it in my world.

LEON. Even with your white nigger.

REVA. We're trying to change that world.

JOYCE. If you were really smart, you'd forget all about being a . . . a great white savior and get the hell out of here.

LEON. Joycy would if she could.

JOYCE. Shut up, Leon. (*To Reva.*) You'd grab your Sergeant Save-the-World and go live in Palmer Park with him.

LEON. I saw Palmer Park once. From the streetcar.

REVA. You know I'd hate that.

LEON. Joycy wouldn't. You should've let her have him.

JOYCE. Stay out of this.

LEON. 'Cause she don't want me. (*To Joyce.*) It's okay, Babe. You don't have to be my woman. I just like hearing you say so. Makes me feel good. (*Falls asleep.*)

REVA. You wouldn't really . . . be with him . . . would you?

JOYCE. (*Cynically.*) Why not? Why wouldn't I want to live in a slum and support a man who's in and out of the pen?

REVA. I'm sorry, I didn't mean—

JOYCE. Why wouldn't I want to raise a dozen pickaninnies to carry on the family tradition?

REVA. Joycy, I know you want better than that.

JOYCE. You don't know nothing. You don't know . . . Do you know how jealous of you I am? Always been? Since we were kids?

REVA. I was jealous. Of you.

JOYCE. Your whole family was right here, near you.

REVA. Right on top of me.

JOYCE. You had a car and you went places together.

REVA. You had lots of friends.

JOYCE. You had nice clothes.

REVA. You were prettier.

JOYCE. Hell, girl. I'm black.

REVA. I once painted my face black with coal. (*Off Joyce's look.*) I wanted to be you. All the kids liked you. And they treated me like . . . They made me feel like . . . nothing.

JOYCE. That's how I've felt all my life.

REVA. Oh, Joycy. (*Lights dim down on the alcove. Lights come up full in the office: Chris is asleep, leaning against Danny's chair. Danny suddenly thrashes about, then sits bolt upright.*)

DANNY. They have guns!

CHRIS. (*Leaps up.*) Who? Where? (*Realizes.*) You had a nightmare.

DANNY. There were . . . they filled the street. Both sides, moving toward me. I tried to run but my feet were melted into the sidewalk.

CHRIS. It was a dream, Danny.

DANNY. One side was Negroes. The other, cops.

CHRIS. White cops.

DANNY. Colored. I tried to jump over them. But I couldn't.

CHRIS. In my nightmares, I was always about eight inches tall and there were these ten foot guys surrounding me.

DANNY. White.

CHRIS. Like milk. I'd try to get out between their legs, but they'd all get webbed together. And they'd close in on me. And I'd open up my mouth to scream—

DANNY. Only nothing came out.

CHRIS. And just before they got to me, my mom would be there, shaking me, waking me up.

DANNY. For me, it was Reva, holding me, telling me . . . Where is she?

CHRIS. In there.

DANNY. Is he—?

CHRIS. Alive. So far.

DANNY. Maybe if I try again . . . (*Danny starts toward the alcove. Joyce sees him approaching.*)

JOYCE. Stay out of here. (*Danny backs away.*)

CHRIS. There's an ambulance coming, Danny. They'll take care of him.

DANNY. It was the damned gun. I should never have taken the gun. But he was grabbing at it, and I—

CHRIS. I believe you, Danny.

DANNY. But will the cops believe me?

CHRIS. Probably. Because it was a white man shooting a black one.

DANNY. It was a Jew. They can get rid of us both. . . . You going to take me in?

CHRIS. No.

DANNY. Because of Reva.

CHRIS. Because you have to live with you, not me.

DANNY. You think I'm wrong.

CHRIS. I think you have to go for what you want. Wading through shit if that's the only way.

DANNY. You sound like Reev's kind of guy.

CHRIS. Because I'm . . . holier than thou?

DANNY. Because she gets an idea, she doesn't let go.

CHRIS. Yeah.

DANNY. Not like me.

CHRIS. Or me. I could have waited to be drafted.

DANNY. You didn't want to go?

CHRIS. I didn't know what I wanted.

DANNY. Pa said I was a coward.

CHRIS. And if you didn't join up, you'd be responsible for the destruction of your whole tribe. (*Off Danny's surprised look.*) I was supposed to turn my tribe into national heroes.

DANNY. And here we sit, prisoners in an accessory shop. (*In the alcove suddenly, Leon begins to shake, violently.*)

JOYCE. Leon?

REVA. Leon, wake up!

LEON. (*It's his death rattle.*) Mama! (*Leon falls back inert. Joyce screams.*)

JOYCE. Leon! (*Lights come to full in the office, the alcove and the secret room. Chris and Danny race into the alcove. Nate and Esther sit up.*)

NATE. What was that? (*They go to the alcove door as lights dim down in the office and the secret room. Lights stay up in the alcove. Danny pushes Reva and Joyce aside.*)

DANNY. Let me! (*He applies mouth to mouth resuscitation to Leon—breathing, pounding on his chest, sobbing.*)

DANNY. Breathe, damn you, Leon! Breathe! (*Chris tries to pull Danny off Leon. Reva looks more closely. Esther and Nate hurry into the alcove.*)

JOYCE. Is he . . . ?

REVA. He's dead.

JOYCE, DANNY, AND NATE. No!

ESTHER. *Oy guttenuh!**

DANNY. (*Still working on Leon.*) He can't be dead! He can't be dead!

CHRIS. There's nothing more you can do, Danny. (*Suddenly, Joyce throws herself at Danny and pounds on him.*)

JOYCE. Murderer!

ESTHER. (*Pulling Joyce off Danny.*) No, Joycy, it's not his fault! (*Chris pulls Danny off Leon. Danny backs into the office. The others, looking at Leon, don't notice.*)

NATE. Why didn't the doctor come?

JOYCE. Why should he? It was just for a nigger.

REVA. Joycy . . .

JOYCE. Just for some dumbass nigger who doesn't count.

ESTHER. Nobody here feels that way.

JOYCE. Nobody?

ESTHER. We have to tell his family.

JOYCE. He doesn't have a family. He doesn't have anyone. . . . Not even me.

REVA. You're not responsible for him.

JOYCE. Nobody is! Only your . . . your brother, the pacifist. He's responsible.

ESTHER. No!

CHRIS. (*To Joyce.*) Hey, come on. The way they were fighting over the gun, it could have been either one of them.

JOYCE. Right. It went off all by itself.

ESTHER. (*Realizing.*) Where's Danny? (*Lights come up in the office and stay up on the alcove. Esther goes into the office, with Nate right behind her, just as Danny backs toward the store, his eyes glued to the alcove.*)

ESTHER. Danny?

JOYCE. (*Kneeling at the cot.*) You dumbass nigger. (*Reva and Chris try to console Joyce. Lights dim down on the alcove and stay up full on the office.*)

ESTHER. Danny? (*Danny freezes.*)

NATE. Where are you going?

DANNY. I'm . . . I'm . . . I can't stay here.

ESTHER. (*Going to the safe.*) Wait.

DANNY. I can't wait, Ma. I have to get out of here.

NATE. (*To Esther.*) What are you doing?

*God!

ESTHER. He can't go without money.

DANNY AND NATE. No!

ESTHER. (*To Danny.*) Get the coat. You'll need the coat.

NATE. No, Esther. We need that money!

ESTHER. Our son needs it more.

DANNY. Ma, I don't need money. Please don't open the safe! (*Esther does. Danny dives for his note—too late. Esther takes it out and, holding it, looks into the safe again.*)

ESTHER. Where is it?

NATE. (*Looking into the safe.*) The money's gone?

DANNY. Pa . . .

ESTHER. (*To Nate.*) Why did you take it out? (*Nate picks up the note. Danny tries to take it away from him.*)

DANNY. Don't read it! (*Danny and Nate grapple over the note.*)

ESTHER. Reva! Come here!

REVA. (*Running in.*) What is it? (*Seeing Danny and Nate.*) What are you doing? (*Calling.*) Chris! (*Chris runs in and helps the women separate Danny and Nate. Joyce comes to the doorway and watches. Nate has the note.*)

DANNY. Please don't read it.

NATE. (*Reading.*) "Dear Ma . . ."

ESTHER. (*Taking the note.*) It's for me.

DANNY. Ma. Don't. (*Esther just starts to read the note. Nate grabs it back and opens it. As he does so, Danny backs toward the store.*)

DANNY. I can explain.

NATE. Not if you run out. (*Reading.*) "Dear Ma, I'm sorry. I needed the money to get away." (*To Danny, seeing what he's doing.*) You stay right here! (*Back to reading.*) "Please forgive me, but I can't be a soldier. I can't kill anyone."

JOYCE. (*Calling into the alcove.*) Hear that, Leon? He can't kill anyone. You're not dead. (*To Danny.*) But you are. And I hope you live a long life with it.

ESTHER. Joycy, don't—

DANNY. . . . . I'm sorry, Joyce. (*Reva goes to embrace her, but Joyce pushes her away. Nobody notices as Nate finishes reading the note to himself. Devastated, he drops his arm, dangling the note.*)

JOYCE. Sorry? Well, I'm sorry, too. I'm sorry I can't stay to hear the rest of the lies. I have to go out where the shit is at least honest. (*She runs through the store and exits out the front door. Chris starts after her. Lights come up in the store and stay up in the office.*)

CHRIS. Joyce! Wait!

REVA. Chris!

CHRIS. She's not safe out there. (*He exits. Reva exits after him.*)

REVA. Wait! Chris!

ESTHER. Reva, no! Nate, stop her! (*Just now noticing Nate's state.*) Nate? . . . Nate, what is it!? Danny?

DANNY. Pa . . . I'm sorry . . .

ESTHER. What? (*Nate hands Esther the note.*)

ESTHER. (*Reading.*) "Tell Pa I'll pay back the money when I can. I know he'll never forgive me for this. But I'll never forgive him either. I love you, Ma. Danny." (*Doesn't know which one to comfort.*) Nate . . . he was trying to take it back. Isn't that right, Danny? You were trying to take it back? (*Danny can't answer.*)

NATE. Can he take back that he wrote it?

ESTHER. He didn't mean it.

NATE. Or that he stole money from us?

DANNY. (*To Nate, pulling the money from his pocket and putting it on the desk.*) Here, Pa, I don't want it any more. I was trying to put it back in the safe.

NATE. Why suddenly you don't need it? What are you going to do? Kill more people and take their money?

ESTHER. Nate!

DANNY. Why not? You taught me how! (*Danny bolts into the store, and heads for the front door. Esther goes after him. In the store Esther tries to catch up with Danny.*)

ESTHER. Where are you going?

DANNY. I don't know! . . . I don't know!

ESTHER. Wait! I can't run fast like you, Danny. Wait!

DANNY. (*Stopping.*) I can't stay here, Ma.

ESTHER. I know. But you can't leave like this.

DANNY. If you're waiting for Pa and me to make up, . . . it's too late.

ESTHER. If you run out, it's too late. (*She takes his arm and pulls him back to the office. Lights dim down in the store. Lights stay up in the office. Nate starts into the alcove.*)

ESTHER. (*Continuing.*) Nate, you walk out on Danny now, I walk out on you. (*Nate stops, but doesn't turn around.*)

ESTHER. (*Continuing, to Danny.*) Sit down. (*She indicates the desk chair. Danny sits.*)

ESTHER. (*Continuing, to Nate.*) And you sit here.

NATE. I have nothing to say.

ESTHER. Sit.

NATE. I have to go see if Reva is okay.

ESTHER. Reva has a soldier to protect her, she doesn't need you. Danny does. Sit. (*She turns him around and pushes him toward the easy chair. Nate sits. Nobody talks.*)

ESTHER. (*Continuing.*) Okay, Danny, he won't start, you start.

DANNY. I haven't anything to say.

NATE. All of a sudden. (*It's quiet.*)

ESTHER. I'll start. How come a couple of decent men can also be so stupid?

NATE. I'm not stupid. And he's not stupid, he's a deserter.

ESTHER. He's a pacifist.

DANNY. Not since last night. (*They ignore Esther as:*)

ESTHER. Don't talk past—

NATE. To run out when your country needs you.

DANNY. Like Poland needed you, and you hid in a closet? (*Nate looks to Esther. She shrugs. She did tell Danny.*)

DANNY. (*Continuing.*) How the hell you had the gall to make me go into . . .

ESTHER. That's past, talk future.

NATE. We weren't fighting a Hitler then. I would have gone if we were fighting a Hitler.

ESTHER. That's not what you should talk about!

DANNY. What if I'm supposed to fight a Hirohito? What if they want to send me to Japan?

NATE. (*Beginning to falter.*) You . . . you could . . . since when do you want my opinion?

ESTHER. (*Giving up.*) Do it your own way. (*She goes into the alcove, but the lights in the alcove stay dim. Esther stops at Leon's body, touches him gently, and then gets Danny's coat. She covers Leon with it and then sits beside him and rocks herself as if* davening*. *In the office at the same time, Nate sinks into his own thoughts. Danny looks to the alcove, to Leon.*)

DANNY. You remember the BB gun, Pa?

NATE. What BB gun?

DANNY. My birthday present. When I was nine.

NATE. We're not talking about when you were nine.

DANNY. I almost killed someone with that gun, Pa.

NATE. I don't know anything about—

DANNY. Because we didn't tell you. We were playing cops and robbers. Reva and me. And I aimed the gun at her. And . . .

NATE. . . . Reva?

---

*Praying, usually while swaying back and forth.

DANNY. It made me feel so . . . strong . . . and . . . big . . . holding that thing, aiming it, and pulling the trigger.

NATE. You shot Reva?

DANNY. Ma made up that she scratched her face climbing a fence.

NATE. You shot her in the face?

DANNY. Her cheek. An inch over, it would have been her eye, Pa.

NATE. But . . . nobody . . . Esther never told me anything.

DANNY. You know what I did with that gun, Pa? I took it out into the alley. I banged it on the pavement. And banged it. Over and over. Until it was just . . . a bunch of little pieces.

NATE. (*Remembering now.*) . . . And . . . you said you lost it.

DANNY. I could have blinded her! And now I've killed someone. Pa, if I didn't have the gun, Leon would be alive . . . And so would I.

NATE. Nobody told me . . .

DANNY. I should never have joined the army, Pa. I don't belong there. If that's being a coward, okay, maybe I'm a coward. I'm not you, Pa. I'm no hero.

NATE. And I'm a hero?

DANNY. Ma told me about it. I could never have gone into Poland like you did.

NATE. . . . Like I did . . .

DANNY. With Nazis all over the place. I couldn't have done that.

NATE. I could have gone in and saved my father and come out and—

DANNY. You did go in. And I could never . . . didn't you, Pa?

NATE. I wanted to. I tried. I got as far as the checkpoint. At the French border. They made us get off the train.

DANNY. But you had your passport. And all the right papers . . .

NATE. All the right papers . . .

DANNY. But . . . didn't you see your father?

NATE. I saw only them. In their uniforms with their black boots, and their swastikas and . . . their faces . . . those faces. . . . I turned around and went back. I ran back. I didn't stop until I turned a corner and I couldn't see them . . . they couldn't see me . . .

DANNY. Didn't you get back on the train?

NATE. I got back on a train . . . a train going back. Away from them. . . . They had those big rifles.

DANNY. . . . Guns . . .

NATE. He was my father, Danny. And they killed him. And I should have saved him. (*Far off, a siren is heard approaching.*)

NATE. (*Continuing.*) Danny, don't . . . please, don't tell Esther. Or Reva. Please? (*Esther runs in.*)

ESTHER. Police! Come, Danny, hide in the room.
NATE. (*Pleading.*) Danny . . .
DANNY. I won't, Pa.
ESTHER. Won't what? Why are you wasting time . . . ?
NATE. I'm so sorry, Danny.
DANNY. Me, too, Pa.
ESTHER. Okay, you're both sorry. Now—
NATE. What can I do to . . . ?
ESTHER. You can let him go hide. (*The siren is closer.*)
ESTHER. (*Continuing.*) Hurry, Danny! Nate, tell him!
NATE. Tell him what? I don't know any more. I only know . . . I couldn't save my father. And I wish I knew a way to save my son . . .
DANNY. Pa . . . (*The front door is opened from the outside. Nate, Esther, and Danny freeze. But it's not police. It's Reva and Chris.*)
CHRIS. Danny, we have to get out of here.
ESTHER. Where's Joycy?
REVA. We couldn't find her.
CHRIS. Danny, I'm going back to camp. I'm telling them the truth. I went AWOL to protect my family.
REVA. And you can tell them that, too. Chris will back it up.
ESTHER. (*Liking the idea.*) Danny . . . ?
DANNY. No . . .
NATE. But if Chris tells them—
DANNY. I'm not going back.
ESTHER. He's not going back. He'll hide from them.
REVA. The car is right outside—
CHRIS. Hey, if he doesn't want to go—
ESTHER. He doesn't have to go. They won't know he's here.
DANNY. And then what, Ma?
ESTHER. They go away.
DANNY. And then what? What do I do with the rest of the war? What do I do with the rest of my life?
ESTHER. You . . . you . . . tell him, Nate.
NATE. . . . What do you want to do, Danny? (*While Danny tries to find an answer:*)
REVA. You could go to Canada.
NATE. Canada's in the war, too.
REVA. And they need medics, too. (*The siren is closer.*)
ESTHER. All right. Canada. And later, Danny, after the war, you can come home.
DANNY. . . . Pa . . . ?
NATE. If you can get to the border . . .

DANNY. (*A beat, then to Chris.*) Can you take me to the Windsor Tunnel? (*The siren is closer.*)

REVA. I'll take him.

NATE, ESTHER, AND CHRIS. No!

REVA. Give me the car keys, Pa.

NATE. No, I'll take him.

REVA. You stay here with Ma.

CHRIS. (*To Reva.*) You, too. (*To Danny.*) Let's go. (*Chris and Danny start into the store. Reva and Esther are right behind them. Nate starts to follow, then goes back into the office, takes the money from the desk, and rejoins them as:*)

ESTHER. Wait, Danny. (*Hugging him.*) You let me know where you are.

DANNY. I will, Ma. (*To Nate, tentatively.*) . . . Pa . . .

NATE. (*Putting the money into Danny's hand.*) Zei gezunt.

CHRIS. He'll be okay, Mr. . . . Pa? (*Off Nate's unsure look.*) . . . Nate.

NATE. . . . Nate.

CHRIS. Esther . . .

ESTHER. Ma.

CHRIS. Ma . . . take care of my girl.

ESTHER. Why not? She was my girl first. (*Chris kisses her cheek. She grabs him in a hug.*)

ESTHER. (*Continuing.*) And you take care of yourself.

REVA. I'll just go to the corner with you.

CHRIS. No, Reev.

REVA. I'm not afraid.

CHRIS. I am. If anything happened to you, I'd kill you.

REVA. And if anything happened to you—

CHRIS. I'll be all right. I have to be.

REVA. . . . Okay . . . (*They kiss.*)

NATE. (*Aside to Esther.*) See? That's how to talk to her. (*Chris and Danny run out. Reva peeks out through the blackout shades to watch them go. A moment and Nate goes after them, with:*)

NATE. Wait! Danny! (*Stops in the doorway.*) I love you! (*But he knows that Danny didn't hear that. An ambulance comes to a stop and the siren dies. Nate looks back into the store.*)

NATE. It's not police. It's an ambulance.

REVA. A little late.

NATE. (*To Reva.*) You stay sha. I'm still the father around here. (*Looks off with:*) In here, Doctor. He was a looter. He threatened me. I had to shoot him. (*Lights dim to black.*)

THE END

Photograph by Edward Feld

Merle Feld

I WAS BORN IN BROOKLYN on October 18, 1947, the youngest of three children. Jewish communal institutions and the services they provided were beyond the means of my family's modest resources; my parents, Milton and Lillian Lewis, did not belong to a synagogue nor did they send me to Hebrew school. My scant exposure to religious observances was in our home: a seder in English, sometimes the lighting of Chanukah candles. I realize now that although I had no access to the richness of Jewish life growing up, I sensed something important, powerful, in the enterprise. It was mysterious, unknown; being excluded, I wanted "in." In addition to setting me on a course of religious inquiry, the circumstances of my childhood served to make me forever sensitive to those who are invisible, silenced.

One of our few family indulgences was discount tickets to Broadway theater. Theater was of particular interest to my father, who taught me when I was a child to look for Hirschfeld's *Ninas* in Sunday's *New York Times* Arts and Leisure section. I remember *New Girl in Town,* my first play; I sat high in the balcony, transfixed by the live music, the dancing, the spectacle of the opulent theater itself. As a high school student I continued going to the theater regularly, taking advantage of the inexpensive "twofers" that were available in those years. I also have fond memories of listening to the radio station WVNJ, which played cast albums of current and old Broadway shows, working hard to memorize the lyrics so I could "replay" my favorite scores at will.

I always dreamt of being a writer, but, although family and teachers were constantly impressed by my work, I was not encouraged to take myself seriously. Despite my outstanding high school grades, my parents assessed that a "sleep-away" college was beyond their means even with scholarships, and so at sixteen, I entered

Brooklyn College, partaking of the free public education of the New York City system.

I found the college an enormous disappointment intellectually; the hoped-for awakening, when it came, was from a wholly unexpected source. An assimilated adolescent, I became active in Hillel, immersing myself in Jewish observance and thought. The student community at Hillel, under the direction of Rabbi Norman Frimer, provided me entry into a vast and magical world of spirit, fellowship, text, and ritual and was the driving force of my intellectual coming of age.

During my senior year of college I met Edward Feld, a rabbinical student steeped in tradition yet with an independent religious and intellectual spirit. In June 1968 I graduated from college, he was ordained, and we moved to Boston, where he was a founding teacher at Havurat Shalom Community Seminary, a radical experiment in Jewish communal living, text study, and social activism. The year we spent helping to shape Havurat Shalom solidified our shared vision of Jewish community, community that combined pleasure in traditional ritual with the searching, challenging ethos of the sixties. In June 1969 we were married, and we moved to Champaign, Illinois, where I earned a master's degree in literature, worked as a technical writer, and taught freshman composition at the University of Illinois. During this time I began a pattern, which was to last for many years, of mentoring Jewish college students and welcoming them into our home. I also evolved a radical feminist stance that enjoyed much of traditional observance but insisted on egalitarian treatment in all aspects of religious life.

In 1973 Eddie became Hillel director at Princeton University, where we made our home for the next nineteen years and where our daughter, Lisa, was born in 1978 and our son, Uri, in 1982. During the early years in Princeton, I taught at the surrounding community colleges, enjoying especially my work with older students who were returning to school in midlife. Not until Lisa was in nursery school did I take up the writing I had abandoned in adolescence. In fact, I saw the birth of my daughter as having been freeing, empowering, pivotal in the reawakening of old dreams and the creation of new ambition: In having a daughter I saw the danger of displacing my longings onto her and her life's course. I also felt looked down upon as a stay-at-home mom with a baby and was ready to take a chance as a writer. Even if I failed utterly, I felt I had nothing to lose—my status could sink no lower.

Three mornings a week I luxuriated in the solitude of a carrel in

Firestone Library. I began without a plan or even a genre. What emerged was my first play, aptly titled *The Opening:* an artist prepares for her first one-woman show as she tries to come to terms with some of the important relationships from her past. I was acutely conscious of having had no training as a playwright, that I was inventing myself and my art as I went along. A year later I took a workshop with Jean-Claude van Itallie. With Jean-Claude I developed my ear for dialogue, learned to build characters, and acquired the discipline of economy in writing; most significantly, though, for the first time I felt nurtured by a mentor.

In 1983 I began work on my second play, *The Gates are Closing.* The play takes place on Yom Kippur, as ten characters who represent a range of Jewish identity experience self-reflection and renewal. As with all plays, there is a story behind its genesis. Over the course of a number of years I would attend services, and expecially on Yom Kippur I would wonder what was going on inside the people who were praying alongside me. *The Gates are Closing* was an attempt to explore that question.

During the period of time in which I was working on *The Gates are Closing* I also began writing poetry. As a part of the pioneering generation of feminists, I turned my attention to the variety of Jewish texts with an increasing consciousness of the absence, the silence, of women in those texts. I saw myself as attempting to write women back into the tradition, and I began by writing prayers and poems to give voice to women's life-cycle experiences. In the past ten years my poetry has become a mainstay for rabbis, teachers, feminists, and congregants: my work is widely published, anthologized, and even included in several new prayerbooks. My next play, *Moving into the Light,* was written during the period of decline my father suffered at the end of his life. The play explores the relationship between a woman and her widowed father as she spends a few days visiting with him in a retirement home in Florida.

In the summer of 1989 Eddie, the children, and I left Princeton for a year's sabbatical in Israel. Through an old friend, Veronika Cohen, I became intensely involved in a wide range of peace activities: demonstrating, interviewing political prisoners, and most important, helping to organize and facilitate an ongoing grassroots dialogue group with Israeli and Palestinian women, which met regularly on the West Bank at the height of the *intifada.* Upon returning to the States, I drew on the experiences of some of the women I had come to know through my political work, and on extensive research into traditional Jewish source material, to create the characters for *Across the Jordan,* in which the ancient passions of Sarah, Abraham, and Hagar come to life for a young Israeli lawyer assigned her first political case—to defend a Palestinian student accused of terrorism. A winner of several awards, including my second grant from the New Jersey Council on the Arts, the play had a number of readings, most notably one by the Audrey Skirball-Kenis Theatre directed by Jan Lewis. *Across the Jordan* was first produced in October 1994 at Theatre Intime on the Princeton University campus. Multitalented childhood friend Margaret Pine, who had been dramaturg for *Across the Jordan,* directed the production and composed original music for it.

Through my writing I seek to enlarge our experience and understanding by giving voice to the invisible, the disenfranchised. In *The Gates are Closing* I attempt to provide a window through which to glimpse the secret spiritual yearnings of a seemingly ordinary *minyan* of Jews on Yom Kippur, making the overtly religious a legitimate subject of dramatic concern. The feminist sensitivity that allows me to hear the voices of the silenced has matured and ripened in subsequent work. At the center of *Across the Jordan* are ancient biblical women brought to life, women who were there in the text all the time, but who moved about in the wings, in the shadows. I bring them stage center. My methodology in creating Sarah and Hagar was to turn the volume way down on Abraham, to begin to hear what Sarah and Hagar would say if only they were given a chance to speak. Perhaps the preeminent example of allowing the silenced to speak is my choice in the same play to give voice to a contemporary Palestinian woman, Najah. With her radical ideological stance and her political activism against the State of Israel, she is unexpected as a sympathetic figure created by a Jewish playwright who views herself as a Zionist.

Another concern that surfaces in my plays is how identity is expressed through vocation: what is the proper place of vocation in the life well lived, in the healthy psyche? Margaret in *The Opening* struggles for the courage to be an artist and to present her work to the world. Jonah, the young medical student in *The Gates are Closing* needs to learn to submit himself to a discipline, yet longs to run away. Joan, a social worker in the same play, asks where the demand for social justice ends and how to put in the balance her desire for a comfortable life. Jake, the rabbi of *The Gates are Closing,* would seemingly represent institutional certainty and stability, yet through him we learn that even ostensible insiders experience alienation and maintain an uneasy relationship with the Jewish community. At the heart of the character of Arnold in *Moving into the Light* is the story of his life in business, the anger and shame he feels about his failure, and the way in which the entire family's story was shaped by his story as a worker in the world.

Even in *Across the Jordan,* a play with multiple ambitious themes, Daphna is concerned with questions of vocation. Part of her coming of age is her growth in competence as a lawyer. She struggles to learn to do her job well while facing the underlying philosophical dilemma of any good attorney: What is my responsibility as a lawyer to a client who may be guilty of heinous crimes? And, particular to her situation, how do I deal with a client who sees herself—as perhaps I see her—as an enemy of my people?

An even more central and far-reaching concern of my writing is the exploration of connection and of boundaries. My work poses a series of questions: How can we fulfill our longing to connect? How can we bridge the pain of our existential aloneness in the universe? How do we create necessary boundaries to protect psychic health and autonomy? How do we learn to accept boundaries, particularly those imposed by the separation of death? How do we overcome boundaries that isolate us or, in a political context, lead to hostility and violence? And always, the problem of overcoming boundaries, of achieving connectedness, comes down to a question of trust.

Across the Jordan presents an almost dizzying array of variations on these themes. The biblical Sarah we meet here is a remarkable, independent woman, at the height of her powers, yet ultimately destroyed by the dissolution of trust in her marriage and by the simple human longing to have a child and thus to be connected intimately to an other. Daphna, who is at the center of all the stories in *Across the Jordan,* is hard at work simultaneously on two intimate processes. First, in mourning her father, she is struggling to separate from him and his traditional religious and political attitudes: How do I honor him sufficiently so that my soul is not torn apart by guilt? How do I individuate, establish boundaries between us so that I can come to know who I am and what I believe and can have the courage to act on that in the world? Secondly though, Daphna poses the question of boundaries and trust as it is played out in her relationship to her Palestinian client. In my earlier plays, characters strive to establish appropriate and life-affirming connections in relationships where there is an expectation of trust—parent/child, wife/husband, brother/ sister. One way or another, all these characters ask: How can I balance intimacy and autonomy? In the story of Daphna and Najah, however, the women meet against a backdrop of deeply ingrained mistrusts and hatreds: the question initially posed for family, for intimates, is now extended to the political realm, to archetypal enemies. While the ancient Sarah and Hagar cannot extricate themselves from mutual destruction, Daphna and Najah, with great difficulty, are able to form a tentative bond.

As I explained in a newspaper interview before the first production of *Across the Jordan*, "I write about the things I most urgently need to understand. . . . I want the audience to experience both sides of the conflict, to feel viscerally what's at stake. I want my play to disturb the audience as it has disturbed me. I want it to be the beginning of questions for them, questions that challenge what they thought they knew, questions they take home and make their own" (Freedman 1994, 1).

Across the Jordan was first presented by Theatre Intime of Princeton University, opening on October 20, 1994. It was produced by Theatre Intime with associate producer Lucy Hornby. The cast was as follows:

Vanessa Lemonides	Jenn Burnham
Wendy Barrie-Wilson	Taifa Murry
Nick Smith	Heather Fry
Kiersten Van Horne	Cara Reichel
John McHale	Amanda Low

Director: Margaret Pine
Sets: Jennifer Lee
Costumes: Lucy Hornby
Lighting: Jeff Kraus
Muscial Director: J. J. Weiss

Playwright's Notes

It is important in presenting this play to understand the moral universe it tries to explore. To approach these characters with a preconceived political bias is to undermine the work of challenging and disturbing everyone in the audience. The audience must not "know" to what extent Najah is innocent or guilty of the list of charges brought against her. They cannot "know" what she has or has not done because that is the ultimate test of trust that Daphna undergoes, and we must experience this same test, we must live through this tension with her. You can never "know" the other, yet you must at some point decide what it is you believe about them, how you will proceed, how you will behave.

Similarly with regard to Yonatan: most often I have seen actors audition for this part and play him as a Nazi, a stock evil character. To play him in this way destroys the complex moral balance of the play. Yonatan and Daphna are both young Israelis, each with a different job to do, each playing out a different facet of the Israeli psyche. It is Yonatan's job to protect the safety of his civilian countrymen, who have all been made potential victims of terrorism; thus it is his job to suspect the worst of Najah. He comes to believe she is guilty of the murder of innocents and he proceeds accordingly. Daphna, equally, is doing her job—to insure the democratic process, to protect the rights of her client, to understand her client, to establish a relationship in order to best defend her.

Perhaps a brief word is needed for Sarah and Hagar as well. Although each may see herself as victim of the other, to portray one as victim, one as demon, is to miss the tragedy of both. What is needed is to recognize the humanity of each of these characters as fully as possible.

Ancient Sarah and modern Daphna are women who travel over the same terrain but pass each other headed in opposite directions. Sarah begins her journey as remarkably, powerfully independent; she finishes utterly alone, destroyed. Daphna, at the outset, is fragile, in turmoil; by the end of the play she has found her power, her independence.

Acknowledgments

My work as a playwright has twice been supported by the New Jersey State Council on the Arts. The development of this play has been further aided by travel grants from the National Foundation for Jewish Culture and the Dorot Foundation. *Across the Jordan* would never have come to life without the dramaturgy of Margaret Pine and the moral passion of Veronika Cohen. To both of them, my thanks, my love.

Across the Jordan
1995

Characters

DAPHNA, an Israeli lawyer in her late twenties
SARAH, Biblical matriarch, in her forties
ABRAHAM, Biblical patriarch, in his fifties
CHORUS OF WOMEN (three singers)

NAJAH EL DARWISH, a Palestinian student, just twenty
NAJAH'S FATHER
ISRAELI SOLDIER/GUARD
YONATAN, an Israeli Army interrogator in his twenties
DAPHNA'S FATHER
PHAROAH
DANCER, in Pharaoh's court
HAGAR, Biblical Egyptian princess, just twenty
MESSENGERS OF GOD (three singers)
FIRST HANDMAID
SECOND HANDMAID
ISHMAEL, son of Hagar and Abraham, a sixteen year old
Note: Actors may play multiple roles

Places

Daphna's study, Jerusalem
The Negev
An Arab neighborhood in Jerusalem
An Israeli detention center for political prisoners
The land of Egypt
An Israeli prison

Times

Long ago and now

ACT I

Scene 1

Middle Eastern music bridges ancient and contemporary times. A minimal set suggests the very old and the modern. There is a well onstage. The colors of the set are of Jerusalem stone, of sand, of desert, enlivened by the rich reds and blues of Middle Eastern decor. Music fades. Lights down. Sounds of Jerusalem street noise in background. Lights up. Enter Daphna, in a suit, carrying her briefcase. She walks downstage far right and sits in a large comfortable easy chair, suggestive of the study in her Jerusalem apartment.

DAPHNA. (*To audience.*) My father had no son. I was the eldest daughter. He never complained, perhaps because I was both son and daughter to him. I was whatever he needed me to be. Now I am his mourner. As a woman, I am not permitted to say the mourner's kaddish in our synagogue, but I need a way to honor him, so I am studying in his name. It's a tradition to do that—I think it would have pleased him. I began at the beginning, *bereshit,* in the beginning. The study has gone slowly. I work hard all day, I am with a new law firm, I must work to prove myself. It's hard to find the time to open my book and study in his name. (*Daphna removes a book from her briefcase. As she begins reading aloud we again hear the Middle Eastern music. Projected now on the backstage wall are huge blown up shots of the Negev. As Daphna reads, Abraham and Sarah enter from the rear of the theater. They wear colorful Middle Eastern robes. Slowly they walk together in and around the audience as if this were the path of their journey. Over their heads is draped a single large white cloth.*)

DAPHNA. (*Reading.*) "This is the line of Shem. Shem was one hundred years old when he begot Arpachshad, two years after the flood. After the birth of Arpachshad, Shem lived five hundred years and begot sons and daughters. When Arpachshad had lived thirty-five years, he begot Shelah. After the birth of Shelah, Arpachshad lived 403 years and begot sons and daughters . . ."

CHORUS OF WOMEN. (*Singing.*) Sarah is barren, she has no child.

DAPHNA. "When Eber had lived thirty-four years, he begot Peleg. After the birth of Peleg, Eber lived 430 years and begot sons and daughters."

CHORUS OF WOMEN. Sarah is barren, she has no child.

DAPHNA. "When Peleg had lived thirty years, he begot Reu. After the birth of Reu, Peleg lived 209 years and begot sons and daughters . . ."

CHORUS OF WOMEN. (*Louder, bolder.*) Sarah is barren, she has no child.

DAPHNA. "When Nahor had lived twenty-nine years, he begot Terah. After the birth of Terah, Nahor lived 119 years and begot sons and daughters." (*Daphna looks up from her reading.*) Nahor, Peleg, Reu, Eber—father begets son, father begets son—(*She resumes reading.*) "When Terah had lived seventy years he begot Abraham, Nahor, and Haran, and Haran begot Lot."

CHORUS OF WOMEN. Sarah is barren, she has no child.

DAPHNA. "Haran died in the lifetime of his father Terah, in his native land, Ur of the Chaldeans. Abraham and Nahor took to themselves wives, the name of Abraham's wife being Sarah and that of Nahor's wife Milcah . . . (*Abraham and Sarah are now on stage. He banishes the taunting chorus. Sarah refreshes herself at the well.*) Now Sarah was barren, she had no child." (*Daphna looks up.*) Look at this! Father begets son, father begets son—they only mention a woman when the system breaks down!

ABRAHAM. (*To Sarah.*) The first time I saw you, you were dancing with the other girls. I watched for a long time but I don't believe you noticed me. I stood and watched, and my longing grew. From those first moments I wanted you. But you liked your freedom and would not be possessed. Only slowly you came to trust me. You knew of course you would have to accept some man and so, one day, quite suddenly, you agreed to me. . . . Always through the years there has remained a mystery around you. Even though we are joined, and move together as lovers, you've never wanted me to know you completely. That distance served us both. But now, I hear their taunts, their laughter, I feel that you are suffering, and we cannot speak of your pain together.

SARAH. (*To the offstage Chorus of Women.*) I hear your taunts, your laughter, (*mimicking*) "Sarah is barren, she has no child." (*Alternately to Abraham, to the women.*) Sarah is barren, she has no child. The truth is, I've never wanted a child. I was never eager to see my body distorted like the others. You were all in a great hurry for husbands, for babies, as if to fill up some emptiness within. A great lack of imagination. I never needed someone to fill me up. I always felt apart and quite content to be so. As a girl I'd dance with the other girls, but in the midst of the movement, the swaying bodies, my rhythm was my own. At marriage time, why were you the one I chose? You also were solitary, a solitary man with a deep voice, a solitary man, with piercing eyes, caressing eyes. (*Abraham exits, continuing the journey.*) You knew enough to respect me. . . . Then, married, again the expectation—to sit with the others, to gossip with the others. I found them silly, their words bored me. When Abraham was called by God, I rejoiced to break away, to begin a new journey. I did not hesitate to leave behind the old ways, the old home. A new way, I thought, a new sort of home . . .

ABRAHAM. (*Calling to her from offstage.*) Sarah!

SARAH. Together now we move, our rhythm as one, seeking a new way, leaving behind the old home. (*She exits to follow him. Lights down.*)

Scene 2

Sounds suggest a quiet Arab neighborhood in Jerusalem in the middle of the night. We hear banging, then a door opening; the scene is played on a dark stage.

SOLDIER. Is this the home of Najah El Darwish?

NAJAH'S FATHER. At this hour she is asleep.

SOLDIER. Is she your daughter?

NAJAH'S FATHER. Can't this wait till the morning?

SOLDIER. We have an order for her. Tonight. Now.

NAJAH'S FATHER. You can't take a young girl in the middle of the night—I will bring her, in the morning.

SOLDIER. Now. Tell her to get dressed. We have the order.

NAJAH. (*Whispering.*) Father, don't humble yourself. I'll be all right. I've done nothing. Nothing.

Scene 3

Lights up on Daphna in her study, late at night.

DAPHNA. (*Reading.*) "And Abraham took Sarah his wife and Lot his brother's son and all their substance and all their company and went forth into the land of Canaan." (*Music, blown up shots of the Negev. Enter Sarah and Abraham.*)

SARAH. I've never felt so alive before—

ABRAHAM. —leaving behind the old home.

SARAH. I see everything more clearly—

ABRAHAM. —an ordinary mountain goat seems to me a sign.

SARAH. I feel a power,

ABRAHAM. A strength, a joy.

SARAH. At night, in the dark, my pleasure grows, larger, larger, and then I explode—

SARAH AND ABRAHAM. Together, we explode.

SARAH. And in the morning, we walk to the wadi, I hear the wind, you can see forever. I fill myself with this land, with the beauty of this land.

DAPHNA. (*Reading.*) "And the Lord said to Abraham, to your seed will I give this land, and Abraham built an altar there and called upon the name of the Lord."

ABRAHAM. Your hand on my cheek, the air on my cheek, the wind . . . the clouds low on the mountains, the sun on the mountains . . . hills and mountains, they go on forever . . . sometimes, in this land, I feel smaller than myself, then sometimes, larger—a giant—but always, strangely content, at peace . . .

SARAH AND ABRAHAM. I believe the sky is bluer here. (*Music fades slowly, Abraham exits, lights dim on Sarah who spreads a fabric and lies down to sleep.*)

DAPHNA. (*To audience.*) There is a certain type of person who understands the desert, who falls in love with the desert. My old boyfriend Avi had a cousin from America like that. He came to visit with his girlfriend. We took them everywhere—mountain climbing in the North, scuba diving in Eilat, camping in the desert, in the Negev. When it was time for them to go (I think Zurich was next) he wouldn't go, he couldn't go. They postponed, they postponed, they canceled. He stayed, he went to the army. I think he's working in some computer store off Ben Yehuda now . . . (*Daphna absently clicks her remote, sounds of TV program.*) Avi was so funny about that—he was proud, that he lived in a country that could seduce his American cousin, but he also thought the cousin was crazy, for being seduced, for giving up America. . . . (*"Hatikva" starts playing on TV. Daphna stands.*) He was the same with me—he would have laughed at me right now, the way he used to when we were together in bed, late at night . . . I would hear "Hatikva" when the TV was ending . . . he would laugh at the way I was raised to . . . but when they play "Hatikva," you stand up . . . (*Blackout. Daphna leaves stage.*)

Scene 4

SOLDIER. Stand up! (*As the lights come up, Najah is standing at attention, center stage. She wears jeans and a T-shirt. A table and chair suggest an interrogation room. Enter Yonatan.*)

YONATAN. I am Yonatan. Chief interrogator. (*He extends his hand, which she shakes reluctantly.*) If you are cooperative, I am the only interrogator. . . . (*He motions to her cordially.*) Be seated. (*She sits. He stands, leaning easily on the table.*) Would you like a coffee?

NAJAH. We are not friends having coffee. Ask what you have to ask.

YONATAN. Why do you think you are here?

NAJAH. How am I supposed to know why I am here?

YONATAN. You were a student at Bir Zeit?

NAJAH. I am a student at Bir Zeit.

YONATAN. Bir Zeit is closed already a long time.

NAJAH. Still, I am a student there.

YONATAN. You like it there?

NAJAH. You come for me in the middle of the night to ask if I like my school?

YONATAN. Please answer my question.

NAJAH. Is this some new survey for the Americans? Yes. I like my school.

YONATAN. Why do you like it?

NAJAH. I learn there. I have good friends there.

YONATAN. I have spoken with some of your friends.

NAJAH. If you have something to charge me with, charge me.

YONATAN. Najah, I am just trying to get to know you. Your people complain that we don't know each other. I read that all the time in the foreign press. So I want to know you. What did you do with your friends at Bir Zeit?

NAJAH. We are students—what do students do together?

YONATAN. That depends on who they are. Some students, for instance, are active in politics. Were you active in politics?

NAJAH. I was on the student council.

YONATAN. Tell me what you did on the student council.

NAJAH. I worked to improve the conditions of students.

YONATAN. And organized demonstrations for students?

NAJAH. Yes. No. Yes, for improving conditions. I did nothing illegal.

YONATAN. We will see. Tell me about your courses—what were you interested in? Wait—let me guess—a bright girl like you, so involved in the world—you took politics, right?

NAJAH. Yes, political theory. I read many books. I liked Marx.

YONATAN. I am also interested in Marx. You had Ibrahim Abasi for political theory, or was he already in prison?

NAJAH. What does it matter who was my teacher?

YONATAN. I am just curious. I knew him, that's all.

NAJAH. You knew him? How did you know him?

YONATAN. We had many conversations.

NAJAH. When will you charge me?

YONATAN. We will talk more later. (*Yonatan exits. Najah remains seated, looking confused. She closes her eyes, begins to sing softly to herself the 80s pop song "Lady in Red." Lights down slowly, music continuing . . . in blackout, Najah exits.*)

Scene 5

DAPHNA. (*Voiceover.*) "And Abraham journeyed going South. And there was a famine in the land and Abraham went down into Egypt for the famine was sore in the land." (*Lights up. Sarah, who has been sleeping downstage left, is gathering her possessions, preparing to leave. Abraham stands off to the side, watching her, unnoticed. Finally he approaches.*)

ABRAHAM. Sarah, are you afraid to go down to Egypt?

SARAH. I hadn't thought to be.

ABRAHAM. We are a caravan, they are a nation. You have a beauty . . .

SARAH. Am I in danger there?

ABRAHAM. I am the one, I am the one in danger—you will shine in their eyes, they will kill me to possess you.

SARAH. But we are traveling with God.

ABRAHAM. Yes. But what does that mean? If my enemy comes to kill me, will God appear to slay him first? I think not. When the Egyptians see you, they will want you, they will kill me to possess you. But if you tell them you are my sister—

SARAH. Your sister? Your sister?

ABRAHAM. I have heard about them and their ways. But if you tell them you are my sister, all will go well for us. (*They look at each other without speaking further. Abraham exits, she remains in her place, preparing her things to leave. Enter Daphna, in hiking clothes.*)

DAPHNA. (*To audience.*) When I was in high school, one Shabbat, after lunch, my father and I were discussing the Bible reading from synagogue that morning—it was this reading—"tell them you are my sister . . ." (*She puts a white cloth on the interrogation table to suggest a Shabbat setting. Abraham enters as Daphna's father in slacks, white shirt, sandals.*)

DAPHNA. (*To her father.*) It's horrible, this story—"tell them you are my sister." How could he do that—just sacrifice his wife? You wouldn't do such a thing.

DAPHNA'S FATHER. One of the rabbis said, when they entered Egypt he hid her away in a basket and told the border guards he'd pay tax for the gold that was inside. They uncovered the basket, beheld her radiance, and only then does he say "she is my sister."

DAPHNA. What good is this? The simple meaning of the text cries out. He hands her over to be another man's wife—to save himself. This commentary—it's just trying to cover it up. Doesn't it make you feel dirty?

DAPHNA'S FATHER. Daphna, it's not a pretty moment, it's not a proud moment, but it's reality, it's our reality—he does it for survival, Daphna. You do what you have to do, to survive. (*He exits. She begins to cry.*)

DAPHNA. (*To audience.*) I ran from the table. I went to my friend from scouts and I didn't call home after Shabbat was out. I stayed away very late, and when I came in I went straight to bed. . . . I didn't want to talk about it or fight about it. It was the first time I ever thought, "My father is capable of betraying me—(*at this point, Sarah, who has remained on stage, gathers her things and exits*)—under the right circumstances, he would betray me." (*Music for Egyptian court dance. Daphna removes the Shabbos tablecloth, which reverses to serve as a camping blanket. She spreads it out downstage left, lies down and resumes reading.*) "And it came to pass that when Abraham was come into Egypt, the Egyptians beheld the woman, that she was very fair. And the princes of Pharaoh saw her and praised her to Pharaoh . . ." (*Pharaoh's court. Enter entourage of court—the three singers who comprised the earlier Chorus of Women; enter Pharaoh, Sarah, and Hagar. Pharaoh sits in chair with Hagar on one side, Sarah on the other. All watch— including Abraham, from a distance—as dancer performs.*) ". . . and the woman was taken into Pharaoh's house. . . . And Pharaoh dealt well with Abraham for Sarah's sake; and he had sheep and oxen and he-asses and men servants and maid servants and she-asses and camels. . . . And the Lord plagued Pharaoh and his house with great plagues because of Sarah, Abraham's wife. And Pharaoh called to Abraham and said,"

PHARAOH. (*To Abraham.*) What is this that you have done to me? Why did you not tell me that she was your wife? Why did you say "She is my sister" so that I took her to be my wife? Now therefore, behold your wife, (*Abraham approaches, Sarah stands*) behold your wife, take her and go. (*The dance abruptly ends.*)

SARAH. (*To Abraham.*) I did as you asked, and you prospered. But now there is a silent question which stands between us. What happened to me there, you want to know. You are afraid to ask. And I volunteer nothing. I did as you asked, and you prospered. (*Music. Abraham crosses stage left and exits up aisle. Sarah follows him stage left, remaining on stage. As the Chorus of Women in court begin to sing "a princess for a handmaid," Pharaoh motions to Hagar that she is to follow Sarah.*)

CHORUS OF WOMEN. (*Singing.*) A princess, a princess, a princess for a handmaid. (*They continue singing as Hagar exhibits confusion, resistance, finally compliance with Pharaoh's order: she follows Sarah stage left. Sarah and Hagar remain stage left, inhabiting quarters—a rug, some fabric, should suggest tent interiors—side by side, mistress and maid. Singing of the chorus ends, Pharaoh removes ornamental robe, it is Yonatan in his officer's uniform. Chorus of Women at court exits.*)

Scene 6

Yonatan seated in interrogation room. Najah is pushed on stage.

NAJAH. Ask away—I'll tell you nothing—I am an Israeli citizen, I am not from the West Bank. By forty-eight hours you must take me to court. Don't think you can do as you wish because I am some ignorant girl—I know the law—

YONATAN. Listen to that! The little bitch will tell me what to do? You go to court when I say you go to court. You know Ahmed Fousari, little bitch?

NAJAH. No.

YONATAN. He's a student at Bir Zeit.

NAJAH. I don't know him.

YONATAN. He says you're his good friend. He says he knows you well.

NAJAH. I don't know him.

YONATAN. (*Pausing.*) He's on the student council.

NAJAH. There are many on the student council.

YONATAN. He says he knows you well. He says you'd do anything for him.

NAJAH. I don't know him.

YONATAN. He told us everything you did for him. Today we are bringing your father to him. He can tell your father all about you. Ahmed gave us details—he described you in detail. Your father probably thinks you are still a virgin. Your father probably thinks you are still his little girl. Your father doesn't know, does he, little bitch?

NAJAH. My father will not believe you. My father can smell an Israeli pig—

YONATAN. You are right. He may not believe me. But he will believe Ahmed. Ahmed told us—you like it rough. He says you like it from behind. He says—

NAJAH. I won't listen. My father won't listen. And this is not a charge. You play with this because you have no charge—I have done nothing so you have no charge.

YONATAN. We have a charge. Oh yes, we have a charge.

NAJAH. Then what is it? Even if someone says I am a prostitute, for that you cannot put me in prison.

YONATAN. We'll have no trouble putting you in prison.

NAJAH. For what?

YONATAN. Ahmed impressed us with how much you know, how much you taught him. Maybe you will teach us.

NAJAH. I don't know him. You are making all this up. When I am in court today—

YONATAN. You are not in court today. Your charges are in the West Bank—under occupation law. We don't need to bring you to court today. We have time to get to know you. (*Yonatan exits, Najah remains on stage, sitting in her "cell."*)

Scene 7

The Negev. Sarah center stage, Hagar stage left, seemingly busy with some task, but listening closely.

SARAH. (*To Daphna.*) I don't know myself anymore. My body has begun to betray me. I feel an ache, a longing. Some time ago, a while ago, I began to feel small. A hollow inside me was calling out, and a great dark emptiness echoed back. I turned round and round and round, quickly, quickly, and saw—I was connected to no one, to no thing. (*Pause.*) What was I doing when all the time passed? I can't remember. I only know one day I saw it all piled up behind me. There were little lines around my eyes, two thin hairs sprouted from under my chin, and I began to feel small and alone in the universe. Now, when someone comes to visit with her baby, my breasts tingle and harden. I watch his baby hand carelessly caressing her as she suckles him, and suddenly, a hollow inside me is calling out and a great dark emptiness echoes back.

DAPHNA. (*On her blanket, reading.*) "Now Sarah Abraham's wife bore him no children." . . . In the *midrash,* the rabbis wrote, God restrains her from bearing—not that she needs a charm or a talisman—but that God prevents her conception, wills her to be barren. One of the rabbis said, God wills her to be barren because God longs for the prayers of women. . . . I read such words, I want to cry.

ABRAHAM. (*From back of theater.*) God, why do you want to humble her? Because she's proud? Always holding herself aloof? Is that it—is that why she is being punished? Am I being punished too?

SARAH. I want to cry. (*Lights down on Sarah, Hagar, Daphna.*)

Scene 8

Lights up on Najah, sitting huddled in her cell.

NAJAH. (*Crying softly.*) Najah, don't cry, sleep, sleep . . . 99, 98, 97 . . . I must sleep . . . 95, 94, 93, 93, 90, 95. . . . What could they know? They know nothing. I must sleep . . . 99, 98, 97, 95, 94, 93,

92, 92. . . . They have nothing . . . (*She falls asleep. Lights down on Najah.*)

Scene 9

As we hear Daphna reading, Abraham enters and goes to Sarah and Hagar, stage left.

DAPHNA. (*Voiceover.*) "And Sarah, Abraham's wife, took Hagar the Egyptian, her handmaid, and gave her to Abraham to be his wife." (*Daphna enters, stage right, wearing a bathrobe. She's in her study, preparing for bed. Music.*)

SARAH. (*To Abraham.*) Here, here is my handmaid. Go in unto her, that through her, I may be built up. (*Sarah motions to Hagar who joins Abraham. Sarah then goes to sit stage left in her tent. Abraham crosses to stage right with Hagar following. He lingers a moment, his hand on her face, then exits. Music ends.*)

HAGAR. (*To audience.*) I never imagined this. I thought my life would be in my father's court, desired by all the young men. Then suddenly, this foreign tribe, that woman at the center. I am plucked up, exiled, given away to serve, to serve her. Then, just as suddenly, I am given to the man, as wife! I never even noticed him, never thought about him, and suddenly, he is in my bed. I am overwhelmed by desire, I ache to feel his hands on me, his weight on me. I look for him at every turn, I wait for him, humbled and trembling. Will he come again tonight? Does he only come to make a child?

DAPHNA. "And Abraham went in unto Hagar and she conceived, and when she saw that she had conceived, her mistress was despised in her eyes." (*Sarah, unseen by Hagar, watches her.*)

HAGAR. (*To Daphna, to audience, laughing, ecstatic.*) I am with child, his child! Wife to Abraham, bearing his child—I have won! I never dreamt—that I would come here to serve and that that could end in triumph! Now she will see—I am a princess! (*Sarah exits.*) She treated me like nothing, now she will see, she will hear. Now I shall be the one to say—(*pause, now addressing Najah, asleep upstage in her "cell"*)—what?—"Sing some tune, old woman, Abraham's baby needs a lullaby!" (*Hagar bestows a gentle kiss on Najah, who wakens to observe the exiting Hagar, as if in a dream.*)

Scene 10

Najah, sitting on stage in her cell, now awakened by Hagar's kiss, uses her shirt cuff to "brush" her front teeth, tries to fix her hair. Enter Yonatan who sits down next to her.

YONATAN. (*In a teasing tone.*) Najah, why do you bother? Take my word for it, you look ugly.

NAJAH. I would take your word for nothing.

YONATAN. (*Gently.*) You've already ruined your life—no good family will accept you now, no nice boy will marry you. Even Ahmed doesn't want you any more.

NAJAH. I have told you, I do not know this Ahmed.

YONATAN. Why keep pretending? Even your father knows now.

NAJAH. My father would not believe—

YONATAN. Yesterday, when Ahmed told him . . . your father said nothing, but his eyes blazed. I myself blushed for you. And I worried—what will your father do to you when finally he sees you again. . . . Listen Najah, you are smart. If you help us, we can help you. Tell us about your activities and we will get you out of here. We will let you out, to study abroad—Rumania, Germany, even America.

NAJAH. You would let me out all right, you just wouldn't let me back in. You would like that, to get rid of all of us. No. (*Najah angrily gets up, Yonatan also gets up.*) I want nothing from you. I have done nothing. I have nothing to tell you. What is your charge? I demand you tell me your charge.

YONATAN. Your father says you are sick.

NAJAH. You are charging me with being sick?

YONATAN. He says you have been in hospital, in Hadassah, but they cannot find what is wrong. Something maybe with your heart.

NAJAH. What has this got to do with my charge?

YONATAN. He is bringing us your records. . . . You're very skinny but you don't look sick to me. Are you sick in here?

NAJAH. With your fine accommodations?

YONATAN. You are a brave girl, Najah, I can see that. But it is all wasted. Somewhere else you could build a life, but not here. Here there is nothing for you. Your friend, you gave him your love . . . you did . . . maybe terrible things . . . in the name of his cause, but where has it got you? In prison, perhaps for many years. You will be old when you are finished with prison. And if you are really sick, it will not be easy for you to be in prison. You could die in prison.

NAJAH. I have done nothing.

YONATAN. Save yourself, think of your future. I could talk to the judge—show him how you've been used—that you're not at fault. I'm sure that's it—I'm sure that's how it was. An idealistic girl, innocent—mixed in with the wrong people—I understand. But don't waste your life. Please, tell us, tell us everything, how it all came to happen, and then I can help you.

NAJAH. There is nothing to tell you. I don't know Ahmed Fousari. There is some mistake, or he is lying to save himself.

YONATAN. It is getting late. (*Yonatan motions for a guard, then exits. Lights down slowly as Soldier with flashlight enters, leading Najah to a space onstage that suggests greater confinement—the "coffin" cell. Soldier exits, taking the light with her. Najah remains onstage. Music of Palestinian rallying song.*)

VOICEOVER.

> *People, we have to stand up together.*
> *If we don't stand up together*
> *The future will never forgive us.*

Scene 11

Street noises outside Daphna's apartment. Lights up on Daphna, sitting in her study. She is engrossed in reading the newspaper. Slowly she finishes the article, lets the paper drop to the floor.

DAPHNA. Not again, not again. (*Enter Daphna's father.*)

DAPHNA'S FATHER. This is our State, Daphna, we have to guard it, this is the greatest State, we are just, we are the only democracy. Remember the Lechi, the Underground—how they fought, how they died. My whole family was part of it. This is our State, Daphna, the greatest state.

DAPHNA. (*To her father.*) That's what you taught me, that's what I learned in your house. (*Daphna's father exits.*) And then there was Avi, but what is it that *I* believe? (*She sighs loudly as she returns to her Bible reading.*) "And Sarah said to Abraham." (*Enter Sarah.*)

SARAH. (*To Daphna, annoyed.*) If you're not interested in what I said, stop reading.

DAPHNA. I'm sorry. I really want to know. (*Music. Enter Abraham, followed by Hagar, who now wears an elaborate outer robe.*)

SARAH. (*To Daphna.*) I did a foolish thing. (*To Abraham, as Sarah and Abraham walk, with Hagar bringing up the rear.*) I thought to make us a child and so I gave you that handmaid. But now she sees that she has conceived and I am despised in her eyes. She openly mocks me. It cannot continue.

ABRAHAM. She is your maid—do with her as you see fit. (*He exits. Sarah turns and slaps Hagar, they then instinctively move back from each other.*)

DAPHNA. "And Sarah dealt harshly with her. And she fled from her face." (*Sarah exits. Music fades. Hagar, at the well, cools her face with water.*)

HAGAR. (*To audience.*) She began by hitting me, but she could see it did her no good. (*She removes the ornate outer robe she's been wearing, places it nearby as she continues cooling herself at the well.*) Each blow burned the hand which meted it out, but never touched me. So she stopped that, before it demeaned her further. Then I didn't see her for several days—I realize now, she was thinking—

SARAH. How can I destroy her? (*Sarah, unseen by Hagar, takes the robe, enters Hagar's "tent" stage left and rifles through Hagar's things, wreaking havoc.*)

HAGAR. I awoke one morning . . . (*She does her morning ritual of washing at the well, looks, and sees her special robe is missing, enters her tent space and discovers what Sarah has done.*)

HAGAR. (*To Sarah.*) What are you doing here? Where is my robe— the robe—*he* gave me that! You have no right in here. Is that my robe? The necklace! You have no right! Those were gifts from him. I'll tell him—he won't allow this. Give me my robe!

SARAH. (*Throwing her a dress.*) Here! Cover yourself.

HAGAR. This! This is the dress of my old servant. You sent her into the next world in a shroud—you people wouldn't even bury her in her dress, and now you give it to me! Look at this, look at what you've done in here—it's all spilled, ruined. My oils, my perfumes, ruined. You're a fool if you think this will help you. He wants me now, he loves me. It's *my* bed he comes to—I have his child inside me. I am a princess, you're just a shriveled old woman. (*Sarah crosses upstage slowly. Two handmaids inadvertently stumble in on this scene, watch with wordless horror and fascination.*) You think by making me wear this dress and taking away the jewelry he gave me and spilling the perfume—you think you'll make me ugly in his eyes? You can't make me ugly, you'll never succeed, I am strong, a princess.

SARAH. (*By now far upstage, calls back to Hagar.*) Hagar, come into my tent—the slop pots are not emptied. You need to clean them out. (*The two handmaids burst into laughter at this and run off together convulsed in giggles. Sarah exits.*)

HAGAR. Everyone heard her, everyone will know . . . I can't have them see me, not after this . . . (*Sound of wind, change in lighting during the following as we go from late afternoon to sunset to dusk to darkness.*) I could never have them see me again, after that. . . . (*The wind is howling.*) I walked, I walked all day. Now it is cool in the desert, the sun is down, it is cool. . . . (*Pause.*) I wonder what my sister is doing now . . . being bathed, getting ready for the evening meal. I wonder if they've married her off yet. I suppose she's already married. . . . (*She touches her belly, gently rubs.*) I suppose . . . with a child . . . I can't go back there . . . (*Howling wind, Hagar runs in a panic.*) I didn't think to be afraid, I just ran and ran, and here I am, (*she falls down in exhaustion*) far from the place of my shame, the place I now call home. . . . (*Wind's howling intensifies.*) I had forgotten the clean wind, the free wind. Once I was free, and now again, am free. . . . (*Wind howling.*) I am so small in this vast land, maybe I don't exist at all . . . (*Drum beat begins slowly. Music. Hagar now sits far downstage. Three different figures, clothed in darkness but whose faces are lit, each call to her from different places on stage and in the theater. We hear their singing over the howling of the wind—their words should sound like the wind, echo like the wind. Stage and theater are dark, except for their lighted faces.*)
MESSENGERS OF GOD. (*Singing.*)

Hagar	Hagar	Hagar
a child	a child	a son
Hagar	a son	come home
your child	Hagar	a son
Hagar	come home	your son
your son	your child	Hagar
Hagar	come home	Hagar
come home	Hagar	Hagar

(*The Three Messengers of God lead Hagar offstage, the music ends. Total darkness, Daphna exits now. Only the sound of the wind and the drum beat. The drum beat continues intermittently through the next scene.*)

Scene 12

Lights up on Najah in her "coffin" cell. As Yonatan enters, she awakens, goes to sit in the interrogation chair. Yonatan's manner is resolute, closed.

YONATAN. I have completed my investigation. I will have no trouble proving your guilt before the judge. But maybe he will be easier on you if you cooperate.

NAJAH. I have done nothing.

YONATAN. (*Pausing.*) Tell us about the bomb.

NAJAH. The bomb? (*Her mind racing.*) Oh my God! I know nothing about a bomb.

YONATAN. Cut the shit! By the time we are done today you will be begging to tell me, you bitch! I know all about it now, but I want to hear it from you.

NAJAH. I have done nothing. (*He pulls the chair out from under her, picks it up, and continues the scene holding it over her.*)

YONATAN. (*Shaking with rage.*) We are finished with games. Make no mistake about it!

NAJAH. (*On the floor.*) You think you will frighten me? You think I will confess? Look at you! You have the guns, you have the tanks, but you are shaking, you are afraid of a girl on the floor! You are afraid of us though we have nothing. Once *you* had nothing, less than nothing, and it made you strong. Now *we* have nothing. You have forgotten how strong you can be when you have nothing.

YONATAN. (*Furious.*) Cut the shit! You and your friend bombed a bus, and three people burned to death, a twelve-year-old boy and his grandmother—burned to death. You think because you are a woman you will be safe with us? You think you can kill our children, our grandmothers, and you will be safe because you're a woman? You are not some innocent girl on the floor—you're a murderer, murderer! Shimi! Shimi! Come in here, it's time to get this bitch.

NAJAH. I want to go home! (*Blackout, music.*)

ACT II

Scene 1

Music. Lights down. Music ends.

DAPHNA. (*Voiceover.*) "And Hagar bore Abraham a son and Abraham called the name of the son whom Hagar bore Ishmael." (*The phone rings. Lights up on Daphna who's been asleep in her study. She answers the phone.*)

DAPHNA. Hello . . . Levi . . . no, I'm still up. . . . Yes . . . tomorrow morning? HaSharon Prison . . . eight o'clock, yes . . . Can you tell me anything about it? . . . O.K. . . . Goodnight. (*Lights down on Daphna. In the dark, Daphna exits and Hagar replaces her in the bed.*)

Scene 2

Sound of an infant crying. Lights up on the Negev. Two handmaids are downstage center, sifting grain. Sarah is sitting upstage, with her back to the audience.

FIRST HANDMAID. So, Hagar had her baby. But what a night! I never heard such crying—I almost got up to nurse him myself! What was going on?

SECOND HANDMAID. The baby couldn't get suck.

FIRST HANDMAID. Why not? Hagar looks healthy enough—didn't she have milk?

SECOND HANDMAID. He wasn't with Hagar—he was brought in to Sarah.

FIRST HANDMAID. Sarah! Of course he couldn't get suck—Hagar is the mother—Sarah doesn't even have milk!

SECOND HANDMAID. That didn't stop her trying though. All night she lay with him, forcing him to her breast.

FIRST HANDMAID. What happened? (*Enter Abraham, upstage.*)

SECOND HANDMAID. Abraham nearly tore her tent apart! He comes in screaming about the noise—

ABRAHAM. (*To Sarah.*) What is going on here?!

SECOND HANDMAID. And then he sees—this tiny baby, a hungry newborn, fighting with all his might, pushing away her breast! What a lusty boy!

FIRST HANDMAID. She's a powerful woman, but she's a fool. What happened then? (*Abraham takes the baby from Sarah, still with her back to audience.*)

SECOND HANDMAID. Abraham scoops up the baby,

ABRAHAM. I'm taking him to his mother. If he doesn't get milk he'll be dead by the morning.

SECOND HANDMAID. Then Sarah screams, she cries, she's begging him,

SARAH. Give me a little more time. He will suck from me.

ABRAHAM. You don't have milk! And even if you did, the baby wouldn't suck from you. For all the months he was inside Hagar, he listened to her heart, beating out her pain. He knows in his bones you wanted him dead.

SARAH. I didn't! I didn't!

SECOND HANDMAID. It pulled at my heart, to see her brought so low—but he leaves her there, and brings the baby to Hagar. (*Abra-*

ham takes the baby downstage right to Hagar, then sits on the edge of her bed as she tends to the baby. Sarah remains upstage with her back to us.) Hagar, silent, spent from the birthing, waiting. Just lying there, waiting. As if she knew—something. Finally, as the sun came up, the baby sucked and was peaceful.

FIRST HANDMAID. I've never heard of such a thing! The women will live apart and the baby is with Hagar? Will Sarah still claim him?

SECOND HANDMAID. A little piece I didn't tell you—when Abraham took the baby to Hagar—he finished the night there.

FIRST HANDMAID. He slept in her tent? Sarah will never permit that.

SECOND HANDMAID. Sarah has lost a lot this night, maybe even the power to permit and not permit. In all her struggling, with Hagar, with Abraham, she did not take account of the power of a tiny hand which pushes away one breast and reaches out for another. (*Blackout.*)

Scene 3

Background "hum" of prison. Lights up. A table, two chairs suggest prison visiting room. Daphna, stylishly dressed but disheveled, is seated, waiting. On the table in front of her are stacks of papers and the book she has been reading from during Act I. Najah, in dark brown prison shirt and overalls, enters. She sits.

NAJAH. This is your first time, yes?

DAPHNA. What do you mean?

NAJAH. You have never been here before.

DAPHNA. How can you know that?

NAJAH. Your face is red, sunburned, you have no hat. It is already afternoon. I think you were here early in the morning—to get right in, see me, and go. You thought, I am a lawyer, I am an Israeli, they won't keep me waiting in the sun. Next time, if you come back, you'll wear a hat.

DAPHNA. Why "if" I come back?

NAJAH. Why are you here?

DAPHNA. To represent you.

NAJAH. Why now, why not before? Are you a fresh lawyer, just born?

DAPHNA. I am here to work with you, not talk about myself.

NAJAH. Why is this your first time?

DAPHNA. That's not your worry. We don't have time to talk about me.

NAJAH. This is my time. I'll decide how to spend it.

DAPHNA. Do you imagine I am here spying?

NAJAH. It wouldn't surprise me. You are new, like a baby. I want to know why.

DAPHNA. I'm not a new lawyer, but I am new with this firm. The boss is very—everyone takes a turn with such a case. You are my turn.

NAJAH. So, you are here because it is your job.

DAPHNA. Obviously.

NAJAH. You have to be here—you have no choice.

DAPHNA. I chose the law firm.

NAJAH. And what is this book—a law book? Do you need to bring the books along?

DAPHNA. (*Embarrassed, annoyed.*) It's a Bible.

NAJAH. (*Taunting cheerfully.*) Are you religious?

DAPHNA. No. I am reading something, I am thinking through a problem.

NAJAH. You read your Bible to solve your problems? Then you *are* religious!

DAPHNA. (*Impatient.*) Are you done with this? You've heard enough about me, I have to hear about you if I am to help you.

NAJAH. Like you—I am here because it was my turn. They have a certain number of places for us, in prisons of one sort or another. It was my turn to be in this one.

DAPHNA. (*Starting to take notes.*) You have been in prison before?

NAJAH. I was born in a prison. I grew up in a prison.

DAPHNA. Please answer my question!

NAJAH. No, I've not been in prison before! I was a student at Bir Zeit University, I was on the student council there. I didn't know that was a passport to come here. . . . My family is from the village of Silwan—in Jerusalem—the neighborhood—

DAPHNA. —I know it. But you've spent time abroad.

NAJAH. How do you know?

DAPHNA. There's something about you.

NAJAH. I have an uncle, in America. Every year he takes one of us. For a year we get to see what life could be like. So now I know, if I lived in San Francisco, I could have a nice life.

DAPHNA. They have not permitted me to see the charge sheet yet. Why are you here?

NAJAH. In *this* prison?

DAPHNA. Yes.

LOUDSPEAKER. (*Blaring.*) Your time is up. Leave at once. Your time is up. Your time is up. Leave at once . . . (*Daphna and Najah both look surprised, confused. Najah stands, starts to exit. They end the scene urgently, abruptly, as Najah exits.*)

NAJAH. Tell my father I love him. Tell him I am well.

DAPHNA. Do you need a doctor? My office said—

NAJAH. (*From offstage.*) Tell my father I love him.

Scene 4

Enter Sarah, wearing a colorful sun hat.

SARAH. (*To Daphna.*) So very strange, a moment in time, a moment like any other. You make a choice, the choice seems small, but in that moment, in that small choice, your life is changed forever. . . . I wanted a child, needed a child. I thought, God prevents me from bearing, but I could get a son from this young Egyptian. It seemed . . . easy. . . . (*Sarah fusses with Daphna in a gentle way, fixes her jacket, smoothes her hair.*) Before my eyes they act out the love of mother and son, a love I will never know. (*Sarah puts her hat on Daphna.*) The way he slips his hand into hers, the way his face shines, like a new lover, when he looks up to laugh with her. She has stolen from me the shining looks. He was meant to be my delight, instead he is the instrument of my torture. Whatever burden I lay on her—to show her the strength of my hand—whatever I give her to do—she shares with the boy. Together, they make of it a game. And the child—he is rough with everyone, but to her, to her he gives the softest embrace. The sweeter he is with her, the harder I become. They have made me so. I work to destroy her, but she is not destroyed—*I* am the one who is being destroyed—I am becoming something terrible, but I cannot stop. I am imprisoned in this hatred—torturer and tortured both. . . . Abraham is perfectly in love with his little family. He worships the boy, he sits at the feet of my servant. He is in awe of the simplicity of their joy. . . . Yes, he comes to me still, the requisite times, but he mounts me, he rides me, as if hard at work, concentrating on his obligation. I imagine he thinks of her when he is riding me. Did I ever want him so much when he was mine? (*Sarah remains downstage left in her "tent," Daphna walks into next scene.*)

Scene 5

Daphna enters prison visiting room, well dressed again, this time with the hat from Sarah, which she removes. Najah enters and sits.

NAJAH. I am sorry about last time.

DAPHNA. I've seen the charge sheet. It's very long, very, very serious. Apparently I can't give it to you. I will read it: (*She takes it from her briefcase and reads.*) "Membership in an illegal organization for the past three and a half years; recruiting two others for the same illegal organization; buying material for a Palestinian flag; making a Palestinian flag; in December of last year holding said Palestinian flag at a demonstration in Ramallah; distributing directives for an illegal organization; in June of this year buying two gallons of petrol; making three firebombs with this petrol; recruiting one Ahmed Fousari to go to Hevron with you for criminal purposes; on the third of June, in Hevron, throwing one of said firebombs at an Egged bus; responsible for the death of Menachem ben Yakov, age 43; responsible for the death of Yitzchak Pinchas, age 12; responsible for the death of Rosalie Pinchas, age 58, who died three days later from injuries sustained in aforementioned bombing."

NAJAH. (*Trying to control her fear.*) I didn't do that. I never threw a firebomb. I never made or threw a firebomb. How can they prove this? (*Najah seems to have some trouble breathing.*)

DAPHNA. They don't have to show me their evidence. Did they question you about a firebombing?

NAJAH. Not at first, only later.

DAPHNA. (*Angry.*) Why the hell didn't you tell me they questioned you about a firebombing?

NAJAH. You looked so green, I thought it would frighten you away.

DAPHNA. What good could I do you not knowing?

NAJAH. It was only at the end, the last day.

DAPHNA. Did you make any confession?

NAJAH. I confessed nothing. (*Najah is having trouble with her breathing, she seems to be having some chest pains.*)

DAPHNA. You look awful. Are you going to be sick—should I get someone? (*Daphna starts to get up to go for help, Najah motions her not to.*)

NAJAH. They won't help, they'll just cut short my time with you.

DAPHNA. What is it?

NAJAH. (*Crying.*) I didn't think they would really charge me. I thought—maybe they are just playing with me—to accuse me of this—maybe they will use it, to get me to confess to other things.

DAPHNA. Let me call for the doctor.

NAJAH. He'll do nothing. He only gives aspirin.

DAPHNA. It's not just hearing the charges is it?

NAJAH. No. My files are in Hadassah Hospital. They were testing me when I got arrested. I have terrible pain. They say the problem is my heart but so far they have found nothing.

DAPHNA. Then we must get you out—to the hospital.

NAJAH. They won't let me out with the charges you read. I will die in here.

DAPHNA. I'll help you.

NAJAH. What can you do?

DAPHNA. My boss will know. This Ahmed—

NAJAH. I don't know . . . he must have named me to save himself.

LOUDSPEAKER. (*Blaring.*) Your time is up. Leave at once. Your time is up. Your time is up. Leave at once. (*They both get up.*)

DAPHNA. You may not see me for a while—that just means I am busy on your case. Don't be afraid. I will insist on a doctor, one from Hadassah.

NAJAH. My father . . . (*she starts to cry, then in a whisper*) . . . does my father understand?

DAPHNA. I'll talk to him today. (*Najah exits.*)

Scene 6

Enter Daphna's father.

DAPHNA'S FATHER. (*To Daphna.*) This piece of land—this is our State, we have to guard it. Remember Hevron in 1929, how they murdered all the Jews. No one will come to help us, we can never let down our guard. We have to be strong.

DAPHNA. Yes father, we have to be strong. This is our State.

DAPHNA'S FATHER. Daphna, my friends fought for the State. The British captured them, said they were terrorists, murderers. The British took them to Acco Prison and hung them, and the Lechi blew up Acco Prison. They were heroes, the Lechi—because of them we have a State.

DAPHNA. If the Lechi was so wonderful, why weren't you in the Lechi? (*Daphna's father looks wounded, turns angrily, exits.*)

DAPHNA. (*Coming downstage, to audience.*) That enraged him. I guess

that's why I said it. The child always knows how to hurt the father.
. . . But I did always feel, I still feel, we have a right to be here, we
have a right to build a nation. This is our State. We have to guard it
. . . (*Enter the Messengers of God. Daphna goes back upstage and sits,
reading.*)

THE MESSENGERS OF GOD. (*Singing.*) Where is Sarah? Where is your
wife? Where is your wife?

DAPHNA. "And messengers of God appeared and Abraham ran to
serve them, (*Abraham enters and kneels at the feet of the three messengers*)
and they ate what Abraham put before them, and he stood by them
under the tree. And they said unto him: Where is Sarah your wife?"

ABRAHAM. (*Pointing.*) Sarah is there, in the tent.

DAPHNA. "And the messengers of God said,"

MESSENGERS OF GOD. (*Singing.*) We will certainly return to you
when the season comes round, and lo, (*Music accompanies their singing
now.*) Sarah your wife shall have a son, Sarah your wife shall have a
son, Sarah your wife shall have a son . . . (*Sarah, who has been sitting in
her tent downstage left, begins laughing.*)

DAPHNA. "And Sarah heard from behind the tent door and Sarah
laughed."

MESSENGERS OF GOD. (*Chanting softly throughout Sarah's speech.*) A
child, a son, a child, a son.

SARAH. (*Laughing.*) Ridiculous! Ridiculous! "Sarah shall have a
son." How I've wanted a son, longed for a son, longed so, that finally,
I must have willed him into this world. Can this be real? Lord of the
world, why do you play with me? (*Exit Sarah, laughing.*)

MESSENGERS OF GOD. (*Singing.*) Sarah your wife shall have a son . . .
(*The Messengers of God and Abraham exit. Daphna remains seated where
she was reading, now again it is the prison visiting room.*)

Scene 7

Visiting room in prison. Najah enters and sits.

DAPHNA. Did the doctor come?

NAJAH. Yes.

DAPHNA. What did he say?

NAJAH. That I am sick. That the cold and the food here will kill
me. He wants to send me abroad for tests.

DAPHNA. Good, I can use that. I will try with international pressure, humanitarian groups. I'm in touch with Amnesty International,

ACRI, Women for Political Prisoners—(*pause*)—but I must tell you, it is bad. There is a lot in the press about you now. They are making you out to be a real terrorist. Once the press gets hold of something like this . . .

NAJAH. You look frightened.

DAPHNA. You lost more weight.

NAJAH. I get strength from the other women here. We have classes, we teach each other—English, Hebrew, political history. And we exercise—all on a strict schedule. (*Pause.*) Why are you helping me?

DAPHNA. I thought we finished with all that.

NAJAH. No. I think about it a lot—I don't understand you. It bothers me.

DAPHNA. My answer would bother you more! (*Silence—Najah clearly won't let her off the hook.*) I love this country, I want to feel proud. This is still a democracy and you have a right to representation.

NAJAH. (*Angry.*) So you think this is justice? You have a home, you are free to come and go. Your pain—it is only in ancient memories. I long to go home now and cannot. I have not seen my father in over two months.

DAPHNA. You're accused of a serious crime! (*Pause.*) I have seen your father.

NAJAH. (*Excited.*) How did you see him? How is he?

DAPHNA. I went to your home. I met all of your family. Your father loves you. More than anything, he's worried about your health—I didn't realize you'd been in and out of hospital so much. He is suffering, but he will be all right. I think I was able to reassure him. . . . (*Pause.*) You never ask for your mother . . .

NAJAH. I know how she is without asking. She will survive whatever God gives her.

DAPHNA. I think you're right. My mother too—what God gives her, she will take.

NAJAH. Are you a mother?

DAPHNA. Me? No. I am alone, and anyway, it's hard for me to think of having children in this land, the way things are now.

NAJAH. This land is hard on mothers. (*Najah turns upstage, Daphna packs her briefcase and as she walks into the next scene, Najah exits.*)

Scene 8

DAPHNA. (*Walking into her study, addressing the audience.*) It's getting harder and harder to see this study as a way to honor my father, but I need to honor him, in *some* way. . . . If he were alive now and saw me working on this case—(*pause, then, surprised by her thought*)—it would not surprise him, but he would be angry. Maybe he would even tear his shirt and sit shiva, as if I were dead to him. (*Music. Daphna opens her book and begins to read.*) "And God remembered Sarah, (*enter Abraham, Sarah, and handmaid. Abraham is carrying a baby*) and she conceived and bore Abraham a son and Abraham called the name of the son that was born unto him, whom Sarah bore to him."

DAPHNA, ABRAHAM, AND SARAH. Isaac.

DAPHNA. "And Abraham circumcised his son Isaac when he was eight days old, as God had commanded." (*Abraham holds the baby aloft, then passes him to Sarah.*)

SARAH. God has made laughter for me and whoever hears of this will laugh for me! For who would have said that Sarah would give children suck? (*Lullaby is sung by handmaid and Daphna as Sarah speaks.*)

> *Koo-ooh koo-ooh ah*
> *sweet sweet child, oh sweet sweet child*
> *I love you child, I love you so*
> *never never will I let you go.*
> *My sweetest child, my sweetest child*
> *you are my joy, you are my greatest joy*
> *I never thought to have a boy.*

SARAH. How my heart sings! Look at you, sweet baby. Praise God! I will be worthy, protect you, nurture you, never will I let harm come to you. Thank you God. Thank you for this. You gave me a miracle. I thought I was far beyond a miracle, I had long since forgotten miracles, but You gave me a miracle. I will be deserving and merit this child. Anything, to merit this child. Thank you God. Thank you. (*Abraham bounds downstage, addresses audience.*)

ABRAHAM. Come join us! Come celebrate with us! (*Sounds of a great crowd, a celebration. Festive music with drums.*) Drink a toast to the child! Have you seen the child? Strong and hearty, he'll live a full life, father many sons and daughters! (*To Sarah.*) Look! Everyone is here! Every king, every nation! What a tribute for the son of Abraham and Sarah! (*To audience.*) Look at this feast, have you ever seen a feast like this before? This is my gift to all of you. You have all come to celebrate with us, to share in the fullness of our joy. Never before have I been so blessed! Lord, I sing your praises! Thank you Lord! On this day, (*the adolescent Ishmael enters, approaches Sarah and the baby*) I lack for nothing. Thank you Lord, thank you! (*Music ends.*

Abraham sees Ishmael.) Ishmael, my son! (*Ishmael motions for permission to see the baby, Abraham signals "yes," he approaches them, Sarah pulls away, nervous. She moves with the baby toward Abraham.*)

SARAH. Abraham, cast out the bondwoman and her son, for the son of the bondwoman shall not be heir with my son, with Isaac. (*Abraham is immobile.*)

ABRAHAM. (*Stunned.*) No. Sarah, do not ask me to do this.

SARAH. You must. Our son can never be safe with him.

ABRAHAM. I know that you've suffered, I know—

SARAH. That's not it—

ABRAHAM. —and I know that you fear them, but he also is my son. (*Sarah now shows the baby to Ishmael, who turns away in hostility. She gives the baby to the handmaid for safekeeping; handmaid exits with Isaac, Sarah goes to sit in her tent.*)

ABRAHAM. (*To Daphna.*) And the thing was very grievous in my sight on account of my son. And God said unto me, "Let it not be grievous in thy sight because of the lad, and because of thy bondwoman; in all that Sarah says to thee, harken unto her voice, for in Isaac shall seed be called to thee. And also of the son of the bondwoman will I make a nation, because he is thy seed." (*Enter Hagar, upstage, with a long veil on her head. As Abraham talks, she slowly comes downstage center to where he and Ishmael are.*) All night Hagar and I lay awake, neither of us saying a word. In the morning I brought her food and water. She never said a word. And the boy, (*looking at Ishmael*) he wouldn't look at me at all. . . . And I rose up early and I wrote a bill of divorcement, and gave it to Hagar, and I sent her and her son away from me, from this world and from the world to come. I sent her away with a bill of divorcement, (*Abraham begins preparing Hagar and Ishmael for their journey; he gives them food, water. Finally, he ties the long veil around her waist; it reaches to the ground like a train.*) and I took her veil and tied it around her waist, so that it should drag behind her, to disclose that she was a bondwoman, (*Hagar and Ishmael exit slowly up the aisle through the audience. Abraham remains looking after them.*) not only that, to disclose the way that they went, for I wanted to follow them. (*Abraham now also exits up the aisle. The phone rings, Daphna answers it.*)

DAPHNA. (*In her study.*) Hello . . . Dani, what is it? . . . (*Pause.*) Oh my God! Oh no! What happened? . . . At the bus? . . . Is there anything I can do? . . . No, I can't come in the morning. I'm working. . . . Tell them I'll come in the afternoon. Thank you for calling. Please, give them my love. (*She hangs up the phone. Blackout.*)

Scene 9

Lights up. Sounds of visiting room of prison. Najah sits waiting. Daphna enters, sits.

NAJAH. What's wrong?

DAPHNA. Nothing.

NAJAH. What's wrong?

DAPHNA. What makes you think something's wrong?

NAJAH. Your face.

DAPHNA. (*Irritated.*) Can you read my face?

NAJAH. We learn to read your faces, for survival. Just as you learn not to see ours—also for survival.

DAPHNA. You're wasting time. Another doctor from Hadassah will come to examine you next week. They still haven't sent your hospital records. I'll have to go there myself and get them released to me directly. Anyway, apparently we need two opinions—and then we can appeal to the judge.

NAJAH. —if the doctor finds the time to come, if they let him in, and if the judge will look at what he writes. (*No response.*) What happened? What's wrong? It's not about me, is it?

DAPHNA. No. Maybe. . . . There was another bomb. At the bus stop—my bus stop. . . . My neighbor's son was on his way to school. He's eight. He's a dreamer, always late. He imagines he's a knight, an astronaut. This month he's a soccer star. He's very bright—a beautiful shining face. There was a shower of glass—from the bomb. He looked up at the noise, and the glass from the store window—all in his face.

NAJAH. Is he alive?

DAPHNA. Yes. But he will need a new face. And he has lost his sight.

NAJAH. I am sorry.

DAPHNA. You are sorry because I know him, because I told the story, because he is eight. What if you read it in the paper? Or what if I knew him but he wasn't eight, he was eighteen—then would you be sorry?

NAJAH. If he was eighteen, he'd be a soldier.

DAPHNA. Yes, that's right. When I was eighteen I was a soldier, when my father was eighteen he was a soldier, when my mother was eighteen she was a soldier—we are all soldiers, forced to be soldiers. Yes, OK, let's say it's the same story, but he's eighteen with a shining face, a dreamer. Are you only sorry because I know him and he's eight?

NAJAH. Our children don't die? Our children don't lose hands and legs and eyes? Please! The difference is your children die one at a time, a few a year, in big headlines. Our children die every day, on the back pages.

DAPHNA. *This* little boy—his life is ruined—someone threw a bomb and ruined his life. Six months ago, on an Egged bus, another boy died—someone threw that bomb! Was it you Najah? Did *you* throw that bomb?

NAJAH. Now we get to it, the question that has sat in this room with us, silently, there, in the corner. "Did she throw that bomb?" You finally found the courage to ask me! I was waiting for that to come from your lips! That last day, when they had me, your soldiers, those were the words, again and again—when they beat me, when they spat on me, when they called me "bitch, dirty bitch," when they promised to fuck me, (*Najah and Daphna each get up—Najah on the attack; Daphna offended, shaken*) yes, your soldiers, when they promised to fuck me till my blood covered the floor—those were the words— "Did you throw that bomb? We know you made it, but did you throw it also? Tell us already, tell us you did. We know you did!" I was stupid to trust you! Go, go on, go! Don't come back. Tell your boss: "She did it, I cannot defend her, she did it!" (*Najah exits. Daphna stands numbly.*)

Scene 10

Abraham begins speaking from back of theater as he comes down the aisle and onto the stage. There is music with drums for this scene.

ABRAHAM. (*To Daphna.*) And God tested me, and God said to me, "Take now your son, your only son, whom you love, Isaac, into the land of Moriah and offer him there for an offering (*by now he's on stage*) upon the mountain which I will show you. And I rose early in the morning and saddled my ass and took two of the young men with me and Isaac my son, (*Abraham takes Daphna by the hand and begins to walk with her*) and I cleaved the wood for the offering and I rose up and went toward the place where God had told me. On the third day, I lifted up my eyes and saw the place far off. And I said to the young men, "Wait here with the ass and I and the lad will go off over there and we will worship and I will come back to you." And I took the wood of the offering and laid it upon Isaac my son and I took in my hand the fire and the knife, and we went both of us together. And Isaac spoke to me and said,

DAPHNA. My father

ABRAHAM. And I said, "Here I am my son."

DAPHNA. Behold, the fire and the wood, but where is the lamb for an offering?

ABRAHAM. It is God who will provide the lamb my son. . . . (*They walk hand in hand.*) And we went both of us together. And we came to the place which God had told me of, (*Daphna approaches the "altar" and as he continues speaking, she lies down on it*) and there I built the altar, and laid the wood in order, and bound you and laid you on the altar, on the wood. And I stretched forth my hand and took the knife—(*Music ends. He takes out a knife and begins to raise his hand, he and Daphna form a frieze; the lighting on them changes to backlighting so that they are now seen in silhouette. Sarah, who had been asleep in her tent, sits bolt upright, screaming.*)

SARAH. Isaac! (*Sarah, screaming, runs to find Isaac. Hagar appears at the back of the theater.*)

SARAH. (*To Hagar.*) Have you seen Isaac? I dreamt—something terrible—and now I cannot find him.

HAGAR. (*From the rear of the theater.*) Did you think to find him here?

SARAH. A man, a man with a knife—where is Ishmael?

HAGAR. Ishmael? Leave him alone. He knows nothing.

SARAH. But who else would hurt my son?

HAGAR. What was it you dreamt?

SARAH. A man with a knife. . . . *Please,* if you know something, tell me, help me, for the sake of my son.

HAGAR. (*Coming up the aisle and onto the stage.*) Your son, your son. You destroyed us in the name of your son. You hated me and then you feared me because you hated me so. You hated me, you feared me, but you never *saw* me, never saw that I suffered, never saw that I also was a mother. What of my pain, what of my son?

SARAH. I know you hate me for this exile, but when *you* had the power, when yours was the boy and yours the man, did you care for *my* suffering? No—you enjoyed it. And if you had the power now, you would enjoy it still.

HAGAR. In your dream, this man, with the knife—

SARAH. It is impossible!

HAGAR. It is impossible that Abraham would sacrifice a son? Betray someone he loves? You know better. We fought with haughty looks and jealous stabs. But Abraham and your God—they play for higher stakes than we do, and it is our children who must pay. Exile and sacrifice. Our children are the ones who pay.

SARAH. I beg you, help me!

HAGAR. (*Pause.*) Your son is with Abraham—Go!—(*She motions the direction, exits. Drum beat. Sarah runs off. Abraham raises his hand with the knife, Sarah approaches from behind, stays Abraham's hand, takes the knife. Blackout.*)

Scene 11

Drum beat ends. Lights up. Visiting room of prison. Najah sits waiting. Daphna enters, out of breath.

DAPHNA. I have wonderful news, remarkable news!

NAJAH. (*Quietly.*) Your boss wouldn't let you quit?

DAPHNA. Did you think I would quit?

NAJAH. (*With great difficulty.*) I was afraid you would quit. I don't understand you, but you are here.

DAPHNA. Listen to me! After I was here last time, I went to Hadassah, to get your records myself—I was sick of waiting for their red tape. You're charged with throwing one of the bombs, but that is impossible. On that date, on June third, (*she shows Najah a piece of paper*) you were in Hadassah Hospital. You could not have thrown that bomb.

NAJAH. (*Looking at the paper.*) I never thought about the date—I was in and out so much—(*pause—she is struggling to absorb the news*)—I never thought—there are other charges—preparing the bombs, recruiting Ahmed, all of it. How do you know I'm innocent of that?

DAPHNA. (*Slowly.*) I can't know. I wish I could know, but I don't. What I know is, I'm your lawyer.

NAJAH. Is that all? You're my lawyer?

DAPHNA. That's a lot. Let's get back to business here. What is their case? Ahmed Fousari says you made the bombs, but he also says you threw one, and that we can prove is false—you were in Hadassah. If they have no other evidence, if he's their only witness against you, we can get you acquitted.

NAJAH. You look happy.

DAPHNA. Aren't you?!

NAJAH. I suppose so. I should be.

DAPHNA. We've won—you will be free!

NAJAH. Someday. Maybe. But now I am here. And just because you can prove it wasn't me, with that bomb, on that day, doesn't mean they'll let me go. And if they let me go—in six months, in two years—if they let me go—I'll go home to Silwan, which is also a prison. What is my future there? You'll tell some of your friends that I am one of the ones who can be trusted, and they will let me come to wash their floors and scrub out their toilets—

DAPHNA. What are you doing?! Stop it!

NAJAH. —until the police take me again, because they have said I am bad and they will not let it rest now until they have proved it.

DAPHNA. No! Stop it!

NAJAH. If you can't hear the truth, then you are too fragile for this work.

DAPHNA. That's what my mother says.

NAJAH. Listen to your mother. (*Pause.*)

DAPHNA. (*Quietly.*) I wanted this case. I couldn't admit it, but I did. I've been at war with myself, with who I was raised to be, but I came to a point—I was looking for someone to reach out to. Najah, don't give up now.

NAJAH. You are excited because you discovered I didn't throw the bomb. You forget—I have known all along I didn't throw that bomb.

DAPHNA. Please. We can work together.

NAJAH. How is your little neighbor boy, with the shining face?

DAPHNA. He's at home. He won't go out. His face is still bandaged. His schoolmates come, by two's. They bring him little treasures. They are afraid, but they come. They won't give up on him. Najah, tell me what you need. (*Daphna takes notes at the beginning of this, then toward the end, when appropriate, stops.*)

NAJAH. What I need? I need—a pair of shoes that fit. I need a heavy blanket. I need writing paper, and books, and newspapers. I need food a human could eat, and real toilet paper. I need relief from this pain. I need to feel my mother's hand on my face. I need to sit in my olive grove and be with those old trees. I need to walk to the wadi and hear the wind and be under the open sky. I need to end this waiting. Outside, life goes on, but in here, my life stands still. (*Pause.*) I need to be free. I need some hope of a future.

DAPHNA. I am moving for dismissal. I'll send the doctor again. I will be here again and again until you are free.

NAJAH. They will force me into exile, force me to leave.

DAPHNA. We won't let them.

NAJAH. For all this I thank you.

DAPHNA. Don't thank me, Najah. I also need hope of a future. (*They look at each other, then Najah faces upstage as Daphna reads.*)

Scene 12

DAPHNA. "And the life of Sarah was one hundred and seven and twenty years. And Sarah died in Kiriat-arba . . ." (*Abraham enters, comes downstage center.*)

ABRAHAM. (*Kneeling at Sarah's grave.*) The first time I saw you, you were dancing with the other girls.

DAPHNA. And he buried Sarah in the cave of the field of Machpelah. And he said to his servant, "Go to my country and to my kindred, and take a wife for my son, for Isaac." And he did. "Isaac brought Rebekah into the tent of his mother, and she became his wife, and he loved her. And Isaac was comforted for his mother." (*Abraham walks slowly up the aisle to the back of the theater until he reaches Hagar. Abraham takes Hagar's hand, and as Daphna reads, Abraham and Hagar walk together, through the theater, onto the stage, evoking the entrance of Abraham and Sarah at the beginning.*) And Abraham took a wife again, and her name was Keturah. Who was this woman, Keturah? Some of the rabbis said Keturah was the real name, the original Egyptian name, for Hagar. That "Ha-gar" means "the stranger"— that the young Egyptian was taken from her home and known as "the stranger" until Abraham married her again, only this time as a woman who was free. (*Celebratory music. The Chorus of Women come on stage as at the beginning and sing the final text, which Daphna is reading. Abraham and Hagar come on stage as Najah turns to watch them. Abraham and Hagar exit slowly up the aisle, while the Chorus of Women exit up the other aisle at the same time.*)

DAPHNA. (*Reading.*)/CHORUS OF WOMEN. (*Singing.*) "And she bore him Zimram, and Jokshan, and Medan, and Midian, and Ishbak, and Shuah. And Jokshan begot Sheba, and Dedan. And the sons of Dedan were Asshurim, and Letushim, and Leummim. And the sons of Midian: Ephah, and Epher, and Hanoch and Abida, and Eldaah . . ." (*Daphna and Najah are now alone on stage.*)

DAPHNA. These too were the children of Abraham. (*The celebratory music ends, only a rhythm sound continues. The lights come down slowly on the two women who sit facing each other in the prison waiting room. Lights out. Middle Eastern music as at beginning.*)

THE END

Works Cited

Alter, Iska. 1994. "Wendy Wasserstein." In *Jewish American Women Writers,* edited by Ann R. Shapiro, 448–57. Westport, Connecticut: Greenwood Press.

Baskin, Judith R. 1994. "Women at Odds: Biblical Paradigms." In *Feminist Nightmares,* edited by Susan Ostrov Weisser and Jennifer Fleischner, 1209–224. New York: New York Univ. Press.

Beck, Evelyn Torton, ed. 1982. Introduction to *Nice Jewish Girls.* Watertown, Mass.: Persephone Press.

Betsko, Kathleen, and Rachel Koenig. 1987. "An Interview with Wendy Wasserstein." In *Interviews with Contemporary Women Playwrights.* New York: Beech Tree Books, 418–31.

Botto, Louis. 1984. "Blood Relations." Playbill, Westside Arts Theatre, 48.

Chasnoff, Sally. 1991. Program notes for Northwestern Univ. production.

Cohen, Arthur A. 1981. *The Tremendum: A Theological Interpretation of the Holocaust.* New York: Crossroad Press.

Cohn, Robert A. 1990. "Humor Triumphs Over Despair in *Ladies Locker Room.*" *St. Louis Jewish Light,* 30 May.

Current Biography Yearbook. 1989.

Fiedler, Leslie. 1991. *Fiedler on the Roof: Essays on Literature and Jewish Identity.* Boston: David R. Godine.

Freedman, Marcia. 1982. "A Lesbian in the Promised Land." In *Nice Jewish Girls,* edited by Evelyn Torton Beck, 211–21. Watertown, Mass.: Persephone Press.

Freedman, Sally. 1994. "Working on the Questions." *Princeton Weekly Bulletin,* 17 Oct.

Gussow, Mel. 1983. "New Romantic." *New York Times,* 15 Dec., C3.

Koblenz, Eleanor. 1992. "Theatre Facts." Program, Siena College, Feb.–Mar., 2

Lester, Jules. 1994. "The Lives People Live." In *Black and Jews*, edited by Paul Berman, 164–77. New York: Delacorte Press.

Lyons, Bonnie. 1986. "Lillian Hellman: 'The First Jewish Nun on Prytania

Street.'" In *From Hester Street to Hollywood: The Jewish-American Stage and Screen*, edited by Sarah Blacher Cohen, 106–22. Bloomington: Indiana Univ. Press.

Mersand, Joseph. 1937. "When Ladies Write Plays." Quoted in *Plays by American Women 1930–1960*, edited by Judith E. Barlow. New York: Applause, 1994.

Nathan, George Jean. 1941. "Playwrights in Petticoats." Quoted in *Plays by American Women 1930–1960*, edited by Judith E. Barlow. New York: Applause, 1994.

Odets, Clifford. 1995. *Awake and Sing*. In *Awake and Singing*, edited by Ellen Schiff, 223–84. New York: Penguin.

Ozick, Cynthia. 1988a. *Art and Ardor*. New York: Knopf.

———. 1988b. Letter to author, 5 Dec.

———. 1988c. "Notes Toward Finding the Right Question." In *On Being a Jewish Feminist*, edited by Susannah Heschel, 120–51. New York: Schocken Books.

Rosen, Norma. 1974. "The Holocaust and the American-Jewish Novelist," *Midstream* 20 (Oct.): 58.

Schiff, Ellen. 1995. Introduction to *Awake and Singing*, edited by Ellen Schiff, xv–xxxvi. New York: Penguin.

Solotaroff, Ted. 1988. "American-Jewish Writers: On Edge Once More." *New York Times Book Review*, 18 Dec., 1, 31, 33.

Wasserstein, Wendy. 1991. *Bachelor Girls*. New York: Vintage Books.

West, Cornel. 1994. "On Black-Jewish Relations." In *Black and Jews*, edited by Paul German, 144–53. New York: Delacorte.